# HOT ART,
# COLD CASH

Joan Withers

# HOT ART, COLD CASH

*Michel Van Rijn*

LITTLE, BROWN AND COMPANY

A *Little, Brown* Book

First published in Great Britain in 1993
by Little, Brown and Company



A CIP catalogue record for this book
is available from the British Library.

ISBN 0 316 90474 0

Typeset by Hewer Text Composition Services, Edinburgh
Printed and bound in Great Britain by
Clays Ltd, St Ives plc

Little, Brown and Company (UK) Limited
165 Great Dover Street
London SE1 4YA

# CONTENTS

| | | |
|---|---|---|
| Acknowledgements | | vii |
| List of Illustrations | | viii |
| Author's Note | | ix |
| 1. | A Painter's Palette | 1 |
| 2. | Turkish Delight | 2 |
| 3. | Go East, Young Man | 17 |
| 4. | Behind the Icon Curtain | 32 |
| 5. | New Icons for Old! | 50 |
| 6. | Operation Attila | 61 |
| 7. | Anything to Declare | 69 |
| 8. | Saints and Sinners | 79 |
| 9. | 500 Mothers of God | 94 |
| 10. | Rembrandt's Castle | 104 |
| 11. | A Private Viewing | 114 |
| 12. | Stop the Plane! | 126 |
| 13. | On a Plate | 146 |
| 14. | Dealers and Double Dealers | 163 |
| 15. | The Treasure of the Avar War Lord | 168 |
| 16. | La Comedie Française | 187 |
| 17. | Grimm's Fairy Tale | 215 |
| 18. | The Challenge | 229 |
| 19. | The Madonna Takes Wings | 251 |

20. Madonna at the Disco 261
21. Museum Piece 272
22. Veni, Vidi, Vinci? 287
23. Whitewash and Black Money 291
24. ¡Bienvenido a España! 297
25. Welcome home, Leonardo 306
26. Michelangelo 312
27. The Giant in the Shoebox 322
28. Whose Modello? 357
29. Enter the Lawyers 363
30. Coupe de Carabanchel 369
31. Gangsters 385
32. The Integrity of Daniel Wildenstein 389
33. Mosaics 420
34. How to Acquire a Stolen Masterpiece 429
35. Trial in Indianapolis 450
36. Win the Appeal! 461
37. The Clergyman and the Colonel 469

# Acknowledgements

I wish to acknowledge my sincere gratitude to Eric Kohn for his advice on literary style.

Also I thank Interpol for their generous cooperation: their persistent interest in my activities so complicated my life, particularly by restricting my travel arrangements, that they provided me with the leisure without which I would never have written this book.

# LIST OF ILLUSTRATIONS

1. The author with his brother Guy, as children.
2. The icon of St Peter.
3. Franz Hals' portrait of a man seated.
4. A painting by Rembrandt van Rijn.
5. Patrikiades' silver dish from the Kumlucu treasure.
6, 7 & 8. Part of the Avar treasure.
9. Leonardo sketch of the head of a girl.
10. The author with Professor Carlo Pedretti, Madam Nakamura, Mr Sasaki and Rosanna Pedretti.
11. The author with Paul Petrides.
12. 'The Menil Christ'.
13. Peg Goldberg and Stewart Bick.
14 & 15. The 'Feet of Christ' mosaic.

# AUTHOR'S NOTE

On occasions I have taken the artistic licence to recreate a dramatic scene while staying between the bounds of information and conversation as I recall them. This recollection of dialogue in exchanges that sometimes occurred many years ago may be queried by some but it is nonetheless intended to be true to the dramatic integrity of each episode as I experienced it.

# 1

# A Painter's Palette

'It will feel good to start working again,' I said, as I rowed the little boat across the bay to my fish trap.

'It should do after half the cops of Europe have been chasing you,' Eric replied.

I looked back to where the rose roof and cream walls of the church gleamed in the Caribbean sunshine.

'Don't exaggerate,' I told him. 'It was really a problem with the French.'

'And the Swiss, the Dutch, the Italians and the Spanish,' said Eric. 'And to cap it all, an Interpol warrant. So, Michel, how the hell did you get it all straightened out?'

'Don't bust my balls, Eric.' I pulled the heavy basket into the boat. 'Just look at the fish. Doesn't that look like a painter's palette?'

'How did you get into the art business in the first place?'

'Maybe I was bound to end up in the art world. My father's name is van Rijn, my mother's is Rubens, and I was born in the rue Vincent in Paris.'

I put the emptied fish trap back over the side and started rowing back towards the shore.

'Why don't you tell me how it all happened?'

# 2

# TURKISH DELIGHT

I had the good fortune to spend my teens in the Swinging Sixties. Of course there were things to get het up about, but it was a damned sight better than the Aching Eighties. We were not preached at that if we ate we would die of a coronary, if we smoked we were doomed to cancer, that God had decided to punish sex with the scourge of AIDS and the whole damned generation would probably end up addicted to cocaine.

My second stroke of luck was to be born into a family which, while not ostentatiously rich, was sufficiently wealthy to indulge its taste for culture. My father, a successful dentist, was a keen collector and my mother a talented painter. She has great strength of character and during the war was very active in the resistance. As a child, I spent hours posing for her and learned that good art is the product of hard work. When I was a bit older, I decided that buying and selling works of art would be less arduous than creating them. Years later, I am not so sure. However, watching my mother at work, I did discover something else which was to prove invaluable in my career. She taught me the difference between simply looking at something and actually seeing it. I acquired, if not the eye of an artist, that of a connoisseur and an art dealer.

But my first venture into commerce had nothing to do

with art. I was still at school, but I wanted to break out. It was a warm spring evening and I was sauntering along the Prinsengracht, one of the picturesque canals which almost encircle Amsterdam. These were the streets on which had lived the wealthy merchants who had made the city the centre of the world's commerce in the seventeenth century and had built the dignified brick houses with stone steps which flank the canals. Now, some of these lovely buildings were dilapidated and many had been broken up into apartments, store rooms or tiny shops. One such space stood empty. It was a perfect location and I knew it would make an ideal gallery or showroom. It could be rented, and I suddenly realized that I had just about enough money to take it for a few months, long enough to acquire stock and sell it and earn enough to pay the next instalment of rent. It was crazy – but I simply had to take the place.

So there I was, Michel van Rijn, trader, with nothing to sell and all my capital tied up in taking the premises. I discussed my problem with Pieter, a classmate and trusted friend. He too was broke, having splashed out on a small secondhand van, which had seen better days, but which Pieter assured me still had plenty of life in it, if treated with care and the respect due to its age.

'The first thing,' I told Pieter, 'is to decide what to buy for my stock.'

'And what are you going to use for money?'

I dismissed this trifling detail. 'We'll deal with that later.'

I did not appreciate it at the time, but instinctively I had hit on the right approach to commerce. If you can get your hands on whatever the public really wants, somehow or other you will be able to find the necessary captial.

'Well,' Pieter said, 'the one thing everybody is buying now is sheepskin coats.'

'Fine,' I said. 'I'll buy sheepskin coats. When I find out where to get them, can I use your van?'

'Of course. What's my cut?'

'Let's work something out when I have found out where to get coats and what they cost.'

Pieter was a friendly sort of guy and was prepared to accept that I would somehow arrange things and that he would be looked after.

So now I still had nothing to sell, but I had acquired a transport manager. The more I looked into it, the more convinced I was that sheepskin coats were dead right, and by the time I next saw Pieter I had discovered that the best source of cheap supply was Istanbul.

'Jesus Christ, you want to take my truck to Istanbul?' Pieter shrieked. 'You must be out of your fucking mind. I thought you might have to drive to some out-of-the-way farm in Friesland. Istanbul is the arse end of Europe. And have you forgotten about school?'

'We could slip off for a few days,' I suggested.

'No dice,' Pieter retorted. 'My van would be clapped out after a trip like that.'

'Hold your horses,' I said. 'I have made a few calculations.' I told him what I reckoned we could make on each coat, allowing for travelling expenses.

Pieter listened attentively. 'OK,' he said. 'When do we start?'

'When we have scrounged the money to buy some coats.'

We stared at each other, racking our brains. Then, as if by magic, the answer came to both of us at the same moment.

'Jaap!' we shouted. 'Jaap de Vries.'

Jaap was at our school, a year ahead of us. His aunt had just died, and rumour had it that the old lady had been loaded. We hurried round to see the bereaved.

'Sorry to hear about your aunt,' Pieter said cheerfully as Jaap opened the door. 'Listen, we have a business proposition for you.'

Jaap turned to me. 'Do you think this is the right time to talk about some deal?' he protested.

'Of course not,' I agreed. 'Pieter is so insensitive. Here, let me show you the figures.'

Half an hour later, I still had no stock but I had a financier and a transport manager.

'So when do you leave for Istanbul?' Pieter asked.

'As soon as you have fixed up the green card,' I told him. 'I am too young to drive, and anyway, since I was the original entrepreneur, I deserve a chauffeur.'

'How do you make a sheepskin coat?' asked Jaap.

'Take a sheep and turn it inside out,' I replied. 'When can we have the money?'

My parents had witnessed my leasing of the tiny space on the Prinsengracht with a mixture of scepticism and amusement. After all, I was hardly committing myself to a mammoth emporium, and they probably considered the venture a harmless stage in my education. When I announced that I was taking off for Turkey, that did raise their eyebrows. My father understood that I needed to assert my independence, so he was too tactful to offer me money directly, but asked casually how I intended to cope.

'My financial associate has provided me with sufficient working capital,' I replied.

My mother confined herself to recommending me to spend some time at the Archaeological Museum and to be sure to look at Dubrovnik en route. So Pieter and I set out in the great tradition of the Dutch merchant venturers; the old boys who once lived on the Prinsengracht would have been proud of us.

We did not linger in Dubrovnik or anywhere else; we had neither the funds nor the inclination for sightseeing. Pieter's aged van coped valiantly with the *Autobahnen* at first, but as the road became hillier it developed a worrying wheeze, and we drove on in dread of a major breakdown. Yugoslav customs officers looked at our dusty, mud-bespattered truck with amusement and curiosity but they let us enter the country without raising any problems. However we had not gone far into Slovenia before the engine began to splutter ominously; eventually it gave up the ghost and we came to a halt on an empty stretch of road in the middle of a dense pine forest. Pieter opened the bonnet and peered helplessly at the vehicle's entrails.

'What's wrong with it?' I demanded.

'It won't go,' was the laconic reply. Pieter explained that his knowledge of motors was confined to that of a chauffeur, not a mechanic. Some way down the road was the city of Ljubljana where presumably we could get help but it would be a damned long trek. Pieter tinkered about, but with an air of defeat. We became more and more depressed, but suddenly we heard something approaching and an even more decrepit-looking truck than our own came into sight. Pieter stood in the road and waved frantically. The truck stopped and a burly man in workman's overalls jumped out. We begged him to give one of us a lift into the nearest town – we tried German, French and English but clearly he did not understand a word. Ignoring our entreaties, he strode over to our stricken van and proceeded to probe about with a much greater sense of purpose than Pieter. He straightened up, having detached as if by magic a part of the carburettor, into which he proceeded to blow.

'What's he doing, giving it the kiss of life?' I asked.

The stranger rubbed the casing and wrinkled his nose disapprovingly.

'I think he is trying to tell us there was dirt in the carburettor,' I said.

Whatever the explanation, when the offending mechanism had been reassembled, the engine once more came to life. We thanked our saviour effusively and offered him money which he refused. A bottle of Genever, however, was accepted with alacrity, and we parted the best of friends.

Fortunately that was the worst of our misadventures. We did get a puncture in Macedonia, but Pieter was able to change the tyre. After five days on the road, unshaved and smelling of stale sweat, we drove into Istanbul, welcomed by the strident call to prayer by the muezzins, echoing from the slender minarets which reached like questing fingers into the purple and golden sunset.

In Istanbul the past and the present meet more dramatically than in any other city in the world. But when we arrived, we were in no mood to take in the cultural rich of the city. Hot, dirty, tired and thirsty, and without the slightest idea of our way around, we wandered into the first *taberna* and gulped down ice-cold lemonade. Then, having rejoined the human race, we looked around us. A group of Turks were earnestly playing dominoes and smoking cigarettes which smelt like exhaust fumes. They sipped glasses of tea and barely gave us a glance, but a couple of young men at another table looked up from a tric-trac board and gazed at us. One spoke to the other in Dutch.

'I bet you a glass of raki they're Dutch.'

His companion shook his head. 'Kids on the hippie trail,' he concluded. 'Probably from Scandinavia.'

Pieter turned to the first speaker. 'Since we have been good enough to win your bet for you, I think you should stand us a glass of raki each, whatever that may be.'

'Bloody poor deal this turns out to be,' he laughed. 'I win one drink and end up paying for two.'

They told us they had been in Istanbul for three days, but that they made frequent visits and knew the place pretty well.

'So you aren't tourists?' Pieter asked.

Klaas, who had bought our drinks, answered. 'We are here strictly on business. We are in the secondhand car trade.' His companion seemed to find his words one hell of a joke.

'We sort of help the cars to become secondhand,' Klaas said by way of explanation. Then, seeing that we were intrigued, he continued: 'You see one of the great businesses in Turkey is stealing cars from foreigners and handling cars which have already been stolen – it's quite a national industry. But don't worry. Nobody is going to pinch your old jalopy.' He made a face at Pieter's travel-stained van outside the door.

'Can you tell us a decent, cheap place to stay for a few days?' I asked.

They consulted, then Klaas drew a street plan.

He marked the spot with a big cross. 'Here's a pension. It gets a bit noisy at nights but it's cheap and reasonably clean. There is a bathroom and hot water which you can obviously do with. Ask for Firman.'

'Firman the Spy,' amplified Henk, with a grin.

'Spy?' echoed Pieter. 'What do you mean?'

'A Russian spy. At least that is what he pretends to be this year. I'm sure he was on the CIA payroll last year.' Klaas laughed.

'Probably still is. Gets paid by both sides and doesn't declare it for social security,' Henk commented. 'Don't look so shocked, kids, you'll soon get the feel of Istanbul; all the men are spies and all the women whores. Have a good time.'

'CIA, KGB? Say, he has to be kidding,' Pieter said anxiously as we made our way through a mini-maze of narrow streets, 'hasn't he, Michel?'

The pension was a dingy building in a street which seemed to consist entirely of cheap hotels interspersed with eating houses and *kahves*, those coffeehouses where paradoxically most people drank tea. Coming in from the bright sunlight, the lobby seemed dark, even ominous. A few circling flies welcomed us. As we grew accustomed to the gloom, we saw that the walls were lined with blue and white tiles, but the place had more the air of a public lavatory than of a hotel. From a cubicle, there issued wailing Arabic music. We called out but to no avail. Then a woman bustled in. She might have been thirty-five or forty and thickly coated with cheap cosmetics. Behind her trailed a shy little ferret of a man. The woman banged on the counter and called out in what we took to be Turkish. A shifty-looking bald man emerged from the cubicle and threw her a key. She hurried off to her room, hanging on to her victim's hand.

'Are you Firman?' I just checked myself from saying Firman the Spy.

He nodded and when I explained that we had been recommended by Klaas, he assented that he had a double room and pulled open a drawer from which he took a ledger. But what riveted my attention was a glimpse of a couple of dozen passports inside the drawer. I spotted several American, Dutch and a couple of French ones before he snapped the drawer shut.

'Are there many foreigners in the hotel?' I asked. There seemed too many passports of different nationalities for such a shabby pension.

'Don't ask stupid questions,' he snapped. 'There are a lot of sneak thieves about after foreigners' passports, so watch out.'

Bathed and wearing clean clothes, we wandered around, taking in the unfamiliar sights and smells of this other world. And in Istanbul, a sixteen-year-old schoolboy could come across plenty of educational experiences. After all, this was where the sultans maintained their harems, and I soon realized that the tradition, on a strictly commercial basis, still flourished. I gave Pieter some money and told him to have his truck thoroughly serviced.

'Don't you want to come with me?' he asked. 'It will give you a chance to see the place.'

'That's all right,' I assured him. 'I'll do a bit of exploring on my own.'

So it was that while my trusty comrade was negotiating an oil change and checking his brakes, I hopped into a *dolmus*, one of Istanbul's shared taxis, and made my way to a house which had been highly recommended by Firman while Pieter was taking his shower. The exterior was unimpressive, a plain unvarnished door beneath an old-fashioned lantern. I rang the bell: a small lattice slid open and a pair of cold, dark eyes contemplated me.

'Firman from the Bahar Pensiyon gave me this address,' I said nervously.

There was a rattling of a key, the door was opened, and for the first time in my life I ventured into a brothel. I could not have had a more colourful initiation. The man on the door was one of those immense Turks who carry off Olympic awards for weightlifting or wrestling. He neither spoke nor smiled but led me into a small, rather shabby room where a fifty-year-old madam in a flowing pink robe informed me of the house tariff. Young and eager as I was, I was not such a sucker as to agree terms without inspecting what was on offer. The lady of the house nodded and beckoned me to follow her. We entered a large salon and I gasped for it was nothing like the parts of the premises I had seen so far. The walls were hung with scarlet velvet curtains and a blue and cream tiled fountain played in the middle. But what riveted my attention was the occupants. Standing around or sprawling on divans, were perhaps a dozen girls. And what girls! Blue-eyed blondes, dark-eyed brunettes, coffee-skinned Levantines, slant-eyed Asiatics, a longlegged black girl with her hair in corn rows, girls from each of the continents, giggling little doll-faced girls, hardly more than children, serious-featured madonnas – and every one absolutely beautiful.

I blinked and then gaped in amazement. Madam had tweaked aside a curtain and in a deep recess stood half a dozen iron cages. Behind the bars were more women, stark naked.

'They are the wild ones,' confided madam. 'You are just in time to see a little of our special cabaret.'

I looked around me. There were a number of men at tables, some sipping drinks, and I smelt the sweet odour of hashish which was being smoked in *narghile* 'hubbly bubbly' water pipes. All were gazing expectantly at the beauties behind the bars. I took a seat and the show started.

A high-breasted girl with hair to her waist, modestly wearing a jewel in her navel, flashed a haughty smile at me, and turning to a very pretty girl with an unexpectedly fair complexion proceeded to engage in a sensuous dance. Soon the others joined in, their bodies twisting like serpents, as they fondled each other and taunted their audience with proferred breasts and buttocks.

At the end of the show, the girls joined the clients. Many of the men were greeted like old friends. Madam came to my table and smiled knowingly.

'It's the first time, isn't it?'

I wanted to say that I was a seasoned veteran, but I knew there was no way I could deceive the hawk-eyed old harridan. I nodded, feeling as if I were back at school and had been caught cheating.

'Then we must give you something to remember,' she laughed. 'You are still young but you are already a fine, upstanding man.'

I looked down and could see what she meant.

Then she waved her hand at her assorted wares. 'Well?' she queried. 'Is there anybody here with whom you would like to get better acquainted?'

I forced myself to remember that I needed to conserve some capital if I were to get back to Amsterdam with enough sheepskin coats to make my journey worthwhile, made a rapid calculation and pointed to a girl with hair like burnished copper. But there was also something special about her neighbour, dark-eyed and with skin like ebony. Madam deliberately checked the notes I had crammed into her palm and called to my pair of houris to take me into the Sultan's Room and 'look after me properly'.

The Sultan's Room was decorated like an oriental tent and strewn with richly coloured carpets. I went in a boy but I came out a man – or so my charming partners assured me.

'How did you get on?' asked Pieter when I returned to the pension. 'I found some very attractive merchandise,' I told him.

Next day, we went to the covered market in the huge, rambling Çarşi, the Great Bazaar. All around us were shops piled with every sort of merchandise, the owner seated in the middle of his wares, like a dragon watching over his treasure or sipping a glass of *çay*, hot, sweet tea, and playing tric-trac. At first we were bewildered by the sheer variety of goods; jackets of softest leather, gold coins, woven carpets, water pipes and chess sets. Objects in the richest jade or onyx nestled beside plastic miniatures. We found embroidered robes and kaftans, copper pots, brass trays, elaborately chased silver teapots and jewelled daggers, ancient watches and even older flintlock guns with ornately decorated stocks. In one street adjacent to the vaulted arcades of the market proper, pirated cassettes of European and Arabic pop songs blared out; all was noise, bustle, chaos. However, after a while, we realized that there was a sort of order in the apparent confusion; shops specializing in certain goods were clustered in the same street. This was the case with those selling leather goods, and it was here that we ran to earth our sheepskin coats. They had probably been banished to a far corner by the other shopkeepers, since the stench of partly decomposing animal flesh, drying skins and the sharp tang of the acids used in the vats would have made them lousy neighbours for stalls offering Turkish Delight or attar of roses. We screwed up our nostrils and plunged into the maze of narrow alleys which enclosed the bedesten, a quaint little building with tiny twin domes which used to be the cloth market.

Buying in an oriental bazaar is a serious business, nothing like our supermarket mentality. Imagine sitting on a scarlet and maroon leather pouffe, sipping strong, sweet, black coffee while carrying on a leisurely but purposeful discussion about quality and price in the middle of Sears or Marks & Spencer! Of course the diplomatic exchanges take time. Give the impression that you are in a hurry, and the owner is likely to feel slighted and the heartbreaking sacrificial bargain which he was on the point of giving such a nice guy will be lost to you for ever. But after the third cup, you reluctantly settle for Mustafa's final price, something so ludicrously cheap, he tearfully assures you, that you will have eaten up his profit for the entire week and his wife will tear his eyes out when he gets home.

So we bargained, haggling until we had bought our coats at a fraction of what we had been prepared to pay, and as we left Mustafa wished us a safe journey, prosperity and a speedy return – as well he might since he had sold at a multiple of what the goddamned coats had cost him. But he was entitled to whatever super-profit he had screwed out of us; even after deducting the cost of the trip, I would be able to unload the consignment of two hundred coats at prices which would leave me smiling. I have since bought and sold many precious objects, often at substantial profits, but a dealer's first coup is something special, like one's first love, and I have a warm spot in my heart for that truckload of sheepskin coats.

We strolled out of the Grand Bazaar, and found ourselves facing the oldest surviving mosque in the city, the Beyazit Mosque. It was remarkably like a less spectacular version of Hagia Sophia, but it is a favourite with the locals for the swarms of pigeons which flutter round it. Directly behind it stands a pleasant park which we strolled across. On the other side of the park is a high tower, the Serasket Tower. We trudged our way to the top and were rewarded by a super view. Over the grounds of the university, there reared the dome and the four minarets of the Suleymaniye and beyond the Golden Horn, spanned by the Ataturk Bridge. We decided on the spot that while we waited for Pieter's van to be serviced, we should indulge in a little sightseeing. It was in Hagia Sophia, as I gazed at the tremendous deesis, a tripartite icon depicting Christ flanked by the Virgin Mary and St John, that an almost obsessive interest in icons was quickened in me. We walked round the grey walls of the university and there was the Mosque of Suleiman the Magnificent. In the spacious courtyard, we got caught up with a gaggle of American tourists and tagged along to the adjoining graveyard, where they duly boggled at the splendid tombs of Suleiman and his wife.

'Observe the diamonds in the tiled roof over the sultan's tomb,' ordered their guide.

'Gee, this place must be worth billions of dollars,' gasped an impressed matron.

'It is not for sale,' retorted the Turkish guide.

I was not so sure. Istanbul appealed both to my aesthetic and my business sense. I had come upon a treasure house in this city, but at the same time, it was a marketplace. Marvellous – one could handle things of such beauty that merely touching them was a joy, and get rich at the same time! What more could an ambitious boy with artistic interests ask for?

As we made our way across the market area, we were constantly propositioned by eager, intense kids, of whom the oldest was about ten, offering us introductions to their sisters who were without exception young, virgins and as beautiful as the moon. When we declined, they fell back on their second line of merchandise, their brothers or black market exchange. All around were stalls with the usual tourist garbage on offer; the whole wide open space presented a fantastic spectacle, clamorous and vibrant. To me, it was a challenge. I was fascinated by the place. A fiercely bearded man with wild staring eyes plunged blazing brands into his mouth and all around were singers, dancers, hustlers, pimps and pickpockets. Pieter shuddered.

'This place is a dump. I'll be glad to get back to civilization.'

'I like it here,' I answered. 'As soon as we've sold those coats, I'll be back. There's a hell of a lot more to Turkey than we have seen in a couple of days in Istanbul.'

Pieter sniffed, unconvinced. But then he had not made the acquaintance of Isdel and Soraya and the rest of the harem.

On the journey home, however, my feelings were far from tender. Mustafa, blast his eyes, had not bothered to warn us that one of the reasons the coats were cheap was that in order to speed up his turnover, he had not waited until the tanning process had been finished. The process was completed in the warm fug in our truck. The aroma of rotting sheep blended with the smell of hot oil from the engine and our own sweat. With each kilometre, the stink grew worse. We drove on grimly, resolved to douse the coats with strong deodorant before offering them for sale. But even this annoyance turned to our advantage. At the Dutch border the customs officers hurriedly waved us on our way.

'We have a few sheepskin coats,' I called, with an innocent smile.

'Just get the fucking things out of here,' snarled the half-asphyxiated officer.

My optimism over the demand for the coats was justified. No sooner had we unloaded the shipment than the first customer walked through the door. Within a couple of days, all two hundred had been sold and we held a celebration dinner. Jaap, clearly relieved at the quick return on his investment, told us that the school staff had taken a dim view of our absence.

'Old Kremer will give you hell,' he said.

'Well, he can't have us hanged,' Pieter retorted.

'He will probably settle for having you castrated,' grinned Jaap.

'He can go fuck himself if we don't bother to go back,' I pointed out.

Jaap stared at me. 'But you have to go back. You have another year before you can go to university.'

'What for?' I demanded. 'To plod away at subjects I don't give a damn about and end up like Kremer, a boring old schoolmaster?'

'It's a good job, safe and not too badly paid,' Jaap objected.

'Do you realize that with this one trip, I am already earning more than old Kremer who has been working for years?' I retorted.

'So what are you going to do now, Michel?' asked Jaap.

'I am going straight back to Istanbul to pick up another couple of hundred coats.'

Jaap shook his head. 'It was a good idea for one trip, but to go on is risky. You don't know how long this fashion will last. Maybe next year it will be back to leather jackets or military tunics.'

'All the more reason to hit the market while it lasts. Look,

Jaap, I am grateful to you for backing our first trip but get this clear, I'm going on.'

'So what will you do when people stop buying sheepskin coats?'

'Sell something else. I spotted so many things in that bazaar that I am sure I could have sold in Amersterdam.'

It was a parting of the ways. I did not need Jaap to finance my next trip and he had no desire to get involved in what he saw as a dicey gamble. But he had not been to that teeming bazaar. He had not listened to that cacophony of Arabs and Armenians, Turks and Lebanese: chattering, arguing, wheedling, threatening, bargaining, bribing. He had not sniffed that mixture of every possible aroma; fruits and spices, the tang of leather or of carpets, the strange hashish odour, and of course he had not sampled the delights of the modern harem.

I turned to Pieter who had said nothing. I knew he had neither the eye to choose stock nor the patience to deal with Turks, Greeks and Armenians, but he was a sound, reliable guy – and a good driver.

'How about it?' I demanded. 'I'll buy your bloody old van and take you on as my assistant with a salary big enough to turn old Kremer green with envy.'

So I dispensed with my transport manager and my financial associate, but acquired a chauffeur and my first company vehicle. Not exactly an executive limousine, but what the hell.

And that is how I decided to quit school and devote my time to my little shop, or rather to the travelling, the bargaining and the constant looking out for things that would sell. I was about to swap the classroom for the saleroom, and to enter a very special sort of university where the professors were buyers, sellers, middlemen and downright thieves, along with bent customs men, civil servants, art experts, all of them on the make. The geography might be haywire, but I crossed my Rubicon on the banks of the Amstel – or the Bosphorus. As Kremer might have said: *Alea iacta est.*

# 3

# Go East, Young Man

I was soon back in Istanbul but, with quite a bit more money in my pocket, I was able to look out for other things besides sheepskin coats, things which interested me more both for artistic value and for potential profitability. As a mark of my growing affluence, we stayed in the Pera Palace, one of the better-class hotels. I kept thinking of those passports in Firman's desk and wondering what exactly was his racket. A remark by the hotel receptionist gave me food for thought.

'Watch your passport, sir,' he said as he handed it back after we had registered. 'A lot get stolen, especially around the bazaar.'

'Is that so?'

'Sure. Istanbul is a centre where all sorts of people buy passports, genuine ones. There are plenty of experts who can doctor them for the new owner.'

'I'll remember,' I promised. I did not realize then how soon I would be going into the passport business myself.

Although Pieter drove us to Turkey, the journey was a strain, and I resolved that after this trip I would retire the ageing vehicle; present it to a museum if I was not able to sell it. It was certainly not the sort of conveyance to park outside the Pera Palace, so we hid it in a side street.

As Klaas had said, nobody was going to be tempted to steal it.

The hotel was on the other side of the Golden Horn from Stamboul and the bazaar, an area less frequented by tourists but the most prosperous part of the city. I chose rooms at the back looking out onto the quiet Tepebasi Gardens. It was definitely an improvement on the Bahar Pensiyon!

Knowing our way around, it did not take long to buy our quota of coats and I discovered a lot of shops outside the bazaar and the tourist trek where I came across all sorts of quaint and curious objects, some undoubtedly old, others probably contemporary but of traditional design which made them difficult to date. However it was in the Divan Yoli Cad, the street just outside the bazaar, that I strolled into the welcome shade of a small carpet shop. I was alone; Pieter had taken time off to photograph the sights. The owner greeted me courteously and asked if I had anything particular in mind.

'I'm just looking,' I replied.

He motioned to me to wander around. Every conceivable size of carpet was standing rolled or hanging from the wall and a great pile had been spread on the floor.

'This is something special which might interest you,' said the shopkeeper with the air of a magician about to perform a mind-blowing trick, and he pulled out a rug. It was quite a jazzy piece, which I recognized as being *kayseri*, shoddy, and of practically no value.

'Persian?' I asked innocently.

'But of course,' smiled the Afghan, scenting a sucker.

'I think I'll wait until I go to Teheran to buy Persian things,' I told him.

'But you will find they are cheaper here,' he persisted.

'How about something more traditional?' I suggested. 'I could be tempted by a good *kilim* carpet. One of those floral patterns from Anatolia. Do you have any of those?'

His expression changed. Perhaps I was not the world's leading authority, but clearly I knew enough not to be stuffed with any old rubbish. Glasses of *çay* were produced, and so were some very attractive carpets. We discussed prices, and half an hour later I was the owner of a three-square-metre carpet for which I was to pay the equivalent of $380 on delivery to my hotel. I was happy, since I knew I could sell it back home for at least double that. Less than a block up the street, I came across Ali Pasa's Bazaar, one of those lively teahouses where a man can sample a *narghile*, drink tea and chat with the regulars.

I found a table and declined a tube of a pipe but ordered a yoghurt drink, *aryan*, as a change from the incessant *çay*, and a portion of *baklava*. A tall, heavily moustached man had followed me in and he now approached and gazed at me enquiringly. I beckoned to him to take a seat.

'Let me introduce myself,' said the stranger with a smile. 'My name is Dergazarian – that's Armenian, you know. I was passing and happened to hear the end of your bargaining with that carpet seller. You did pretty well, but do you know that they have a recognized two-price system? If you had got a Turk to buy the carpet, he would have got it at least twenty-five percent cheaper.'

I nodded. 'I'm not staying here long enough to make it worthwhile setting up scouts, and I know I can make a good profit on it back home.'

'So you are in the business?'

'Sure. I have a gallery in Amsterdam.'

'What sort of things do you sell?'

'A whole range of art objects and antiques,' I answered. I did not add that so far I had only sold sheepskin coats; I could already imagine that the little shop had been transformed into a real gallery with marvellous paintings, ivories, bronzes, fabrics, glass, ceramics – the whole gamut of precious things.

'So you are on a buying expedition. Where are you going after Istanbul?'

I had not considered venturing further afield, at least not on that trip, but now I thought, why not? Pieter could take the coats back, and he could easily sell them without my being there.

'I'll see what's going in Izmir,' I answered. 'And then, I haven't made up my mind, perhaps down the coast to Selçuk and Bodrum.'

Dergazarian shrugged. 'You never know, you might strike lucky, but if you want to deal in any volume, why don't you really take the plunge and come to Beirut?'

I had never thought about visiting Lebanon.

'It's the obvious place,' Dergazarian said. 'Instead of traipsing all over the world finding one thing in one place and another God knows how far away, come to the marketplace where the goods come to you. I guarantee that whatever you are looking for, someone in Beirut can supply it – and at a reasonable price, no tourist hype.'

'If it's so great, why are you in Istanbul?' I challenged.

Dergazarian laughed. 'I live there. I've come here to unload some merchandise which I know sells dearer here.'

'Not *kilims* by any chance?' I asked anxiously.

'No way,' he grinned. 'As a matter of fact it was a few icons for which I had a customer.'

'Now that is something I would like to get into,' I enthused. Those vivid impressions from our first trip of the deesis in the Hagia Sophia welled up and something of my earnestness must have got across.

'If you really mean that, come to Beirut and look me up.' Dergazarian scribbled an address and phone number on a scrap of paper. Then he got to his feet and held out his hand. 'I am serious,' he added. 'You won't regret it.'

I fished out one of my cards from my pocket and gave it to him. Who knew? Perhaps I would go to Beirut some day.

I explained my change of plan to Pieter who was only too pleased to get back to what he termed civilization.

'The trouble with this arsehole place,' he grumbled, 'is the way they drape those bloody great sacks over their women. You can't see what's on offer.'

'When it's heavily veiled, it's not on offer,' I told him.

So early next morning we checked out and Pieter started back to Amsterdam.

'Take it easy,' I warned him. 'That van has just about had it but what you are carrying is worth real money, so don't do anything stupid.'

'You're the one who might get into trouble,' he replied. 'They'll probably cut your balls off and you'll end up as a eunuch in some filthy cat-house.'

'You're too young to know about those things,' I grinned. 'On your way!'

He thumped the van into gear and I waved farewell. I breathed a sigh of relief. I got on well enough with Pieter but I wanted to be on my own, to seek out new people in exotic places – and to sniff out deals which would take me out of the class of humdrum Holland.

Dispensing with breakfast, I bought some fruit and boarded the daily ferry for Izmir, and a few minutes after nine I watched the domes and minarets of Istanbul slip past as we nosed our way into the Sea of Marmora. There were quite a few tourists aboard, many of them hikers and backpackers; the more affluent class of tourists usually waited for one of the cruise liners, but we businessmen could not hang about for days for the next sailing.

I was lounging by the rail watching the coastline disappear and reflecting on how boring a whole day confined to a ship can be. A girl in her twenties walked over and stood beside me. I made some conventional remark on the view. She spoke excellent English, and in a short time we were chatting and I was congratulating myself that perhaps the trip would not be so boring after all. I had just offered to buy her a drink when she clutched my arm.

'Wait,' she said, and there was an urgency in her voice which made me stiffen. She was staring at a lean-faced man whose hooked nose and long, black moustaches brought to mind childhood stories of bandits in equatorial jungles or the wastes of Asia. He was lithe and sinewy. Beside him were two other men, rather similar in build, and all three gave off an aura of tremendous tension, of latent violence.

'Kurds,' she whispered. 'Be careful: there could be trouble.'

'What sort of trouble can there be with all these people about?'

She shook her head impatiently. 'You do not understand these people. There are Kurds in Turkey, in Iraq, in Iran. They want their own state and they commit all sorts of atrocities to get publicity against all three countries. But above all, against us Turks.'

I shook my head in disbelief. Even modest Turkish girls were seeing too many Hollywood movies. The trio of Kurds walked purposefully towards the bridge. A couple of passengers lounged against the handrail of the iron stairs, only a few feet from us. As the Kurds reached them, some sort of scuffle broke out. There was a quiet plopping sound and a whirring sound past my ears. One of the Kurds crumpled and sagged to the deck. I had the weird illusion that he was dropping to his knees in prayer. At the same instant, his companions were seized by the two Turks with whom they had been grappling. I wheeled around to see where the shot that had felled the Kurd had come from. In the hand of my pretty acquaintance was a snub-nosed pistol, fitted with a silencer. Unconcernedly, she stuffed the gun into her shoulder bag. Three or four policemen materialized from nowhere and lugged the body of the Kurd down a companionway. The two prisoners and their escorts went with them. In seconds, the incident was over: peace had returned and the few passengers who had witnessed what had occurred decided it was wiser not to have noticed anything. The body had been whipped away so quickly there was hardly a trace of blood.

'We were tipped off,' the girl said softly. 'I'll have that drink now.'

I stared at her, too shaken to reply.

'An iced *raki* will do,' she prompted.

Since there was no decent beer on board, I had the same. The taste of *raki* is distinctive but it always reminds me of Dutch liquorice.

My most vivid recollection of Izmir was that for the first time in my life, I knowingly slept with a member of the secret police. She called herself Derya, and when she was not toting a gun she was friendly enough.

I found Izmir disappointing; noisy, crowded, polluted and infested by tourists. However, the excursion paid off for as well as enjoying my luscious super-cop, I came across a lovely Byzantine incense censer, fashioned with devotion.

I had decided to pay a flying visit to Ephesus, one of the most historic sites of the Ancient World, since it is only about seventy kilometres from Izmir. Just before Ephesus is Selçuk, an unassuming little town on the banks of the Lesser Meander, overawed by an old castle. It is so close to Ephesus, indeed part of the town is built from stones carted from the site, that tourists tend to rush through. But there, close to the Isa Bey mosque, a strange building with twin domes and twin pediments, looking as if it were its own mirror image, I found a shop, tucked away off the main street, with all sorts of bric-a-brac inside. The owner proudly displayed several pieces of brightly coloured rubbish which I politely declined. Then I saw the silver censer, a genuine Byzantine piece which seemed to shine out among the modern imitation antiques. I picked it up, glanced at it and put it down again, apparently dismissing it. The elderly Turk recognized this as a ritual gesture and proceeded to extol the virtues of the piece.

'But if it is so valuable I shall have trouble if I try to take it out of the country,' I objected.

'No, no, no!' He waved his hands in simulated horror. 'See, I shall give you a receipt for a few thousand lira, or maybe better in foreign currency, let us say twenty dollars. Then you can show it to the customs: they will see that for that price it must be of no historic importance. And since I will have charged you in foreign currency, they will assume that it is overpriced anyway and that I had fleeced some ignorant tourist.'

'If they will believe that, it cannot really be much good, or they would spot it.'

He laughed. 'Do you honestly believe that some boy from a village in Anatolia who has been given a uniform and a rubber stamp will know the difference between something that was made six hundred years or six days ago? Pack it with any cheap presents you may be taking home – pretty boxes, a bottle of *raki*, T-shirts.'

I knew I was going to buy it and so did he but we went on discussing. I could see he was enjoying this little game, and before we came to a conclusion, I took an antique ring, a nice thing, quaint rather than lovely, but the sort of object that could be sold easily.

'Genuine Selçuk, before the Ottomans conquered the country,' he assured me without a blush.

His asking price was less than a tenth of that of the censer. I frowned and haggled for a little but then agreed with a reluctance more apparent than real at a figure which obviously gave him a glow of pleasure. I reckoned that by playing the ring easily, I would be able to squeeze a better deal on the censer, and I had instinctively hit upon the basis of oriental bargaining.

As the old man prepared the false receipt, he asked if I were a dealer.

'I have recently opened a gallery in Amsterdam,' I told him proudly. 'I hope to be travelling around quite often. Turkey, Greece, perhaps Beirut,' I added.

A young boy, presumably his son, had entered the shop and was sent off to bring us coffee. His father smiled at me and murmured.

'You should do well. Already you understand *kavla*. It is a rare gift among Westerners.'

'*Kavla*?'

As we sipped our coffee, he explained. 'I have lived in Turkey most of my life, but I am Greek and *kavla* is a Greek word. But we all have it – Turks, Syrians, Armenians, Greeks – everyone from this part of the world who is a trader, and which of us is not? If we are to trade happily and fairly with somebody, the first deal must be a sort of triumph.'

'You mean the way I let you screw me for the ring?' I asked mischievously.

'I thought you understood. Well, it was only a little bit of a screw, but it was worth it for the censer, wasn't it? You see, with us, buying and selling is not simply calculation of profit or loss, it is a matter of the emotions. Think back to your first girlfriend, how you would gaze at her, the first time you took her hand, the first kiss. How you let your hand brush against her breast, wondering whether she was going to push you away, then bolder and bolder until at last she opened her legs to you and what it felt like when you first entered her, that moment of complete possession! Well, good trading is like making love. There is the same sense of gradually working up to a climax. And then, just as with sex, when you actually come there is a tremendous feeling of relief, the tension is over, but afterwards, well it is a bit of a let down wouldn't you say? Think of that moment before your orgasm. If only that could last, but it is too intense. Every nerve is in ecstasy. That, my friend, that is the moment of *kavla*. Remember: give pleasure, *kavla*, on that first deal and you will do well.'

My only regret on reaching Ephesus was that I could not spare time to wander through the immense site. With such cities as Ephesus, Pergamum, Miletos and a host of less famous sites, I realized that there are more great Greek remains in Turkey than in Greece itself. Later I discovered that many of the finest Roman monuments were not in Italy but in Lebanon. For the first time, I appreciated the richness of the Hittite civilization. Everybody seemed to have marched through Asia Minor and left behind marvellous artefacts. Each revelation – a marble statue, a gold brooch, a Hittite basalt frieze, a shard of pottery – made me more determined that after this expedition I would devote myself to dealing in such works of art and remains of ancient times.

But not all the charms I encountered belonged to the past. I was relaxing in a *taberna* close to the deserted port of Ephesus, gazing past the rocks and golden sands to the sea. I could imagine how men had visualized the birth of Venus, goddess of love, rising from the waters to make her home on this shore. My parents had taken me one year on holiday to Italy while I was still a child and I had been enraptured in the Uffizi by the Botticelli painting of *The Birth of Venus*. I found it erotic even then! As I recalled that impression, a girl appeared on the beach. She had been on the other side of a headland and had just walked into view, but I could not help kidding myself that she had emerged from the waves for she bore an uncanny resemblance to one of Botticelli's maidens – fair hair rippled by the breeze, skin pearly white and those lean, sensitive features and clear blue-grey eyes. A Greek goddess had returned to visit me. I willed her to come to me, and, as if summoned by the force of my desire, she walked straight up to the *taberna*. I rose and signalled her to join me. She looked surprised, as well she might, but presumably deciding that I was respectable, took a seat opposite me.

How do you speak to a Greek goddess? Did they understand Dutch on Mount Olympus? Could I offer her tea or a beer, or would she only drink nectar? She solved my dilemma by speaking first.

'Where are you from, Britain?' she asked.

Her voice had an attractive lilting quality, but it was obvious that my Greek goddess would be more at home in Ilium, New York than in Homer's city.

'I'm Dutch,' I informed her. 'May I buy you a drink?'

My Aphrodite settled for white wine. I guess things must have changed on Mount Olympus, but she rekindled my classical fantasy when she told me her name was Helen.

'Helen of Troy,' I grinned.

'Nearly right,' she admitted. 'Helen of Ithaca actually.'

She told me that she was a member of a research team from an American Ivy League college. They were excavating a site at Sart.

'So what's at Sart?'

'That's the modern Turkish name. It was Sardis, one of the greatest of the Ionian cities before the Persians knocked hell out of the place. There's a lot there, but the work has only just started. Why don't you come and have a look – unless you have something else arranged?'

One look at her figure was enough to convince me that I had nothing better to do. After all, it was a divine invitation.

'Is it far?' I asked.

'About twice as far as Izmir, but there shouldn't be much traffic. My car is outside.'

I left some money and she led me to a small red Alfa Romeo. I looked at it approvingly; it surely was an improvement on Pieter's van. Helen was watching me.

'Would you like to drive?' she asked.

'I'd better,' I answered. 'You've been drinking. A whole glass of wine.'

She laughed. Nice teeth, I thought. American academics could certainly teach the Greek gods a thing or two about dental care.

It was quite a long drive along a road which twisted among the mountains but since most of the traffic to Sart and beyond took the main road out of Izmir, it was, as Helen had predicted, almost deserted. As I swung the sports car around the tight bends, she swayed against me. Her body was firm and warm; it felt good, so on the sharper corners I put my arm around her shoulders to steady her. She snuggled closer, and then started to unbutton my shirt. I don't think Botticelli's demure goddess would have done that, or what came next.

'Keep your hands on the wheel and your mind on the road,' Helen coaxed.

She had bared my chest and began to run her fingers through my hairs. She then turned her attention to my pants which she unzipped with a nimbleness which suggested that this was not the first time that she had set about a seduction on the move.

'Drive faster,' she urged.

The car streaked through the countryside, always with the unknown round the next bend. The risk that we might be about to crash into some lumbering truck added to my sexual excitement, and to hers. The gods must have taken us under their protection and we came, unscathed, to Sart at around five in the afternoon, but I came quarter of an hour earlier. Maybe that was how Aphrodite persuaded Paris that she was the fairest of the goddesses.

There was not yet a lot to see at Sardis, the dig had a long way to go, but I was intrigued by some of the coins which had been discovered. The American archaeologists were enthusiastic at the prospects.

'This was the city where the Greeks first used coins,' one of Helen's associates told me. 'Just think of all the trouble they started.'

Helen drove me back to Izmir where we dined on dainty *mezes* of aubergine, peppers and dolmes, grape leaves stuffed with rice, followed by juicy steaks of grilled *kiliç baligi*, which turned out to be swordfish.

'What did you think of Ephesus?' Helen asked.

'I never got a chance to look at the place. I had just arrived when I stopped for a drink and somehow I got diverted,' I explained.

'I'll take you back tomorrow and show you around,' she promised.

That night neither of us got much sleep, but I was not complaining and Helen seemed contented. As we lay back and recovered, I stroked her hair.

Helen asked jokingly, 'So when was the last time you picked up some unknown girl and made love to her?'

'Yesterday,' I told her, 'but she pulled a gun on some guy.'

'You shouldn't have hustled her,' Helen rebuked. 'Women need wooing.'

'Is that so?'

'Sure. Now why don't you stop talking and fuck me!'

I don't know what Helen of Troy was like in bed but if she was half as accomplished as Helen of Cornell, I can quite understand why the Greeks went to war to get her back. The next morning I was content to sit back and let Helen drive back to Selçuk, weaving through the convoys of elderly lorries. As we passed through the old town, I pointed to some enormous nests which appeared to be about to fall out of the roofs of some of the buildings.

'Who says elephants don't fly!' I exclaimed. 'Just look at the size of those nests.'

'Storks,' said Helen. 'But don't get any crazy ideas about babies.'

'Glad to hear it,' I replied.

Ephesus must have been one hell of a place. The drive off to the entrance to the site was three kilometres along the road, but Selçuk is built on part of the land occupied by the Roman city. As Helen reminded me, in its heyday it was second in size only to Rome itself. Helen the sex bomb now gave way to Helen the archaeologist. She led me along the road, lined with ruined columns which ran down from the old port, now far from the sea, up to the enormous theatre – it seats 25,000 people – which has been beautifully restored and is used in festival productions of classical dramas. It is an acoustic miracle. A mere whisper on the stage can be heard perfectly in every seat, more than can be said for many modern, scientifically planned auditoria.

We halted on the marble street in front of the Upper Agora. Helen pointed to a small excavation. 'That was the library of Celsus,' she informed me. 'The much larger building on our left was the brothel.'

'They didn't have to walk far to pick up their pornographic literature,' I observed.

'Mr van Rijn, I am beginning to suspect that you are a frivolous person.'

'Sorry, teacher. I promise to be a good boy from now on.'

'You had better be kidding,' Helen said.

Some of the buildings, like Hadrian's Temple and Trajan's Fountain, were still remarkably well preserved and they, together with some reconstructed terraced houses, were already thronged by tourists.

'So what do you think of the place now?' she asked.

'The trouble with the Romans was that they had no respect for the past,' I said. 'Where is the Greek city? I believe the Romans invented the real estate business. Still, I must admit that I was impressed by the superb mosaics and the friezes in those houses.'

She nodded. 'So you're not really frivolous? Come on, I'll take you to the museum in Selçuk where you can see the fine things that have been taken from the excavations here. And they have that statue of Artemis with breasts all over her body. That should give you some ideas.'

It was getting late when we came out of the museum and I asked Helen if she did not have to get back to Sardis.

'No, sir. I am absolutely free,' she told me with a broad grin of pleasure. 'I have just quit to take up a university post in the fall. But ought you to be heading back to Holland?'

I calculated that by now Pieter would probably be stopping for a beer somewhere near where we had our breakdown on our first journey and saw no reason to hurry home.

'Well, if you really want to see something of this part of the world, why not take a few days off? I could show you a lot of things during the day and I suppose we could think of some way of passing the nights. What do you say?' It seemed a great idea.

We spent a marvellous week sightseeing, bathing, eating freshly caught fish and drinking heady wine, and making fabulous love, but there came a day when we had to get back to our own lives. 'I guess we might never meet again,' Helen said softly.

'We must,' I replied. 'Is this university appointment back in the States?'

'No way. I have a research post at the American University of Beirut.'

First Dergazarian, now Helen. Fate obviously intended me to go to Bcirut.

# 4

# BEHIND THE ICON CURTAIN

It was drizzling when we touched down at Schiphol. I had slipped my censer into a plastic bag from a tax free shop at Ataturk airport. If challenged, I would pass it off as a gift; well, it was really, a gift to myself. However, nobody wanted to know. I think it was the moment when my parents looked at that Byzantine censer that, in their eyes, I ceased to be a schoolboy. Sheepskin coats were merely fun; this was different. For my part, I knew that the time had come to find a place of my own. No man can be truly independent living with his parents, no matter how tolerant and understanding they might be.

Meanwhile there was the shop in the Prinsengracht and a truckful of coats to be sold.

'Do you honestly expect people to buy sheepskin coats in the middle of summer?' my father asked incredulously.

'Summer in Holland was yesterday between three and half-past five,' I announced. 'And people will buy anything at any time if they think they are getting a bargain. You'll see.'

The coats went all right: they were still in fashion. And there were other things in the shop by now. I began to look around for antiques and curios. Imperceptibly, I had changed from being a shopkeeper to being a dealer, and had outgrown the Prinsengracht premises both mentally and literally, for there was simply not enough room for the stock I wanted to carry. As luck would have it, a larger gallery on one of the side canals, right in the heart of the city and a situation much in favour with antique and art dealers, became vacant and I took it.

Shortly afterwards there was another change. Pieter was not really interested in fine art, nor had he the patience to spot unusual objects. The first trip to Istanbul had liberated him from school and he soon went off to do his own thing. And I was haunted with the desire to get back to the East, and the days when I would travel in a clapped out truck had gone, so there was a natural drifting apart, but I have always kept a warm spot in my heart for him.

At this time, I came across Robert Roozemond. His wife, an actress, was a friend of my current girlfriend who was also an actress. He was quite a bit older than me, in his early forties, and an entertaining character, chirpy as a cricket and lively as quicksilver. The son of a street singer, he had become the lord of a fine castle although at the age of twelve he was singing in cafés for his living. He had bright red hair and a face so mobile it might have been made of rubber. I was not the first to remark on his resemblance to Danny Kaye, and maybe that encouraged him to play the clown, which he did sometimes in the most incongruous settings.

The Roozemonds were handling the collection of an important foundation called de Wijenburgh and they were buying works of religious art. I was keen on acquiring a collection of icons myself, and at the same time, here was an opportunity to buy for a museum. Soon there were other customers too. I rapidly acquired expertise in assessing icons. Not that I dealt exclusively in them: in quite a short time, I became known as one of Amsterdam's most enterprising dealers with a constant supply of ceramics, antique jewellery and coins, and the whole range of *objets de vertu*. My preoccupation was keeping the gallery stocked and finding interesting items for my increasing numbers of customers. More and more of my time was spent in travelling, and repeatedly dealers urged me to take a trip to Beirut.

'Get off your arse and go to the Lebanon,' growled one grizzled dealer, noted for his shrewd brain and coarse tongue. 'The place is a bloody paradise for someone like you. You can deal all day and fuck all night.'

I decided the time had come to take the plunge. Fate was calling me to Beirut, and I had Helen's address. I had been making good money and could afford the time to look around, establish new contacts and generally get the feel of the place. I took a plane and checked into the St George's Hotel.

All around me were signs of opulence. White-robed sheiks flitted in and out of the jewellers' and boutiques, escorted by shapely nymphs, usually European and blonde. It seemed to me that the girls dripped diamonds while their protectors dripped oil! Sober-suited Americans represented the almighty dollar and the multinationals, rubbing shoulders with smooth French and aristocratic British members of the diplomatic corps. But if these were the exotic blossoms in the Beirut jungle, the predominant flora were the Levantine traders. Lebanese, Syrians, Egyptians and Iraqis thronged the souks, calculating to the last cent what they could make in Cairo or Baghdad. Sephardi Jews traded happily with uprooted Palestinians: in Beirut, nobody took sides. Beirut meant business – if only it could have stayed that way!

And Beirut was rich. That was evident when one visited the golf courses, the race track or the casino. Concrete and glass offices of banks and international corporations reared up along the Avenue General de Gaulle and the Avenue de Paris. The restaurants served the subtle Arabic cuisine or meals which could have graced the best tables in Paris.

There was no problem in getting to know people. Reticence was for old-fashioned Europeans and very soon I had found a niche among the business community. I dealt with everyone, but more and more I came to realize that the smartest guys were the Armenians who had their own quarter in the city.

Not for them the ostentation of the Saudis or Americans; small shops in shady side streets jostled noisy bars and shops selling hot *chawarmas* or *falafel* sandwiches. The housing was old-fashioned tenements, the streets narrow, the air filled with a language which was foreign even in cosmopolitan Beirut. And there, once more I came across Dergazarian.

Shortly after arriving, I had left a message at the number he had given me, asking him to call me at the hotel. A girl, speaking French with a strong foreign accent, said that he was away but she would pass on my message on his return. She did not know where he was or when he would be back; indeed, she was unwilling to tell me anything except that Dergazarian was not in Beirut. So I was surprised when he walked into the bar in the Armenian quarter where I had stopped for a glass of freshly crushed orange juice. He smiled at me.

'You will learn that we Armenians are a very close people. When a stranger looking for rare and beautiful things asks for me, it is noticed. I knew of your shopping expeditions the moment I returned. And, let me see, this morning you were in the Sunrock Museum before you began nosing around the shops and stalls here. Right?'

I nodded. 'Where have you been, back to Turkey?'

'Not exactly.' His expression was enigmatic. 'What are you looking out for?'

'All sorts of things,' I answered. 'I have quite a lot of regular customers now, each with his own preference.'

Dergazarian nodded as if assessing this. 'Still after icons?'

'You remember. Can you put me on to anything special?'

'I have a few things you might fancy. How about this evening? Shall I bring them to your hotel, let's say around six?'

That afternoon, I visited the Korban Gallery. I had been told it was one of the best and most professional in the city, and I was not disappointed. There were no icons on display but there were plenty of other good things. I bought a small, finely wrought ivory Byzantine plaque depicting a madonna, a very rare piece, but first I went through the *kavla* routine with a small purchase.

I liked the look of Korban, a Marronite Christian, I felt at home among the Armenians, and later tonight would be my reunion with Helen. What more could a man ask for? I found out when Dergazarian strode into the hotel lobby, carrying a bulky parcel.

In my room, he unwrapped the package and produced two icons, each about forty centimetres long, and laid them on the bed.

'Well?' he growled.

They were superb, far finer than anything I had seen in the shops, stalls and galleries. One was the familiar image of the Virgin holding the infant Christ, the diminutive child, three-quarters turned towards the viewer, tenderly resting his cheek against his mother's. I had expected something from Greece or perhaps Crete or Cyprus. This was, without any shadow of doubt, painted in Moscow in the fifteenth century; the luminous, almost transparent colours and the elegance and balance of the composition were unmistakable. It was the work of an accomplished master, free from any trace of provincialism, the sort of piece in hot demand among Western collectors.

'The Mother of God of Vladimir,' I mused.

The archetypal icon of the Mother of God of Vladimir is in the Tretyakov Museum in Moscow. A similar icon had been brought to the city of Vladimir from Byzantium in the twelfth century and the Russian copy had served as a palladium, a sort of religious banner to protect the armies of Vladimir against their enemies. Miraculous powers had been ascribed to it and it had been adopted by Moscow. Eventually it had become a sort of emblem for the whole of Christian Russia and many examples were painted throughout the centuries. This was undoubtedly a very fine one, in good condition and free from any trace of 'restoration' and overcleaning.

The other icon was also Russian, but from Novgorod, and also a very desirable painting.

I bought the two and Dergazarian indicated that he would be able to lay hands on more of similar quality.

I was so excited by what I had acquired that when Helen arrived, looking ravishing, I had quite forgotten our date, but I soon remembered. I have never been accused of neglecting a lady.

'You see, I made it,' I told her with a smile. 'Just as you prophesied, here I am in Beirut.'

It was a blissful reunion. We made love and our formal dinner date was forgotten but I ordered sandwiches and beer to be brought to the room. I had opened the curtains to reveal a sky like deep velvet in which the stars shone like diamonds sewn into a sumptuous robe. Helen slipped one of my shirts over her shoulders. The wardrobe door was ajar and she nodded at the brown paper which was visible. 'What have you got there, Michel? Have you been buying already?'

I unwrapped the icons. 'What do you think of those?'

She whistled. 'Jesus H. Christ! Where the fuck did you get those?' She stared hard at me. 'You do realize they must have been spirited out of Soviet Russia and are probably looted or stolen?'

'That's a matter between my source and his conscience.'

'Sure, honey. I just want you to be aware of what's going on. It could turn risky, so watch you don't get caught being the patsy in some little game with the KGB.'

She had a point. I knew that I could get the icons out of Lebanon and into Holland without any problem, and that I would be able to sell them for a lot of money without any trouble from the Russian authorities. But would I come under observation, and if so what might happen when I returned to Beirut to buy more? I did not know Dergazarian, and for all I knew he could be playing a double game. Armenians had a reputation for deviousness: could my friendly icon dealer be an undercover agent for the Soviet security police? I resolved to be on my guard but to keep in contact; after all, he had brought me first-class merchandise. So I started to shuttle to and fro between Amsterdam and Beirut and at the same time to buy and sell inside Beirut through the Korban Gallery, but Dergazarian remained my best source, specializing in Russian works. Back in Holland, I rapidly acquired a reputation as the leading dealer in icons and I began to form my own collection.

So, in addition to my gallery, I had an office in the centre of Amsterdam employing a full-time staff, including a chauffeur. However I looked after the selling myself, and as I was spending longer and longer periods away from Amsterdam, I frequently left the gallery closed and eventually sold it. My operating base was really Beirut, and I decided to get an apartment there. But before that happened, I made one of the most extraordinary trips of my life.

I had met Dergazarian several times, and as my own collection took shape, I would tell him what I was looking for. Naturally, he could not always come up with what I wanted but he repeatedly told me that there was a great deal available.

One evening, we had spent a few hours together, looking at things which he offered me, eating and drinking. There was nothing that really attracted me this time and Dergazarian looked at me thoughtfully.

'You know where I get things don't you, Michel?'

'If you mean from what country, it's not difficult to guess.'

'Well now, I have told you, absolutely everything is there for the asking. So why don't you come along on my next trip and see for yourself? You can choose what you want on the spot. It would be a lot simpler and we can come to some sort of arrangement. What do you say?'

I was amazed. 'Do you mean to say that I should go to Russia, buy illegally and smuggle the stuff out? Do you think I am crazy?'

'Not Russia, Armenia,' Dergazarian replied.

'Same thing.'

'Not at all. I promise you that in Armenia, my country, you will be able to walk and talk freely, buy whatever takes your fancy and have no problem in getting the goods and yourself safely out of the country.'

'Freely?'

'Well, at a price,' he grinned. 'But you will find it money well spent. Look, I am offering a partnership. You have the contacts to sell the things, I know how to get hold of them. In Armenia there is a treasure trove, and there is nothing which cannot be fixed for roubles.'

All my former suspicions surged up again. Was he aiming to get me into Soviet territory where I could be seized redhanded? I had no desire to see the inside of a labour camp in Siberia; on the other hand, I had detected a very independent spirit among Armenians, combined with a mixture of scorn, contempt or downright hatred for Moscow. And all the Armenians I had talked to in Beirut spoke well of Dergazarian. He should be on the level; it was inconceivable that they were all members of the KGB. I took a stiff swig of Stolichnaya, then nodded. After all, Helen had told me everything was possible in Beirut.

'OK. When do we leave?'

'First, you had better get hold of some money. We Armenians are a goodnatured people, but don't expect credit.'

'No problem. I'll go to the bank tomorrow and draw dollars.'

'Use your head, Michel, who wants dollars? We are going to Yerevan, not fucking Disneyland. The man who sells you his grandmother's wedding ring needs roubles. He can hardly wander into the local GUM store and pay in greenbacks, can he?'

'Rouble notes?'

'That's right. We sew them inside the linings of our clothes. You can buy them cheaply in Zurich, so you had better book a flight. I'll make the travel arrangements here; it will take you a couple of days to get a visa. Don't forget that you are a tourist when you apply to the embassy. I'll meet you here in a week's time.' With a twinkling smile, Dergazarian bade me goodnight.

It took me a few days to complete these preparations. I have never been much of a needlewoman and I did not feel inclined to ask a hotel maid to sew money into my clothes. I did drop a hint to Helen, but she voiced strong feminist objections. Luckily, Dergazarian had that side of the operation organized and so, feeling like someone in a second-rate spy movie, I arrived at Beirut International Airport and took the short hop flight to Aleppo. There, I sauntered up to the Aeroflot counter and checked in for the direct flight to Yerevan. There was not much of a crowd and all the other passengers seemed to be Russians or Armenians, so I felt uncomfortably conspicuous but nobody paid any special attention to me. A Syrian girl handed me my boarding card and wished me a good flight. I stood for a moment watching my suitcase containing a large part of both my wardrobe and liquid capital bump on to the conveyer belt and disappear from sight. I recalled those occasions when my baggage had got loaded on to the wrong plane, despite prominent labels, and shuddered at the thought that if the loader was thinking about his girlfriend, my case might arrive anywhere from Melbourne to Montevideo. The flight was called and there was no sign of Dergazarian. What would I do if he did not turn up? Advertize on the local TV – 'Wanted, rare works of art and icons. Best prices paid. Strictly cash, non-deductible for taxes'?

We shuffled through the departure lounge and took the airport bus. Still no Dergazarian. I was beginning to feel very ill-at-ease. On board the Tupolev, there was the usual confusion as some smoker found himself in the non-smoking area, and while people were still pushing through the cabin, Dergazarian slipped into the seat next to mine.

I remember very little of the flight. Dergazarian busied himself with a chess problem and I consoled myself with the thought that if I were shipped off to a Soviet jail, it would give me an excellent opportunity to learn to play chess really well. But as we began our descent to Yerevan, I got my first sight of Armenia, and what a beautiful country it is! Snow-capped mountains dominated a landscape of fields and forests, interlaced with rivers and lakes, blue as sapphires. As we skimmed over the fir trees which fringed the airport, I felt close to panic. Why on earth had I come on this crazy expedition? Even if we got in with our smuggled money, how the hell were we going to get out again with our booty? Then I thought, Well, Dergazarian has done it plenty of times, so there must be some way, but I was not convinced.

There were the usual forms to be filled in when we landed but nobody was particularly concerned with our baggage, which mercifully had been loaded into the same plane as ourselves after all. It stood to reason that they would be more worried about what we might be taking out rather than what we might be bringing into the country, or so I reckoned, and that thought did not fill me with much joy. However, as we prepared to leave the terminal, Dergazarian went over to one of the offices reserved for customs and emerged a few minutes later, chatting amiably with a uniformed giant who was clutching a bottle of good French cognac. They exchanged cordial farewells.

'One of my most useful contacts,' he explained. 'It is always a good idea to renew his goodwill when we arrive.'

We took a taxi into the city. 'Welcome to Armenia,' beamed my companion. 'And what do you think of Yerevan?'

I did not say so but I thought the city dignified but dull. There were monumental buildings in glistening white stone and fine, broad tree-lined avenues, but precious little traffic. And of course there were no lurid hoardings, urging us what to smoke and what to drink. There were posters exhorting workers to exceed their production norms, but they didn't do much to cheer the place up. However the streets were clean, and our hotel, a long two-storied affair in red tufa stone, with a distinct resemblance to a nineteenth-century museum, was reasonably comfortable. Situated on one side of Lenin Square, it looked on to neat gardens where fountains played in an ornamental lake. It rejoiced in the name of Hotel Armenia. No marks for originality, I thought. As I anticipated, Dergazarian greeted the manager like a long-lost brother.

My bathroom was a splendid piece of nostalgia with gleaming copper tubes, polished brass taps and an enormous tub. Not bad, I reflected as I enjoyed the steamy water, I have been in the Soviet Union for nearly two hours and I haven't been arrested yet.

Then off to dinner. I had expected to be taken to one of the restaurants which Intourist recommended, but that was not the Armenian way. We had been invited to the home of one of Dergazarian's friends, a key figure in organizing 'our sort of business' as he diplomatically described it. Any preconceived idea about the austere character of Soviet socialism was shattered by what I saw. But then this was Armenia, which I was learning was something different.

Aram lived in a detached bungalow on the outskirts of the city, standing in its own parkland. Richly decorated rugs were scattered over the marble floor and there was an impressive display cabinet filled with the distinctive pottery of Transcaucasia. But what dominated the room was an enormous table, groaning under the weight of great platters of every sort of smoked meat, a monster dish on which a whole sturgeon reposed, buckets of ice in which stood bowls of glistening, large grey grains of the finest Beluga caviar. On one side of the room was a hot-plate contraption on which *shashlik* sizzled. There were creamy goats' cheeses, peaches, grapes and apricots. Bottles of the local wines and the blood-red vintages of Georgia were drawn up in ranks, their flanks guarded by decanters of cognac. And vodka! Clear vodka, cloudy vodka, vodka in which lemon peel floated, vodka in which were submerged tiny red peppers.

'You must be famished after your journey.' Aram, a large, shaggy man, gave me a hug of welcome. 'My house is open to any friend of Dergazarian, and he commends you highly,' he continued. 'Come, let us drink to a successful and enjoyable visit, your first to Armenia.'

My memory of that feast is fragmentary, great chunks of it were effaced by the deluge of alcohol. Aram was one of the bosses of the black market network in Yerevan. After the fourth or fifth vodka, a toast to Dergazarian, another in response to our host, more to the other guests, Aram raised a glass and we all drank to Armenia. I was surprised to see tears starting in his eyes. He wiped his sleeve across his moustache and turned to me. He had a deep, booming voice and it was charged with emotion.

'Everybody has heard of the Holocaust and all decent people feel shame, horror, disgust, yes? But the same thing happened to my people forty years earlier, and nobody gives a damn. The fucking Turks carried out a policy of genocide and they still pretend it never happened. Not surprising, is it, when some Armenian knocks off a Turkish diplomat now and then? There ought to be one Armenian land, like the Jews got Israel. We are scattered among the Turks who still hate us, the Iranians where the Shah's police murder anybody they consider a danger, and that goes for us, and some in Iraq, the most bloodthirsty of all.'

'What about here?' I asked.

'Yes, here we live in peace. But make no mistake, beneath the surface friendship of the three Transcaucasian republics there is mistrust and tension. Who knows? One day blood might flow. Look, Azerbaijan is Moslem, Armenia was Christian while the savages in the north were still swinging their clubs in the forest. Islam talks toleration, but there is a fanaticism which runs deep. As for Georgia, they are about as straight as a corkscrew. Remember a guy called Jozef Stalin?'

'So you see,' Dergazarian chipped in, 'why we Armenians tend to run our own show. You will find out how deep Armenian friendship runs. If you want to do business here, nothing is barred to you, everybody will help.'

'It's just that we don't play ball with foreigners,' growled Aram.

I turned to Dergazarian in confusion. He laughed. 'Not you,

Michel, you are one of us. Foreigners are busybodies from Moscow.'

We then drank toasts to people I had never heard of and although the conversation grew less serious, voices were raised and local issues debated with considerable heat: Armenians are passionate, especially in their cups. Dergazarian took the opportunity to introduce me to some of the guests, including the freight manager for Aeroflot.

'He is a very good friend,' he told me. 'He's never failed to be helpful.'

The Helpful One shook my hand and assured me effusively how he looked forward to our friendship maturing. We drank to it; I presumed he had just been paid off.

A middle-aged man with a well-filled belly waddled towards me.

'Be especially nice to Victor. He is important,' Dergazarian whispered.

I guess that I must have put on a satisfactory performance since Victor insisted on proposing another toast to me.

'Who the fuck is he?' I murmured to Dergazarian. 'Everybody seems to be making a great fuss over him.'

'So they should,' he replied. 'He is the local KGB boss.'

'Jesus! Who else is in on the racket?'

'Practically all the Armenians in the republic,' Aram answered. 'Let's drink to the system.'

After that, as I recollect, we drank to an icon which I would buy, to the memory of a favourite poet, to Aram's armchair, and God knows what besides. The food was terrific too, but it was relegated to blotting paper for the vodka. Somebody sang what I was told was an old Armenian folk song – it sounded pretty bawdy to me – and there was an energetic bout of dancing which soon subsided since the dancers rapidly became too thirsty to continue. The festivities went on for hours, and I lost track of time.

Next day's hangover deserved a special mention in Dante's

Inferno, but somehow we got down to business, and yet more eating and drinking. I met dozens of people and was everywhere given a warm welcome. I was getting plugged into the Armenian network: it was more than a black market, it was a sort of alternative society, a submerged people. I was offered silver art deco objects, antique watches, elegant boxes which I recognized as being the work of Fabergé. And I found a number of superb icons, older works from Moscow and Novgorod and later examples from the Stroganoff school. I was surprised at the variety and the remoteness from Armenia of so many of these objects.

'How did so many good things get to Armenia?' I asked. 'I would have expected to find this sort of stuff in Leningrad or Moscow.'

'In what we call the Great Patriotic War, the Germans never got as far as Yerevan, but plenty of refugees from the north did,' I was told.

My eyes were really opened to the extent of graft in the Soviet system in a place called Echmiadzin. It was a leap into a remote past. The cathedral, which goes back to the fourth century, has dumpy spires shaped like wizards' hats surmounting a round tower and open-sided cupolas.

'Nothing like those weird candy-striped onions they stuck on top of churches in the north, is it? But then that came a thousand years after our churches.'

My companion called himself Alyosha. Doubtless he found the Russian name more convenient since he worked largely in Russia proper. He was one of the main restorers at the Hermitage Museum in Leningrad.

'Have you visited the Hermitage?' he asked. 'You must go. It is a marvellous place – everything from the paleolithic to Picasso. Do you realize that they have more than two million exhibits?'

I admitted that I hadn't.

'Neither do they,' he chuckled. 'So when a few of them go astray, well, who is the wiser? Of course they would notice if their Michelangelo or Leonardo went missing, but who is likely to worry about a few damaged icons?'

He took me back to his house where he offered me several icons. I couldn't believe my eyes. His words had led me to expect some insignificant pieces, but what I saw were magnificent and highly important.

'Do you want proof of provenance?' Alyosha asked. He had a cherubic face which seemed to light up with innocent pleasure. He had produced a catalogue of an exhibition held at the Rublov Museum in Moscow. There were photographs of some of the outstanding exhibits among which were three Tver panels of archdeacons which I bought. They were superb, and worth a small fortune in the West, but how the hell was I to get them out of the country? I supposed Dergazarian would make light of the problem. I was right.

'They are great, aren't they?' he said. 'Let's see what else you can pick up to make a respectable load.'

'And just how do you propose that we export what we have already?' I asked. 'You can't sew these into the linings of your pants.'

'We'll have to crate them up,' he said, as if it were the most normal thing in the world for smugglers to take things out by the crateful. 'I have that in hand, don't worry.'

After that, things became insane. At the health centre of Dilizhan, an elderly merchant on a cure sold me valuable Oriental carpets and I bought a rare triptych with a rizza from the workshop of Carl Fabergé and some pieces from that of Pavel Ovchnikoff. We had resolved to take out some gold, strictly forbidden of course, which we hid by buying a few old samovars, having the gold melted down and poured into them.

The day before our departure, we got together all our acquisitions which, to my consternation, filled several enormous crates. But that night we were treated to a farewell dinner, a repetition of the one with which we had been welcomed, except that we drank even more. It was an emotional occasion.

We swore eternal friendship and I promised I would be back as soon as I had disposed of my purchases.

'If I can ever help you or any of your people, just say the word,' I told Aram.

'I am sure that there will be such times,' he said. 'What is important is that we can trust you and that you can trust us.'

Even after enough vodka to sink a battleship, I remembered those words clearly. Aram had been deadly serious and the moment when I was to be put to the test was soon to come. Everybody kissed everyone else. The KGB boss was especially tearful at my leaving. I just hoped that he was not tempted to protract my stay in order to have the pleasure of my company longer.

The next thing I recall was being roughly shaken by the shoulder. 'Wake up, Michel! For fuck's sake, what's the matter with you? You have a couple of drinks and you want to sleep for a week. We have a plane to catch, remember?'

I opened one eye and regarded the devil in the shape of Dergazarian. 'Leave me be,' I mumbled. 'I've made up my mind to die today. I'll take the plane tomorrow.'

He went on shaking me and swearing. He was making so much noise that I decided to humour him and survive, if only he would be quiet. He was going on about our things being loaded on to a truck to go to the airport and slowly an appreciation of my situation began to filter through to my mind. Somewhere outside were jumbo-sized boxes, containing a fair sample of the treasures of the Soviet Union, which represented practically all of my liquid resources. The chances of this lot slipping unnoticed through Soviet customs were as remote as my being elected Pope. But even after that miracle, there would be the little matter of bringing the stuff into Beirut. The only thing which would keep me out of jail, I judged, would be to plead insanity. No sane man could have undertaken such an expedition.

My reflections were interrupted by Dergazarian pouring coffee into me. My morale recovered a bit as we left the hotel and the manager wished us a good flight, adding that he had seen to the disposal of our luggage.

'Luggage?' I croaked. 'He calls an entire baggage train luggage?'

'Everything is arranged,' Dergazarian soothed me. 'In Aleppo, it is merely a matter of trans-shipment. And as I told you, I deal with the formalities in Armenia and back in Beirut.'

I sank back in the taxi. There was nothing to do now but wait and see. I was relieved when we arrived at the airport that there was not a firing squad already in position. There were our crates, piled up in the freight area, as inconspicuous as a dinosaur or two.

Our drinking buddy the freight manager sauntered over.

'Your things are going on first,' he said.

And it was as easy as that. Forms were stamped; nobody appeared to read them but all the formalities were complied with. I squinted at our fellow passengers. Suppose they were in the same line of business and had a similar amount of freight? The goddamned plane would never take off. Our carpets alone must have come close to its authorized maximum load. Maybe the floor of the hold would fall out? I was brought back to reality by the flight being called. To my amazement, the plane took off without apparent effort.

In Beirut, we walked through immigration and had a drink in the VIP lounge. When we emerged, our crates had cleared customs with no questions asked. The journey had proved quite an anti-climax, but I surely was not upset by that! That afternoon, I retrieved my treasures and took stock of my position. I knew the value of what I had brought back. My previous deals had made me good money: this one trip had made me a rich man. And I had laid a foundation on which I could build a flourishing business. From now on, virtually anything I desired was within my grasp.

Gazing at the splendid icons, I grasped the essential difference between them and the religious paintings of the West.

Whereas the magnificent paintings of medieval and Renaissance Catholicism are triumphant representations of objects of worship – Christ, the Virgin, the Saints or the Crucifixion – icons of the same subjects are actual objects of worship themselves. It is as though there has been a second incarnation of God, not into flesh and blood, but into gold and gesso. Whatever we may judge their artistic merits, the great icons are spiritually more exalted, more intense, than their Western counterparts. They are literally inspired art for it is as though the Divine has breathed its own life into their austere formality. An icon does not portray Christ, it embodies Him. This is the secret of the power of the icon, and its personal appeal to the worshipper. The icon confronts the viewer with the subject so directly that there appears to be no intervention by the painter. The strength of the image arises because the icon is no longer the image but the reality, prayer given form and substance, a God who can be touched and kissed. I dreamed that I would build an icon collection, something outstanding which I could display. That was not simply arrogance. Icons were not then widely appreciated in the West and even less understood. Of course, there were some knowledgeable collectors; many of the most active were customers of mine. But I wanted more people to have a chance to see these marvellous objects and to get the same emotional experience from them as I did.

Another dream of that afternoon also came true – to live at least part of the time in Beirut. Not only would it be convenient for future raids into Armenia, there were also happy hunting grounds for icon collectors in Greece, Cyprus and Turkey, while Beirut itself attracted many dealers with things to sell as well as wealthy buyers. And I knew that here I could live well; in comparison, Amsterdam seemed dull like its weather and prosaic. I felt comfortable in the exotic, colourful kaleidoscope which was Beirut.

# 5

# New Icons for Old!

I had been drawn to Istanbul by its bustle and its clamour, the spot where Europe and Asia confront each other, but Beirut was altogether more exotic and more of a mystery, since it seemed that anybody who had anything to sell or any way-out proposition to finance, headed for the capital of Lebanon. I am certain that if the Martians had invaded Earth, their first colony would have been established in Beirut and that they would have mingled unnoticed in the crowds.

But I had not settled in Beirut merely to watch the world go by, nor solely because it offered beautiful women, good food and a great night life. Life was pretty good and after my successful invasion of Russia I was able to afford the things I appreciated. I reckoned I had done a hell of a lot better in my Russian campaign than either Napoleon or Hitler!

I bought a superb penthouse apartment in Hamra, the wealthiest part of the modern city. Next door to the Middle East Airlines building, it was reached by its own private elevator. The rooms were light and spacious, but what I most enjoyed was the extensive terrace which ran right around the building. On one side it commanded a panoramic view of the city and the mountains, while on the other side one took in the sparkling expanse of ocean beyond the sweep of the bay. The place was lavishly furnished and one could sit on that terrace of an evening, listening to the splashing of the fountain, sipping a chilled kir royale, and gaze down at the stream of toy automobiles, so far below that the traffic noise was reduced to a soothing hum. There were times when friends would sit around and talk and smoke the *narghile*, stretched on divans, like characters from the Arabian Nights. There were more lively evenings when I would entertain a succession of soft-eyed but surprisingly knowledgeable young ladies, and then it would be their turn to entertain me. It was a marvellous setting for subtle seduction. Beirut was a rich man's paradise, a perfect combination of the comforts of the West and the exotic richness of the Orient.

But I could not relax indefinitely; I was still engaged in my hunt for outstanding icons for my own collection and proposed exhibition. The work provided a profitable and interesting distraction from the constant round of pleasure. During the next few years, Beirut was to be my main base. In Russia, I found myself increasingly involved in helping desperate men and women, sometimes persecuted as dissidents, to slip through the security net and start a new life in the West. Consequently, there were times when I would be living under great strain and sleeping rough. So, when I returned to Beirut, I really appreciated my apartment and I felt that I not only deserved its conveniences but actually needed them to recuperate from hardships in the field.

I would wander through the Armenian quarter, savouring the restaurant aromas and chatting with the world's most quickwitted dealers. It was in Beirut that I first heard that celebrated definition of an Armenian as a man who will go into a revolving door behind you but come out in front.

I kept in touch with the respectable antique dealers in their shops or in the lobbies of the luxury hotels, but in the less classy bars and restaurants I would run into my Armenian connections and others like them whose business methods ranged from the unconventional to the shady or the downright illegal.

In a sleazy nightclub where wise men would have avoided contact with the booze or the birds, I came across Antoine. He was a short, prematurely balding Lebanese in his mid-twenties with soft, friendly eyes, the sort of fellow you knew you could trust the moment you met him – but of course you couldn't. I had heard of his skills, and news of my dealings had reached him along the grapevine. Antoine was a restorer of paintings, especially icons, and he was damned good at it. But he also knew how to take advantage of his specialized knowledge and of his contacts in Turkey, Lebanon, Greece, and especially Cyprus. We went through the courtesies, such as getting drunk together, and there was an immediate rapport. I inspected some icons he was selling and it was obvious that he was able to sniff out excellent pieces, but it was some months before I learned how an impoverished picture restorer was able to acquire first-class works of art. It was too easy to assume that he had stolen them; he lacked the aggressiveness of the robber or the furtiveness of the petty thief.

'How well do you know Cyprus, Michel?' he asked one night. He had come back to my place for a nightcap.

'Hardly at all,' I replied. 'Is it worth getting to know?'

'Bloody godforsaken hole,' he complained, 'but it does have something going for it, if you know your way around.'

He gave me a knowing wink and his usually frank features assumed a foxy expression.

'Tell me more,' I cajoled.

He looked around as if to make sure no eavesdropper had crept in and took a good swig of Moskovskaya. 'Who was that guy in a story who found a cave of treasure? He was Chinese or Japanese or something?'

I shook my head.

'Had an old, battered lamp which he used to rub and, hey presto, some damned great genie would appear and do whatever he was ordered.'

'Aladdin?'

'That's the fellow. Well, it was his wicked uncle or somebody who persuaded Aladdin's girlfriend to swap his rotten old lamp for a nice bright new one. Remember?'

I nodded. 'New lamps for old.'

'That was his slogan. Well, that's who I am, Aladdin's uncle.'

When Antoine had first gone to Cyprus, he explained, the British were in control, but they were being harassed by both the Greek and Turkish communities and, as long as they were able to retain the use of their military bases, were only too willing to get the hell out and leave the natives to come to some sort of arrangement, or to fight it out among themselves. The politics of Cyprus were, however, of no interest to Antoine; what mattered to him was the existence throughout the island of Greek churches, often with their original icons. Fine icons had been painted in Cyprus certainly as early as the tenth century, and the capture of the island by the Turks in 1570 had not marked the end of the tradition although the later icons were increasingly influenced by Venetian and Western styles. But there was no register of the paintings, and precious few people outside the island cared about them or were even aware of their existence for they were for the most part in tiny isolated villages. It was to one of these out-of-the-way hamlets that Antoine came one day. He had completed some restoration work in Nicosia and an acquaintance had recommended that he spend a few days looking around the countryside since often the icons in the old churches were dilapidated and he could earn a little money doing repair jobs.

He had been disappointed in the first few villages in the rough, hilly country beyond Nicosia, and was on the point of giving up when he arrived at a tiny village, hidden away in a valley. There was a fresh fragrance of wild sage and rosemary and the earth was carpeted with wild flowers. There were half a dozen tumbledown cottages and a posse of semi-wild goats patrolled the one track through the place. The ruins of a few larger houses and the stumpy remains of Roman columns indicated that once the village had been rather grander. That its origins went back to the remote past was evident to Antoine when he peeped inside the austere, post-Byzantine church.

Coming as he did straight out of the brilliant sunlight, it was dark inside despite the guttering candles, and the iconostasis, the five-storied screen which separated the altar from the body of the church, appeared a dingy affair, the dozens of icons with which it was panelled almost invisible beneath the thick encrustation of soot from the incense of centuries. But Antoine was too much of an old hand to be put off by the grime and he peered closely at the images.

'I am afraid they are too decrepit to bring home to the people the nearness of the Mother of God and the holy saints,' murmured a voice behind him.

Antoine started. He had been too engrossed in the icons to notice the approach of the priest, and before he had recovered sufficiently to answer, the old man rambled on.

'The other day I was in a village, not more than ten kilometres from here, the priest there is a cousin of mine, and it did my heart good to see the fine ranks of icons in his church. The whole building seemed to be illuminated by their freshness and the bright colours.'

'I restore icons,' Antoine replied. 'It was probably some of my work. Maybe I could do something for your church too.'

The priest shook his head sadly. 'There is nothing you could do with these. They are too far gone. And besides, this is a poor village, we could never afford to have them restored.'

Antoine took a candle, approached the screen and gazed into the gloom. The panels were worm-eaten and ravaged by weather, but that was only to be expected and Antoine possessed the skill and experience to deal with that sort of damage. Faintly he made out the sad features of a Mother of God Hogoditria, She who shows the way, and he recognized the work of a fine artist – and a work of the late-fifteenth century which would command a high price back in Beirut, and an even higher one in Europe or America.

'You are young and probably consider these icons as just so

much old rubbish,' the priest said, 'but to the men and women of our village, they are old friends, and it grieves us to see them, as it were, ill and aged.'

Antoine could not believe his luck. 'I understand, Father,' he answered, 'but perhaps I can nevertheless be of some service. I not only restore icons, I also paint them. Why don't you let me paint you a whole series to replace these?'

'My son, you have not followed what I have been saying. We don't have the money to have the icons restored. How could we pay for new ones?'

'Pay!' cried Antoine in mock horror. 'Who said anything about paying? God gave me this talent and it would be humble service to Him to adorn His church. How could I think of demanding money for such a thing!'

'Would you really do that for us, whom you do not know?'

'It would be for the glory of God,' answered Antoine, a confirmed atheist.

The old man's eyes were shining. 'It must have been the mercy of God which led you to us,' he said.

'And I'll tell you what I shall do,' Antoine waxed enthusiastic. 'I shall paint you the finest, brightest icons you have ever seen. Why, your cousin will be so jealous! What is more, I shall take away the old, ruined icons which now disfigure your iconostasis so that you won't have the trouble of disposing of them.'

The priest shook his head. 'They are old friends: I would not like to think of them being destroyed or used for firewood.'

'Have no fear, Father,' Antoine told him. 'I know places where old icons are cherished. I will see that no harm comes to them.'

By the evening, the good news had spread through the village like wildfire. It was an occasion for celebration; a goat was killed and the strong, red wine with its penetrating resin aroma flowed so freely that the midday sun was beating down before Antoine staggered out of the priest's house to commence his charitable work. Once his head had stopped trying to go into orbit, he made rapid progress. In Nicosia he was able to buy cheap wooden panels by the dozen, with a special discount for quantity. He was running short of ready cash and had to scrounge around to borrow enough to buy the paint. The actual time it took to knock out a few Saints Peter, Paul, George and Demetrios and a Virgin or two was amazingly short, but then he was not decorating a Sistine Chapel and as long as the colours were bright, the features of the subjects familiar, and the general effect warm and cheerful, the rustic worshippers were well satisfied. Indeed, their recommendations were so enthusiastic, their praise of the itinerant genius so fulsome, that long before he had finished refurbishing their iconostasis and relieving them of their tatty old paintings, men from the neighboring villages had come to inspect his work and offers flowed in. If the artist would paint nice new icons for them too, he would be welcome to the old ones. It was unbelievable that this young man, so talented and so devoted to the Church, who might have been having a good time in Nicosia, should labour for months to create an entire new iconostasis for the poor people of an obscure village, without asking payment, merely for the greater glory of God. Why, Antoine must have been an angel sent from Heaven.

And it was with something resembling religious devotion that Antoine eventually packed the dirty, discarded icons into strong crates and arranged to have them sent away. The wise men of the village smiled secretly at his naive ardour since they knew that the crates must have been worth more than the decrepit paintings, but it was heartwarming to see the holy objects treated with such respect.

Shipment and customs formalities in Cyprus and in Lebanon posed no problems to Antoine. But even when one had paid the right guys to look the other way, there was always the possibility of something going wrong, and he was gnawing at his fingernails until the precious boxes were safe in a Beirut warehouse. However, Antoine was not in close contact with the most interesting buyers, and that was where I could get into the act. I could also help with the financing of the operation since he needed cash quickly to repay the sums he had borrowed. In no time at all, together with some associates, I had turned an improvised bit of business into a smooth organization, a moneymaking machine. Officials were paid off, sales arranged, and the trickle of icons out of Cyprus broadened into a flow. Everybody was happy. Priests and villagers had their pretty new icons and we had a steady income. Nothing could go wrong – but it did.

Archbishop Makarios was then President of Cyprus. The saturnine prelate possessed true charisma, as befitted a man of his cloth, but it was as the political leader of the Greek Cypriots rather than for his religious fervour that he had gained a worldwide reputation. *Enosis* had been the rallying cry – self-rule for the people of Cyprus – with which Makarios and the underground military leader of the revolt, Grivas, had won their struggle against the British, but it was the Archbishop who emerged as the statesman, a leader with a touch of Ghandi's adroitness but without the drawback of his attachment to the ideals of non-violence and the simple life. Indeed, Makarios had a keen interest in worldly things, and one of his enthusiasms, unfortunately for Antoine, was his valuable collection of icons. It might have been considered irregular for a religious leader to acquire objects which must have been looted from churches and the purchase of which by private citizens was frowned upon, but then the good Archbishop was presumably able to grant himself political pardon as well as spiritual absolution. He had eyes and ears everywhere on the island, and it was only a matter of time before he learned of the goodhearted young man who was giving new icons to embellish the churches and disposing of the old garbage. A man of Makarios's intelligence understood immediately what was going on, and the Archbishop decided to take a hand in the game.

Antoine had stripped a church of a particularly fine set of icons and had consigned the crates in what had now become a routine. But this time he waited in vain for their arrival in Beirut. It was incredible; the regular goodwill offerings had been made to the customs officers, but a squad of specially imported officials had made a beeline for Antoine's crates and seized them. Since they had not gone for any other cargo, it was obvious that they had been tipped off. Antoine came to see me in a state of frenzied despair.

'What the hell am I going to do?' he wailed. 'There was a fortune to be made out of that shipment. And what do you think will happen if I stick my nose back into Cyprus? They'll shove me into some stinking jail and throw away the key.'

I soothed him as best I could with vodka and endeavoured to conceal my own anxiety. We could do nothing until we had more information and even then we had to resign ourselves to the fact that the consignment was irretrievably lost.

The next day, I heard of the arrest of Youssef, a close friend of Antoine. Youssef, a Lebanese, was one of the ablest dealers in Munich, then the centre for trade in Middle Eastern antiquities, and a key figure in the arrangements I had made for my exhibition. He was also one of our smuggling team; he had nothing to do with the acquisition of the icons or their transportation but he had been in Cyprus, assessing some of Antoine's finds as well as looking out for items which might be purchased in a more conventional manner. This was serious; we had to get him released. It also confirmed my fears that the seizure of the crates was not an isolated strike by the authorities; our cosy little racket had been blown. Youssef was accustomed to ease and comfort. Nature had not intended him for incarceration in some smelly cell.

While I was agonizing over his predicament, Youssef called.

'You mean they actually permit you to phone from jail?' I cried in amazement.

'I have to pay for the cell,' he replied, 'and you know what damned thieves these hotels are, so let's make it brief.'

'Hotels?'

'Sure, Michel.' His tone was impatient. 'Didn't anybody explain that I am under house arrest in the Hilton?'

I learned that he had been treated with almost exaggerated courtesy, and was able to enjoy all the amenities of the Cyprus Hilton in Nicosia, except the use of the exits. There could only be one explanation: somebody with the power to have things handled the way he ordered wanted to do a deal, and it was not long before an approach was made to me. The sober-suited young man with the button-down shirt and horn-rimmed glasses might have been kitted out by the CIA; actually, he informed me, he was an emissary from the Archbishop and had a proposition to make which I would find irresistible. After he had left, I summoned Antoine.

'You are going back to Nicosia,' I told him.

'Like hell I am!' he retorted. 'Aladdin's lamp has run out of oil. Get it straight, Michel, we are getting no more icons out of Cyprus.'

'You are not going there to beg, buy, borrow or steal icons,' I informed him. 'You are returning to your highly respectable profession. Your services as a repairer and restorer are demanded.'

'By whom?'

'By His Reverence Archbishop Makarios.'

Antoine stared at me in disbelief. 'You are out of your mind. And this little mouse is not going to stick his nose into the lair of that big pussy cat.'

'This little mouse will do as he is told if he does not want God knows how many charges thrown at him by an angry Archbishop. Use your head, Antoine. They've been following you for months and if you don't play along you are going to have problems, no matter where you hide.'

He would have gone on arguing, but I pointed out that until he agreed to take an unofficial appointment as Makarios's personal restorer of icons, Youssef was going to stay in confinement and it was likely that he would ultimately be sent to a less comfortable residence.

Miserably, with bad grace and shaking in his shoes, Antoine returned to the scene of his earlier exploits. He was taken to view the Archbishop's very private collection. Despite his predicament, he was unable to conceal his admiration for Makarios's taste, that of a true connoisseur, and as he became engrossed in the restoration of the beautiful and rare objects, he found that he was actually enjoying his enforced labour.

Makarios himself came to view his progress and the two struck up a strange friendship based on their mutual love of the icons. Youssef was freed, and no obstacles put in his way as he went about his legitimate business but, as Antoine had predicted, Aladdin's lamp had been extinguished.

Antoine was commissioned to restore the icons in several churches as well as those in Makarios's own collection. A discreet watch was probably kept on him, just in case he reverted to his old habits, but he was well paid, and controlled any itch he might have had to 'liberate' the paintings. Ironically, we were able to turn this confrontation with the Archbishop to our advantage, for with Antoine working for him, and as it became known that we shared his passion, we were allowed to continue operating in Cyprus under his unofficial protection. And with the help of Antoine's network in Greece, I was able to get on with amassing the items for my exhibition.

However these satisfactory arrangements were shortlived due to the revolt of the Cypriot National Guard and subsequent invasion of the island by the Turkish army in 1974. Three years later the Archbishop suffered a heart attack and died, bequeathing his magnificent collection to the nation. By then, I had set up my own organization in Cyprus, but I have always retained a soft spot for Antoine, the Aladdin of the icons.

# 6

# OPERATION ATTILA

In July 1974, Makarios was driven from power by a coup, inspired by the dictatorial regime of the colonels in Greece, and dedicated to *enosis*, the absorption of Cyprus into Greece. The immediate reaction was an invasion of the island by the Turkish army, the so-called Operation Attila, avowedly to protect the Turkish Cypriot minority, but this drive, and the subsequent Attila II after the breakdown of a ceasefire, were the occasions for brutal persecution of the fleeing Greek Cypriots and wanton destruction of property, particularly items of Christian worship. Hostilities came to an end with the intervention of a United Nations peace-keeping force, UNFICYP, and the establishment of a buffer zone, dividing the Turkish-occupied north from the Greek south. The Attila Line became the Green Line. The island was effectively partitioned, military checkpoints were set up and there were no formal communications between the two sectors, other than those channelled through the United Nations in the divided city of Nicosia.

These conditions virtually eliminated the simple smuggling operations, such as those of Antoine, but were ideal for people with privileged access, either to the British military bases or to the UNFICYP organization, and Aydin Dikmen was specially favoured. Although a Turk, he also held a Cypriot passport and had property in both the Turkish north and the Greek south of the island. His relations with senior officers in the Turkish army were so good that he was referred to sometimes as the official archaeologist to the occupying force, which he was not. Not long after the arrival of the United Nations troops, he reached an understanding with important officers in the Finnish contingent which made it possible for him to slip from one sector to the other.

Aydin became my main source of supply, but since I had been operating in Cyprus well before the invasion, I had my own organization on the island as well, both Greek and Turkish Cypriots. I was in the southern part of the country during those troubled months and saw the streams of refugees, fleeing from the north, often having abandoned virtually all their possessions.

Before the hostilities, I had visited the little church of St Euphemianos, just outside the village of Lysi, about eight miles from Famagusta. The church was famous for its outstandingly beautiful frescoes, dating back to the fourteenth century. But Lysi was later in the Turkish sector and I was told that the church had been abandoned. Then Aydin came to me in Munich with a proposition.

'We have removed the complete fresco,' he informed me. 'Obviously we could not take out the entire wall in one piece, but you will see, all the bits can be reassembled once we have brought them out.'

'You must have a whole bloody trained team working for you,' I gasped.

'Of course. They were hand-picked and given an intensive course, some in Budapest, the others here at the Dorner Institut.'

I had to admire his style. He recruited a gang of church robbers and had them trained at one of the most famous centres for the study and restoration of classical and medieval works of art.

'And do they go in for much restoration work?' I asked mockingly.

'They are good skilled workers, but most of what goes on around them is not restoration but destruction. Look here, Michel, you would like to buy this fresco, wouldn't you? So we remove it from a church which has been deserted and already partly ransacked. But what would happen if some inquisitive bastard wandered round the church and found it had been stripped? Somebody might remember there used to be an old fresco there, but it had been removed by a squad of men, disciplined, not ordinary soldiers. That could lead to trouble simply because we saved beautiful, religious objects before the church was blown up by the army.'

'They blow it up?' I gasped.

'You do not understand the mentality. There is such religious bitterness. You don't want to buy a derelict old church, do you? The attitude in the army is that the places are falling apart and anyway there are too many churches in Cyprus, so why not get rid of a few? But they warn us and we first take out the things which matter.'

'And nobody objects?'

'Use your head. There are so many mobs wandering around, pillaging and wrecking the place, that it is taken for granted that it was the work of an army unit or maybe freelance looters. Once the building no longer exists, nobody is likely to trace these frescoes, or any other good things, back to their original homes, are they?'

I still looked dubious, so Aydin turned to the moral argument. 'OK, so you don't approve of blowing up the odd church. But first I carefully take out anything worth saving. What would happen if we left the churches alone? You know as well as I do that being in countryside occupied by the Turkish army, they would either be destroyed or left to fall into ruins. In either case, precious works would be lost. So what do you prefer? A nice clean conscience, or my programme of conservation?'

'Stop fucking around, Aydin,' I retorted. 'You're in this for the money, not for pure-hearted love of the Cypriot cultural heritage.'

'Sure, I'm in business, I've never denied it. But my motives should not be your concern, and I don't need you to be the keeper of my conscience. What matters is that I am saving beautiful things which would otherwise perish. If you don't approve, nobody is going to force you to buy them.'

I believed Aydin's account because I had been in the north and seen some of the buildings which had been vandalized. And I knew that Turkish soldiers were involved; I had seen them take icons from churches and use them for target practice.

He told me that the frescoes were stored away with other pieces he could offer me in a depot in the north. There were a number of such depots used by Aydin and other groups, sometimes even guarded by Turkish soldiers.

I took a regular flight into Cyprus. Aydin was waiting for me and we drove into the Turkish north, using an illegal route avoiding checkpoints. Not far from the village of Psillatos stands a barn, and this was the depot which housed the Lysi frescoes and other treasures. Aydin led me past a Turkish army sentry, and I saw how the frescoes had been carefully crated to avoid damage. I agreed to buy them and some important icons removed from the Monastery of St Chrysostomos which he offered, as well as another great fresco depicting the Tree of Jesse which had stood in the Monastery of Antiphonitis. I took photographs to record the state of the pieces when I bought them. Then we supervized their loading on to a Turkish truck. I handed over half the agreed purchase price; Aydin was to receive the balance when he had shipped the pieces out by way of Larnaka and they had arrived safely in Munich.

'What happens now?' I asked.

'We drive back the way we came,' he answered. 'The crates will be taken to a rendezvous close to the Green Line. There will be a UNFICYP truck waiting, and they will be taken into the south by UN soldiers. In the morning, we meet the truck and I take over from there.'

Aydin wanted to get back over the Green Line, so we drove off first. I was well satisfied with what I had bought.

Next morning, he took me to a deserted spot close to the Green Line. A truck bearing UN insignia was waiting for us, manned by Finnish soldiers.

'OK, let's check the load,' I called.

The soldiers unloaded the crates. Something was wrong: there should have been more. So we looked inside each one. All the other pieces appeared to be there, but there was no trace of the Lysi frescoes.

'What the fuck is going on?' I shouted.

Aydin questioned the soldiers but they were adamant. They had loaded every single thing that had been delivered. If anything was missing, it had been taken before.

'It has to be those thieving bastards in the depot,' Aydin exploded.

'I thought they were your men?'

'Sure. But other people use the depot. Some of them must have got their hands on our crates during the evening before our men drove off.'

'What about the guards?'

Aydin laughed bitterly. 'It's easy enough to bribe a few soldiers to look the other way while a case or two is taken off the truck when my guys are busy or having a break.'

I was pretty sure the Finnish soldiers were not responsible. They would have neither the specialized knowledge nor the outlets to dispose of that sort of merchandise. Aydin's conjecture seemed to be the only possible explanation.

'Look here,' I told him. 'You take the rest of the stuff to Larnaka and go ahead as planned. I have some business here in the south.'

I spent the day getting together some of my own trusted men. They came from both communities, tough, seasoned men, all armed, and knew every track in that part of the island. At nightfall, we stealthily made our way across the artificial border and during the next day, keeping to the country, we moved close to the barn at Psillatos.

Throughout the night we kept the depot under observation. There was a handful of Turkish sentries, but they appeared relaxed, chatting and smoking, clearly unaware of our presence or of any likely threat to the depot. There were a few trucks parked nearby, but no sign of any activity.

At the first glimmer of dawn we crawled, inch by inch, until we were practically on top of them. Then, all hell broke out. We stormed into the depot: there was a fusillade of shots, but it was over in seconds. The guards were taken competely by surprise, and soon overpowered. Nobody was killed but there were some wounded on both sides.

Apart from the soldiers, the depot was deserted. We took our prisoners inside and bound them securely. There were a number of packages inside which we took out and loaded on to a truck.

'Drive over one of the cars,' I ordered. 'We need one back-up vehicle. Sabotage the rest!'

It was still early morning when we drove off, heading by a roundabout route for the coast. I kept a fishing boat standing by outside Karakumi, near the port of Kyrenia. I had fitted it out with sophisticated communications and navigational equipment. We loaded the crates on to the boat and I embarked with a few men. On board, I was able to call up the base I used in Athens where I had a yacht anchored.

The yacht and the fishing boat made a rendezvous at sea, and once more the crates were transferred. Only when we were safely back in Athens was I able to examine in detail what we had captured. Most of the pieces were icons, some valuable; the Lysi frescoes were not there. I presumed that whoever had stolen them had moved them out of the depot before we had returned.

I went on making trips into Cyprus, north and south, and on my next excursion with Aydin came across some of the most famous pieces ever to be taken out of Cyprus. We had met up with a local Turkish army commander and he offered icons looted from St Chrysostomos. Aydin bought a large, tremendously moving fourteenth-century Virgin, and another icon depicting the Virgin, St John the Almoner and donors, which we agreed he would sell to me in Munich. After he had pocketed the money, the commander called up his soldiers.

'Tear the eyes out!' he commanded, pointing at the second icon.

We were forced to stand by while these barbarians gouged the eyes from this painting. He probably thought that he had destroyed its value. What we witnessed was an expression of black fury and religious fanaticism. Both of these icons are famous, illustrated in *Icons of Cyprus* by Athanasius Papageorgiou for which Archbishop Makarios wrote a foreword.

One day in 1979, I was called by Aydin to come to Munich as he had something very special to show me.

'What a stroke of luck,' he enthused. 'After all this time, those frescoes from Lysi have turned up. I have them, and since you bought them before, of course I will let you have them at a special price.'

At that moment, I was pretty sure that the story about the theft in the depot was phoney and that Aydin had screwed me. However, I went on working with him. He did get hold of exceptionally fine pieces, and I had to recognize that the black market is a jungle in which one has to look after oneself.

But I decided against buying the frescoes. I reckoned they were so well known it would have been necessary to break them up and sell them piecemeal, and I was repelled at the thought.

Aydin had something even more spectacular: mosaics from the church of Panagia Kanakaria in the village of Lythrankomi. They were superb but absolutely unique, and therefore, I judged, virtually unsaleable. During the rule of the iconoclast emperors of Byzantium from 726 to 843 AD, all such representational religious art was systematically destroyed and only three sets of mosaics of this quality have survived, at Ravenna, Mount Sinai, and these sixth-century works – a superb mosaic of the adolescent Christ held by an enthroned Virgin, with a series of roundels of apostles and archangels.

'I saved them,' Aydin told me. 'The church has been utterly destroyed, there is nothing left but rubble. The mosaics were in pieces, but I collected the fragments and it was an enormous work to reassemble them.'

I admired his skill and patience, but told him that he ought to keep both the mosaics and the frescoes back from the market. But I was so struck by the beauty of the mosaics and their historical importance that I concluded a deal by which I would buy them for later settlement just to make sure I did not lose track of them.

'I make you a promise, Michel,' said Aydin. 'Whenever I get an acceptable bid for the frescoes, you will have the chance to match it.'

He kept that promise a couple of years later.

# 7

# ANYTHING TO DECLARE?

My work was based in Beirut, Munich and Amsterdam, but I travelled all over Europe and the Middle East, even the Americas, seeking old and precious things. The hunt for icons and my ambition to mount a really splendid exhibition kept me occupied. I began to make frequent visits not only to Armenia, but increasingly to Moscow and Leningrad. Because of the stringent law against inherited wealth, plenty of people were ready to dispose of family treasures on the black market; the real challenge came when one attempted to take them out to the West.

Of course, I was not the only person involved in the trade, although I think my activities had helped to stimulate interest, and I received a lot of dubious propositions. A highly respectable diplomat at the British embassy sidled up to me at a Moscow cocktail party and whispered out of the side of his mouth.

'I say, Michel, old boy, there is a story going around that you are buying up these icon things.' He waved his hand as if to indicate that such baubles had little charm for him.

Although I had not been meeting dealers openly, my interest in works of art was widely known and I reckoned I had enough influential contacts in Moscow and outside to keep me out of serious trouble, so his revelation left me cold.

'Now you don't want any aggro with these Russkies, you know. They can be very nasty if they catch you trying to smuggle the damned things out.' He adopted a grim expression, then winked at me. 'But I can solve your little problem. I'll tell you where to bring them, a few at a time you understand, and we can slip them into the diplomatic bags without any fuss. No trouble then with some nosey customs johnny. You'd be surprised at how many of you fellows I help this way. And you won't find it expensive, not considering the risk-free service.'

I shook my head. 'Thanks for the offer. I appreciate your efforts to open up Russia to enlightened Western trading practices, but I have no idea what you are talking about. What is more, I would not like to feel I was tempting you to abuse your diplomatic privilege by betraying the confidence with which our host country treats the members of your embassy.'

He stared at me in disbelief. Then, muttering something about impudent young pups, moved away. In fact, I distrusted any course so obvious and so conspicuous as using the regular diplomatic channels. If the authorities wanted to get tough, sooner or later they would pounce on me and my contact at some rendezvous outside embassy property, and that would mean far worse trouble than a straightforward case of smuggling. And there had been a number of incidents where diplomats had been stopped at the border with undeclared art treasures in their baggage, with embarrassing consequences. Only a few weeks previously a member of the Finnish embassy had been stopped at the airport. The Russians, if they suspected someone or had been tipped off, didn't give a damn about diplomatic immunity. Despite his protests, they opened his case and impounded his loot. Although his diplomatic status saved him from a prison sentence or a fine, he was given quite a hard time before being sent home in disgrace.

In fact, I had built up an extensive and efficient organization, based on my friends in the Armenian mafia. The news that I could be trusted had spread, and I had been able to go seriously into the smuggling business: not merely works of art but also men and women who had to get out of the Soviet Union. It was a bit like the underground railway that used to spirit runaway slaves out of the South before the American Civil War. Not that my efforts were entirely altruistic; it was natural that people I helped to escape should turn to me if they had valuable objects to sell.

So I did not think it necessary to mention to my helpful diplomat that after the cocktail party I was going to a noisy café, much frequented by students, to make arrangements for my next unofficial export.

Moscow is full of students, many of them foreign. Indeed, an American survey has stated that there are more institutions of higher education in Moscow than in any other city in the world except Boston. Students going home, especially those from black Africa or other countries which the Russians felt to be friendly, were hardly ever frisked at the frontier. Their customary route was via Berlin, and one did not need to be an organizational genius to establish a reliable Courier service, a hell of a lot cheaper than that which my embassy bagman would have provided. One dealer, who owned a prestigious gallery in Berlin just round the corner from the Kurfurstendamm station, where he would meet returning students, became rich on the proceeds of the parcels they took across the Wall.

However the snag with students was that their carrying capacity was limited, and I was buying stuff by the crateful, so they were not my chosen couriers. That was where the coaches came in useful. My contact that night was the driver of a coach which would be taking Dutch tourists back to Amsterdam.

I went back to my hotel and changed into jeans. I handed in my key to the concierge, and my departure was noted by the sad-faced man beside him whom I took to be my friendly, neighbourhood KGB representative. I took the metro to the café, and found my driver Vinnie already at a table. We took the customary vodka, then went to Nadya's apartment.

She was a beautiful, green-eyed blonde who helped me reserve seats for concerts or the ballet and provided translations of learned articles and catalogues. She was one of the hopefuls of the Bolshoi's *corps de ballet*, but had not progressed beyond seventeenth little swan, counting from the left. Some members of the *corps de ballet* were like Soviet geishas. It was common knowledge that some of the girls slept with top Politburo members and so they had access to the shops reserved for party officials. Dealing with the complexities of illegally buying and then surreptitiously shipping works of art, which themselves met with official disapproval, was quite a strain, and I welcomed the sensuous charms of a passionate, living woman as a break from the sad, unchanging stare of images of the Mother of God. However, I stored some of the icons in Nadya's bedroom, so that even when we made love the image of the sorrowful Virgin was still with us.

Vinnie and I carried the boxes down the stairs (seventeenth swans did not qualify for apartments in blocks with elevators) and packed them into the luggage compartment of Vinnie's coach. From the apartment, I called an associate in Amsterdam and, using a prearranged code, instructed him to pay cash to Vinnie's wife; then we waited for a call from her which indicated to Vinnie that she had received the money. Of course there were a lot of rogues in the smuggling business. It was vital to use a courier one could trust, like Vinnie.

I got back to my hotel very late (to have spent the night in Nadya's apartment would have been an indiscretion) and collected my key from the hall porter who was probably keeping a check on my movements but who also became more amenable when presented with a handful of roubles.

I was still in bed when the Dutch tourists filed on to the coach, their piled-up suitcases hiding my boxes, and Vinnie prepared for the long drive across the breadth of Europe. I had three days before I needed to fly out to take delivery of the icons and I did not expect to hear anything from him until we met in Amsterdam. But when I was sitting in

Nadya's lounge-cum-kitchen, sipping indifferent coffee, the phone shrilled.

'There has been a problem. I wanted to warn you that there could be trouble,' Vinnie said.

'Trouble?'

'On the road to Smolensk there was an accident. A tanker skidded, hit the coach and then crashed. The tanker caught fire and the coach was scorched by the flames.'

'Christ! Are you OK?'

'Yes. None of our people were injured. Everybody piled out of the coach and I was able to put the fire out without serious damage. We are driving on now and we shall probably not be too delayed getting to Holland – that is, unless the police make trouble.'

I felt my guts turning to water. 'What sort of trouble?'

'Well, before I could get the fire under control, there were hordes of police on the scene and they swarmed all over the place.'

'What about the passengers' baggage and the presents for your mother?'

'When it looked as if the coach might be burned, we pulled everything out of the coach. The cops didn't open the luggage but everything was stacked by the roadside.'

I told Nadya what had happened. 'It sounds as if they didn't ask any questions about my boxes.'

'No, they wouldn't, would they?' she said. 'They must have been traffic or municipal cops. Poking their noses into luggage is not their job. But they might have informed the security police if they thought there was something suspicious, and they in turn could alert the border guards. I don't think Vinnie is in the clear until he is across that frontier.'

For the next few days, I sweated, fearing every knock on the door. The British diplomat would have had a damned good laugh if he could have seen me. Nadya did her best to take my mind off the prospect of a cosy chat with the KGB but my anxiety mounted every minute.

Yet the hours went by without incident. I booked my flight and when I presented my passport at Sheremetyevo airport, my nerves were twanging like bedsprings. There was the usual delay, one unsmiling official handed the passport to another, and they stared at the photograph then at me. I felt sweat running down my spine. Then, when I was bracing myself for the worst, they banged an exit stamp in my passport and handed it back. I was still inwardly shaking when I boarded the Aeroflot Tupolev and for once I gratefully gulped down the sweet champagne offered to first-class passengers.

I was safely outside the USSR but still I had no news of Vinnie – or of his precious cargo. In fact, as Nadya had predicted, he was left unmolested until the frontier. As the overloaded coach pulled in, a posse of police made their way towards it without waiting for Vinnie even to produce his documents. It was clear that they had been waiting for him, and the Dutch-registered vehicle, scorch marks visible beneath the coating of grime, was easily recognized.

'Driver, come with us.' Vinnie was quaking as they entered an office, and reckoning how many years it would be before he could lay his head on his own pillow next to his wife. There was quite an array of police waiting for him. An elderly colonel got to his feet and made a long speech. Vinnie could not believe his ears. A report had been sent on the courageous behaviour of the comrade driver of the coach who had, virtually singlehanded, extinguished a fire which imperilled not only the lives of his passengers but also the property of the Soviet state, namely the tanker. Sod the tanker, Vinnie thought, the property of Michel van Rijn was worth a hell of a lot more than it and the Dutch bus together! Then, with a flourish, the colonel announced that in recognition of his devotion to duty, the comrade driver had been awarded a decoration. Half an hour later, with a splendid bronze medal pinned to his chest and several tumblers of vodka in his belly, and surrounded by admiring frontier police, Vinnie sauntered back to his coach with its load of contraband which he drove across the border without any formalities. Nobody was going to subject a popular hero to the indignity of searching his vehicle.

The unfortunate consequence of Vinnie's exploit was that he started to think that a Dutch hero of the Soviet Union could be better employed than in acting as chauffeur to ordinary tourists. He remained a coach driver, but insisted on more prestigious itineraries, and I lost one of my better couriers.

Not long after Vinnie quit the Russian route, a new and unexpected ally arrived on the scene to help in the transporting of works of art to the West – no less than the Soviet government itself. Of course, they knew there was a steady stream of goods leaving the country and they could always do with hard currency, so why not sell some national treasures and permit them to be exported legally? I was one of many dealers who went to inspect what was on offer at the converted church that was now the headquarters of Novo-Export. What a disappointment! The Russians must have dcided it would be a privilege for the ignorant capitalist world to acquire even the dregs of their cultural heritage; the stuff was terrible. I suppose that if they could get away with keeping the really lovely things inside the country and be well paid for rubbish, nobody could blame them. Indeed, I showed my approval of this Soviet initiative by supporting their sales and buying several items. They were painstakingly listed and labelled, and lashings of official stamps gave the paperwork a truly impressive appearance.

Meanwhile, I played the eager tourist, visiting such historic cities as Novgorod and Vladimir where good Soviet citizens were only too willing to trade family relics for the cash to buy Japanese cameras and electronic goods from the decadent West and, most important of all, food from the special shops.

I refreshed my memory of such famous collections as the Hermitage in Leningrad and the Tretyakov Gallery in Moscow where the display of icons was staggering. Yet such was the extent of old-fashioned graft that I was even able to buy from a restorer well-known works from the cellars of the Tretyakov, icons which had been displayed in exhibitions, still with their catalogue numbers attached.

As I expected, it was possible to get hold of some valuable items in Kiev the Golden, where Christianity first entered Russia in the ninth century. But it was in Zagorsk, not far from Moscow, that I found some of the best quality icons. The Trinity Cathedral boasted an icon of the fifteenth century which they claimed was the work of Andrei Rublov, perhaps the most famous of all icon painters; not surprisingly, this particular specimen was not on offer.

There was a whole network of black market dealers who bought from the ordinary Russians and, as I had been given clearance by the Armenians and had helped with the 'underground railway', I was accepted by them.

So I bought some fine icons. To these I attached labels which belonged to official rubbish which I then got from Novo-Export to match the subjects of the good pieces. The first time I had taken things out on Novo-Export labels, I had used the real things to make sure the system worked. As I had anticipated, the customs officers carefully examined the lists and labels, but hardly studied the actual icons.

I had the good luck a little later to come across another way of removing icons. Back in Holland, at a reception at the Polish embassy, I was told about a new workshop near Warsaw specializing in the repair and restoration of such things as icons and was invited to visit. When I arrived, I was given real VIP treatment: limousine at the airport and a suite at the best hotel. All very pleasant, but what caught my attention was the customs declaration form I was given. It was the usual sheet of bureaucratic bumbledom with lines for the traveller to fill in with details of items which he was bringing into the country. I noticed that the customs officer signed and stamped the form even when I left lots of useful blank lines between entries in which other items could be added later. At the end of my tour of inspection, I thanked my hosts effusively, announced that I had been greatly impressed and would certainly be sending them icons for restoration. Then I called on a friend, Joseph, who lived in Warsaw and was a trader in a small way in antiques, curios and plain junk.

It was not long before I made my next trip to Warsaw. Getting stuff from Russia to Poland presented no problem, so I was able to send a shipment of valuable icons to Joseph. I waited until I heard from him that they were safely in his basement, then, armed with impressive official forms from the embassy, I flew to Warsaw with the same number of icons. However these were of mediocre quality, mostly disposed of by Novo-Export at auctions in London, which matched the black market pieces in subject and size. These I duly declared to the customs, stating that they were being brought to Poland for restoration and re-export. The forms were produced, the icons examined, and once more stamps and signatures were affixed on the forms; the icons were not marked in any way.

The rest was child's play. At Joseph's place we switched the icons, delivering the fine pieces for restoration while Joseph retained the others. While I waited for the restoration work to be completed, I enjoyed myself looking around Warsaw, which has been rebuilt with dignity and good taste after the devastation of the Second World War.

But I kept my eyes open and found a few good pieces, often things which had been seized by the Germans and those Poles who played along with them, from Russia and all the countries of occupied Europe during the Second World War. The descriptions of my new purchases were carefully added to the customs declarations I had filled in when I imported the third-rate rubbish. When the repairs to the valuable icons which I had switched had been completed, I took the whole lot to the airport and consigned them to Amsterdam, all declared with transparent honesty and officially approved.

The junk which I had brought into Poland was peddled by Joseph to Western tourists on street corners. They thought they were being offered priceless treasures and doubtless found all sorts of ingenious methods of getting them out of the country. Back home they presumably explained to their friends and to experts the risks they had taken bringing these extraordinary pieces through the Iron Curtain, only to find out that some had been included in catalogues from Christie's or Sotheby's, having sold for less than it had cost them in their illicit adventure with Joseph. But then they would not have had the thrill of being smugglers!

# 8

# Saints and Sinners

I was on my beloved terrace, gazing down on the tranquillity of the Beirut sunset. I had got back that day from a particularly hazardous flit through the gloom of Soviet officialdom. While I felt relaxed in Yerevan, in the north of the country the protection of the Armenian mafia was remote, and when I was carrying passports and false identity papers there was always the threat of running foul of some over-zealous cop or KGB agent. I had an iced drink by my side and a dish of juicy olives. My companion Fatimah was wearing a slinky Valentino robe of scarlet silk with a slit in the skirt which revealed her long, sleek legs. I did not need to say a word, the look in my eyes was sufficient. Fatimah sidled over and I undid the button at the top of her dress and laid bare her firm breasts. As I did so, there was a strange rattling noise outside, like a handful of pebbles thrown against a distant window. Fatimah looked at me questioningly. The same sound again, this time closer. There was no mistaking it: the staccato tattoo of rifle fire.

'Raad,' I called. 'What the hell is going on?'

'It is bad, Monsieur Michel,' he said. 'Those damned Moslems, they have started killing each other.'

'But you are Christians, they will leave you alone?' I demanded.

Raad spread his hands. 'Who knows, Monsieur! We are not involved in their squabble, but both groups hate us. And this part of the city is not the safest.'

'What are you talking about?' cried Fatimah. 'This is the heart of Beirut. Look over there: that's the American University. Downstairs are the best shops, the offices of the most important companies. Why, this must be the last part of the city to get caught up in gang warfare.'

Raad shook his head sorrowfully. 'Hamra is the richest part of the city and the most tempting for looters. This will be the heart of the trouble when it starts.'

'Sounds as if it already has,' I commented, as another volley of rifle fire was answered by a burst from a machine-gun. 'As long as we stay up here on top of the world, nobody can touch us,' I assured them.

Although I was convinced we were not in any immediate danger, it was a new experience, making love to the accompaniment of a battle. Then the firing stopped as abruptly as it had started and the newspapers next morning reported a skirmish, nothing more. Whatever the tensions between the Moslems, peace had returned to the city – or so it seemed.

'How would you like a trip to Athens?' I asked Fatimah.

'Athens? What's so great about Athens?'

'I want to talk to some people at the Benaki,' I explained.

'Are you still working on this exhibition idea?' she asked.

'Sure. I have found the ideal spot. I'll show the best collection of icons in private hands, and it will be in Delft. It's a wonderful location.'

'And you hope to get hold of icons in Athens?'

I laughed. 'Let's say maybe something will turn up.'

As it happened, something extraordinary did turn up in Athens, one of the most exciting discoveries I have ever made. I was by now well known to the senior officials at the Benaki, one of whom showed me an icon which had been beautifully restored. I expressed my admiration.

'Ah,' he grinned. 'That is the work of our good Nicholas. He is a genius. I've never come across anyone who has his feeling for the things he restores. You should meet him.'

'I'd love to.'

'Well, you are in luck. Most of the year he and his father work together up in the mountains, in some isolated village or in a monastery about as approachable as the summit of Everest. Every now and then, he gets back to civilization. It so happens that he is in Athens now.'

That evening, I met this fabulous restorer. A night out in Athens was a great treat for Nicholas. When he hit town, it was a case of down to the Plaka for grilled fish and *souvlakia*, jugs of cheap red wine until he could hardly see straight, a night with whichever girl might grab him and an imperial-sized hangover in the morning. This time it was going to be different.

Although Piraeus is crowded and polluted, like any busy seaport, the bays on the east side of the peninsula no longer berth heavy freighters, cruise liners or American aircraft carriers. A long line of restaurants overlook the yacht basin. Sellers of postcards, flowers or pistachio nuts thread their way between the tables. It is a vibrant, noisy, colourful scene of unpretentious gaiety.

Nicholas was perhaps in his mid-twenties with dark, lank hair and large, questioning eyes. I don't think he would have trusted me had it not been for the good report from my friend at the Benaki – and the promise of a first-class meal and maybe some business. He was very reserved, but when he realized that I did not merely buy and sell icons but that I loved them, he opened up a bit and by the third bottle of wine he had become positively talkative. When we got to the Metaxas brandy, he was talking very confidentially, even if his voice was a bit slurred.

'You must have seen some wonderful things,' I said. 'Tell me, which icon was your own favourite? There must have been one that meant more to you than all the others.'

'There was one . . . no, there *is* one.' His eyes grew misty as he recollected. 'You have never seen anything to touch it, a St Peter.'

'Where is it?' I asked.

He shook his head. 'Let's go on somewhere else,' he suggested. 'I feel like some music and a bit of life.'

My curiosity had been aroused but I knew there was nothing to be gained by pressing him, so I settled the bill. We found a cab and went off to the liveliest *bouzouki* joint at Asteria Beach. This was the real thing, not one of the phoney tourist tavernas which infest the centre.

'Great!' enthused my guest when he found that none other than Marinella was singing that night. The place was packed with an excited, enthusiastic audience. Under the stars, shining in a velvet black sky, with the murmur of the waves lapping on the shore behind the stage, the setting was romantic but the entertainment was throbbing with vitality and the audience soon became roused to a frenzy.

Since the imposition of the colonels' regime, *bouzouki* places had become much more than just somewhere for a night out. They were symbols of freedom, of defiance. Everything short of actually closing them down was done: shows had to finish not much after midnight instead of going on until six or seven in the morning to try to stop the excitement getting out of control. Instead of throwing glasses, people had to make do with camellias and plates. The more popular the performer, the more intense is the barrage from their public. By the end of the night, everyone on stage was ducking and dodging and the great crowd beneath them was singing or whistling, dancing and swaying, snapping their fingers and shouting: '*Ela*, *ela*, Marinella!' The whole place seemed to explode in a carnival riot of exultation. 'Bravo, bravo, Manouli!' they screamed. Nicholas was swaying in time with the music which grew ever wilder and more abandoned.

Shortly before we left, I managed to steer the conversation back to the wondrous icon of St Peter.

'It's not just mine,' Nicholas shouted over the din. 'There were four of us. We were all icon restorers, you see, so it was no problem getting them out. A quick lick of overpainting was all it needed. The St Peter wasn't the only one,' he told me in a confidential shout. 'When we were sent to clean them, nobody seemed to give a damn when the best of them disappeared.'

'Is that so?'

'Well, I mean to say, if those bastards did not even know what they had, they did not deserve them, don't you think?'

'Quite right,' I assented. 'Let's get something more to drink. Which bastards?'

'The monks, of course.' Nicholas seemed quite surprised that I did not know that he and his pals had removed St Peter and sundry other saints from a monastery somewhere in northern Greece. 'But, you know, I don't trust those crooked sods who were working with me. I'm damned sure they have been slipping back without telling me and selling some of the icons. That way they wouldn't have to pay me my share and by the time I found out they would be God knows where. I couldn't go to the police, could I?'

'Not really,' I agreed. We had both drunk a skinful, but I was sober enough to see my chance. 'Have you seen your St Peter recently?'

'How the hell could I when it's – ' he checked himself – 'a long way away.'

'Well, how do you know the treacherous bastards haven't already taken that one?'

He shook his head and tears of frustrated anger welled up in his eyes.

I had found that people from the Eastern Mediterranean, like the Armenians, are intensely suspicious; if one tries to hustle them, they shut up like clams and the cosy relationship is destroyed. So I did not press the point but paid our bill and led a very unsteady restorer of icons out. I knew he would not get much sleep that night; doubts about the fate of his beloved St Peter would prey on his mind.

'Let's have lunch tomorrow,' I said. 'I think I might be able to help you. How about at Jerophinicas, let's say at one?'

'Make it half-past, or better still at two,' Nicholas mumbled as I bundled him into a cab.

At lunch, Nicholas seemed a different man from the night before, tense, subdued and reticent. Whether it was due to his monumental hangover or merely a resurgence of his native caution, his enthusiasm over the icon was muted. He was in no mood for discussion; his only concern was whether St Peter was still safe in the bank vault. The lyricism of yesterday had vanished. Conversation was monosyllabic until he had absorbed sufficient *souvlakia* and salad to neutralize some of the booze which was still hurtling around his system.

'That icon you were talking about last night,' I said casually. 'Why don't we go and look to make sure it is still there? Listen, Nicholas, I'll make you an offer. I would love to see this icon. If you say that it is an outstanding one, I guess it must be. So I am prepared to pay your fare if you will let me come with you, just to look at it, you understand. And if it means staying in a hotel, you will be my guest. What do you say?'

I could see that he was in two minds.

'And you will be able to make sure that it is safe. If you like, you can move it somewhere where the others will not be able to get their hands on it.'

'Yes,' he breathed. 'It is mine, not theirs. Why not?'

'I'll book the tickets this afternoon,' I promised. 'Just say where.'

'Munich,' Nicholas replied.

At once he brightened up, but I was careful to avoid any suggestion that I might buy the icon. I had learned from years of dealing with Levantines that business has to be conducted in their own time and in the right mood.

When I met Nicholas at the airport the following morning, all his former edginess had returned and when we were airborne I demanded to know what was causing him such excessive anxiety.

'It's all right for you,' he answered reproachfully. 'You are used to rushing off all over the world. This is the first time I have ever set foot in an airplane, and I'm shit scared!'

'But when you took the icons to Munich, didn't you fly?'

'We drove. That's the only time I have ever been out of Greece.'

I began to understand the sort of life Nicholas led. Weeks or months would go by between his trips to the city; his life was spent in the wild places. Sometimes he would work in a village church, but more often he was to be found in a monastery which had purposely been built in a wilderness. He worked alone, or watched by silent monks. He was devoted to his work and treated the icons with love and reverence. A factory worker would have a radio going full blast. To Nicholas, delicately cleaning or repairing an image of a saint or a representation of a miracle, that would have seemed a sacrilege. So in Athens, he was as abandoned as a mercenary on leave from war. His pleasures were simple, and he took them with such gusto that a stranger might regard him as vulgar and stupid. Yet he was gentle beneath the bravado and his simplicity manifested untutored wisdom; all his words and deeds were so totally sincere that I found in him a wonderful and winning innocence. He was as remote from the trappings of modern civilization, such as the jet in which we were hurtling through the sky, as the hermits among whom he spent the greater part of his life.

As we walked out of the Munich terminal, I asked, 'Is it far?'

'Why do you want to know?'

'Goddammit, man, if it is near here we can take a taxi. If it is outside the city centre, it might be easier to hire a car.'

Nicholas nodded. 'That's a good idea. Let's get a car.'

I told Nicholas to tell me which road to take when we got into Munich.

'We aren't going to Munich,' he answered. 'Head for Heidelberg.'

I swallowed my anger at his deviousness. It was typical, I

thought, that he would keep his secret until the last moment. Heidelberg is quite a way so I put my foot hard down, but when we arrived, it was obvious that Nicholas had only the vaguest notion of the whereabouts of the bank. We had to ask directions, but finally we arrived at a branch of the Bayerische Vereinsbank which he claimed to recognize.

Nicholas disappeared into the vault and emerged carrying five bulky packages. 'We can't very well look at them here,' he said nervously.

'Bring them to the car,' I ordered. 'We can check into a hotel, examine them at our leisure and bring them back here when we are ready – or take them to another bank if you prefer.'

I was consumed by curiosity to set eyes on this icon, but I restrained myself. Driving back, I took a roundabout route. Nicholas, now speaking volubly, and not being able to read the German road signs, did not even notice how much longer the return journey took until we were back in Munich and had registered at the Continental Hotel.

I had taken two adjoining rooms. The packages were on the floor of Nicholas's and he was fussing with the string.

'Look at the time,' I said. 'We can't get them back to Heidelberg today.'

'So we put them in a bank here in Munich. I'd prefer that.'

'Sure, Nicholas, but it will have to be tomorrow. The banks close at four. We can put them in the hotel safe for tonight.'

He was not very happy, but as there was no way of getting the icons into a bank that night, he assented.

'Now we have come all this way, how about showing me what you have there?' I invited.

I had been struck by the fact that there was not one crate but five, and my excitement mounted, but I controlled myself and waited, apparently calm to the point of indifference, for Nicholas to make the first move. He was quite a master of the dramatic. With quiet deliberation, he unpacked the first crate and there emerged a very early, beautiful icon of St Procopius. It was good, very good, but I was keyed up in anticipation of this fabulous image of St Peter, and Nicholas sensed my impatience.

'It comes from the same iconostasis as the St Peter,' he explained apologetically.

'I thought that the St Peter was earlier.'

'Yes, it is, a full two centuries, but it was overpainted when this icon was painted. Still, it is very fine, don't you think?'

'Let's get to the St Peter,' I said impatiently.

But Nicholas was eager for me to see everything and he left me in suspense until the last crate. However, the intervening icons were quite fine enough to maintain my interest. After Procopius came two more warrior saints, with those strangely sensitive faces which are so incongruous a feature of the likenesses of the Byzantine soldier-saints. Then he produced a panel, painted around 1500 in Crete, of the forty martyrs of Sevastos, huddled together in the frozen lake in which they were compelled to stand, naked according to the legend but here decently swathed in loincloths, within sight of the heated bath-house, ready to welcome any of them who would renounce his faith. And only thirty-nine chilled martyrs were standing in the lake; one could be seen scurrying towards the bath-house. He was to drop dead an instant later, but next to him stood a red-cloaked soldier, one arm raised in exaltation, who was about to join the martyrs in the lake.

And then, the revelation. I was transfixed by the power and the pathos of those beautifully moulded features of St Peter, who wore his two keys round his neck. It was as fine as anything in the choicest museum collections in Greece or Yugoslavia. It simply hit me, I could not bear to take my eyes off it. Just being in the same room with so wonderful a thing gave me joy. To this day I have never come across a finer piece and only perhaps three or four which could stand comparison with its simply dignity and natural majesty. It was the face of a man who could stare into the very soul of the viewer. I was deeply moved and ached to possess it, not out of greed, but simply from love. I looked up at Nicholas and there were tears in his eyes. Both of us stared at that face which contemplated us over seven centuries. It was a proud face, but one which had seen much suffering. Many icons have a formalized beauty, depicting a divine image: here was a real, living man. And it was imbued with tremendous strength, a man who would not accept defeat but would fight with all his soul. The artist must have admired and revered him and all his emotion flowed through the ages. Nicholas, after perhaps a quarter of an hour, moved to wrap up the icon, but I stopped him.

'Let it be. I want to go on looking at it.'

'We ought to take it to the safe.'

'Please. Let us keep it for the night.'

Nicholas understood. He too loved this icon, it was a bond between us. But in the morning our ways would part: the icon would be his and I would have to resign myself to its absence. I wanted to fill this one solitary night with the love affair of a lifetime, for how else can I describe this passion? And Nicholas understood, so he agreed that the St Peter would stay in my room. We kept open a connecting door and so it was an experience shared.

I took him to a simple Greek restaurant for dinner, but even as we ate I had the urge to run back to make sure that the icon was still there and just to set eyes on it again. Throughout the night I was conscious of that brooding image in my room, a living presence; and I know that it had the same power over Nicholas.

In the morning, I spoke frankly. 'I want to buy all your icons,' I told him. 'They are all fantastic, but you know that well enough and I am prepared to pay their true worth. The St Peter is wonderful,' I said. 'If you can bring yourself to sell it, I will buy it from you, along with the others. And I give you my word, it is not to sell on to some avaricious collector or to a museum where it will be buried. I want it for my own collection. I am crazy about it, you can see that. So, what do you say?'

He looked pained. 'I believe you, Michel, and I give you

my word that if I ever find myself obliged to sell it, I shall offer it to you. But there is no way that I will sell it unless circumstances force me to. As long as I live, that St Peter is part of my life. And as for the others,' he hesitated, 'no, not yet. Perhaps later, but I want to enjoy them for a bit longer.'

I offered him hundreds of thousands of dollars but he was adamant. As for the St Peter, I did not argue. I understood the obsessive force of the icon, for I also was infected by it. And that was the end of the matter, or so I thought.

I took Nicholas to another bank in Munich where I was a good customer, introduced him to the manager, and he deposited his packages. Since Nicholas did not speak German, I could have instructed the bank manager to put the deposit in both of our names with a power of attorney to each of us, returned later and made off with his icons. What chance would a penniless Greek have of pursuing me and reclaiming property to which he had no legal title? They were great icons and I loved the St Peter, so why didn't I cheat him? Not because I would have nothing to do with anything questionable – it was impossible to deal in the art market in such places as Yerevan or Beirut if one were over-scrupulous. But I had respect for Nicholas, a respect I did not feel for men who regarded great works of art merely as money in a different form. God knows, Nicholas needed money and, with a nod, could have become by his standards an unbelievably rich man. But the icons meant more to him than wealth. Maybe he did not own a spare shirt, but he had something a damned sight rarer: dignity. There was no way I could have brought myself to steal from such a man. And I felt a warmth in his regard for me; maybe he understood that these beautiful paintings forged a bond between us. He was in love with his superlative icon, and I could share that total devotion. I have come across very few people with that passion. We left the bank and looked in at my apartment I wanted to check that there were no urgent messages.

'You never told me you had a place here,' Nicholas said reproachfully.

'If I had, you might have thought I was setting some sort of trap to lure you here and steal your icons, mightn't you?'

He winced. 'Maybe.'

Then to the airport, Nicholas to return to Athens, me to go to Amsterdam. My preparations for the exhibition in Delft were going ahead rapidly and I regretted that I could not have his icons there, with St Peter as the centrepiece. Nicholas took my hand and thanked me for his outing and for my help in arranging the safekeeping of his icons.

'Perhaps one day,' he started, but then stopped. 'Goodbye, Michel, I hope to see you again soon.'

It was an emotional parting. Did I have some premonition? I cannot truthfully say but I remember the sad, serious look in his eyes. I kissed him on both cheeks and watched as he walked off through passport control.

I never saw Nicholas again. Six months later, he was dead. I heard the news from his sister. 'He had been out at a night club in Athens,' she said. 'You know how Nicholas loved a night out when he got the chance. He was hit by a car. The driver did not stop and has never been traced.'

Could he have been one of those other restorers whom Nicholas suspected of having swindled him? I had my suspicions, but I shall I never know.

'He lay in a coma for ten days,' continued his sister. 'But after he met you, he spoke of you many times. It was as if he felt that something bound you together. I suppose it was your feeling for beautiful things. So I think he would have wished you to have those icons he loved so dearly. We have discussed this in the family, and we would like to sell them to you.'

And so I lost a friend and came into possession of one of the supreme works of the icon painter's art. I am not easily moved, but when I heard of the death of Nicholas, I was moved to tears; not only because of his great talent and his willingness to suffer hardship for little material reward. He was so young, but more than that, he had such a tremendous enjoyment of life, it was unfair that he should have been snuffed out by some drunk, hurtling along, or as a cold act of vengeance. I could not sleep: I kept seeing him as he was at the airport, as withdrawn as a figure in one of his beloved icons. I had known him so short a time, yet I felt as if part of me had died with him. I would have many friends, but there would never be another Nicholas. There was something special about the man, a sort of grandeur.

For days, I walked about as if in a trance. But life had to go on, and I had become more and more absorbed in getting my exhibition staged. Although still in my early twenties, I was already regarded as an authority on icons, not only for my knowledge but also because of my being the source of so many good pieces. I had icons in bank vaults in Amsterdam, Geneva, Zurich, Brussels and Munich. I was hearing reports of more unrest in Beirut and so I had moved stock from there to Europe but I was still journeying frequently to Greece and Turkey. At the same time our 'underground railway' was active, running refugees as well as relics out of the Soviet Union. But I was not satisfied. Icons were not yet appreciated or understood by as wide a public as they merited. I hoped that my exhibition would help to put that right and I started to write a book, a lavishly illustrated affair, to complement the show.

However, as I pointed out to Roozemond, I was faced by some tricky problems.

'Do you have any idea,' I asked 'how many of the icons which will go on show in Delft have been smuggled out? Unless I can find some way of keeping the wolves away, there will be howls for the return of masterpieces from just about every country where Orthodox Christianity has ever been practised.'

'We don't want that,' Roozemond agreed.

'I shall have to get some respectable people to come and make the thing look kosher.'

'Well, I guess that the Pope wouldn't be interested in the Greek Church, so you had better sign up the Queen.' Roozemond, the joker!

But he had the right idea, only he did not go far enough.

What I needed was not one eminent person but a team of them. With my experience of awkward customers, devious dealers, thieves, priests, ministers and bandits, there was little I did not know about lobbying. My first sponsor was His Excellency, the Minister of Justice, Professor Dr Andries van Agt, whose unimpeachable presence would erase any hint of doubt as to the provenance of the works. And just to show how wrong Roozemond was in dismissing the idea of the Catholic Church, I then enlisted the support of the head of the Church in Holland, Cardinal Alffrink. With these two on board, it was plain sailing getting other celebrities and businessmen. And Roozemond's facetious suggestion of the Queen was not that wide of the mark since I had the honour to receive the Princess Beatrix, as she was then, later Queen of the Netherlands.

The Princess was clearly impressed by what she saw. I don't suppose she had ever been in the same room with so many smuggled works of art! But she is a truly cultured woman and I cherish her letter complimenting me on my book.

The exhibition was opened by the mayor of Delft, Dr Ing J.P. Oele. The bare white walls and time-worn green and white tiled floor were a perfect, austere setting and I did not detract from their dignity by inappropriate music or handing out canapes and glasses of wine at the opening. The event was such a success that I followed it up with a second show in the same museum. Icons were news; there were articles in the serious newspapers and features in the magazines. For the second show, I produced a catalogue with articles and descriptions of the works by the most celebrated authorities in this field. And on the cover, I had displayed a reproduction of the St Peter which I installed as the star item in the exhibition. In a way, both the exhibition and the book had become a private tribute to Nicholas.

After I had exhibited the St Peter, I learned how it was that although it was on the Interpol wanted list, the Greeks made no attempt to reclaim it. As Nicholas had told me, it had been overpainted when the St Procopius was painted and that was how it was listed. Nicholas had removed the overpainting. Also the Greeks did not have a record of its exact dimensions and would have been unwilling to risk putting in a claim in view of the distinguished patronage of the exhibition.

I was doubly contented. I had succeeded in getting icons recognized as a major form of art, and while reserving many of the better pieces for my private collection, I had sold practically all my stock.

I was spending more and more time travelling, consequently it made sense to have a partner in Amsterdam and I thought I had the ideal man in Gerrit Daleboudt. Still young, he had a degree in economics and was a co-founder and partner in the country's most important employment agency. I learned that he was selling his stake in the firm and was on the lookout for a fresh challenge. Although not an expert in art or antiques, he took an intelligent interest. I found him serious-minded without being pompous and learned that he was extremely involved in church affairs. Unfortunately, there were other things about Gerrit Daleboudt which I did not discover until much later.

And there were changes in my private life. I was forever away on trips and Fatimah and I had our own separate lives to lead, so gradually, and without any bitterness, we drifted apart. We remain friends but to share my life I came upon Lesley, beautiful, witty and full of fun. What more could a successful man want?

# 9

# 500 Mothers of God

Back in Amsterdam after a trip to the Soviet Union during which I had acquired a lot of good, black market pieces, I was greeted by Lesley.

'Did you have a good trip, my darling?'

'I was able to buy a few good things,' I told her.

'There was a call for you this morning. From the cultural attaché at the Soviet embassy. I said I expected you back today and he asked if you would get in touch with him at once.'

My blood ran cold. Since I had been buying from Novo-Export, during my last trips I had used my real name. Although safe in my own country, I did not want to find my name on a Russian blacklist while I was still actively in business there.

The attaché was most cordial. 'Mr van Rijn, so good of you to call. I very much want to meet you, I have heard so much about you. Why don't you come round for a drink?'

Like hell, I thought, you won't catch me venturing on to Soviet territory. 'I have enjoyed such lavish hospitality in your country, the least I can do is to invite you. Let's say, the terrace of the American Hotel?'

The attaché was a jovial little man with a round face and red cheeks which suggested that he and the vodka bottle were on friendly terms. He was accompanied by a woman with a worried expression whom he introduced as an assistant commercial attaché.

'We have been told about your interest in Soviet art and the good work you have done in bringing our artefacts to the West,' he beamed, 'and we have a proposition for you.'

He either wants to enlist me in the KGB or defect himself, I thought.

'Actually it is your own idea, something you mentioned to one of the officials at Novo-Export. You said that if we were to open a department store, on a temporary basis to start with, in Amsterdam, it would be a wonderful outlet for Soviet goods. Well, the idea was passed up through the Department of Foreign Trade, and the Minister has given us the green light. We have found a suitable site, and are of course prepared to finance the venture and provide staff, but it requires a first-class Dutch entrepreneur to organize it for us. Would you be prepared to do this?'

I was amazed. I remembered putting the idea up and had met somebody in the middle echelons, or so I thought, in the Ministry of Foreign Trade. Then it had been swallowed up in the black hole of Soviet bureaucracy. Now it had re-emerged, could I turn it to my own advantage? The attaché might have been reading my thoughts.

'We would be honoured if you would accept, and I am sure you would find some way of ensuring that you would profit from the publicity such a store would attract,' he said smugly. 'We look upon you as more than a trading partner, a good friend.'

Daleboudt, my new partner, was very doubtful about the scheme.

'But don't you see,' I exclaimed impatiently, 'the perfect setting for selling black-market icons smuggled out of the USSR is a department store owned by the Soviet government?'

'They would never let you do that,' he objected.

'Of course they wouldn't,' I chuckled. 'Just you watch.'

Roozemond and I ran the thing together. The Russians scurried about importing everything we ordered, from fabrics to furniture, lithographs, posters, Palech papier mâché, *matryoshkas*, and every kind of trinket, together with a mind-boggling variety of culinary concoctions. For our part, we leased a massive building just around the corner from the Royal Palace. We devoted one floor entirely to Russian antiques, icons and similar works of art. We laid out chairs and tables in the street and waiters dressed as Cossacks served *shashlik* and vodka. From loudspeakers, the Red Army choir boomed out lively songs and a large red flag adorned with hammer and sickle floated over the building. As the attaché had forecast, we got tremendous publicity.

So while the Soviet government paid for their elaborate sales promotion, we experienced a boom in demand for works which had been spirited out of the country.

The cultural attaché visited our stall and picked up an icon.

'Looks more like Moscow than Novgorod,' he pronounced. 'I must congratulate you on your enterprise in finding such good quality works. I am sure Novo-Export would be amazed if they could see what they have exported.'

I liked his sly humour and he deserved the case of Davidoff cigars which I sent him.

The store was a great success but after several months I quit to continue my activities with such organizations as Novo-Export and left Roozemond to continue.

But there were many other visitors, including a whole posse of Japanese who were beautifully polite and totally unfamiliar with the art of the Russian Orthodox Church. One man introduced himself as a Mr Fujiwara of the Gekkoso Gallery in Tokyo and gave me his card. I thought no more about him until some weeks later, when I received a telex.

PLEASE SEND 500 ICONS SOON AS POSSIBLE. SUBJECT MOTHER OF GOD. STYLE PERIOD 19TH CENTURY. DIMENSIONS 30 × 40 CMS. PRICE RANGE US$2,000–10,000. TELEX CONFIRMATION OF ORDER. KIND REGARDS ISSEI FUJIWARA VICE PRESIDENT GEKKOSO.

My first reaction was one of indignation. Didn't the Japanese realize that icons were works of art, not factory products churned out on a belt like Toyota cars? Did they think I could call some painter in a remote monastery in Russia or Macedonia, living two or three hundred years ago, and place an order as casually as they might ask for hamburgers at the local McDonalds?

Then the challenge of the thing got through to me. After all, if anybody could locate five hundred icons portraying the Mother of God, it was me. And were the Japanese behaving any differently from the Americans at the turn of the century or the Arabs after the oil boom? As soon as a people become rich, they set about buying up culture, and their methods are usually those of the marketplace, which they understand. So when investment banker Julius Bache bought Italian paintings from that greatest of art hustlers, Joe Duveen, he acquired selected masterpieces in much the same way as he would build up a balanced portfolio of stocks and bonds for oil-rich Texan investors. Indeed even the museums of Europe and the United States are the homes of many paintings wrongly ascribed to a famous artist to justify a higher price, or downright fakes and forgeries. But as long as some respected authority gave his opinion that the work was genuine and artistically significant, then it was so, regardless of the evidence of one's eyes, or of scientific tests. And in the end, something valuable was achieved, despite the trickery and the deceptions. After Duveen and his rivals had sold countless paintings, all verified by unchallengeable pundits such as Bernard Berenson, many first-class paintings did end up in private and public collections, and a real knowledge and taste developed. It was what is called education, and it had to be bought.

I had no doubt that most Japanese were absolutely unaware of alien forms of culture and would behave with the same crassness as former nouveaux riches, but I was just as sure that, with their intelligence and eagerness to learn, they would soon surpass their mentors. Meanwhile, why not sell them some education?

So, instead of answering by telex, I flew to Tokyo to explain how we could go about building up an awareness of the true nature of icons; their singularity, their spiritual intensity and that each one was a prayer in paint.

But education is a two-way process. I was overwhelmed by the frenetic activity of Tokyo, which made even New York or Hong Kong seem quiet. The solid mass of traffic, the jostling sushi bars and stores crowded to suffocation – the city was a surrealist dream inspired by Hieronymus Bosch! And what a contrast with Moscow, where the streets were almost empty of private cars and where instead of neon signs, red stars crowned official buildings. Tokyo was a blaze of advertising signs, flashing psychedelic messages. If you can imagine Times Square superimposed on Piccadilly Circus and the whole thing intensified by mirrors, that's Tokyo's Ginza. What a contrast with the perfect symmetry of snow-capped Mount Fuji, the exquisite harmony of flowers, water and stone in their gardens, the tranquillity of the Shinto shrines or the simplicity of the garden in the Zen temple at Kyoto which, using nothing more than raked white sand and a few rough rocks, seems to provide a miniature landscape, the perfect setting for meditation!

I got a clue to the Japanese character from their paintings. Sometimes little more than a wash of colour, subtle and mysterious, at other times vivid and virile, the brutality of modern Tokyo apparent in a depiction of a samurai warrior, or a cat baring its teeth. Even more eloquent were the extraordinary works of calligraphy, a whole concept expressed in a brush stroke, a symbol expressing a word or an idea, and at the same time, a gateway to mood, an inner calm, a whole philosophy of contemplation.

More relevant to my mission was the different way that works of art were being marketed, and here Gekkoso was like something from a different planet. It was much more than a gallery for displaying and selling art, and it organized lavish exhibitions in the big department stores. A Frenchman would not dream of going to Au Printemps to buy an Old Master painting or sculpture but the great stores of Tokyo deal in just such works. Then Gekkoso had its Cercle de Crillon, a magnificent club where politicians, industrialists and other prominent figures would meet. Here, they exercised their creative talents, working with their hands, getting away from the terrifying stress of their responsibilities. They would exchange views and information – and look at and buy works of art. On my first visit, I inspected a clay mask made by Premier Nakasone. Later, he was to become embroiled in many financial scandals, and even then I came to know him as a man who could and would lend his powerful presence to influence the sale of specific works of art in Japan.

I was given VIP treatment by Gekkoso and lodged in the Okura, the most luxurious hotel in the city. My first night was devoted to work. Fujiwara had brought catalogues of exhibitions, brochures and books, all devoted to Gekkoso's operations. To my surprise, I found that Gekkoso had for some years been operating in the USSR and even had an office in Moscow, but it was not until later that I learned of their agreement with the Soviet state workshops and the price-fixing arrangement they worked. They deliberately fostered a cult of contemporary Russian painting and were able to meet the demand they had generated thanks to the efforts of a hundred employees. The painters had no idea that their canvases were sold in Japanese department stores for up to fifty times the prices they commanded in the Soviet Union and that some of them had become quite famous in Japan. When I was there, they had ten thousand of these bland, well-executed but thoroughly conventional Russian paintings in their warehouse.

This brilliant strategy was the brainchild of Madam Yoko Nakamura, the president and chief executive of Gekkoso, who created this completely artificial market of pictures, made to order and of a size dictated to fit Japanese houses. It was completely protected from competition since the Japanese customers were not going to go to Russia to seek out such works at source as they could have done if she were promoting works from France or Italy. It was enormously profitable, although sales fell off somewhat after the Russian invasion of Afghanistan. In part, the success of this project was due to the extraordinary way in which the painters were promoted. Lavish catalogues, openings attended by high-ranking officials from the Eastern Bloc, all created the illusion that these artists were of the first rank. So dominant was Madam Nakamura's position, a member of important government delegations to the USSR and honoured by the top officials of the Soviet Union, that her monopoly of the market was complete; she could destroy any other Japanese concern rash enough to compete. Gekkoso had its own museum where exhibitions were staged of works borrowed from such famous museums as the Hermitage and the Tretyakov Gallery.

So why should anyone as well connected in the Soviet Union and as influential as Madam Nakamura turn to me for icons? It was a mark of her intelligence that she recognized that these works were part of the national heritage and that, with their strong religious significance, to move openly into the market could be unpopular and jeopardize her privileged position, so it was prudent to deal at arm's length, through an intermediary.

On my first morning I was whisked off by Fujiwara to meet other vice presidents of Gekkoso. I was impressed by their seriousness and ability, but their knowledge of European art was superficial. They were well read but clearly quite unfamiliar with the products of our culture, though ever ready to absorb the best from other countries. Japanese galleries and collectors, I was told, were now in the market for just about everything. Our discussion was interrupted by the arrival of Madam Yoko Nakamura herself, and I had my first experience of this phenomenal personality.

She was in her fifties, still attractive and exuding an aura of authority. She listened to the views of the others but when she announced what was to be done, there was no further argument. Not that Madam Nakamura was a tyrant; she was a learned woman and had been given the extraordinary honour of being appointed to a special professorship in a Russian university as a result of work she had done there during numerous visits as part of official government delegations. Also present was a Mr Hashimoto, who said little but watched carefully. When I checked him out later, I found that he was the major shareholder in Gekkoso.

I had brought extensive literature on icons and Russian ecclesiastical art. I had a very difficult task. These people were learned yet naive when it came to European art. They would rightly resent any apparent condescension on my part but I had to get across the very different way in which we operated.

As our talks progressed, I in turn had to learn how they operated. I found that Madam Nakamura seemed to know everybody who mattered. Just how far her political antennae extended I was soon to discover. Gekkoso was typical of the Japanese system; the whole country was, and still is, covered by networks of power associated with one or other of the trading groups such as Fuji, Sumitomo, Mitsui and Mitsubishi. I learned how Mitsukoshi who controlled, among other things, the most important department stores group in Japan, had become involved with Tamanaga, the owner of the celebrated gallery in Paris. Some idea of the importance of the Tamanaga operation is given by the fact that the Paris gallery became one of the top fifty exporters in France. I remember their accountant being sent to London to buy about three hundred paintings for the Paris gallery, which could ship almost anything at any price to the art-hungry, enormously wealthy, but relatively unsophisticated Japanese.

The more I learned about the Japanese way of running things, the more I felt comfortable with them, as I had with the Armenians, but here they had virtually unlimited money, and they were the official, not the underground government of the country. I also realized that I had stumbled upon one of those powerful groups. Gekkoso even owned a banking company, Luna Trading, which advanced money to other galleries, providing up to 50 percent of the finance required to acquire stock, taking works of art as collateral. It was a heads-I-win, tails-you-lose operation. The rate of interest could run up to forty or fifty percent annually and if the minor gallery owner was unable to repay the loan, his stock would be taken by Gekkoso who would have valued it for collateral at far less than its market value. Gekkoso could be the sleeping giant which would transform my own business, provided I could earn their confidence and respect. I was to realize how typical this operation was of Madam Nakamura. In addition to the purely financial aspect, she learnt a great deal from applicants for loans of the financial standing, the supply of art works and all kinds of background information of her competitors who became increasingly dependent on her.

I had brought presents, but I was embarrassed by the number of gifts showered upon me. That was another aspect of the Japanese way, and of course our meetings were conducted with a courtesy which has vanished in almost every other part of the world. I managed to explain that they should not approach acquiring icons as though they were identical objects in a supermarket. I was delighted that everybody got the point.

There was a sumptuous dinner in my honour on my last night in Tokyo. The venue was Maxim's Tokyo, if anything superior to its Parisian parent in cuisine and the service is superlative. Even the wine cellar is amazing, with its wonderful selection of Bordeaux and Burgundies. Indeed, since the decor faithfully copies the Paris parent and nowadays most of the clientèle in both restaurants is Japanese, you might make believe that you actually were dining in the Rue Royale. Yet I could not help feeling that there was something incongruous about the violinist soulfully playing La Vie en Rose in the middle of Tokyo. Despite the enormous pains they took over the ambience, it was just not the same.

Next morning, I got a call from Yoko Nakamura. Would I mind calling in at the gallery before I went to the airport? It would be a pleasure, I assured her. So, once more off to the Ginza, where the full complement of vice presidents were waiting for me – and more gifts. Madam Nakamura took me on one side.

'We had a meeting earlier this morning,' she told me. 'Now we would not want you to feel that in any way we were insulting you or contradicting what you told us. We absolutely understand your position but we came to the conclusion that it would be better for you as well as for ourselves if we could modify very slightly the order. Could you ensure that all five hundred icons are the same size and of the same century?'

I was staggered. All my eloquence, all their agreement, had counted for nothing. I realized why many European or American businessmen give up trying to deal with the Japanese. All too often they go back on what had apparently been agreed and start the discussions all over again. So often Western business people lose patience and treat them as if they were idiots, which their prosperity shows they are not. But they have a different approach, and it is necessary to get inside their heads if one is to succeed.

This problem had to be tackled once and for all. I cancelled my flight. For two more days I explained, persuaded, answered their questions, virtually ran a seminar; I left with a firm order for five hundred Mothers of God, dimensions and period at my discretion.

For months I scoured every shop, gallery and auction room and I pressed every runner, restorer and robber I knew. It was an enormous task, but I assembled the whole shipment. I don't suppose that ever before five hundred virgins had boarded the same Jumbo! For years, I was known in the trade as Mr Mother of God. Madam Nakamura was overjoyed and so was I at the profit I made and on pulling off the first major icon sale in the country, and in the growing interest in these beautiful but neglected works of art.

# 10

# A Rembrandt's Castle

Since I had a partner, I felt I could travel for longer periods, sniffing out new sources and prospective buyers; somebody was looking after the shop. Gerrit Daleboudt, since selling out his business, had become something of a dilettante, collecting mainly Dutch nineteenth-century paintings by such artists as Schelfhout and Leickert; dainty, romantic works, executed with taste, but untouched by genius. The dealers homed in on Daleboudt like buzzards. As at that time it was not generally known that we were associated, I had an excellent opportunity to observe as my competitors tried out their tricks on my associate. The buzzards thought they had found a pigeon!

A couple of years had passed since my buying up every Mother of God I could lay hands on for the Japanese when a well-known dealer named de Boer called on Daleboudt with an exciting proposition. A long-time patron of de Boer's gallery was the owner of a self-portrait by Rembrandt and would be prepared, if satisfactory terms could be agreed, to sell it. Would Daleboudt like to buy it? Just consider the enormous reverence in which such paintings were held; a Rembrandt self-portrait is a star item in the great national collections fortunate enough to have one. Here was a unique opportunity for a private collector. And, regarded simply as an investment, this was something which must always be attractive to the richest galleries and collectors, regardless of the whims of fashion. Daleboudt agreed that it sounded interesting, told de Boer that he would be in touch within a few days – and hurried off to consult me.

Now I had not long returned from one of my Japanese trips during which I had visited a lot of museums. The Japanese economic miracle was in full swing and money was flooding into the country. They were buyers of every sort of art and rapidly building up impressive collections. However, they were not always too well informed. I saw canvases exhibited, even in Tokyo's National Museum of Western Art, still proudly displaying labels which informed the world that they were VENDU. Presumably these had been left attached in the belief that they were testimonials to the works' provenance. There were fine paintings by many of the great names in European art, but I realized I had never come across a single Rembrandt. For such avid collectors as the Japanese, that omission had to be rectified. So I told Daleboudt to play de Boer along, act intrigued but drag his feet a bit. Meanwhile I sent off a telex to Gekkoso for the attention of Mr Issei Fujiwara, asking if they would be interested in an important self-portrait by Rembrandt. The same evening, I had their reply. They were not merely interested, they were *very interested*. A most important client had just demanded a major European work. What was the price, and also, please send details of the work? What sort of a serious institution could this be, I wondered, which wanted to know the price before they had seen the painting, or even a photograph of it? This was to be my first contact with the MOA, a museum owned by the Sekai Kyusei Kyo (SKK), a religious foundation of immense wealth.

The MOA was the realization of a dream. Mokichi Okada had intended to become a painter but instead had made a fortune, first as a haberdasher and then in the wholesale business. But he could spend a whole night discussing the nature of art with leading painters. Ruined by the economic depression and desolated by his wife's death, Okada resolved to promote a new religion, devoted to the creation of a new civilization in which the suffering of society would be conquered by the establishment of an ideal world through the pursuit of truth, virtue and beauty. Militarist Japan, engaged in the invasion of China and preparing for the Second World War, was hardly fertile soil for such ideas and Okada's activities were curtailed by the police. His prophecy that Japan would be defeated in a war with the United States did little to endear him to the warlords, but in the aftermath of atomic devastation and defeat, his influence, and presumably his wealth, increased enormously. In 1952, he opened the Hakone Gallery of Art to house many of the works he had acquired and by the time he died in 1955, Okada had amassed more than three thousand.

But the gallery, beautiful as it is and set in unspoiled landscape, was not the culmination of his dedication to art and beauty. He aimed at creating 'earthly paradises' in Hakone and Atami, areas of outstanding natural beauty, and at Atami a superb ultra-modern building was being completed, the MOA (Museum of Art). Already there were rich collections of Japanese and East Asiatic art and the foundation was beginning to expand its horizons. Henry Moore's King and Queen sit in majesty on the terrace. In the years to come, the MOA would play its part in spurring on the incredibly costly purchases of Impressionist paintings by the Japanese, but at that time they had virtually nothing from the West. My friends at Gekkoso were eager to remedy this deficiency.

It must be admitted that with affluence, the men who ran the SKK had lapsed from the austere moral ideals of its founder. Inevitably they got involved in the corrupt politicking of Japan. They whisked around in their private jets and their relations with pretty girls were definitely unmonastic. Scandals abounded, culminating in the flight of the president of the order to Brazil. I was not aware at first of this lurid reputation, but its corruption and warring factions were to have a great impact on my own career. Of course, Madam Nakamura knew the score exactly.

Next day, Daleboudt visited de Boer, examined the painting and spoke in general terms of the possibility of his buying it. Just how much was de Boer asking? Four million guilders, he was told. To keep things simple, I decided to propose four million also to Gekkoso, but dollars, not guilders; I would be content with the modest profit on the foreign exchange! I received an immediate telex. Never mind the price, would I give the gallery a ten percent discount? I was fast learning Japanese commercial practices.

Gekkoso was so enthusiastic that I might have been tempted into getting Daleboudt to buy the painting without waiting to have a definite deal. There was, however, apart from normal prudence, a compelling reason for acting otherwise.

'These Japanese,' Daleboudt said. 'They ordered five hundred icons, didn't they. And they paid up. So you must have the funds necessary to stake the Rembrandt.'

'No way. Remember, I had the Beirut penthouse completely redecorated before all that trouble. Then there is the place in Munich, and you've seen the house I have bought in Amsterdam, not to mention the cars.'

I had taken him to see the splendid modern house, standing in its own grounds in the snootiest, priciest part of town. Apart from my real estate commitments, I must admit to enjoying as exalted a standard of living as I could afford, or even rather more. But I had a wealthy partner, so I turned the proposition back to him.

'Besides, I don't believe in financing my own deals. How about you forking up with some of the proceeds of your share in Randstad?'

'There is a problem,' Daleboudt told me. 'Although the sale was agreed long ago, I still have not received all the money. I am flat broke – temporarily, of course.'

There was indeed a problem, but it was not one of which I was then aware. Daleboudt had taken to frequenting the illegal casinos which had sprouted up in Amsterdam, and had become an addicted gambler.

So there was no way either of us, or the two of us together, could come up with the sum demanded by de Boer. We would have to seek a way to finance the deal, and that was to lead to complications.

First, however, there was a little matter of authentification to cope with. The Rembrandt Research Committee had been established to look into the legion of paintings all over the world which were, so their owners all too often erroneously claimed, genuine Rembrandts, and it had started work in 1968. When the first of their authoritative volumes appeared in 1982 the Committee made itself very unpopular as it gave the thumbs down to many well-known, well-loved and often very expensively purchased 'Rembrandts' in important museums and private collections. The entire art market and the world's museums hung upon the words of the Committee and since advance knowledge of their conclusions would have enormous financial implications, comparable to illegal insider-trading in shares, they made it a rule that they would not express opinions or issue certificates prior to publication. The primary examination of Rembrandt's early paintings (those dating from 1625 to 1631) was completed by 1973 and this first stage finalized at the end of 1979. It covered, in addition to the painting which de Boer was offering, two other paintings which had a direct bearing on our deal.

The Bridgestone Museum in Tokyo, founded by a tyre manufacturer called Ishibashi (Bridgestone was a literal translation of his name), had taken great pride in the acquisition of a Rembrandt entitled *A Nocturnal Scene*. This picture had been in the celebrated Matsukata collection, many of whose paintings had been bought before the war from the Wildenstein Gallery. After the defeat of Japan, Daniel Wildenstein went to Tokyo to see what he could buy back, but this painting remained and it was claimed to be the first Rembrandt to have been brought into Japan. So it was a shattering blow when the Committee indicated that it was possibly the work of Gerard Dou.

As soon as I offered de Boer's picture, Madam Nakamura, knowing that this other 'Rembrandt' was in the Bridgestone Museum, summoned the museum director, Dr Kamon. Beneath her placid, innocent features, the mask of a kabuki actor, she was one of us, a street fighter. She could immediately sense weaknesses and vulnerability, and knew instinctively how to turn them to her own advantage. She was as dominating a woman as the great matriarchal figures of feudal Japan, and to achieve such pre-eminence in as male macho a society as contemporary Japan was phenomenal. Leading industrialists and politicians, even prime ministers, danced when she pulled the strings, so Dr Kamon told her the bad news about his painting, even though this disclosure to somebody active in the art market was clearly improper. Madam Nakamura was quite prepared on top of this to pay to make sure that what I was offering would not share the same fate, so she asked me to demand clearance from the Committee.

The other painting important to us was an early self-portrait which the Indianapolis Museum of Art had acquired as part of the Clowes Collection. There were a number of versions of this portrait, six recorded by the Committee, and one was our painting. Only one version was approved by the Committee, so it followed that if the Indianapolis picture were genuine, as had been generally accepted, then ours was at best a copy. The other versions were of no practical consequence.

The first step therefore was to discover whether the decision of the Rembrandt Research Committee was favourable, but how was I to persuade the members to break their rule and commit themselves? Madam Nakamura refused to accept that when the Committee stated that they would not 'leak' their findings, they really meant it. In Japan, a series of real-estate and share scandals have subsequently demonstrated how corruption ran right through the business community, and Madam Nakamura could not be convinced that the Rembrandt

Research Committee could not also be purchased. The painting had been examined by two members of the Committee, Dr Simon Levie and Professor Josua Bruyn on 7th April 1976. Dr Levie, in addition to other prestigious appointments, was director of the Rijksmuseum, and undoubtedly in the eyes of the world the most important person in the Dutch art establishment; and he was the chairman and leading member of the Committee. So if he inspected it personally and if his opinion were favourable, I knew this would be the strongest possible endorsement.

Madam Nakamura contended that whatever had been decided after that examination would ultimately be published, so why not say now whether the picture would be approved? And please could she have it in writing! Of course I wanted to pull off the deal, so I racked my brains furiously to solve this problem. Then I thought of Bottema.

To the delight of the press, Jan Bottema, the editor of *Antiek*, a highly respectable magazine dealing with antiques, had a few weeks previously been detained by the police in connection with the murder with a pair of scissors of a young woman. After holding him for a week, they were forced to admit that they had not a shred of firm evidence against him and he was released. I had contributed some articles to his magazine and knew the man. He was a strange, unsociable person and generally disliked. The scandal of his arrest won him a measure of sympathy but, more important, people did not know how to react to him. The case was still pending; Bottema, although free, had not been cleared and he carried an odour of suspicion. This was to be my secret weapon against the Committee. It would be virtually impossible for them to refuse him without giving the impression that they were condemning him as a murderer without fair trial.

So I approached Bottema and proposed that he undertake two functions. First, it would be natural for Daleboudt to provide himself with an expert adviser but it would not have been a good idea for me, a known dealer, to put in an appearance since de Boer would surely tumble to our plan to sell on. Since his commercial interest in art was confined to publishing of an academic character, Bottema was a natural intermediary and he readily agreed to accompany Daleboudt at his next meeting with de Boer.

But more crucial was his role as go-between with the Rembrandt Research Committee. We put them on the spot. They had to receive him and their predicament was all the more embarrassing since he knew personally one of the members, Bob Haak, the director of the Amsterdams Historisch Museum.

The members of the Committee and the scientific experts who would be required to examine the painting were uncomfortably aware of the publicity given to the dubious arrangements where an 'independent' expert who certified a work as authentic was found to be rather too friendly with the dealer offering it for sale. Bernard Berenson's knowledge of the great masters of the Italian Renaissance earned him a reputation for infallibility which rivalled the Pope's, and for integrity which far outstripped that of the Pontiff. The artistic establishment had been shaken by the disclosure that he had a contract to receive twenty-five percent of the proceeds on all works sold by Duveen on his introduction, and that he had at the same time been approached by prospective buyers for authentification of paintings, some of which were downright forgeries. Even the trustees of Britain's National Gallery were on Duveen's payroll and many of the greatest collections in the United States, amassed in the early years of the century, still display works acquired from Duveen which had helped to enrich not only Duveen but also Berenson.

In our own time, that charming cheat Fernand Legros peddled far more canvases by Derain, Dufy, van Dongen and Modigliani than they ever painted, many verified as genuine by revered authorities.

Now it was the turn of the Japanese to play big spenders and they naturally wanted to make sure that they got a really independent and authoritative opinion: the approval of the Rembrandt Research Committee.

To push things along, I flew out to Japan and had meetings with Fujiwara and Madam Nakamura. Although they still had not seen the painting, this did not deter them from arguing fiercely for a reduction in price. I was prepared for this tough approach, but another tactic took me by surprise and faced me with one of the strangest problems of my career: how to acquire a castle within a week – and without the necessary money!

'So, Mr van Rijn, we are greatly honoured that your family should consider selling this masterpiece to our gallery,' Fujiwara told me.

I had no idea what he was talking about. I never claimed to be connected with the owners of the painting, so I made noncommittal noises.

'And to think that this painting has remained in the family of Rembrandt van Rijn for more than three hundred years. Remarkable,' Fujiwara observed.

My head swam. Remarkable? It would have been a bloody miracle! Then I recalled a conversation I had had with Fujiwara the first time we met.

'My name is Michel van Rijn,' I had told him. 'Like Rembrandt van Rijn, you know.'

Fujiwara nodded knowingly. 'And you are from Amsterdam, Mr van Rijn?'

'Yes. Although my family come from Leiderdorp, a little place you would not have heard of, but it was the home of Rembrandt.'

And now it appeared that Rembrandt was my long-lost tenth cousin or great-great-grandfather. It was news to me, and it would have been just as big a shock to Rembrandt. But this family connection clearly impressed the folk at Gekkoso; it would have been cruel to disillusion them.

'Madam Nakamura has expressed a desire to see the self-portrait before she decides whether to buy it,' Fujiwara informed me.

'That seems very reasonable,' I answered. It was about time somebody thought of actually looking at the painting, but of course I would have to find a way of showing it to her without alerting de Boer.

'So, if it is agreeable to you, Madam Nakamura will come to Holland next week with a small group of colleagues including myself.'

'I shall be delighted to extend hospitality to all of your party.'

'Ah, yes, hospitality,' Fujiwara murmured. 'You are so kind that I am reluctant to impose upon you, but Madam Nakamura has made a further request.'

'You can be assured that I shall do everything possible to make your president happy.'

'To someone with your family background it may seem unimportant, but our business will be greatly facilitated,' smiled Fujiwara.

What the hell can they want, I wondered, dinner with the Queen, a guided tour of the red-light district?

'It would be an act of homage,' Fujiwara droned on. 'And it need only be for an hour or so, if it would not too greatly inconvenience you and your family. However, she really does want to pay a visit to your castle.'

'My castle,' I repeated, dumbfounded.

'Well, the castle of Rembrandt,' Fujiwara amended apologetically. 'I presume that it is somewhere near Amsterdam.'

'Oh surely,' I assented. 'But who told Madam Nakamura about,' the words hung on my lips, 'our family castle?'

'But it stands to reason. So great an artist must have been much revered and honoured. It is unthinkable that he had not a castle and that your family would not have retained the place where he lived and worked.'

'Unthinkable,' I agreed.

'So, please, may we pay a visit to your ancestral home?'

'It will be an experience to which I look forward with the greatest anticipation,' I lied.

So back home to Amsterdam to acquire my family castle.

# 11

# A PRIVATE VIEWING

'A bloody awful mess you've got us in with your precious ancestor,' commented Daleboudt bitterly.

'Screw my illustrious family,' I said. 'You're the one with the connections today. Think, Gerrit, don't you have just one pal with a castle? We only need it for a day. Less, a couple of hours would do.'

'I know a few hotels where you can hire rooms by the hour, but I'm a bit short of castles for the moment,' he growled.

'It's no joking matter,' I complained. 'We both need this deal, and I tell you, no castle, no sale.'

'Bloody ridiculous! You know as well as I do that Holland isn't castle country. No Crusader sites, the Rhine castles are all in Germany, and Vauban built his pretty forts on the French-Belgian frontier. Why can't they settle for a windmill?'

'It doesn't have to be a great big castle,' I protested. 'Just a bijou residence suitable for an artist, preferably with a good north light.'

'Seriously,' said Daleboudt, 'practically every decent stately home has been turned into an hotel or some sort of upper-class amusement park. Blame the tax system. And even if we were to pretend one of those was your family seat, how long would we keep your Japanese shrewdies fooled with hordes of screaming brats rushing in and out?'

'Do you know anybody in the real-estate business who might be able to help us?' I implored.

Daleboudt considered. 'Well, I could give Zadelhoff a ring,' he said. 'I guess if anybody knows where we can buy a castle it will be him.'

I knew Dr Zadelhoff by reputation: he was probably the most important property dealer in Holland. Daleboudt phoned.

'Does he happen to have a nice castle on his books?'

'Not exactly,' said Daleboudt. 'He wanted to know if we could make do with a mere palace?'

'Stop fooling.'

'I mean it. You know Amstelrust?'

Of course I knew Amstelrust, from the outside. In common with most large cities, Amsterdam sprawls across the surrounding countryside, depositing depressingly uniform little houses over what once was meadow or woodland. As if by some miracle, the banks of the River Amstel provide an exception to this urban pollution. Follow the river upstream towards the picture-postcard village of Oudekerk, and within a kilometre of the city centre you are in practically open country. The highway dwindles to a riverside lane. An occasional car or bicycle passes and, apart from the quiet chugging of a barge nosing along the placid water, the only sound is the chirping of birds. There, set at an angle to the road, Amstelrust stands in its own parkland, a compact, classical mansion, perfectly proportioned, with its ranks of tall windows and pediment-crowned doorway. The house is not large as palaces go, perhaps twenty or thirty rooms, and it is screened from intruders by an elegant gateway of iron railings, surmounted by gold curlicues in which its name is spelled out. Its stones have mellowed with age; otherwise it is precisely as it was in the seventeenth century.

'Zadelhoff told me that Amstelrust is for sale,' Daleboudt continued. 'It's all very hush-hush at the moment – not officially on the market, you understand.'

'Amstelrust would be perfect. If only we could borrow it. I suppose you don't know Zadelhoff well enough to ask him?'

Daleboudt shook his head. 'Frankly, I was surprised he opened up as much as he did.'

'I suppose he has heard that you sold your business and thinks you might want to retire to your own private palace with the proceeds.'

We racked our brains as to how we could wangle the use of the palace. I waved aside a suggestion from Daleboudt that we could pretend to be shooting a film. Our time was ticking away. Then came a second unbelievable stroke of luck.

The following day I had to see my notary, an old friend. His phone buzzed and I heard his receptionist say, 'It's Dr Zadelhoff on the line for you, sir.' He apologized to me and took the call. They did not speak for long, but judging from the tone of voice and the enquiries about family health, they were on friendly terms. As soon as he had finished, I asked how well he knew Zadelhoff.

'I've known him since he started to deal in real estate,' he replied. 'But I would not say we are particularly close.'

He did not need to say more. I had met Zadelhoff a number of times and not found him lovable. A tall, brisk man in his forties who had made a lot of money in a hurry and was not reluctant to spread it around in order to advance his social standing.

'I want you to do me an enormous favour,' I said. I told him the whole story. He was a bit reluctant to fall in with my plan but when I pretended that we might indeed buy the stately house, eventually he agreed to make the approach.

The next day, I received a phone call from Fujiwara confirming their flight.

I offered to reserve rooms for the party but Fujiwara assured me that his staff had taken suites at the Okura. I promised to be at Schiphol to welcome them; we were positively purring at each other by the time I hung up. All we lacked in order to show them the Rembrandt in the castle were the painting and the castle.

There were just two days to go before the party arrived when I got a call from my friendly notary.

'I had quite a session with Zadelhoff,' he informed me with a chuckle. 'He was a bit doubtful whether you would be able to afford Amstelrust but I assured him you had made a lot of money, becoming the leading dealer in icons and opening up the Japanese market. Anyway, we have an agreement, completion date to be decided.'

'Terrific! Has he agreed to our looking the place over for one afternoon?'

'Yes, but there is a condition. The owner was a bit tricky. He has always been worried that some idiot might burn the place down or scrawl graffiti over the walls. I gave my word that you were a responsible person but the owner has agreed to let you have the run of the building, not for the whole afternoon, just until five, prompt. That's his last word.'

I felt a glow of satisfaction. The whole crazy scheme was working out. 'That's fantastic. We'll get them in and out in time. I can't thank you enough.'

'I hadn't finished,' he cut me short. 'That was not what I meant by a condition. He insists that Zadelhoff or the manager of his company be present all the time you are in occupation.'

'Oh Christ! You mean he'll be sitting there like a bailiff?'

'The manager's quite a decent chap. Maybe if you speak nicely to him he will make himself unobtrusive. Get him to take his clothes off and pose as a statue.'

No sooner had I hung up than Daleboudt appeared. I told him the situation.

'Now it's up to you,' I said. 'I've got the castle; you get the picture.'

'And just precisely how am I supposed to do that?' he demanded.

'Think of something. Tell de Boer you want to show it to your wife.'

'So why doesn't my wife come with me to his gallery?'

'Use your imagination, man. Perhaps she wants to see it on your own wall. After all, it might clash with the wallpaper.'

'Do you think de Boer is such an idiot as to fall for that sort of yarn? I suppose that if she doesn't like it, we get Rembrandt to come round and change the colour of the background?'

'Look, old de Boer wants to sell this painting as badly as we do, so he will fall over backwards to bring it off. Just think of the trouble we're going to to humour this crazy idea of the Japanese. Why? Because they have the money and we want the sale. De Boer will behave in exactly the same way.'

He was still grumbling as he left. At the door he turned.

'And what happens if their bloody plane is delayed?'

'Negative thinking!' I shouted. 'The plane is due in at seven in the morning. They are flying JAL, not some damned wing-and-a-prayer airline.'

He was mumbling about hijacks, strikes at Schiphol and engine failure as I bundled him out.

Meanwhile Bottema had been busy with the Committee. With typical Dutch thoroughness, they were going through the whole gamut of scientific testing, but I had been told that the initial reaction of Dr Levie had been entirely favourable, and that was good enough for me.

But I knew it would not be good enough for the Japanese. Even when I was able to inform them that I had been told in confidence that the painting would be included in the forthcoming book, they could not understand the emphasis the Committee put on discretion and avoiding contact with the commercial side of the art world. As I was to realize, the Japanese were so routinely accustomed to corruption that they had no conception of the Dutch view that experts must be above suspicion. If the painting were to be listed as authentic in the book, we should get the Committee to provide them with a certificate to that effect. No certificate, no sale!

Bottema's role was crucial; his ambiguous position over the murder did indeed work to our advantage. Nobody knew quite how to treat him. Not being a dealer, and representing his magazine, he was received everywhere usually with a degree of sympathy.

The Japanese were packing their bags when Daleboudt finally persuaded de Boer to let the painting out of his possession for the day, and we were hard pressed to complete the arrangements for it to arrive at Amstelrust in time for it to be displayed in the spot where it had supposedly been hanging for three centuries.

I was at the airport at the crack of dawn, making myself a nuisance to the staff. It was after eight when the Jumbo landed and nearly another hour before Fujiwara shepherded his team, complete with baggage, into the VIP lounge, where I regaled them with coffee and rolls.

'I know you must be tired after your flight, so let me get you to your hotel where you can rest for a bit. If it is agreeable to you, I shall call on you, shall we say at one, and take you to lunch? Afterwards, we go to my place where you can inspect the painting.'

I think they were impressed by my consideration. Actually, I was dying to get the whole crowd off my hands so that I could go ahead with the final preparations for our pantomime. Once the Japanese party were installed in the Okura, I raced back to my house where the manager of the real-estate firm was eagerly waiting.

'I want to talk to you in the strictest confidence,' I told him. 'I have been requested by somebody of the greatest importance to find a palace for him somewhere in Europe.'

'You mean you are not buying Amstelrust for yourself?' asked the puzzled manager.

'Not even Mr Zadelhoff yet knows. Discretion is vital, otherwise there could be not merely a scandal, but an international crisis.'

His mouth sagged open.

'I shall be bringing some people with me to Amstelrust,' I told him. 'In a few hours you will see them for yourself, so I might as well tell you now that this is a deputation from the very highest authority in Japan.'

'You don't mean that the Emperor— '

I interrupted him. There are limits to the credulity of even Dutch estate agents. 'His Imperial Majesty is to the best of my knowledge quite satisfied with his official residence, but there are other members of the Imperial family and of his official household. I must not say more; my lips are sealed.' I endeavoured to look both conspiratorial and the soul of integrity.

'Yes, but what's all this about some painting being brought to the house? Mr Zadelhoff didn't say anything about it.'

'I'll come clean with you,' I confided, 'but this is strictly between ourselves, understood? It is what might be called a package deal. Your Japanese client would want Amstelrust perfectly furnished.'

'But it is perfectly furnished,' he protested. 'Why, the carpets, the chandeliers, you won't find better – '

'No, but what is missing is one sublime example of Dutch art – a truly magnificent Rembrandt. I know the people involved and you can take my word that it is the Rembrandt that will sell them Amstelrust. After all,' I said airily, 'there are lots of pretty little palaces about, but masterpieces like this painting turn up only once in a lifetime.'

'Is that so?' he breathed, wide-eyed and quite overwhelmed.

I could see that I had him hooked and this was the moment to press home my advantage. 'Now you play it my way this afternoon,' I urged. 'Don't say anything about the house. Their interest is supposed to be completely confidential and they don't know you, so they will pretend that it is only the painting they have come to see. Any attempt at a sales pitch would be thought so vulgar as to ruin the whole deal. Anyway, they will be able to get all the details of the property which they then have to report back to Tokyo.'

'I could hand them a printed brochure,' he suggested hopefully.

'Absolutely not, that would be fatal. In fact, it is better if they don't think you have any connection with the people selling the place. You have no idea how delicately these Orientals carry out their business. Everything has to be implied, nothing is said openly, and above all show them every courtesy.'

'Every courtesy,' he echoed.

'Why don't you get one of the girls from your office to come and make tea in the house?'

'You honestly think that will help?'

'I am certain of it,' I told the eager beaver. 'But we ought to have a proper butler to serve at table. The girl can prepare the tray and hand it to you.'

'To me?'

'Why not? You have to be there but you must not let on that you are only a real estate broker. And since you have nothing to do with the painting, they will wonder why you are there. You don't look tough enough to be a security man. No, you have to be the butler. And you know, you really look the part, dignified and efficient.'

He was still a bit doubtful, but I stressed that the sale of the house depended on his performance, and his resistance caved in.

I got a call from Daleboudt. Having deposited the deeds of his house in exchange for the Rembrandt for the day, he was picking up the painting with a posse from a security firm and would be delivering it to Amstelrust at two. I told him I would bring in the cast of *Madam Butterfly* no earlier than three to give him time to have it hung and to get my household staff on parade.

My chauffeur drove me to the Okura, where they were waiting in the lobby, lined up in order of seniority.

Fujiwara confided in me that there was considerable political influence behind the MOA. 'Our Prime Minister, Mr Nakasone, is most interested in its progress.'

Later I was to appreciate that this was a masterly understatement, but at that time my mind was fully occupied. I took Madam Nakamura and an interpreter from Gekkoso in my car and the other members of the delegation followed in Daleboudt's. I kept one eye on my watch and took it very easy on the road to The Hague. Amstelrust should be unlocked by now and butler and kitchen scullion in place.

I had taken pains to order the meal in advance. The service was impeccable and the Japanese congratulated me on the excellence of the food.

'They have great respect,' I said modestly, 'for members of the Rembrandt family.'

Conversation during the meal was polite but inconsequential; neither Madam Nakamura nor her subordinates were inclined to open up before they had seen for themselves that I had been able to come up with the goods, and I switched to automatic. At half-past two, the last plate had been cleared away.

'A cognac before we leave?' I offered.

Madam Nakamura declined and everybody followed her lead. 'We are so anxious to view your family castle, van Rijn *san*,' she said with an enigmatic smile. Was she calling my bluff?

'I fear you may be disappointed,' I said. I saw Fujiwara stiffen, but Madam Nakamura, as befitted the daughter of a general who had committed *seppuku* to relieve his men from the disgrace of surrender, betrayed no emotion. 'We Dutch based our prosperity on commerce rather than warfare. So, like the French châteaux, our castles are really glorified houses, not bleak fortresses. But we of the family are very attached to the place.'

We set out in the same order and I took a short diversion in order, I explained, to let our visitors see some of the countryside immortalized in the landscapes of such masters as Jan van Goyen and Jacob Ruysdael. Actually of course, it was to make time for Daleboudt to bring in the Rembrandt.

Just before Amstelrust, we passed an impressive statue of Rembrandt at work. Its position is sheer coincidence, but it was as if the gods had conspired to create the illusion that this was truly his home territory. At twenty past three, the great ornamental gate swung open and the two cars swept into the driveway. The palace was immaculate, the grounds idyllic, but with the air of a home which was still lived in. Just looking at it made me feel proud. Madam Nakamura was duly impressed.

'You were too modest, Mr van Rijn,' she said, as we were escorted into the principal reception room by my real-estate butler. There, with the sunlight glinting on its heavily gilded frame, stood the self-portrait, looking for all the world as if it really had hung on that wall since the seventeenth century. Each of the party admired the painting: the play of light and shade, the expression on the face of the artist, so typical, both artful and yet imbued with a magnetic charm and vitality. I glanced at the real estate manager's expression, hopeful yet mystified.

'James,' I called, 'see about a little refreshment for our guests.'

For a moment he looked as if he were about to tell me to get stuffed, but he remembered just in time – no painting, no real-estate sale – and with a nod he retired to the servants' quarters.

'It is strange,' observed Madam Nakamura, 'that the great artist, living in so beautiful a castle, did not leave us paintings of his residence.'

'My ancestor became more and more obsessed with portraits and paintings dominated by people, as his art matured,' I explained, adopting my most professorial tone. 'Like Goya, he turned from being a court painter, paid to flatter the noble or the rich, to portraying the humanity of his subjects, even if they were beggars or street traders.'

'Even so.' She was not wholly convinced.

'Also,' I improvised hurriedly, 'there was a strong feeling at the time against the aristocracy. He did not want to display the family wealth.'

I'll bet he didn't, I said to myself, great genius that he was, freezing his arse off in a dingy attic in the middle of the city because he had turned away from purse-proud, demanding patrons, but Madam Nakamura seemed happy with my explanation.

My butler returned bearing a silver tray, and a moment later my housemaid appeared, tastefully mini-skirted, bearing a large silver teapot like some medieval chalice. The Japanese indulged in the Dutch tea ceremony.

'I would have liked to entertain you to dinner in Amstelrust,' I announced, 'but practically all the staff are at our country house – a little place of no historic interest,' I added hurriedly. 'So I have reserved a table at a very pretty spot called Waterland. Meanwhile, perhaps you would like to see something of the house? James, lead the way, please.'

The frown lifted from the real-estate manager's brow. 'Not one word of your sales patter,' I hissed in his ear, 'or you will ruin the sale of the palace.'

He looked hurt, but confined his comments to the age of the furniture and the layout of the gardens. The tour took about half an hour, and when we returned, our guests went into a little huddle. Then Fujiwara approached me.

'We would like to express our gratitude for all the trouble you have gone to. As for the painting, it is most satisfactory. We are willing to proceed.'

I sighed inwardly with relief. My butler sighed outwardly with relief. He was busily working out the price of Amstelrust in yen.

'Since your stay is so short, let me take you straight back into Amsterdam,' I said to Madam Nakamura. 'I have called Dr Levie who has agreed to receive you in the Rijksmuseum and afterwards some of your party might care to do a little shopping before we go to Waterland.'

No sooner had I quit my family seat than Daleboudt whipped the painting off the wall and rushed it off home. De Boer was probably biting his nails in agitation as he waited.

In his office in the Rijksmuseum overlooking the gardens, Dr Levie talked quite freely about our Rembrandt with Madam

Nakamura. Although he did not offer to put it in writing, he confirmed that the favourable opinion was to be printed. He was very friendly and accepted my invitation to join us that evening. It was very rare for him to accept invitations from dealers entertaining clients, so this was quite an honour.

I escorted Madam Nakamura to Waterland, a picturesque rustic inn situated, as its name implied, among the drained fens which had once been marshy swamps. When Dr Levie joined us, Madam Nakamura made a great fuss of photographing the party. Since Japanese visitors to Europe habitually take pictures of people and places, this seemed to be normal behaviour. But nothing she does is without ulterior motive. Back in Tokyo, she would be able to show the MOA board that she had involved Dr Levie and our other guest, Mr Uchida, the Japanese ambassador to the Netherlands. And by her guiding the conversation with apparent innocence to his discussing the painting with her that afternoon, Dr Levie could be compromised by this evidence of her friendliness with the chairman of the Rembrandt Research Committee before the sale of an important painting which he had authenticated. However, when Madam Nakamura proposed that he should be their guest in Tokyo, he replied that he would be delighted to visit Japan and to talk about the Rembrandt but not before it had been bought and was hanging in the museum.

Mr Uchida was a friend of Madam Nakamura and I was beginning to appreciate just how extensive was her network of contacts among the rich and the powerful and how strong her influence with the Japanese establishment. Whenever a deal was important to her, she would pull out all the stops and unashamedly exploit the prestige of her family name, the glamour of her own personality and her unrivalled intimacy with the leaders of her country.

# 12

# STOP THE PLANE!

I slept soundly that night. The deal was as good as done. The Japanese were pleased with the painting, I was confident it would stand up to closer scrutiny when the time came, and they had paid homage to the shade of Rembrandt in his own castle. All that was needed now was to keep de Boer sweet until we had completed the formalities of the sale.

But formalities which can be brushed aside at night have a habit of growing far more formidable in the morning.

'So what do I tell de Boer?' asked Daleboudt.

'Your wife's making up her mind,' I replied.

The dealer was disappointed, but did his best to disguise his irritation. 'Come now, Mr Daleboudt, I have been more than reasonable. You and your wife have seen the painting in your own home, what more do you want before you can come to a decision? Do bear in mind that this is a unique work, and I have refrained from offering it to other collectors in deference to you, but I cannot go on indefinitely leaving the offer exclusively with you.'

My partner was enough of a gambler to know that the only way to play a weak hand is by bluffing.

'Personally, I like the thing well enough and I have made up my mind to buy it. However, you know the way women like to dither; it will take a little while for me to persuade my wife that she was the one who wanted the picture all the time and that she had to talk me round to it. Of course, if you cannot be patient for a few more days, that's an end to the matter. I am not prepared to have a quarrel with my wife for the sake of this one painting. If I don't buy the Rembrandt, something else of the same quality will turn up. I am in no hurry, and practically every dealer and gallery owner in Europe and America is chasing me with some masterpiece.'

'You say you have decided to buy it?' De Boer pounced on the words.

'Yes, but in my own time. I refuse to be hustled.'

'Well, my dear fellow, there's no need for any unpleasantness between old friends. It goes without saying that I'll hold it for you for a while.' The old dealer was falling over himself to save the sale, but his natural caution reasserted itself. 'That is, for a little while longer,' he added.

Daleboudt favoured him with a brusque nod and strode out of the gallery.

'Old friends,' he snorted when he recounted the conversation. 'I had never seen or heard of the old rogue until it got out that I had come into money.'

'While you have been amusing yourself in town, I called Dr Levie,' I told him. 'I suggested he might come to Tokyo and give a lecture on the work of the Committee, perhaps with special reference to this panel. A spot of publicity never did a good sale any harm, you know.'

'What did he say?'

'He will be delighted, but he repeated only after the picture is hanging in the museum in Tokyo. He refuses to do anything which might be construed as getting involved in the commercial side of art.'

'Good God, you mean he's honest?'

'I am afraid so. He must be the exception that proves the rule. But even getting him out there after the sale will be terrific for our prestige with Gekkoso.'

'So when are Gekkoso going to pay up?'

'Hold your horses. They have to get formal approval from the MOA board. I expect it will take a few days.'

Daleboudt looked unhappy. He could see himself having to go back to de Boer with some other story about his wife.

Next day, Fujiwara rang me. Since nobody from the Rembrandt Committee could properly be asked to a meeting to approve the painting, before finalizing the purchase, as a pure formality of course, they would like to bring along a Japanese expert whose favourable opinion could be passed to their client. 'We are certain that the painting is absolutely genuine,' Fujiwara assured me. 'What better provenance could it have? But you know the Bridgestone Museum fake caused a dreadful scandal, and the MOA people have become very nervous. And while they have implicit trust in the Rembrandt Research Committee, there is something to be said for an additional opinion by an authority who is Japanese and therefore better known to them.'

'I quite understand,' I told him. 'Who is the expert you wish to consult?'

'Well, that is supposed to be confidential, but I don't mind telling you that it will be Dr Kamon.'

The name had a familiar ring. 'The Director of the Bridgestone Museum,' Fujiwara added.

'An excellent choice,' I chuckled. 'He ought to be uniquely qualified to recognize a fake Rembrandt.'

'We would hope then to complete the purchase. Presumably a letter of credit drawn on a leading Swiss bank would be acceptable?'

'Absolutely.' And the sooner the better, I said under my breath.

'In which case, I suggest we complete formalities in Zurich. That is unless you insist on the painting remaining in your charming palace until payment has been effected. Dr Kamon could then see it in situ.'

'No, Zurich will be fine,' I hastened to assure him.

'So all you have to do,' I told Daleboudt that afternoon, 'is persuade de Boer to let you take the painting to Switzerland.'

He shook his head. 'No dice. Somehow we have to find at least part of the money.'

'When do you expect finally to get paid for your business?' I demanded.

He waved his hand vaguely. 'I can't explain: the whole thing has become incredibly complicated.' He relapsed into silence.

I had no inkling then that most of the proceeds of his sale had already vanished over the roulette wheels. 'Don't you know anybody in your church who would lend you what we need, or just put up a guarantee?'

One of the reasons I had taken him as a serious-minded person was that he was an enthusiastic supporter of one of the old-fashioned, very strict Christian sects. I was to be utterly disenchanted when I learned more about them. However, he ruled that course out, and then I remembered an old friend, Jonathan Bear.

'I don't know him,' said Daleboudt.

'He's an interesting person.' I replied. 'Comes from an orthodox Jewish, South African family, very sensitive and keen on art but also a shrewd businessman. On the surface, he is a cautious, orthodox banker, preferring to earn a safe ten percent than to go for a hundred percent return if there is the slightest speculative risk, but there is another side to his personality. He took a doctorate in philosophy and mathematics, and is still prepared to look at any proposition with an acute and open mind. He is not frightened to take up a position at odds with what is socially accepted. He is just the person to back me.'

Jonathan listened attentively; I think Rembrandt's ancestral castle appealed to him. Anyway, he agreed to help.

'If you will lend me the money to buy the painting, I can ship it out to Zurich where it can be seen by as many experts as the Japanese care to send,' I told him.

But that would have made life too simple. Jonathan trusted

me, but a straight loan would leave him unsecured and I was unable to give him a firm date for repayment since that would depend on the Japanese.

'Instead of being out of the interest on the money for God knows how long, why don't I arrange for one of my banks to put up a guarantee for what you will be paying de Boer?'

So there was one more formality. Daleboudt had to get de Boer to accept the guarantee and release the painting.

'I don't understand,' complained the long-suffering dealer. 'You say you want to buy the painting, so why this rigmarole of a bank guarantee?'

'It assures you that you will get your money, but I told you before, I am not prepared actually to buy it until my wife is happy with it.'

'You must be terribly in love with your wife to go to all this trouble. Very well. Which bank is going to put up the guarantee?'

'The Bank Hapoalim.'

'Who? They don't have a branch in Amsterdam, do they?'

'In Zurich,' Daleboudt answered nonchalantly. 'They do a lot of this sort of thing – it's an important bank, you can check them out.'

'Mr Daleboudt, you live in Holland. Wouldn't it be simpler to get a guarantee from a bank here?' de Boer pleaded. 'Why bring Zurich into it?'

'Because we want you to send the picture to Zurich. That's where my wife will be examining it.'

De Boer stared at Daleboudt with glazed eyes. 'First you had to have it in your home to see it in that setting. Do I take it that you are having your house done up by a Swiss interior decorator?'

'Don't be facetious. We are going to Switzerland for winter sports: my wife is a keen skier. I am sure she will agree that we must buy it while she is enjoying herself in the mountains.'

By now, de Boer was convinced he was dealing with a lunatic, but provided he had a cast-iron guarantee from the bank, he was ready to send the Rembrandt to whatever mental hospital was going to accommodate his client. He had one more surprise awaiting him. A few days later, he called Daleboudt.

'The guarantee from the Bank Hapoalim has arrived and is in order,' he told my partner. 'But why do they want the painting delivered to a different bank?'

Daleboudt told him that the Rembrandt would be displayed to greater advantage at the Volksbank. I don't suppose de Boer believed him, but we didn't want to admit that the Hapoalim did not possess a vault and deposited all their valuables at the big Volksbank building in the Bahnhofstrasse.

Jonathan's careful arrangements complicated things for me also. It was a condition of the letter of guarantee that I was not authorized to remove the painting from the Volksbank without the permission of the directors of the Bank Hapoalim and this was to prove an apparently insuperable obstacle. I had undertaken to pay Jonathan 150,000 guilders plus his expenses on completion of the deal, and I deposited with the Volksbank for the account of Bank Hapoalim works of art valued by Sotheby's at £200,000 as collateral.

Meanwhile, Fujiwara and I agreed to meet in Zurich. I went on my own; Mrs Daleboudt suddenly lost her passion for the ski slopes, so her husband stayed in Holland to look after our business, or the croupiers'! The Japanese however arrived in force, with their distinguished expert, Dr Kamon.

I travelled to Zurich a few days before our rendezvous and got busy. I was armed with the formal letter from the Rembrandt Research Committee stating that our painting was the original, that any other example would be at best a copy, and confirming that this endorsement would be printed in their catalogue. I had paid Bottema twenty-five thousand dollars; he told me that he used this to obtain the certificate, but that was his affair.

In Switzerland, I was able to arrange for the self-portrait to be shown to members of the Swiss Institute of Art who gave me a highly favourable official report on its condition. Consequently

I was in good spirits when I awaited the Gekkoso invasion in the lobby of the Dolder Grand.

There is one suite in the hotel at the top of a small tower which I had obtained as a favour from the manager since it is much in demand by celebrities who wish to remain anonymous or businessmen who wish to remain invisible. The occupant has the key to the staircase, so there is no other person in the whole tower, a veritable hotel within the hotel. In this fastness Fujiwara and I had a discreet chat.

'I would not worry about Dr Kamon being anything other than enthusiastic,' he assured me. 'A substantial honorarium has been promised; I am sure that he will earn it.'

'I was not worried,' I replied. 'I don't think he would have the nerve to contradict Dr Levie anyway.'

'That is why Madam Nakamura chose him,' said Fujiwara. 'When Dr Levie and the Committee pronounced their verdict on the Bridgestone painting, it was removed from exhibition. So we know Dr Kamon will endorse their judgement.'

The following day, we staged the viewing of the Rembrandt: it was a most impressive piece of theatre. I arrived with the Japanese at the Volksbank and a few minutes later, the Dutch contingent arrived from the airport. I had summoned my lawyer and my notary but de Boer also sent a representative. With the guarantee behind us, Daleboudt had finally let himself be persuaded into giving a firm commitment to buy the painting. Old de Boer had heaved a sigh of triumph: he had landed the big fish. Only after he had accepted our letter of intent did Daleboudt reveal that he was not the fish, only the worm on the hook. But the sale had not yet been consummated, so de Boer sent his man along. There was now quite a crowd of us in the main concourse and a receptionist hurried over to find out whether we were going to transact banking business or were holding a Revivalist jamboree on their premises.

'Don't hurry us,' I told him. 'There are plenty more to come.'

Next on the scene was a group from the Swiss Institute of

Art, followed by representatives of the Swiss legal profession, all out to make a buck. By now, the general manager of the Volksbank had been summoned.

'We have come to inspect the Rembrandt self-portrait deposited in your vault,' I announced.

'I regret it is not possible. The painting is being held to the order of the Bank Hapoalim. We require their authorization before we can permit your party to enter the vault.'

One more trifling formality! But I had already called the bank, which is only a few blocks from the Volksbank, and one of their directors entered, slightly breathless, and flanked by a couple of his staff. I saluted the Volksbank manager smartly.

'All present and correct, sir,' I reported. 'Request permission to enter vault.'

He regarded me coolly then led the way, and the whole party, about thirty-five souls, straggled after him into the bowels of the earth where men bury anything they regard as precious. The heavy armoured door swung open, the manager unlocked the grille, and we entered the Temple of Mammon. The painting was produced. In the diffused light of the vault, it had a mysterious, luminous glow, its outlines softened and subtle, reminiscent of the delicacy of a Japanese watercolour. The unlikely setting could not have been better calculated to appeal to Madam Nakamura and her colleagues. Everybody made way for Dr Kamon. He regarded the panel closely and for a moment I wondered whether he was going to sniff it to see if it smelt genuine. Then, with a little bow towards Madam Nakamura, he uttered his verdict.

'It is good. I have no doubt as to its authenticity.'

He had earned his honorarium, but the ceremony was not yet over. The head of the Swiss Institute of Art, together with his associates, took the stage and produced X-ray and infra-red photographs which were carefully examined.

Fujiwara drew me to one side. 'But look, Mr van Rijn,' he whispered, 'are you sure that the picture has not been damaged?'

I was puzzled. The panel was in excellent condition; none of the experts had raised any objections. He explained to me quietly that the hairline of the portrait was marked by a thick black line quite different from brush marks.

'That is a very characteristic Rembrandt touch,' I explained. 'He sometimes lost patience with the limitations of mere brush strokes. He would seize a pencil and, using the back of it, give weight and emphasis to a line. It is as though he were giving the kiss of life to a dead image. Such genius is fiery, incandescent!'

I think my genuine passion and reverence impressed Fujiwara. We turned back to the crowd round the panel. Everybody was nodding or making reassuring clucking noises and I felt a wave of exultation. I was going to pull it off! I was on the point of selling the very first real Rembrandt into Japan. All that remained were a few trivial formalities.

One not so trivial formality was to determine the price Gekkoso were willing to pay. I had asked for four million dollars and had already conceded their ten percent discount, but Madam Nakamura had adeptly avoided committing herself to a figure. She invited me to breakfast with her next day to, as she delicately expressed it, clear up the few details which needed to be clarified.

I knew Madam Nakamura to be a skilful negotiator, intelligent, quietly persistent and, when necessary, charmingly persuasive; a formidable adversary. I had gone to a lot of expense, but as she had carefully kept her hand hidden I had no idea how hard I could press without jeopardizing not only this deal but future relations with Gekkoso. I badly needed information and instinct prompted me to work on Fujiwara.

My opportunity came after dinner. The supporting cast had departed, leaving only the Japanese and myself. We were taking coffee in the lounge of the Dolder when I drew him aside.

'You haven't seen much of the night life of Zurich?' I enquired with a sympathetic smile.

'It is always like that,' Fujiwara smiled. 'We fly into some city, rush from one meeting to the next and fly out again. I have been everywhere and seen nothing.'

'We could go into town tonight,' I suggested. 'I know a bar you might find amusing – very lively and plenty of congenial company.'

Fujiwara nodded gravely. 'It would be a pleasure to accompany you to a place of that nature.'

When I had been their guest in Tokyo, Madam Nakamura would preside over sumptuous dinners and after much winking and laughing Fujiwara would announce that Madam Nakamura had requested him to show me around the town. This was a discreet way of ordering him to take me to one of the Turkish baths, which were in fact incredibly expensive brothels. There, to save me any embarrassment, Fujiwara would choose for me the most expensive and reputedly prettiest girl. Unfortunately, beauty is in the eye of the beholder, and I was invariably awarded the girl whom I considered the least desirable. Now I would have the opportunity to repay him in kind and perhaps, as a treat, let him profit or suffer from my powers of selection.

We took a cab to the Limatquai, and got out by the Gothic arched arcade. I led my companion up a steep, cobbled alley, pushed open a door and led the way down a flight of stairs. There was a small booth where I paid the stiff admission charge.

'Welcome to Die Rote Hutte,' I told him.

We went through into a large cellar with tables grouped above a diminutive dance floor. Against one wall was a long bar. The place was dimly lit, and the furnishings were strictly functional; wooden tables and chairs and wall-to-wall girls. Fujiwara blinked until he grew accustomed to the semi-darkness.

'It's best to take a table,' I said, steering him away from the bar.

A tall blonde sauntered over. 'Wouldn't one of you gentlemen care to invite me to a drink?' she asked. She spoke English with a marked accent and her voice was rich and husky. I reckoned she would make a change for Fujiwara from the home products on the Ginza.

'Whisky?' he offered.

'Champagne is customary,' replied the blonde. A bottle of Dom Perignon in an ice bucket materialized at our table.

'My name is Ingrid,' she announced. 'Meet my friend, Graziella.'

A cute little kid with a pert face perched herself on the chair beside me. 'Is this your first time in Zurich?' she asked.

'What she really wants to know,' I explained to Fujiwara, 'is do we know the tariff or can they take us to the cleaners?'

Ingrid giggled and playfully pinched Fujiwara's thigh. He didn't object, so she kept her hand there.

We had poured our second drinks and the girls were comfortably installed. I turned to Fujiwara.

'I hope that Madam Nakamura is satisfied with the price she will be getting for the picture. I presume she has already arranged the sale.'

'Oh yes, Madam Nakamura is very well organized,' Fujiwara said. I did not need him to tell me that.

'Obviously it would be useful for me to be aware of just what Gekkoso is prepared to pay, now they know what they are getting from MOA. Tell me, hypothetically of course, how much do you think such information would be worth to me?'

There was an excited glint in Fujiwara's eye, which had nothing to do with Ingrid's hand creeping up his thigh.

'I would have thought perhaps a hundred thousand dollars,' he murmured.

'That is precisely the figure I had in mind.'

Sensing that we were engaged in serious discussion, Ingrid signalled and another bottle of champagne was brought.

'The MOA have already committed themselves to a certain amount,' Fujiwara murmured. 'I have seen the terms.'

'I would have thought that it would be convenient for that hypothetical hundred thousand dollars to be paid to the Bank

Hapoalim,' I said, as though talking to myself. 'They seem very discreet, and I would have no difficulty in opening an account there for anybody.'

Fujiwara absentmindedly fondled Ingrid's buttocks. 'Trust is so important in our business, Mr van Rijn.' He wore an expression of total honesty as he scribbled figures on a piece of paper.

I read the figure, nodded and burned the paper in the candle on the table. With a smile, I scolded him. 'You should relax while you are here. We are neglecting the ladies.' I led Graziella onto the dance floor to give Ingrid a chance to warm up her reticent playmate.

By the time we returned, Fujiwara was sufficiently stimulated to be chafing to get away with his willowy blonde. While he was getting his coat, I paid the girls generously and asked them not to bother my friend.

'You have been most kind,' beamed Fujiwara, as we left.

We took two taxis back up to the Dolder, and I wished Fujiwara and his companion pleasant dreams. I never enquired how he fared, but I guess it was a night he would remember.

Next morning over breakfast Madam Nakamura and I dealt with the little formality of price. She made it clear that my original demand of four million dollars, even allowing for the discount, was not to her liking.

'That was the figure we talked of before we had seen the painting,' she pointed out, as if it were my fault that they demanded to know the price before they had anything more than a general description. 'It was not that we had accepted your figure, but there would have been no sense in attempting to finalize discussions at that time.'

I conceded that this was reasonable. When it came to bargaining, the charming, elegant Madam Nakamura was hard as steel. However, knowing what they were getting from MOA, I knew exactly when I could stand firm. I think she must have guessed I had the information for she suddenly stopped bargaining and we agreed that Gekkoso would pay me 6,350,000 guilders and would open a letter of credit immediately. Fujiwara had earned his hundred thousand dollars.

When I received the letter of credit, everything was fine – except for another couple of infuriating formalities. Madam Nakamura had left me to arrange the insurance, and a special policy was demanded. Since the terms of credit also insisted that the painting left on the Tokyo flight in five days' time, things had to be arranged without delay. My broker got on to Lloyds. The underwriters promised a policy would be sent by courier that afternoon.

The other problem was more complicated. The letter of credit insisted that the painting should be delivered to Kloten, the airport at Zurich, before the Credit Suisse would hand over the money. But the painting was still in the Volksbank and Jonathan Bear's guarantee stipulated that the Bank Hapoalim must be paid before they would agree to its release. So how the hell could I get the damned thing to the airport in order to collect on my letter of credit? I was crazy with frustration.

The insurance policy arrived from London. I had it rushed round to the Credit Suisse who immediately rejected it since they spotted two mistakes. I rang my broker. He was with a client.

'I don't care if he is with the Queen,' I thundered. 'Get him on the phone at once.'

Within seconds he had picked up the receiver. He called me back half an hour later. A revised policy would be with me first thing in the morning.

'Make sure it is,' I ordered. 'I am running out of time, and if the Japanese sense something is wrong they can back out of the deal as long as I have not complied with the terms of their letter of credit.'

He gave me his word that the policy would arrive as promised. It did – with a further error. I was hopping mad, and Fujiwara, seeing the deal and his hundred thousand dollars evaporating, was also fuming. Several times Madam Nakamura called me, but I assured her that everything was under control. 'These formalities take a little time,' I said. 'There is nothing to worry about.'

My conversation with the broker was very different. 'What the fuck do they think they're doing?' I shouted. 'The whole deal is going up in smoke because of their idiotic ignorance.'

He did the necessary howling and screaming, and Lloyds produced a third policy, which they confirmed by telex to the banks concerned, while I chartered a private plane to bring the policy to Kloten.

That last day is one I shall never forget. The Tokyo flight was scheduled to leave at four in the afternoon, and the painting had to be on board or the sale could collapse. And we had undertaken to buy the painting from de Boer!

Naturally, the insurers insisted on every precaution and I also wanted to impress the Japanese that I could match the best of them in the thoroughness of my preparations. I had contacted an important firm of shipping agents and arranged for them to have an armoured truck and security guards outside the Volksbank, and I ordered a fireproof packing case to be made to measure for the painting. I had it lined with red velvet, in accordance with the Japanese concept of luxury packaging; it was a sort of professional visiting card so it had to be impeccable. Then, off to the Credit Suisse to assure them that the insurance document would be with them that day and that all the conditions of the letter of credit would then be fulfilled. My next stop was the Bank Hapoalim to persuade them to authorize the Volksbank to release the Rembrandt. In the lobby, I ran into Fujiwara who was clearly ill-at-ease and wanted to engage me in one of his rambling conversations.

'No time now,' I called as I leaped into a taxi. 'Meet me at the Volksbank.'

The directors of the Bank Hapoalim were unhappy. Officially the bank was shut since this was Yom Kippur, the most solemn day in the Jewish calendar. Mr Falkhoff, the director with whom I was dealing, had warned me that they would not be available for business.

'But I shall need your authorization to get the painting out of the Volksbank,' I protested.

Falkhoff refused to act before the certificate of insurance arrived and there was no way it could be in Zurich before Yom Kippur. This appeared to be impasse. I had my suspicions, however, that his spiritual devotion could be overruled through an act of generosity on my part. Indeed, after soul-searching he agreed that the bank would be open just for me.

For the bank to release the painting without having received payment was against all the canons of Swiss morality. What was more, the clause had been inserted on the instructions of one of their most important clients; if he were to learn that he had been disobeyed he might withdraw his business.

A call to London confirmed that the insurance policy was speeding to Heathrow where the chartered jet was waiting. Today, documents can be transmitted by fax, but then the original certificate had to be delivered. The policy should arrive at Kloten at just about the same time as the truck with the Rembrandt, provided Falkhoff got his skates on. I pleaded, argued, cajoled but he would not budge. So I tore around to the Credit Suisse and demanded to see the president.

'Have you an appointment?' asked a receptionist.

'No, but it is a matter of the utmost urgency.'

His secretary was called down. She wrinkled her nose and consulted his diary. 'It is absolutely out of the question,' she pronounced. 'You should have made an appointment days ago.'

There was no point in arguing with her so, resisting the temptation to curse all dimwitted functionaries, I bolted back to Falkhoff at the Bank Hapoalim, where I gave vent to my frustration. 'As a director of this bank, please insist on my seeing the president as a matter of extreme urgency.' He picked up the phone and speaking directly to the president of the Credit Suisse made an appointment for the two of us to see him at once.

This time, we were ushered straight in. I explained my predicament. Falkhoff wanted every kind of written undertaking from me, but he nodded confirmation of my story.

I have nothing but admiration for the president of the Credit Suisse. As soon as he heard my request, he told Falkhoff to go ahead. There was no need to call a committee meeting or prepare special forms of indemnity or consult legal experts. A decision had to be made at once. He made it and accepted unreservedly the responsibility. Maybe that was why he was the president. Falkhoff, who lacked that sort of vision, was happy; he was covered.

It was already two o'clock, the last moment when the Japanese ought to have been checking in, when the order was given to hand over the painting to me with my security escorts. But to make sure there were no further complications, Falkhoff insisted on accompanying me, and he would not authorize the painting leaving until he was satisfied that the insurance was in order.

In the lobby of the marble mausoleum we were confronted by the Japanese deputation, entirely at a loss as to what was going on. I brushed them aside and, with a manager of the Volksbank and the director of the Bank Hapoalim, descended into the vault. Then, at last, I held the Rembrandt in my arms and was free to take it to the airport. Smiling broadly, I approached Fujiwara.

'Right. Let's get this into the security van.'

'What security van?'

I ran to the door. There was no sign of the van or of its guards.

'Are you looking for that MAT Securities truck that was blocking our doorway?' one of the porters called.

'Yes. Where the hell is it?'

'The lads have gone off. I asked them to move the van out of the way.'

'Where have they gone?'

'They said something about a packing case for that painting.

One of the locks doesn't work so they went to get it fixed. I don't suppose they'll be long.'

So much for Swiss efficiency! After having the case specially made the blasted thing was defective. Goddammit, it was three o'clock! They had probably dropped into a café while they waited for some elderly locksmith to get round to repairing the case. I had no time to play hide-and-seek all over Zurich with coffee-swilling security guards. I flagged down two taxis and bundled the bewildered Japanese inside. Clutching the painting, I dropped in beside the driver.

'Kloten. Terminal A, and push the fucking thing!'

'Wait a moment, what about me?'

I had forgotten about the Bank Hapoalim director. 'See you at the airport,' I shouted, and left him to arrange his own transport.

By some miracle, the two taxis arrived together. As we had left, I had warned the Japanese to have their passports ready, and I herded them through passport control, shouting 'VIPs, VIPs. Urgent. Let us pass.' In the face of such insistence, nobody was going to be so unreasonable as to examine their documents and we all rushed through. I had not brought my passport, but the Swiss are so well disciplined they stood aside and let me through as well.

The last passengers had already embarked but the doors of the Jumbo were still open. As we hurried in, Fujiwara turned to me with a frown.

'Mr van Rijn, shouldn't the painting be in the safe deposit on the plane?'

Of course it should have been, but we had broken so many regulations one more was no problem, and I certainly was not going to try to persuade the captain to hold up the flight any longer.

'Just visiting,' I called to the stewardess who wanted my boarding pass, and we scurried inside.

I dumped the painting on a seat in the first-class compartment, flopped down beside it and started furiously writing out invoices for the Japanese to hand in at the customs at Tokyo.

'Say, that's real pretty,' drawled a lanky American, gazing at the Rembrandt. 'Now why didn't I think to buy something like that on my last trip?'

The other passengers clustered around and the self-portrait was generally admired. Fujiwara proudly informed them that this was the very first Rembrandt to have been acquired by a Japanese museum.

'That really is something to celebrate,' enthused the American, and the next thing that I knew, we were all drinking champagne.

A steward, with an expression of extreme annoyance, tapped me on the shoulder.

'We are already overdue, and the captain says we are getting clearance for take off,' he informed me.

'Just finished,' I said, and thrust the invoices into Fujiwara's hand. 'Have a good trip.'

I waited in the departure lounge and it was with enormous satisfaction that I watched the Jumbo taxi out on to the runway.

'Stop the plane, stop the plane!'

I turned to find myself surrounded by airport officials, at their head the director of the Bank Hapoalim, red-faced, puffing and waving his arms. For one ghastly moment I feared there was a bomb scare and the plane would be ordered to return.

'The painting must not leave,' gasped the bank director. 'The jet from London had an engine failure and had to turn back. The insurance policy is not here. I cannot permit the painting to go without the original certificate.'

I heard the roar of the Boeing's engines as it started its takeoff.

'Take it easy,' I told him. 'The policy wouldn't have been valid anyway.'

I informed him gleefully that instead of being consigned to the special safe area of the plane, the precious Rembrandt was lying on a first-class seat, surrounded by a crowd who were probably at that moment spilling champagne all over it. He turned bright purple and I thought he was going to have a heart attack, but he settled for howling that he would have me locked up for the rest of my days. The Jumbo disappeared into the clouds. I had made it.

I imagine that none of the Bank Hapoalim directors slept very soundly that night, and that they were haunted by nightmares of planes plunging into the sea. However the flight arrived in Tokyo, Madam Nakamura proudly displayed her purchase, and I cashed the Credit Suisse letter of credit.

'Did you have any problems?' Daleboudt asked when I got back to Amsterdam.

'Nothing to speak of,' I answered, 'just the usual formalities.'

A few days later, we settled accounts with de Boer. He had been screaming for a commission and he held our letter of intent, but the terms had not been absolutely finalized and, bearing in mind that he had not even had the painting authenticated, I saw no reason to be charitable. He had sent a representative to Zurich called Sjalo Roelofs who met with my notary and me to conclude a contract. The document stated that I would pay de Boer a commission but it did not say how much and Roelofs was so excited at the deal actually having been done, that he did not trouble to read the thing thoroughly. As soon as it was signed, he and the notary hurried away for the flight to Amsterdam.

When they were airborne, my notary passed him a message from me. De Boer would have his commission, but five percent, not the ten he had demanded, and only after we had knocked the purchase price down from four million to three million guilders. After all, I had graciously consented to give a discount to Gekkoso, so it was reasonable for me to recoup from de Boer, but I don't suppose he saw it that way.

The only other disappointed party was Zadelhoff who had hoped to sell me Amstelrust. Years later, I met him in the south of France, at the Eden Roc, one of my favourite hotels. Chagall lived nearby in St Paul de Vence and he would come down to the hotel where he was treated like a revered prophet. So I had drinks with him and sat fascinated, listening to him discoursing on art, on Russia and everything under the sun. It was as if I were living out one of the fantasies which inspired his rhapsodical pictures.

So I was in a happy frame of mind when one morning I ran into Zadelhoff and his wife, and invited them to lunch.

He had not changed for the better. He glared with apparent disfavour at my exceptionally pretty companion. Perhaps he felt that being with his wife put him at a disadvantage. We had scarcely sat down before he asked me why I had not gone ahead with the purchase of Amstelrust. I was delighted to enlighten him about the way my temporary occupation of the house had helped to clinch my deal with Gekkoso. I thought it rather an amusing episode but Zadelhoff did not seem to appreciate the story.

He said he would kick out his manager which was a pity because he was quite a passable butler and it revealed what a small-minded man Zadelhoff was. I paid for the lunch and wished his wife good luck with such a man as her husband. I could see he did not know whether to take this as a compliment or whether I was being ironic.

# 13

# ON A PLATE

Selling the Rembrandt, as well as making me three million florins, opened up the prospect of dealing in Japan in the whole spectrum of Western art, not just Orthodox religious. I took a short holiday; then back to Tokyo, and work.

First I had to redeem my promise to Fujiwara. I don't think that he doubted I would keep my word.

One place I particularly wanted to see again was the MOA, destined to be the new home of the Rembrandt. The museum was not yet ready to welcome the public, but its site at Atami was breathtaking. Mount Fuji floats above Lake Ashi and all around the snow-capped summit are volcanic hot springs which serve the health spas among the wooded hills. The museum is on a crest, called Phoenix Hill, commanding spectacular views over the Izu peninsula to the ocean and the dim outline of Hatsushima Island beyond. I visited the Hakone Gallery, a placid monument which seemed to have grown out of the landscape. Its curved roof and the nearby timber teahouse emphasized the traditional, as did the feathery blossoms of the Plum Garden, white against the dark branches. But the MOA was a startlingly modern building.

I studied the sort of art which appealed to the Japanese. It avoided vulgarity or clumsiness, a line would suggest rather than state, and the total effect was of lightness, of delicacy and of a misty vagueness, a dream world; I was to recall this a few years later when I was shown a drawing by Leonardo, with dramatic consequences.

Meanwhile business was prospering and I was able to establish new contacts. But my closest associates remained Madam Nakamura, the Gekkoso gallery and, of course, Issei Fujiwara. But beneath the surface, there were already some tensions in the Gekkoso team which emerged one evening.

Fujiwara was restless; some incident in the gallery had irritated him and, abandoning his customary reticence, he gave vent to his feelings.

'Do you know what I would really like, Michel? To set up a gallery of my own where I can do things the way I want and not have to conform.'

'You mean follow the line laid down by Madam Nakamura?'

'It's not just her. There are powerful people involved, so she has to keep looking over her shoulder as well. Once you are caught up in a highly successful organization like Gekkoso, you lose all your independence.'

I was taken by surprise. Usually, Japanese who work for important corporations stay with them for the whole of their working lives. And Fujiwara was not some minor executive; he was vice president of a powerful organization, the last person one would expect to consider quitting. And the fact that he spoke so openly to me also amazed me. He was discreet and reticent with strangers, but I suppose that with the sale of the Rembrandt, he felt that he had got to know me and that I could be trusted with his innermost feelings.

I considered carefully. At the back of my mind I had an idea of starting a gallery in Tokyo myself. I knew I would need a Japanese partner. I had not intended to make the leap yet but it would have been foolish to let slip such an opportunity. I suggested that I might be able to offer Fujiwara a chance to be, if not the sole boss, a joint boss of a less authoritarian outfit than Gekkoso. He was enthusiastic and in no time we were getting down to specifics. And that was the conception of the Fumi Gallery, the name reflecting half Fujiwara, half Michel.

During my stay in Tokyo, Fujiwara made the break with Gekkoso and we found a splendid location for the Fumi Gallery on the Ginza. It took some time completing all the formalities and decorating the gallery but when it opened with an outstanding Picasso exhibition, it was an immediate success and this was followed by another fine show of works from the école de Paris.

For a foreigner with a successful business, life in Tokyo meant working like hell but there were plenty of cultural diversions. Many simply spent each night in restaurants, nightclubs and discotheques and ended up in bed with the current pretty model. Lovely girls came from all over the world, generally on a three-month contract, and they would frequent the trendy clubs and discos. Very often they did not fancy the Japanese men, and lots of the handsome male models preferred each other's company, so a European or American who was reasonably presentable and who could afford to entertain them could have a good time. I enjoyed this constantly renewed supply of nubile companions, but after a while I began to fret for the simpler life. Tokyo was a great place for business, but it did not appeal as an adopted home.

Fujiwara was one of those men who make excellent lieutenants but are not cut out to be commanders and the sudden strain of running the gallery proved too great. Although still only forty, he suffered a heart attack. I felt a responsibility for Fujiwara, but I no longer found Fumi a happy business. The decision to quit Gekkoso had been his, but my offer of a partnership had encouraged him and I could not simply sell my half of the business to some outsider and walk out on him. However, as soon as he had recovered sufficiently to handle the day-to-day administration of the gallery alone, I gave him my share and took a couple of pictures instead of payment, which preserved his self-respect and left him with a valuable investment.

'Just get on with making Fumi as big as Gekkoso,' I told him.

I decided to go to Greece. After the pressure of life in Tokyo, I needed to recuperate somewhere tranquil but first I made a stop over in Amsterdam, to check on how my partner had been getting on. I found Daleboudt in good humour but without any real progress to report. This did not worry me since there seemed to be a natural division of functions between us. My strength lay in finding good things and in selling. I am not good at administration and financial management. What could be better than to have a trained economist, with experience in running a business, to look after such things? While money continued to flow into our joint account in Zurich, I saw no cause for disquiet.

In Athens, I went nautical. Not all the Greek islands had yet succumbed to tourists and the most idyllic existence on earth was still to sail over the calm Aegean to the tiny, rocky isles with magical names from Homer and mythology. Even if one was not classically minded, the sight of the clusters of white houses, lining the curve of a bay and surmounted by a stone church, while gulls swooped for their morning fish, was enchanting. So I bought a boat. Not a floating gin palace, but a real boat, an old wooden ketch which seemed to be part of the seascape. Although lacking the marvels of modern gadgetry, it was comfortable, and I was not ashamed to invite friends or clients aboard.

One of my first guests was a Greek dealer called George, an invaluable contact since he commanded the respect and admiration of most of the black market operators. He had been arrested during the brutal regime of the colonels, and had undergone ghastly tortures which had left him scarred in body and mind. He knew the names of all the men the police wanted to seize, men for whom he had sold works of art abroad, but he kept his mouth shut. So here was a man I knew could be trusted.

We were lying at anchor in the yacht basin at Tourkolimano

and I was preparing to put to sea. That night we dined on board. George seemed thoughtful.

'Tell me, Michel, are you in a hurry to get away?'

'Not particularly,' I answered, 'but it will be good to clear out of Athens and enjoy some clean, fresh air. Why?'

'It's just something I heard today. Nothing definite, but a man I know was telling me there is some really outstanding stuff possibly coming on to the market. It is supposed to be a major discovery.'

I knew better than to press for anything more definite. George would talk when he was ready. 'I don't mind hanging around for a few days to see if anything turns up,' I said. 'But I do have a trip to Egypt planned, so I shall want to leave before too long.'

George nodded. He got the message that I wanted to know if this story was serious or just one more rumour.

It didn't take long to find out. The next day George was back, carrying a large buff envelope.

'Have a look and tell me what you think,' he said.

I tore open the envelope and pulled out a batch of sketches. What I saw sent shivers down my spine.

'Jesus! These things are fabulous. When can I see them?'

'First we have to find out where you can see them,' George answered. 'Have you ever met Patrikiades?'

I had not, but he was well known to me by reputation. Patrikiades was super-rich, owning a great deal of property, including a large part of Pandrossos Street in the centre of Athens in which are concentrated most of the city's antique dealers. He was known to have a great collection of art treasures and a sizeable fortune in gold bullion. I had learned that he had come from Alexandria as a boy and appreciated that as a foreigner in Greece, he must have had to fight hard to get to the top. There would always be the feeling that he was not completely accepted, that his success was resented and that there were plenty of people who would attack him, given the slightest opportunity. So he had to watch his step, and he avoided the ostentatious lifestyle. Patrikiades did not need to prove his wealth, yet he was dogged by this sense of insecurity, a foreigner among his own people.

And now he was faced by a dilemma. George made it clear that the objects in the sketches were not to be viewed in Athens. I understood that he would try to avoid the slightest danger of being denounced to the authorities; he was reputed to have been something of a buccaneer. But showing them outside the country presented the danger of illegally exporting them and there was the risk that we would not strike a deal and the trouble would have been for nothing. Well, that was his problem; meanwhile I studied the pictures of some amazing treasures. George told me that some of the prize pieces had been bought by Robin Symes, an influential London dealer, for the Getty Museum and by George Ortiz, the owner of an outstanding Classical and Byzantine collection in Geneva, but I was more than satisfied with what remained.

There were Cycladic idols as fine as even the celebrated examples in the museum in Athens or the collection of the wealthy shipowner, Goulandris. There were fine Greek statues, but the piece which excelled even these was a great silver dish, a marvellous example of Byzantine art. In the centre was a gold, embossed medallion depicting a lamb.

'He has to be careful,' George said. 'That is from the Kumlucu treasure.'

Ever since the news of the discovery near Antalya on the southern coast of Turkey of that extraordinary treasure had got out, there had been a constant battle by the Turkish authorities to try to prevent valuable objects being spirited away by enthusiasts whose entrepreneurial instincts proved stronger than their archaeological devotion. They had even resorted to providing an army cordon to isolate the site. Part of the treasure was recovered by the Antalya Museum, yet ways had been found of evading the guards and precious silver objects disappeared.

The other objects in the sketches were also of such a high

quality that the governments of the countries where they had been found would have taken drastic steps to prevent their export. I had to admire Patrikiades as much for his ingenuity in getting his collection together as for his impeccable taste.

'It's a pity you have to go off to Egypt,' George commented. 'I told Patrikiades that you were the sort of person who would be interested in buying and he was ready to make an appointment with you to view these, and a few other things.'

'Oh, well, in the circumstances, I think I could put the trip off for a while,' I said.

'I thought you might.' George's smile widened. He had seen through my story of an imminent voyage for the ploy that it was.

'How much do you think he will be asking? He knows the value of these things.'

'The price you will discuss with him,' George replied. 'But don't let that worry you. He won't screw you. But think, Michel, he is an old man and does not want to go traipsing across the world for nothing. He wants a message from you. Are you sufficiently interested to buy these objects provided you consider the prices reasonable?'

'I give you my word that I am willing to meet him wherever and whenever suits him. Is that positive enough?'

'I'll let him know. Stay around for a while.'

A few days later George reappeared. I invited him on board, but he shook his head.

'Feel like a little walk?' he asked. He started walking along the quay and I fell in beside him.

'Where are we going?'

'Patrikiades would like to see you. I've told him you are OK, but you know how it is. He wants to judge for himself.'

'I can't blame him: he has a lot at stake.'

We walked in silence for a while. Then we entered a rather dingy café. At the threshold, George paused. 'Talk about anything that comes into your head, but don't breathe a word about his collection or your business. The old man is as tight as a clam; he doesn't let his own family know what he owns.'

Inside were the usual scrubbed wooden tables, benches and hard chairs. A smell of frying oil wafted in from the kitchen and a large black cat wandered between the tables. A tall, heavily-built man with a mop of snow-white hair was seated between two small, birdlike Greeks. He was shabbily dressed; the aged coat might have been worn by one of the less discriminating beggars in the street, but looking into his face, I got the impression of a man as tough as the rock of the Acropolis and instinctively I knew this must be Patrikiades. He rose to greet me and clasped my hand which disappeared in his great paw. He must have been eighty, but he stared at me with shrewd, ice-blue eyes. His gaze never wavered and I felt myself being weighed in the balance. Then he turned to George.

'*Endaxi*,' he pronounced and I understood that I had been accepted.

We took the customary coffee and ouzo. The others talked in Greek for a few minutes, then, after a few sentences of polite but utterly inconsequential conversation with me, Patrikiades got to his feet.

'I enjoyed meeting you,' he said, 'but I am afraid I have to leave now. I am just going to look at some shops which I am having built.'

So I was dismissed and George and I walked back to the boat.

'Now what?' I demanded.

'Just wait,' George told me. 'You will hear.'

Waiting was a torment, but the memory of those sketches strengthened my resolve. After a fortnight the summons arrived, as always, by George.

'Be in Zurich on Monday morning,' he said. 'The old man is already there.'

'Right. Where?'

'At his hotel, the Limat.'

'What?' I thought I knew every first-class hotel in Zurich, but this was a new one to me.

I flew into Zurich on the Sunday and first thing next morning I went to my bank and drew out three hundred thousand Swiss francs. Then I grabbed a cab.

'Do you know the Hotel Limat?' I asked.

'Sure. It's on the Limatquai near the Rathaus bridge, before you get to the Odeon,' said the driver.

I realized it must be only a few metres from my favourite restaurant in the city, the Kronenhalle, yet I had never noticed it. It was soon obvious why. It was small, shabby and had the air of having been neglected for years.

I ventured into the poky lobby. A girl peered at me from behind the desk. I asked for Patrikiades, and she called him.

'Mr Patrikiades will be right down.'

I looked around in amazement. How could it be that this multi-millionaire was staying in what was little better than a dosshouse? But I had to be on my toes, Patrikiades had not achieved such success without being cunning and having a streak of ruthlessness, so I wanted to make sure he was not dealing with someone else behind my back. I passed the girl a fifty-franc note.

'Tell me, has Mr Patrikiades had many visitors?'

She shook her head. 'He only arrived this morning. You are the first person to call on him.'

'But I suppose he has been on the phone quite a lot?'

'Oh, yes. He has kept me busy.'

I looked at her enquiringly.

'There is no direct dialling from the rooms,' she explained. 'Every call has to go through my switchboard.'

I pushed another fifty-franc note across. 'So you must have a note of the numbers he has called.'

She shot me a disapproving look, but pocketed the note and handed over a list. There had been quite a few calls but every one was to a number in Greece. I sighed in relief. So far, at any rate, he was keeping faith with me.

I stuffed the paper in my pocket as Patrikiades came down the narrow staircase. Zurich is a very formal city: businessmen walk sedately between the solemn bank buildings clad in dark, conservatively cut suits, neat ties, discreet shirts and perfectly polished black shoes. Patrikiades wore the same scruffy clothes as when I had met him in that Athens café. Again his huge hand swallowed mine and he greeted me with a hearty good morning. He invited me up to his room, about the size of a closet in a mediocre hotel. George was seated on a plain, hard chair and half of the place was occupied by a single bed. An ashtray was full of cigarette ends and the room smelled of stale tobacco. As we entered, Patrikiades stubbed out one cigarette and immediately lit a fresh one. I could not help wondering whether, if I reach his age, I shall be fit enough to trot up a couple of flights of stairs, and I don't smoke.

Without any formalities, he dropped to his knees and pulled some plastic airline bags from under the bed. 'Sit down,' he said with a wave.

I squatted on the bed. From the first bag, he took out the silver dish – and it was even more wonderful than in the photograph, with regular repoussé ornamentation around the rim above a Greek inscription, and in the centre the Christian symbol of a lamb in soft, glowing gold. I held it in my hands; it was very heavy and the workmanship was superb. I did not have to say a word. Patrikiades saw that I was captivated.

'There's more,' he grunted.

And out came a succession of gold and silver pendants, brooches and crosses and vases of pure silver, a whole treasure!

I prepared for a bout of hard bargaining. He was experienced enough to know the value of what he was offering and he would not be deceived by a show of indifference. To my surprise, he asked only what was fair; prices which would ensure that I could sell at a good profit. All the pieces were first-class with one exception. There was a cross, not in any way crude or offensive, but which I felt was at best doubtful. I fingered it thoughtfully. We had arrived at an understanding; I could have the whole lot for a quarter of a million Swiss francs. I could bargain over each piece, but what the hell. Even if that one cross were worthless, the parcel was a bargain.

'It's a deal,' I said.

Patrikiades' face creased into a smile. He nodded at the cross.

'You are already wise for your years,' he said. 'You understand *kavla*.'

Just like the humble dealer who had sold me the Byzantine censer, Patrikiades, a prince among dealers, needed his little triumph, one dubious piece passed off, and I could have the rest for far less than he could have screwed out of me. I counted out the notes and handed them to him.

'So you brought the money with you. Very good,' he beamed, as he repacked everything into the plastic bags.

Since he was in a good humour, I ventured to ask about the possibility of doing more business.

'We do not talk about that now,' he answered. 'Stay in touch with George.'

One more firm handshake and then I negotiated the cramped staircase. I was staying in my usual suite at the Dolder and in the cab back I pondered on the contrast with the wretched Limat. Patrikiades was certainly rich enough to have stayed at the Dolder, indeed he could probably have bought the place. He had to be weirdly eccentric to have chosen the sort of place which catered for commercial travellers without an expense account or backpacking students.

Then the truth struck me and I had to laugh at myself. Some of my customers were rich snobs; it was necessary for me to impress them and the Dolder was an ideal setting. But Patrikiades had no need to impress me. His problem had been getting antiques worth a fortune out of the country without attracting suspicion. And it was typical of the man not to trust anybody but to bring them himself. What customs officer was going to stop a man in his eighties wearing cheap clothes and carrying his luggage in plastic bags? And nobody would bother the poor old fellow lodging in one of the humblest hotels. He had used his natural indifference to appearances to provide him with the cover he needed. I could still learn a lot from the old fox.

There were more deals with Patrikiades.

George explained. 'The old man has taken a liking to you. I think he was pleased by the way you accepted that cross; that showed maturity in his eyes. More important, he was impressed that you brought the money with you. That meant that you were serious about doing business, you trusted him to turn up with the goods and that they would be as fine as you had been led to expect. Trust is a great thing in our business, Michel, there are so many rogues about.'

I was not quite sure how to respond to George's last thrust.

Meanwhile, I had all those good things to dispose of, and I made for London and the premises of Sotheby's in New Bond Street.

But first, I wanted an authoritative opinion on the silver plate which I saw as the star item. So I took my prize to John Beckwith at the Victoria and Albert Museum who I knew would be able to interpret five stamps which had been applied to the plate's foot ring. When I unwrapped the plate in his study, Beckwith's eyes lit up and he whistled.

He confirmed that the symbols appeared to be genuine imperial stamps, applied in the correct order. Fortified by his glowing approval, I called Sotheby's and spoke to one of their directors, Richard Camber.

'I just wanted to make sure you will be in your office this morning,' I said. 'I have something to show you.'

Sotheby's principal premises look more like an early Victorian townhouse than a fortress. It has a certain domestic dignity, but inside is a rabbit warren of corridors and staircases, spacious showrooms and cramped offices. A uniformed porter politely directs visitors, but security is unobtrusive. Nevertheless, there is ceaseless vigilance; there has to be in view of the torrent of valuable things which pour in and out of the building. The guard on the door nodded and I went through. Members of the public wait at the porter's desk while they state their business but a select group of dealers are told the sequence of buttons on the doorpost to push to obtain access, so they do not have to wait while they may be carrying priceless things. I hurried along to Camber's room, knocked and strode in.

I produced the Byzantine plate, and watched as he examined it. This was a scene the two of us had often played. I would show him something I had decided to keep for my own collection or merely to get his opinion of what it might fetch and he would do his damnedest to talk me into letting him put it up for auction. He often succeeded, partly because of his eloquent pleading and also because any serious dealer wants to keep on cordial terms with such houses. Besides, they will often offer a highly attractive price without your having to negotiate with a private client. They are not merely auctioneers but command enormous power in the world of art and antiques: immense wealth is stored in their cellars, but even more important is their access to virtually unlimited finance. They possess unsurpassed systems for gathering intelligence since now almost every wealthy person aspires to be a collector; often they do not know or trust individual dealers, so they go for advice to the great auction houses. Yet Christie's and Sotheby's look to independent dealers such as myself to provide them with a significant part of their business, not all of which passes through their auction room. These are private deals when there are some questions surrounding the pieces for sale. Christie's generally skies away from such transactions as a point of policy. However, it is well known than Sotheby's can get around questionable pieces through such methods using dealers such as myself.

Richard Camber was positively lyrical in praise of the plate. But he was too old a hand to suggest that it be put up for auction. Such a valuable piece going on public display would almost certainly provoke demands from either Greece or Turkey for its return.

'What had you in mind?' he asked.

'I am ready to sell it when the price is right,' I told him.

'And would you allow us to act for you? I presume there is a question of provenance.'

Such tact! Of course I was not going to declare that Patrikiades had spirited it out of the Kumlucu treasure. But, as Camber knew very well, after a period of from three to ten years, depending on the country, somebody in possession of stolen goods cannot be charged with theft and after thirty years, the rightful owner of the property loses any claim. That is one reason why the wealthy Wildenstein gallery finds it so profitable to bury things in their vaults for generations and why Camber proposed a quietly arranged private sale.

'I would like a statement from somebody on those stamps,' he added.

'I have shown it to John Beckwith.'

'He's not up to it. This should be shown to a specialist on Byzantine stamps.'

I was happy to concur. I was positive the plate was genuine. The obvious person to consult was Erika Cruikshank Dodd who had written the authoritative book on silver stamps for the Dumbarton Oaks Museum.

Mrs Dodd was an extraordinary woman with a reputation for great learning. She had brought up her handicapped daughter in most difficult conditions and I had great respect for her. I located her in Beirut and invited her to come to London. So, two days later, I was waiting in the lobby of the Intercontinental when this formidable scholar arrived. I took her to my room and handed her the plate. Despite my confidence in the object, it was a tense moment for me. Erika Dodd was not only an eminent art historian but also a brilliant mathematician and it was this combination of the rigorous discipline of the mathematical mind together with aesthetic sensibility and an encyclopedic knowledge of her subject which caused her pronouncements to be accepted with such reverence. An adverse verdict by her would render my wonderful plate unsaleable.

For what seemed an age, she stood there looking at it. She studied the lamb, then turned her attention back to the stamps and frowned. Carefully putting it on a table, she looked hard at me. I felt that it was me, not the plate, that was under scrutiny.

'I would like to examine this more carefully, alone. Do you have any objection?'

Her voice was cold, almost hostile. I was shaken. What could have aroused her suspicions? Surely she could see that the piece was authentic? I did not have her scholarship, but I never had a moment's doubt: John Beckwith had practically swooned over it and Richard Camber had not suggested that he entertained any apprehensions about it. With an effort, I pulled myself together.

'Of course not. I shall wait for you in the bar.'

I endured purgatory while I demolished two Bloody Marys, and fumed against academics. Patrikiades had said that the plate had come directly from the Kumlucu treasure; although he was artful and subtle to the point of deviousness, I felt instinctively that his word could be trusted. But I was trapped. How could I tell this wretched woman who must have some crazy bee in her bonnet that, having been stolen from the site, the provenance of the plate was unassailable? Every professor, every curator, every 'expert' ought to be marooned on a desert island where they could do no more harm to honest dealers in hot art! I had worked myself up into a state of fury when Mrs Dodd asked me to come back to my room.

I tried to put together a form of words which would express how stupid she must be to condemn such a lovely piece of honest workmanship without actually being insulting, but I had not got very far when I entered the room.

'Sit down, Mr van Rijn, while I explain why I first judged this plate a fake.'

My blood was boiling but before I could voice any protest, she asked me what period I had ascribed to the plate.

'With all due respect to you, fifth or sixth century,' I replied.

'Quite right,' she said approvingly.

My speech died inside me. This was a different Mrs Dodd, with a warm smile on her face. She told me she was now completely convinced of the authenticity of the plate and was prepared to give a formal opinion.

'I won't ask for its background because you wouldn't tell me but it is such a fine piece that I would like to publish an article about it. I would not write anything about where it came from or who owned it, that's understood. But I must admit, you did set me a puzzle, Mr van Rijn,' she continued.

'The stamps?'

'Oh, the stamps are exactly as they should be and in the right order, starting with this one which signifies which emperor was reigning. But even in the sixth century, a plate would have been hammered and the stamps punched in. Now, look at the plate and especially that lamb.' She pointed. 'Wouldn't you say that looks as if it had been produced in a cast? And the casting process was not known at that time.'

'You mean that the plate has to be later than the date of the stamps?'

'If the metal had really been cast, the stamps would have to have been added later and have been forged. But everything about the plate seems right, so what could be the explanation?'

Turning the plate over, she ran her finger over the lamb. 'Obviously this ornament was made after the plate had been finished and the stamps applied. See how heavily it is gilded. Then it would have been sculpted with a chisel. But chiselling cold metal is hard work, even with a soft metal such as gold. So the craftsman did the obvious thing. He heated the plate so as to be able to work the metal, and of course he would have held the plate over a fire so that it would have been the bottom of the plate which was heated. That caused the metal around the stamps to melt a little and run so that the plate appears to have been cast, a process which was not discovered until the fourteenth century.'

She stood there triumphant at having solved the mystery, and I was quite prepared to play Dr Watson to her Sherlock Holmes. Richard Camber was similarly satisfied. Sotheby's combed through their large network of clients and they soon found a private buyer who offered two hundred thousand pounds. However, before that I had been to other dealers with the rest of Patrikiades' objects. I sold them for what I had paid for the lot so that I had recovered the whole of my investment and the Byzantine plate stood in for nothing. I told Camber to go ahead and within a couple of days the sale was completed and Sotheby's had their ten percent.

Incidentally, George later told me that Patrikiades had confided in him that though the plate was not exactly a false, he had 'improved' it a little. The centre really was from the Kumlucu treasure, complete with genuine stamps. But he worked the metal to make the lamb and had to heat the plate. This made the stamps look as if the plate had been cast, just as Mrs Dodd guessed. The only thing she got wrong was how the lamb was fashioned – and when, of course.

# 14

# DEALERS AND DOUBLE DEALERS

In all the important cities there are auction houses but Sotheby's and Christie's are in a class of their own. They made London the art capital of the world but as the wealth and sophistication of other countries grew, they turned their eyes outwards. They set up branches or subsidiaries in those European countries which permitted them and Sotheby's absorbed New York's prestigious Parke Bernet gallery in 1964. But they had yet to spread their tentacles as far as Japan and I knew that Japan was ready. It was unique in its combination of culture and commercialism.

And I was marvellously well placed to take advantage of this opportunity. My relationship with Gekkoso had blossomed; the volume of the Rembrandt Research Committee had appeared, and the MOA was duly credited with the possession of a Class A painting, an undoubtedly genuine work. And of course I was well known at Sotheby's.

I suggested to my Japanese associates that they might care to represent Sotheby's. They had considered the idea and thought it would be a splendid development. Could I very tactfully put out feelers? It went without saying that if I could bring together these two powerful houses, my own position would benefit enormously, so I set to work on my new profession of marriage broker.

In London, Richard Camber was all for the idea, but the crucial interview would be with Sotheby's chairman, the late, legendary Peter Wilson.

Wilson listened attentively to what I told him about Gekkoso. He agreed that Sotheby's ought to be represented in Japan without delay. He was impressed by the size and scope of Gekkoso and by the links I had forged with them.

'It would be a good idea if we met their people,' he concluded. 'Perhaps you could extend an invitation to some of their executives for informal discussions? Of course, it would have to be a board decision, but I like the sound of it. Let's see how their people take to us.'

I had started something, and my reputation was on the line.

A regiment of Gekkoso directors and specialists flew into London. I worked hard on each group before they met, trying to convince the sceptics that the firms would complement each other. The concept was so novel that there was bound to be some resistance. However, I thought I had ironed out most difficulties when I took the people from Gekkoso to New Bond Street and introduced them to the home team. I watched anxiously as they behaved so politely to each other. The English and the Japanese are in their own ways perhaps the most courteous people on earth but I could not help thinking of sparring boxers. That evening, I called Richard Camber and asked how things were going.

'Super!' he said. 'They are a lively lot once they stop bowing, and Gekkoso is obviously quite an outfit.'

'And what about Peter?'

'Well, you, know the way he is. I think he has taken quite a fancy to them.'

Peter Wilson called me next day. 'Nothing has been decided yet of course,' he purred, 'but I wanted to let you know that so far things have gone very well and to thank you, Michel, for thinking of Sotheby's. Your little friends have to report back and they and we will be reviewing what we have discussed and seeing where we go from here. Tomorrow, the directors of Sotheby's are holding a cocktail party in their honour. You are invited. In fact, you will be the guest of honour.'

The evening was a resounding success. The permanent smiles of the Japanese seemed much more unforced and some of the English actually unbent to the extent of using first names. Wilson was a charming host and when he proposed a toast to the guests and wished them a pleasant journey home and a swift return, I sensed warmth which was reciprocated by the Japanese.

I saw the Gekkoso people off at the airport and settled back to await developments. I was not in suspense for long. A day or two later, the phone rang.

'Michel? Peter Wilson here. I would like a little chat with you. Absolutely off the record, you understand. How are you fixed this afternoon?'

As I crossed Hanover Square, I took stock of the situation. I was not so naive as to think that Sotheby's had not noticed the way the Japanese market was taking off or that they were being courted by other suitors. But I considered Gekkoso a highly eligible partner and their team had got on well with the Sotheby's board. And without wishing to exaggerate my own standing, I had been a very good customer and was one of the small circle of professional dealers who enjoyed a special relationship with them.

Peter Wilson was all smiles. 'My dear fellow, let me get you a drink. We had a meeting yesterday about future operations in Japan. You'll be pleased to know that we have decided to press on with negotiating a deal with Gekkoso.'

'Will it be all right for me to report that to Madam Nakamura? I wouldn't want to jump the gun and cause any embarrassment.'

'Go ahead. Tell her you have our blessing. Of course there will have to be more meetings to thrash out the details, but we would organize them through you. So let's drink to our future relationship.'

We chatted for a while. Wilson would have done his homework; there was no need for me to tell him that Gekkoso were the biggest gallery in Japan or to stress their intimate links with political leaders and the enormous business combines which dominate Japan. We agreed to stay in touch and if he were not available, my contact would be Richard Camber. I was kept very busy organizing meetings between the two firms, and for weeks I shuttled between London and Tokyo.

The potential was enormous. Gekkoso had their own museum and auction premises, as well as a phenomenal list of collectors and investors which would be at the disposal of Sotheby's; the standing of the two houses together with such people as museum advisers would be unrivalled.

'And you will be right there, Michel,' smiled Camber. 'You deserve it.'

Some weeks passed and, back in London, I received a call from Madam Nakamura.

'I wondered whether you would have any comment to make on this deal by Sotheby's and Seibu?' Her voice, even long distance, was cold and aggrieved.

'What deal?' I was utterly bewildered.

'You haven't heard? Your friends at Sotheby's should have kept you informed. They have just announced a tie-up with one of our leading department stores. I was very surprised, especially as Seibu own half of Wildenstein's business in Tokyo. Is it normal for an auction house to be linked to one gallery, even indirectly? Obviously this rules out any deal with Gekkoso.'

In a fury, I called Peter Wilson, but he was not available. Suddenly, I could not get through to anybody concerned, but after a struggle I cornered Richard Camber. He told me apologetically that one of his colleagues, Peter Spire, had pushed the Seibu deal through. But I knew that such an important move must have been discussed by the full board. Camber, my friend, had kept me sweet while the Seibu deal was done; they had merely been stringing Gekkoso along.

'Of course,' Camber continued, 'I am dreadfully sorry, but I assure you that you will always be welcome at Sotheby's, and I hope you will go on bringing us good things.'

He knew damned well that any serious dealer needs to remain on good terms with the important auction houses. He implied that my resentment was natural but that I would be a good fellow and get over it. I had been screwed by Sotheby's, but I was not the first and I certainly would not be the last.

I was seething. After all the time and effort I had expended in building up my credibility with Gekkoso, to have it shattered by such duplicity! I would lose face, a disastrous setback to my hopes for my business in the East. If the deal had worked out, it would have opened up an enormous volume of business for me and brought me such prestige and goodwill that I would have become a major force, a veritable institution, in the art market. This golden opportunity had been destroyed by people I had trusted.

I needed to think hard about how to restore my reputation and not be dismissed by Madam Nakamura as irresponsible. At the same time, I made up my mind to do something to deflate the arrogance of Sotheby's. They did not give a damn how their manoeuvring might affect me. They deserved a taste of their own medicine.

# 15

# THE TREASURE OF THE AVAR WAR LORD

> 'At the time, a totally unknown and strange people came to Constantinople, called the Avars; the entire city came out to see them because never had men of this race been seen before. They wore their hair plaited with ribbons down their backs, but otherwise their dress was like that of the other Huns'
>
> – Theophrastes

Shortly after I had returned to Athens, still smarting over my treatment at Sotheby's over the deal with Gekkoso, I had received a visit from my old friend, George. He showed me some gold and silver buckles. Little did I know then that I would forge from these impressive antiquities a small but vengeful torpedo to shake the stately hull of the powerful auction house which had so arrogantly embarrassed me.

'What do you make of these?' he asked, offering me some gold and silver buckles.

I examined a beautifully worked piece of jewellery.

'It's a very fine example of work of one of the barbarian tribes,' I pronounced.

'And would you care to put a date on it?'

'Without consulting a specialist, I would guess fifth or sixth century.'

George nodded gravely. 'And I expect that a specialist would agree with you. As a matter of fact, it was made last week.'

I could not believe it. I looked at the other things – all absolutely perfect in craftsmanship and in authenticity of style.

'I have never seen work to equal that,' I said. 'Whoever made them must be a superb artist.' Even the mighty Sotheby's would be taken in by this workmanship – or would they? 'Do you have any more like these?' I asked.

'That would mean going back to the man who made them.'

'George, I would like to meet this artist. I have an idea which could mean him doing some very special work for me. Do you think he would be prepared to make a lot of things like this, a hoard? You could vouch for me never to disclose his name.'

'Your word is good enough for me,' George replied, 'but I must talk with him.'

And George's word was good enough for the artist. A few days later, he returned.

'It might be possible, but you understand it will cost something.'

'Of course. You ought to know by now that I am not mean.'

A few days later, George collected me and I presumed we were on our way to a workshop in some back street. Instead, he led me into a respectable antique shop on Pandrossos Street. To my amazement, Patrikiades came to meet me, his heavy face creased into a great smile.

'I can't take chances, Mr van Rijn,' he chuckled, 'so even after George told me you could be trusted I needed to do business with you, face to face, before I was ready to let you into my secret. All my life I have adored craftmanship and I have never given up working with my own hands.'

George told me later that before he left Egypt, Patrikiades had been a shoemaker.

I told him how much I admired the specimens of his work

which I had seen. 'Tell me,' I asked, 'do you think you can make me an entire treasure, so perfect that the greatest experts in the world would go crazy over it?'

He smiled and said he would think about it and that George would bring me some sketches. Later, everything I saw confirmed my initial view that I was dealing with a true artist with the power to create original works in the idiom of a remote age. It is a great pity that his works remained anonymous and he was denied the recognition his skill and the breadth of his culture merit, although examples of his work are displayed in many museums.

Men like Patrikiades are rare. He was not a book-trained scholar but a true craftsman who thinks with his hands; so great was his instinctive feeling for a style that his creations could mislead the most learned experts. But he was also a dealer who finds fine authentic pieces so that even the few professionals who knew or suspected him of being a faker would buy from him in the knowledge that not everything they take would be as ancient as it appeared. But what does that matter to some people when the instant antiques can be sold off as easily and profitably as the genuine articles? The wisest dealers know that if they want to get hold of the latter, they have to take fakes as well.

The old man, then in his late seventies, had lived a lifetime of adventures, and his name carried clout. If I were going to take on Sotheby's, I could have no better ally.

A few days later, George brought me sketches of intricately decorated belt fittings. 'The old man says these are the sort of thing which could have been found in the burial of some prince. They would probably have been made of gold and silver. He can get hold of old gold and silver.'

'What about money?' I queried. 'Wouldn't a burial contain gold coins?'

I was very happy that I had accepted all the low-quality examples along with the good ones when I bought up those thousands of coins in Istanbul. I had recently begun to hear more stories about Patrikiades, noteably that he was the top forger of ancient coins. So I gave George a few from my hoard to show the old man and asked whether it would be a good idea for some of my coins to be combined with the treasure. But Patrikiades had other ideas, particularly when he heard how many I had.

'Instead of buying old gold, he will melt your coins down and use them for belt fittings. That will look after any clever fellow who examines impurities in the metal,' George told me. 'And he has something better to put into the treasure. He will tell you when the time is right.'

As for silver, George bought fragments of Byzantine silver, bits of broken objects. During the next couple of weeks, he brought me a few pieces of our treasure. I asked him how many pieces there would be and how much the entire treasure was likely to cost.

'Don't worry,' he answered. 'The old man won't screw you. You must know by now that he is too intelligent to ask an unreasonable price. You haven't said what you are going to do with this treasure, and nobody is going to ask, but he would guess that you want to make a profit. So just wait – he'll let you know.'

There followed some hectic weeks while I did my homework. I flew back to London and visited all the museums and bookshops. I bought a veritable library and studied every kind of ornament of the period of the barbarian invasions. Armed with the sketches, I obtained interviews with the experts in the British Museum and the Courtauld Institute, and from them I first learned of the sort of treasure Patrikiades was proposing to reproduce.

More than ninety years ago, I was told, a great hoard was discovered in what is now Albania. Scholars decided it was the work of a people called the Avars. There had been only fragmentary histories written about them, namely a brief account of the arrival of the Avars in the Byzantine capital by the Greek historian, Theophrastes. It was a simple yet evocative account of a barbarian people who had exacted tribute from the Roman Emperors of Byzantium, peace offerings of coins and exquisitely wrought ornaments and ceremonial plates. A custom of the Avars, I surmised from my research, was that a warrior chief would seize every object of gold and silver he could force emperors, kings and nobles to disgorge and then melt these down and have them forged into belts and buckles, armour and accoutrements, things which were finely worked, fit to be worn by a man ennobled by feats of arms, a conqueror.

There had been no important finds of Avar treasure since that Albanian discovery at the turn of the century, the so-called 'Vrap' hoard. So I decided that what I would eventually present to the art world at large and Sotheby's in particular was the 'discovery' of a burial of a leader of the Avars, nomads who might have buried their chief in any one of half-a-dozen countries, thus resolving some of the problems of patrimony. My sketches would reflect just that scenario. I reasoned that the man would probably be interred with the objects he might need in an afterlife, maybe goblets or drinking horns, jewels, but above all arms and armour. Of course, it was probable that such a hoard would not lie undisturbed through the ages; some of it might have disappeared and it was unlikely that different burials would contain identical objects. The Albanian treasure had given scholars a concept of Avar craftsmanship and Patrikiades a standard.

I discussed with scholars the distinguishing features of such items as sword scabbards and belt clasps. In casual conversation, they confirmed that gold and silver were not susceptible to radio carbon or other scientific dating methods. They sent me off to other authorities in the Schweizerisches Institut für Kunstwissenschaft in Zurich and to the highly skilled restorers at the Louvre who explained, however, that impurities in the metals gave an indication of their likely period.

I examined every available work on the period and sent for photographs from collections in Albania and the Soviet Union.

I would create a barbarian treasure as good as the best of them. Once the metal was cold, it would be impossible to differentiate our artefacts from those made more than twelve hundred years earlier. I also learned from the Central Laboratory in Amsterdam that objects such as belts would often retain pieces of cloth and resolved that there would be some authentic shreds which would stand up to analysis.

When last in Egypt looking for encaustic enamels I had picked up a few fragments of Coptic funeral shrouds. Although they might well have dated from earlier than our Avar hero, I reckoned he could easily have acquired clothes from exotic places. All that mattered was that the material should not be of a later period than the armour. This would be the one and only time that I would deliberately set out to fake. My treasure had to be perfect.

When I felt I had a sufficient grasp of the subject, I returned to Athens. Manolis Chatzidakis was at that time a director of both the Benaki and Byzantine Museums in Athens and a good friend of mine. (Alas, he is now dead.) I told him I had the opportunity to buy what appeared to be an important treasure, and would value an off-the-record opinion on the basis of some sketches.

'Where did you come across these things?' he asked.

'It is a burial which has been unearthed in Albania,' I assured him. Obviously, if he thought the treasure genuine and valuable, it would be a serious mistake to let him suspect that it might have originated in Greece. I left the drawings with him and waited impatiently.

'You understand that I cannot give you as definite an opinion as you would like from mere sketches,' he started, with typical scholarly caution. 'However, what you have shown me certainly appear to be barbarian ornaments of the late-sixth or early-seventh century. You say that they were not found in Greece?'

'Definitely not. Do they seem particularly good then?'

'If the objects turn out to be as the sketches suggest, this could be one of the most important discoveries ever made of work of this period.'

I was more than satisfied. Knowing how experts like to hedge and qualify their opinions, Chatzidakis had been more forthcoming and his statement more positive than I had dared hope. I felt confident, but wanted even more confirmation so I gave the sketches to a dealer in Athens and asked him to sound out other important dealers throughout the world. Curators of museums are learned men, but dealers put their money as well as their reputations on the line; what they might say counted more with me than the assurance of any uninvolved academic, no matter how distinguished. Every dealer who saw the sketches was eager to get his hands on the treasure.

Patrikiades was a master who could think himself back into the mind of the artisan of a remote age. He did not copy but created. And he had a great grasp of detail. For example, the Avars held silver in at least as high a regard as gold, and the highest-ranking war lords would wear a pair of belts, one silver, the other gold. But silver was scarce, and Patrikiades purposely made some fittings from very pale gold, just the sort of thing an Avar would use as a substitute for silver. He could not have written a learned treatise on the alliance of the Avar Khanate with the Sassenid Persians against the Byzantine emperors, but he had such an instinctive feeling for their work that his products were utterly convincing. And he owned so many fine things that he had plenty of models to study.

I was totally absorbed by the work. The task could not be hurried, and it was months before George told me that the treasure was finished. 'The old man will let you know where it can be handed over. You remember – he gets there first and tells you where to meet him.'

I was impatient and called the Hotel Limat a couple of times, but drew a blank. Then George said that Patrikiades was ready.

'I shall come with you. Buy tickets to Munich,' he said. 'Check into whichever hotel you like and I shall tell the old man we are there. Before we go to meet him, draw out five hundred thousand deutschmarks.'

I might have guessed Patrikiades would not meet me in the same place twice. Munich suited me as a base; it was where some Greek or Turk who had dug up something he thought might be very valuable would try to sell it.

Next day, George and I registered into the Hotel Continental. George put through a call. I drew the money and we went to the Dresdner Bank where Patrikiades was waiting. In the privacy of the vaults, I examined my newly discovered treasure.

'Wait a minute,' I protested. 'Where are the bits of cloth I sent you?'

'Don't you worry. That has been taken care of,' Patrikiades told me. 'And here, these could have been dug up with the other things.'

He produced a couple of silver plates. 'Byzantine, right sort of period,' he said. 'Look, there are the stamps.'

The plates certainly were more convincing than some indifferent gold coins. I took the money from my briefcase.

'Give me four hundred and fifty thousand deutschmarks,' said Patrikiades. We understood that the other fifty thousand was for George.

Back in the hotel, I waited until any self-respecting English gentleman would have taken himself off to lunch, then called Sotheby's.

'I am afraid that Mr Camber is at lunch,' reported the telephone operator. 'Do you want to leave a message? I pretended to be disappointed, told her to ask Richard Camber to call me back and left my number. So when he rang back, he knew that I was in Munich.

Since the Gekkoso débâcle, I anticipated a certain coolness on the part of the Sotheby's directors, but I was sure Camber would call back; he would be curious about what I was doing. I told him I had been offered a magnificent barbarian hoard. He rose to the bait at once. Rumours had been flying all round the art world and the long ears of Sotheby's were tingling. There are some dealers who habitually buy for some of the world's great collections and who are naturally eagerly chased by lesser dealers when on the track of anything important. Robin Symes, perhaps the most influential of them, had been shown my sketches and had put Sotheby's on the scent.

'From what I hear on the grapevine,' Richard Camber said, 'the thing is worth a fortune. But I imagine that whoever buys it will have one hell of a job with every government in that part of the world claiming it as a stolen trophy from their national heritage.'

'Well, we could always make it a private sale, couldn't we? But I am sure there won't be any trouble and I am willing to face that risk,' I told him.

'Really?' I could tell that he was intrigued by my confidence. 'Well, I wish you luck, Michel, old boy. Do keep me posted, won't you?'

'I keep Sotheby's in mind all the time,' I assured him.

I gazed fondly at the clutter in my room: belts, buckles, clasps, silver plates; these harmless baubles constituted a torpedo aimed at the vulnerable flank of Sotheby's. Now was the moment to launch it.

Next morning I flew into London where I was stopped at customs and the objects of gold and silver examined.

'Are these components of some machine?' asked the customs officer.

'Of course,' I told him, and was allowed to proceed.

I had already made an appointment with John Beckwith at the Victoria & Albert Museum. We had last met when I brought him the wonderful Byzantine plate from Patrikiades. That encounter had assured me that he would given an opinion to a dealer, something which of course he would confirm when he was called by Sotheby's. This was to be by far the most formidable test to date of the credibility of our creation.

I watched his face as each 'relic' was revealed. Curiosity gave way to wonder.

'That is phenomenal,' Beckwith enthused. 'Where the devil did you find such a marvel?'

'I bought it from a collector in Zurich.'

He knew better than to press for more precise information. 'Well,' he said, 'you have there what is clearly an Avar treasure which might have originated anywhere from Bulgaria to China. As you know, those boys got around, so I don't suppose you will be surprised or sorry to know that this would present a serious problem for any country trying to claim the treasure.'

'How would you rate it?' I asked.

'I would say this could be the most important discovery in this field this century.' Such a positive reaction from so respected an authority exceeded my hopes.

Then to Sotheby's. I stifled my amusement as Camber goggled at the wonders I spread before him. No one at Sotheby's seemed to give a moment's thought for how the Gekkoso affair might have affected my business. They were all tainted by the utter disregard of the big corporation for an individual dealer.

Camber was unwilling to have my name mentioned because of the wild stories circulating about my problems with my partner, and he was too experienced to rush into committing the firm. He asked if I would leave the objects with him until he could consult his colleagues. I assented.

'I'm staying in London for a few days. Let me know when it is convenient for you and your colleagues and I shall come round. That is if you are interested,' I added ironically.

That evening our reconciliation was celebrated when I entertained Camber and Sotheby's then icons expert, John Stuart, to dinner at Les Ambassadeurs, my London club. Unlike Richard Camber, whom I have always found a rather colourless individual, Johnny Stuart was exuberant and very open. A brilliant linguist and a fine scholar, he seemed always ready to give freely the benefit of his expertise. He has written learned books on the history of art, has no time for genteel conventions and is incorrigibly absentminded. That evening he roared up with a friend on a motorbike. Other guests left coats in the cloakroom: they deposited crash helmets. They would not have been allowed in if I had not explained that they were my guests.

At the end of a lively evening, Camber and Stuart talked about the sale. There was then fierce rivalry between Christie's and Sotheby's for the most sensational sales.

'I am seeing Peter tomorrow first thing,' Camber confided, as they left. 'I think we ought to consider an official sale.'

I said nothing, but I was thrilled at their even considering making the sale official, although I wondered how Peter Wilson would take to dealing with me again.

Throughout the morning, I wondered how the debate was going in the inner councils of Sotheby's. A great, public sale would give Sotheby's a boost in their gladiatorial contest with their rival. On the other hand, they must have been reckoning that a dramatic intervention by an outraged government would be very harmful to their reputation and a great humiliation. My own impression was that these dignified auction houses would vehemently proclaim their integrity but would sell their own grandmothers if they saw a good deal. If the business was dubious, they could always come up with a hush-hush private sale.

Camber came to see me. There had been a careful discussion with the chairman and they favoured in principle going for a public sale.

'However,' he added, 'I want to make it absolutely clear that two conditions must be met before we could consider selling it. First, we need to be satisfied that the treasure could not be proved to have been stolen. And secondly, there must be no claim from any government. In addition, it goes without saying that we shall do everything possible to establish that the pieces are genuine. You do appreciate, Michel, that this is not in any way a reflection on you.'

'Fair enough,' I replied. 'So let me ask you, if the public sale goes ahead, what sort of figure are you putting on it?'

'Somewhere in the region of two million pounds, but it might easily fetch a lot more.'

'That sounds a good, round figure,' I agreed.

'Now, Michel, you must be patient for a bit. And it is vital to maintain the highest security. Please always refer to the treasure by the code name "Acorn". From small acorns, great oaks do sometimes grow,' Camber reminded me.

'But not always,' I said to myself as he departed.

From Amsterdam, I kept in touch with Camber. As the weeks passed, he informed me that their probing had not turned up any important barbarian hoard which had gone missing. No government was nosing around to recover a filched treasure. By degrees, they came to the conclusion that they were in the clear. The sale could go ahead: my torpedo was on course.

Or was it? I was at home when Camber called, summoning me to London.

Had something gone wrong? Had I overlooked a detail which had blown the whole deception? When I walked into Camber's room, would there be a reception committee from Scotland Yard? I had no alternative but to brazen it out. However, it was a distinctly nervous Michel van Rijn who strode into Richard Camber's office that Monday morning.

'Well,' I said with a forced grin, 'how has Sherlock Holmes been getting on? Has he come up with any acorns stolen from some foreign forest?'

'You may laugh at our deviousness,' he answered, 'but we have had to be very subtle. If we were simply to circulate a description, with photographs, and ask if anything like it had been smuggled out of any country, there are some unscrupulous bastards who would fabricate a claim using the particulars we had provided.'

'People are so dishonest,' I said sympathetically. 'And has anybody lodged a claim?'

'Not a whisper. I don't mind telling you that I am relieved, and some of us were quite surprised.'

It would certainly have been a hell of a surprise to me if any government had recognized my Avar treasure!

'So why the meeting?' I asked.

'We thought you should be present for the tests of authenticity. After all, we would want you to be satisfied that they were fairly conducted. Would you have any objection to some things being sent for analysis to Harwell?'

'The Atomic Energy Research Authority?'

'Yes. Actually, an outfit called the Low Level Measurements Laboratory. Of course, we have a good idea of the date from the stamps on the plates. You remember the work of Erica Cruikshank Dodd?'

I tried not to smile as I recollected her confident assessment of the earlier Byzantine plate. Since the two plates in the treasure were genuine, I was pleased these had been shown to her so that now I would have the backing of her immense authority.

'Still, to make doubly sure we would like to use the traditional carbon-14 dating.'

'I thought you couldn't use carbon-14 on gold or silver?'

'That's right,' Camber answered. 'But the Harwell laboratory can measure the most minute particles of soil or cloth embedded in the metal. It takes months to conclude an analysis, but it is the only way such tiny samples can be dated without vast expense.'

'How many months? I thought you had decided on holding the sale in December. We're halfway through the summer.'

'Yes, I know,' Camber interrupted, 'but we have already spoken with the man in charge of the outfit. He is prepared to work on a sample from Acorn while the equipment is still being commissioned and let us have an interim report before the end of November. So, do you mind if we send samples to Harwell?'

'Go ahead. Why should I have any objection?'

In fact I would very much have liked to object: perhaps the brainy scientists at Harwell had some new and secret way of dating fakes. So, once more, suspense.

But not for long. A few weeks later, Camber told me he had received some startling information. The laboratory had dated the artefacts back to the prehistoric era.

'But don't worry, Michel, the date is a few thousand years too early due to faulty calibration of the machine. They have succeeded in recalibrating it and the carbon-14 counting is going ahead.'

I laughed. 'It would have been awkward if they had made an error the other way and said that the things were made yesterday.' Camber chuckled at the absurdity of such a notion.

On 20th November 1981, barely three weeks before the sale was due, the Harwell report came through. The scientists had been able to extract a tiny sample of flax webbing from a belt strap. Although there were a mere 300 milligrams, they had burned this and purified the resultant carbon dioxide gas, which had then been compressed into the carefully shielded counter. The dating procedure had not yet been completed so background and calibration values were as yet unconfirmed, but after fifty-four days' counting, this interim report stated a radio-carbon age of 'approximately 700 AD' and this was, as Sotheby's exultantly stated in their catalogue, entirely consistent with the style of the belt fittings and the control stamps on the plates.

To have waited for the final report would have entailed delaying the sale for months, and Camber was too impatient for Sotheby's triumph to consider whether by cutting corners he was not possibly working against the interests of the eventual buyers. The definitive report could have provided an additional safeguard but the moment a favourable opinion could be extracted from Harwell, it was 'all systems go'.

I greatly admired the lavish catalogue, not so much a sales catalogue as a commemorative album, even the customary square format being altered for the occasion. Its writer must have been a real expert because he knew a great deal more about our treasure than I did; he identified it as being by the same hand as the Albanian hoard from Vrap. Indeed, he hinted it might well be part of the same treasure. Items of that find had dribbled on to the market over a number of years before the First World War, but there remained a suspicion that some things had been bought by a diplomat in Durazzo and vanished. The definitive book on the Vrap treasure, published in 1917, speculated that other unrecorded items might also be in private hands. Could I have come across the missing pieces? It was just the sort of insoluble problem which bewitches learned pedants. If they were right, I had found part of a noble treasury-cum-workshop and the silver plates had been destined to be melted down to fashion further belt fittings. I would have preferred my version, the resting place of some powerful prince, but who was I to argue with the experts!

I was naturally delighted by all the pre-auction fuss Sotheby's were making. It would make the eventual exposure all the more damning. The torpedo was homing in on its target.

I was at home in Amsterdam when a call from Richard Camber came through. He had just returned from New York and his enthusiasm crackled over the wires. Once Sotheby's had decided on a public sale in order to lord it over their rival, Christie's, they had pulled the stops out in promoting what they now trumpeted would be 'the sale of the century'. Camber had gone to New York for the exhibition in Sotheby's Parke-Bernet saleroom of the whole fabulous hoard. By that time, the treasures had already been showcased at Sotheby's London as well as selected sites in Europe in order to generate enthusiasm among the world's collectors. The sale had been hyped as the greatest collection of barbarian antiquities of this century.

The exhibition in New York had been a great success, Camber told me. I listened to his account of the enthusiasm of the Sotheby's teams who had handled the exhibiting of the treasure, of the interest of the critics and the acclaim of curators. Crowds had flocked to see these strange and beautiful things, although the general public had little knowledge of the art and artefacts of what are still often called the Dark Ages. This sale, he proclaimed, could bring barbarian art out of obscurity and present it to the world beyond the restricted group of specialist scholars and collectors.

'So when are you coming to London?' he asked.

'I can't say,' I replied. 'I'm very busy in Amsterdam.'

'Well, I'm sure you'll get here before the sale. And won't we celebrate when it is all over!'

Actually, I was planning a far different celebration for Sotheby's and Richard Camber's 'crowning' moment.

As the sale approached, I could sense the mounting anticipation in Sotheby's, while for Daleboudt this would be the sweetest, ripest fruit they could shake off the tree. But a few days before the sale, I started calling the influential dealers. Naturally, I did not say I believed the Avar treasure to be fake; that would have suggested I was trying to choke them off so that I or my friends could buy cheap. Asking if they had heard anything about it, and saying that the name of Patrikiades had been mentioned, was enough to sow the seeds of doubt. Rumours began to circulate and the first rumblings reached Camber a few days before the sale, advertised for Monday, 14th December 1981. The lines to Sotheby's were soon buzzing with enquiries from well-informed dealers in New York and London.

On the fateful December morning, the big saleroom on New Bond Street rapidly filled up with dealers from all the important houses, collectors, journalists, and members of the public attracted by the hullabaloo. Daleboudt was in the front row well before the sale began. He had taken the best seat to watch the frantic bidding and listen to the rollcall of his soaring wealth. The morning sale went ahead normally, but as the clock moved towards a quarter to one, anticipation mounted. There were the usual hurried whispered consultations, reporters sat with their pads open. There was a sense of occasion and the sort of tension which mounts before the curtain rises on a great drama. Every man and woman gazed at the solitary figure on the rostrum.

'Now, lots numbers 165 to 180, comprizing a treasure of the Avar period, one hundred and twenty-two gold and silver belt fittings, together with two Byzantine silver plates, bearing Constantinopolitan control stamps of the seventh century, the property of a European collector.'

The first lot was offered, and greeted with a solid wall of silence. The eager owner sat in astounded incomprehension. Eventually the small gold belt fitting was sold for the ludicrous sum of £3,080. But lot number 165 was only a foretaste; 166 was the real thing, a complete gold belt with thirteen fittings, a buckle, strap retainers, mounts, hole guards and a strap end, all intricately decorated with vinescrolls and a strange animal motif; a hundred grams of rich, glowing gold which had been transformed into an astonishing object of complex beauty.

The men from Sotheby's were tense. Daleboudt sat in paralysed expectancy. The belt was shown and bids invited. There was the same desultory interest and the lot was hurriedly bought in for £110,000. Alarm turned to panic as, one after the other, the lots failed to get anywhere near their reserves. Another gold belt was bought in for £100,000 and two belts of silver for £35,000 and £12,000. Two Byzantine silver plates met with a warmer response, fetching £13,200 and £26,400, but the Avar items, on which such hopes had been entertained, had been virtually rejected by the dealers. The sale of the century became the sale that never was!

Daleboudt was not the only person to demand an explanation. After all the publicity, the débâcle came like a bombshell. Hurriedly, a statement was prepared. The reserves were too high, but obviously the owner's expectations reflected the impression given him by Camber and his colleagues. Sotheby's and Christie's have a habit of giving a high estimate when approached by a seller and quoting a far more conservative figure shortly before the sale. This gives them the kudos of announcing fantastic success when sales exceed these estimates.

Also, it was stated, the collection was of 'an esoteric nature'. That was hardly news, and of course it was a negative way of claiming the uniqueness of the treasure which had been the reason for the importance which Sotheby's had attributed to it.

Two other factors were the mystery surrounding its provenance and some doubts about authenticity. They had admitted that the external provenance of the treasure was sketchy, stating merely that its existence became known in London in the mid-1970s and that it had been in the possession of a private collector in Germany. Previously it was reported that some parts had been seen by a Greek archaeologist, now deceased, some time between 1922 and 1938. However, in their catalogue Sotheby's had stated gleefully that the internal evidence was 'considerably more revealing' and while they now admitted that experts at the Metropolitan Museum in New York had cast doubts on the authenticity of the gold belts, other unnamed museums had not agreed with this judgement.

Richard Camber went on to say that negotiations were in the hand for the sale of three lots. In fact, Sotheby's discreetly bought back a couple of lots, the only part of the treasure sold to members of the public apart from the Byzantine plates over which no questions had been raised. Sotheby's could not afford knowingly to peddle fakes under the pretence that they were genuine. They might do a deal behind my back, but even Sotheby's had to draw a line at barefaced fraud.

The day after the sale that never was, I called Camber and asked how the sale went. He was evasive: they might have gone better. Then he asked me outright. 'Michel, were they fakes?'

'Why ask me, Richard. You're the experts.' And I hung up.

That was, however, not the end of it. Ten years later, a letter was sent to Stoop from the British Museum that began, 'Further to Sir David Wilson's letter of 10th May 1991, I am writing to confirm the interest of the Trustees of this museum in the possible acquisition of the treasure.'

Patrikiades would have been so pleased.

# 16

# La Comedie Française

## I

When the dust had settled after the sale that never was, I braced myself to make a fresh start. The ordeal of extricating myself from ruin had strained my relationship with Lesley to breaking point; not long afterwards we split up.

The one good thing about being absolutely down is that the only way to go is back up. I decided that the scene for my comeback should be Paris. Whatever other people may think, Parisians know with utter certainty that their city is the centre of the art world and they are, in cultural if not religious terms, God's Chosen People.

But the international market has long been dominated by the big British and American houses, and any dealer accustomed only to their systems finds the French scene puzzling and apparently chaotically inefficient. But that is a superficial impression. The French art market is well designed to deter foreigners muscling in and works quite well in its unique manner. However, together with my aide de camp, Paul Polak, I descended on Paris to reconnoitre the enemy's entrenched positions.

Paul is a small, wiry man who manages to convey the illusion that he is in an immense hurry even when he is standing still. His expression is that of a tycoon whose every second is valued at millions. Somehow, he manages continually to smoke Davidoff 'A', the most oversized and expensive Havana cigar, even when he is broke, and his habit of never offering his cigar box reinforces the impression of concentrated power and wealth, a man at the heart of great affairs. He has worked for me for years; we are a team, and firm friends. He comes from a well-to-do Jewish family in Amsterdam, but his early life was overshadowed by a domineering father who kept him working like a slave in the big family firm, a furniture factory. Paul virtually ran it, but his father was never satisfied. Our adventures were a liberation for him.

Although most of the more prestigious galleries are in or around the Avenue Matignon in the eighth arrondissement, public auctions were then held in the Hôtel Drouot, a rambling building in a busy part of the less elegant ninth. This was the Bastille we had to storm if we were to break into the Paris market.

That market is highly protected. The only people permitted to sell in the Hôtel Drouot are the *commissaires-priseurs*, approved auctioneers whose numbers are strictly limited. Each of them, alone or with a colleague, organizes his own sale of works of art or anything else he may decide to put on offer. He hires one of the sixteen auction rooms in the Drouot, appoints 'experts' to vouch for the authenticity of works and advertizes the sale in *La Gazette de L'Hôtel Drouot*. To save money, the advertizement might be restricted to the minimum, but regular customers peruse every line. Since the *Gazette* is often received by foreign dealers several days after the sale, the exclusive little clique of Paris dealers tend to have things all their own way.

The works can be viewed in the Drouot only one or two days before the auction, and this is an improvement; previously a morning viewing would often be followed by an afternoon sale, the same day.

The *commissaires-priseurs* are mostly male, and the system

works to restrict the profession to well-to-do, bourgeois families. First, an aspiring youngster must have his baccalauréat in law and the history of art. Then he works in the *étude* of an established *commissaire-priseur* for some years and is paid a pittance, so he needs to have money behind him. Finally, he is obliged to take an examination before he can set up in business. If he wishes to start his own *étude*, he will have to find accommodation close to the Hôtel Drouot, and that is very expensive; and it will be several more years before he is sufficiently established to earn a decent living. Alternatively, he can buy his way into an existing *étude*. Of course, a number of *commissaires-priseurs* are well known and have a flourishing business; they benefit enormously from the way the profession is protected. They have social status and are addressed, like advocates or other professional men, not as monsieur but as maître. They charge up to ten or fifteen percent to both buyer and seller, and the seller also has to pay for production of the catalogue as well as the percentage which goes to the expert appointed by the *commissaire-priseur*.

The fragmentation of the auction market ensures that there are far fewer important or specialized sales than in London. It stands to reason that it will normally take much longer for a *commissaire-priseur* to accumulate sufficient works of any one class to mount a specialized sale. The less favoured auctioneers, competing bitterly among themselves, try to keep down their costs by printing catalogues as cheaply as possible, or simply dispensing with them and lumping together everything which comes to hand in the same sale. A Picasso might be the next lot to a secondhand fridge. Only on the rare occasions when one of them has got hold of an outstanding selection of specialized works of art, does he go to the expense of producing a proper, illustrated catalogue.

That then was the cosy Paris market, undisturbed by unwelcome, thrusting competitors. Sotheby's and Christie's have premises in Paris but are not permitted to carry out auctions in France and although they can collect objects for sale abroad, the delays in issuing export licences cripple their business. To break in, I would have to be accepted by some of the more active *commissaires-priseurs* – but how does one break in to a private club?

Paul and I did not have the money to take an apartment, so the only thing was to check into a hotel where I was well enough known for the management to dispense with such awkward formalities as a credit card or a cash deposit. At the George V we could eat, drink, sleep and use all hotel services, and worry about paying later. It also provided a prestigious address for business meetings; it was our visiting card. In the morning, we set out to explore the Hôtel Drouot.

Outside the hotel was the usual line of taxis. Paul and I ignored them. Being broke, we walked. We fought our way inside the Drouot. The place was teeming with people rushing from room to room, and there was a heavy odour of Pernod in the air. In one room were paintings, drawings and reproductions; in the next, furniture. Upstairs were sculptures and fire arms, musical instruments and books. We pushed our way through, passing old, battered kitchen equipment, and in one room came upon a heap of fabrics, mostly curtains and lingerie. Even here there was a constant jostling of viewers, but I caught sight of a bag of curtain rings. Only one of them, I suspected, was not a curtain ring at all. The bag was pushed over to me. Most were wooden rings from the nineteenth century, but there were metal ones, and I examined a plain golden ring which I tucked away at the bottom of the bag.

'What is it?' Paul asked eagerly.

I handed back the bag and turned away. 'Let's hope nobody else notices,' I murmured. 'We might just be in luck.'

'Michel van Rijn,' said a voice at my elbow. 'I didn't know you were in Paris.'

The speaker was Roy, an Armenian who owned the Galerie Nikolenko and with whom I had done a lot of business. He was a specialist in Byzantine art and noted for his knowledge and integrity. I prayed that he had not seen the gold ring.

'Found any interesting things?' he enquired.

'Nothing much,' I said, edging away from the bag of rings.

He nodded. 'Well, let's get some lunch before the rush starts. May I invite you and your friend to join me?'

Before leaving, I went downstairs to the toilets. I knew that the weekly *Gazette* was indispensable for me, but one had to pay for it. How could I get my hands on nine francs? Outside the loo, a woman was posted before a table on which was a plate onto which people were expected to drop the odd franc. But sitting in the gloomy antechamber to a loo is not an exciting way to pass one's life and she had abandoned her knitting and wandered off for a coffee and a gossip, leaving the plate as a reminder that nothing is for free. There was a heap of francs in the plate. One quick look round, and I scooped up the nine I needed.

I rejoined Roy and he led the way to La Grange-Batalière, a busy, unpretentious restaurant opposite the main entrance to the Drouot. We were just in time to grab a table. Everybody in the Hôtel Drouot seemed to move off to lunch at the same time. Within minutes, the building was deserted and a crowd pushed its way into the restaurant which served virtually as a luncheon club for the habitués of the Hôtel. The place was vibrant as auctioneers and dealers talked shop over their food or pushed their way to other tables to discuss a deal over coffee or cognac; it was even livelier than the Hôtel itself.

'I eat here a lot,' said Roy. 'It serves good Italian and French food, and no bogus snobbery. The place is packed every midday, not with tourists, the location is wrong, but the auction crowd who want good food and wine at a sensible price without any nonsense.'

All around us deals were discussed and bargains struck. Auctioneers and dealers stood talking shop until a table became available. The drama never halted, there was only a change of scene. They argued and struck bargains, formed alliances and made informal agreements, plotted and counter-plotted.

It was a non-stop performance until they all hurried back to the Drouot to bring their schemes to fruition.

At the end of the meal, we walked back with Roy who, to my relief, went off to take part in another sale. But first, he called over one of the porters.

'There is something I want to bid for but I shall be busy in another sale,' he explained. 'Jean here will place my bid for me.'

'Couldn't you leave it with the auctioneer or an expert?' Paul asked.

'Most dealers would rather use a porter. They are honest, down-to-earth types for whom a thousand francs in the pocket means something. An expert works on a commission, so the higher the price, the happier he will be. And remember, he takes a commission also from the *commissaire-priseur*. No, a porter won't push up the price, and they make good money with a thousand francs here, a few hundred there – all unofficial, of course, so there is keen competition for the job. They all come from the same district of Burgundy and even vote on whether to admit a new applicant. Let me present Jean to you. He will look after you if you need someone to bid for you.'

The auction rooms resembled an enormous anthill: a sale taking place in each room, and dealers and experts constantly running from one to another. The smell of Pernod had been overwhelmed by that of garlic and wine and there was a babble of noise as each sale got under way.

The sales were chaos, a sort of sophisticated street market, the whole place buzzing with private pacts and rivalries, and everybody frantically busy. That day, one of the rooms was double-booked, quite a frequent occurrence, so our sale took place in the corridor. It was an inventory sale and was even more chaotic than usual with dealers and experts constantly pushing through the corridor. In an adjoining room was a mixed sale and instead of only one expert there must have been six or eight, who hurried through our corridor sale into the room then fought their way out again to get to their next room. The auctioneer, his hand outstretched like the conductor of an unruly orchestra, noted the bids. Some of the bidders merely raised a hand or nodded, but two *crieurs*, whose job was noting the bids and shouting them back to the auctioneer, marched up and down, pushing their way through the throng, screaming incessantly to encourage the bidding since they also get a percentage.

I waited tensely for the odd lot of curtain rings. When it was offered, there was only mild interest and it was knocked down to me for a hundred and fifty francs. Nobody else had realized just how odd the lot was. What had caught my eye was a Byzantine gold ring, unostentatious but valuable. Paul paid by cheque, trusting in my being able to sell the ring before the cheque was presented. Somehow I found Roy in the crush and showed him the ring. He gave me a cheque for forty thousand francs on the spot. It felt good, as if I had become one of the Drouot insiders.

For the next few days, until the money came in from the ring, we were flat broke and would walk to the Drouot each morning except when we were in a hurry. Then we took the *métro*, leaping over the entrance barrier. I had photocopies made of some items from the *Gazette* for my clients and they were sent out by the concierge on George V paper which made a good impression, the postage being charged to our account.

But I needed good office stationery straight away for a Hong Kong company called Cerbino which I had formed in order to have a non-French company through which deals could be channelled without the complications of French exchange controls. Paul and I asked a number of printers to produce sample sheets of headed notepaper. Cerbino's address was given as a suite in the George V, so they were more than willing to oblige without charge, believing this must be an important company which would place a big order once their sample had been approved. They used high quality paper and printing, but as the paper was used almost exclusively for invoices, their samples were all that was necessary and Cerbino got first-class stationery free.

It was essential to maintain a show of prosperity, and the hotel was a great help. One day, I was being driven in a majestic Rolls-Royce and passed Paul and his girlfriend who had just arrived from Amsterdam. The girl was mightily impressed.

'He must be making a fortune,' she gasped.

Paul shook his head. 'No, that means he's broke.'

He knew that the car was supplied by the hotel and the cost would be charged to our account. The girl, understandably, thought he was either joking or jealous.

The sale of the ring was psychologically welcome. I had both bought and sold in Paris, and this was to be the beginning of a domestic business in this highly protected market in addition to dealing for overseas clients. Prices in Paris, particularly of important works, were usually only a fraction of what could be got abroad because the Comité de Louvre routinely refused export licences so neither French dealers nor foreigners profited from this. And the ban is not solely applied to French works; any object of artistic or historical value, wherever it might have originated, is claimed as part of the national *patrimoine*.

From the sale, I paid twenty-five thousand francs to the hotel. Nobody had yet complained, but we did meet some hard stares and I guessed that the management might be getting restive. Also I had enough to make a special reservation at La Grange-Batalière. I had watched the maître d'hotel closely as he bustled about when the herd from the Drouot came trampling in. He knew them all by name and had a welcome for everyone. A man of about forty, he gave the impression that he was over-qualified for his work. Perhaps there was some incident in his past, maybe connected with his homosexuality which he made no effort to hide, which resulted in his doing a job that must have left his capabilities unchallenged. However, possibly to compensate, he turned everything into part of his theatre, and was perpetually on stage. He was on easy terms with his regular customers, gossiping, discussing, lending a sympathetic ear and swapping scraps of news, a one-man newspaper.

We went back in the evening for dinner. The restaurant was virtually deserted now that the working day was over and the maître d' had plenty of time to talk and satisfy his curiosity about these strangers. I invited him to join us for a drink; some of the waiters were Italians and I chatted to them in their language. By the end of the meal, there was a warm, friendly atmosphere. I told the maître d' that I was a collector and dealer and he was full of information and anecdotes about the habitués from the Drouot.

'We are going to be busy,' I explained to him. 'There are viewings in the mornings and sales in the afternoons, so the only time during the day when we can meet people is over lunch. I like your restaurant and it would be very convenient if I could reserve a table and let people know we can be contacted here for the next couple of weeks. Could you manage that, preferably the round table?'

I am sure I would not have been able to make that sort of reservation had he been the owner. There was only one round table in the little restaurant, close to the door, near which, during the lunch-hour rush, customers would cluster to wait their turn. As he told me, that table was the favourite of some of his regulars, but such was his curiosity that he agreed to my request.

'And I would ask you for one other favour,' I said. 'I would like to let people know they can call me here, if you would agree to take messages?' I thrust five thousand francs into his hand.

'We shall not be able to get here every day,' I explained. 'However, please do hold that table whether we turn up or not. You can pass on any messages to us at lunch, or you can reach me at my hotel.' I handed him my card. 'You will be very welcome to come by the George V and have a drink any time.'

'But of course, monsieur, that is very kind,' he purred. 'And will you be eating here tomorrow?'

'That depends. I have several appointments, but please do keep the table for me. And, at the end of the fortnight, there will be another five thousand francs for your trouble.'

We strode out of the restaurant, and the now thoroughly intrigued maître d'hotel escorted us to the door.

'Are we going back there for lunch?' Paul asked outside.

'Are you crazy? After investing five thousand francs with our public relations manager, we are reduced to foie gras in the George V.'

However, just to make sure that the maître d'hotel was obeying instructions, I asked my brother Guy, who was visiting me, to try to take my table.

'How did it go?' I asked.

Guy laughed. 'It was fantastic. The place was packed, people standing around waiting for a place, and there, slap bang in the place of honour was this empty table. Everybody wanted to know why they couldn't sit there – I heard a trio of his old customers bawling out the maître d'. It was a disgrace, never in all the years they had been coming to the restaurant had they been forced to wait while that table, their particular favourite, was kept for some damned foreigners who might never turn up!'

'And how did our man behave?'

'He was perfect. He regretted, he sympathized, he consoled, but he stood firm.'

I don't want to exaggerate our poverty. We had sufficient funds to take our place at the restaurant a few days later and to bring along an outstandingly pretty girl. We knew quite a few Dutch models working in Paris and I enjoyed inviting them. They must have made the *commissaires-priseurs* even more curious about us. When we came in, the place was full, our table alone standing deserted. Heads turned as we sat down. Who the hell were we?

The maître d' hurried over. 'Oh, Monsieur van Rijn, I am so glad you have arrived. I have just taken a call for you, a Japanese gentleman. He will call back later. And there were three calls before.'

He bobbed with excitement. He sensed that there was something extraordinary going on and he was part of it. I had explained that my business was highly confidential; under no circumstances was he to disclose to anybody the identity of the people who called me. Since he prattled to all the regulars, it was certain that the importance of those urgent calls would be broadcast throughout the Drouot fraternity.

Japanese money was beginning to flood into the European art markets, and top gallery owners in Paris were making fortunes selling at wildly inflated prices to these wealthy but inexperienced buyers. The news that I had connections in Japan spread. These exotic Dutchmen ought to be watched.

I was not in the least surprised at these calls, since they had been placed by Paul and myself or other friends! Another couple of top priority calls came for me while we were at our table. Nobody said anything, but I could see that the fish were eyeing the bait.

The next day there was a repeat performance; then we stayed away for some days. When we were absent, our faithful restaurateur called the George V to relay messages. All sorts of people phoned the restaurant and announced their distinguished, but alas, spurious identities. I was a good client of the hotel, so when calls were made there, the hall porter made a point of reaching me at the restaurant. The maître d' would announce dramatically, '*C'est l'Hôtel George V qui vous cherche, Monsieur van Rijn*,' always in a conspiratorial but audible whisper in front of long-eared auctioneers.

One day when I called he was very distressed. 'Monsieur van Rijn, I have a problem. Tell me, do you yet know whether you will be using your table today?'

'No, I have a meeting and won't be able to get away.'

'Could you as a special favour allow me to give it to one of my very important customers, a Maître Gros? He has just called for a reservation and I have not a single table available.'

'That's all right. Let Maître Gros use the table today.'

The next day, after a morning at the Drouot, we had

finished our meal when one of the young *commissaires-priseurs* sauntered over. He introduced himself as Henri Gros and wished to thank me for letting him use my table.

'*Voulez-vous me permettre de vous offrir un café*?' he asked.

'Please would you be so kind as to speak English to Monsieur van Rijn,' Paul asked.

Paul and I speak French well, but I had decided to conduct discussions in English to exploit the French sense of insecurity and their presumption that business originating overseas must be important. So while Paul answered in French, I persisted in speaking English as long as it suited me.

Gros told us he was organizing auctions, and wondered what our plans were? I gave him to understand that I was a collector who occasionally dealt. That was no more than he had already assumed, but by the time we got to a glass of mirabelle, Maître Gros got round to suggesting doing business together.

'Do you happen to have anything particular just now which you might consider selling?' he asked.

'Not really. I am looking out for things for my own collection, and that covers quite a wide range. As for my clients, most of them are Japanese, and they are still finding their feet in the art world. They buy the names they know, even if the works are from one of the artist's less interesting periods. For instance, the other day I sold them a van Gogh and they paid top price for a picture which would not have caused much excitement in Europe. You might say that they do not yet collect paintings, only names.'

Henri Gros was impressed.

'What about the icon collection?' Paul asked me, right on cue. 'The ones you have in Tokyo.'

I thought for a moment and then nodded. 'Yes, that might be of interest. I had not been thinking about selling them, but why not?'

Gros was enraptured. What other French auctioneer could find a Dutch dealer with icons in Japan?

'A whole collection,' he said appreciatively. 'How many pieces would that be?'

'A couple of hundred,' I told him.

He asked whether they were Russian or Greek, what periods, and whether we had photographs and descriptions. 'I would very much like to handle the sale,' he said. 'It could be a way of starting a business relationship.'

Paul produced his diary. 'I can go over that with you, Maître Gros,' he said. 'Monsieur van Rijn is very tied up, but I have some free time on Thursday, around six. How are you fixed?'

He did not have to look at his diary. 'That will be fine.'

On Thursday in the hotel, we got down to details. Henri was keen to handle the sale of the icons and Paul was able to assure him that we could have them delivered to a customs warehouse for viewing by him and his expert. There was the glint of triumph in his eye; he had landed those strange foreign fish who had swum into La Grange-Batalière. Then the fish bit back.

I had joined them at the end of the meeting. 'Very well,' I said. 'I shall instruct my shipper to consign the icons directly to you. You take them over the moment they arrive and deal with everything – I don't want to be bothered with formalities. As far as I am concerned, I want two things from you, once you and your expert are satisfied. The most important is that you may buy me dinner, not in some great temple but where you go to eat yourself. Right?'

Henri smiled assent. Every Frenchman is approachable through his stomach.

'And secondly, you can pay me a little money, *dix brics*, cash.'

He was amused that after my insistence on speaking English I had picked up sufficient French to demand a hundred thousand francs in good Paris argot.

Paul had asked him about how the Paris market operated. Henri was only too glad to show off his professional expertise and painstakingly described the system we had already studied exhaustively.

'But these dealers who put up works of art for auction – the English auction houses give advances; do French dealers all have the liquidity to buy for their own account and wait until the auction before they are in funds?' Paul asked.

'A lot of them need outside finance,' Henri answered. 'As a matter of fact, we might make an advance, based on the value put on the work by an expert.'

'And that is common practice?'

'It happens a lot,' he assented. 'By cheque of course, cash is not allowed.'

Competition among the *commissaires-priseurs* was intense and whatever they might say in public, cash advances of up to fifty percent were paid, so when I demanded that I receive the same, Henri realized there was no point in arguing if he wished to handle the icons – and who knew what other good things this foreigner might have up his sleeve. At any moment our talk might be interrupted by a summons from a Japanese museum, so he hastened to agree before I got diverted or left for my next appointment.

Henri and Monsieur Roy, his expert, went with Paul to the warehouse and inspected the icons before they cleared customs. Gros had invited me to act as expert on the strength of my book, *Early Christian Art*, but I had declined.

The sale was quite eventful. All the pieces had been smuggled out of Greece or Cyprus, and somehow the Greek embassy got wind of the sale. An irate embassy official turned up and in a white-hot fury insisted that the sale could not proceed. All the pieces are stolen, he thundered. Poor Henri was flabbergasted, but quickly recovered.

'That is a ludicrous assertion,' he replied indignantly. 'They are the property of a gentleman whose name has not been divulged in the catalogue but who is a highly respectable private collector.'

The listing of items in a catalogue as 'the property of Monsieur X' was common practice in Paris, and Henri Gros had convinced himself that his own story had to be the truth. There was a brief screaming match, but the Greek was outclassed. Henri, working on the dictum that attack is the best form of defence, threatened that if the sale were disrupted by this crazy interference, he would hold the official personally responsible and was quite prepared to extend his attack to the ambassador and his entire staff. He emphasized that the *commissaires-priseurs* were directly responsible to the Minister of Justice, and sounded as if he would demand that the French government send an invasion fleet unless my icons were sold without let or hindrance. Before such spirited resistance, the representative of the legitimate owners of part of their national heritage withdrew, routed.

I got to know Henri Gros better as our business developed, and he would sometimes invoke my assistance or advice. On one occasion, I had brought him a collection of African and Pre-Columbian art.

'You know those two Mayan steles among the Mexican pieces,' he said.

I nodded assent. 'I saw them in the catalogue, with no estimate of price.'

It was quite common for objects to be so listed and anyone wanting an estimate was referred to the *commissaire-priseur*.

'That's right. Frankly, I have no experience of those things, so I was at a bit of a loss today when some collector phoned from Switzerland and asked me to quote an estimate. I told him a quarter of a million Swiss francs; it was the first thing that came into my head.'

'What sort of a reserve are you proposing to the seller?'

'That's the point. I went to the expert and asked his valuation. Do you know what he suggested?'

I shook my head. In Paris, any price might have been put forward.

'One hundred thousand French, not Swiss, francs. And that is the figure on which I have based my proposed reserve. The seller is quite happy with it.'

'And the Swiss?'

'He has just put in a bid at two hundred and fifty thousand Swiss francs. Is there some way we could persuade the seller to withdraw the steles and we sell them privately?'

I recalled the fuss with the Greek embassy. Henri put in a call to the owner of the steles.

'I've some bad news for you,' he said. 'The Mexican embassy has heard about those Mayan steles and are up in arms, saying they have been stolen and smuggled out of the country. They're threatening to have them seized.'

'Jesus!' he gasped. 'That's dreadful, what can we do?'

'The safest thing would be if you allow me to pull them out of the auction and try to find a buyer privately. No fuss, no publicity.'

'Sure. Have you any idea of what they might fetch?'

'I would do my best to make your reserve,' answered Maître Gros.

So my company stepped in; the seller was gratified to receive his reserve since the pieces had indeed been stolen. The Swiss collector also was pleased that he had acquired the steles.

But there were other times when one ran up against the French system and it proved invincible. The key to Paris dealing was getting to know the experts with whom the *commissaires-priseurs* worked closely. Their word, no matter how fallible, was law.

On one occasion, I had bought what purported to be a fine thirteenth-century ivory plaque from a *commissaire-priseur* for two hundred and fifty thousand francs. If it were genuine I stood to make a good profit, and considered myself protected since my purchase was covered by the absolute guarantee of the Hôtel Drouot, which it boasts is valid for thirty-three years, not a mere five like Christie's or Sotheby's. I later consulted Kurt Weitzmann, the world authority on such objects, who declared it to be a nineteenth-century imitation. He knew the piece and it was a very good copy, but that is what it was. He detailed convincing reasons for his opinion. Furthermore, it was shown in reference books as a copy, and ought to have been recognized as such by the expert in Paris, so I demanded that the auctioneer take back the ivory. He refused.

'It is perfectly genuine,' he declared. 'It has been so judged by our expert.'

I showed him the opinion of Weitzmann, and even sent him copies of important books the expert had written, but he remained adamant. His expert had said the piece was genuine, so genuine it was.

There could be no appeal against the verdict of a French expert – at least not in France. If the case were taken to a tribunal, it would be composed of French experts, and the experts and the auctioneers back each other up. That is how I learned that the vaunted thirty-three year guarantee, far from offering a buyer protection, is worthless. What makes the system even more of a farce is the fact that experts are also dealers. The so-called expert who stated that this faked ivory was authentic owned an ivory shop himself so he was hardly a disinterested party.

I bought a Marie Laurencin oil on paper, a design for an Aubusson carpet, full of flowers and pigeons. Then I picked up a cheap painting on an old canvas and had the Marie Laurencin mounted on the canvas. It was duly certified by an expert as an oil on canvas, and as such I sold it to Gekkoso from whom it was bought by the Marie Laurencin Museum in Japan. As an oil on canvas it commands a price ten or twenty times an oil on paper. One restoration studio specializing in remounting paintings on to canvas with great skill is owned by an acknowledged expert who can thus certify his own transformations.

Such a system seems designed to encourage malpractice.

## II

To be a successful dealer in Paris needed more than one collection of icons and although the advance payment provided us with much needed working capital, it was a long way short of the money necessary to acquire a worthwhile stock. But I have never believed in tying up my capital in objects and spending my time shut up in some gallery, looking at them. I devised a method by which we could dispense with the necessity of holding stock – it was better to employ that of the auctioneers.

We would write for the catalogues of salerooms in other countries who were only too willing to send them abroad in the hope of business. I had sufficient funds left to buy a first-rate photographic installation which enabled me to photograph illustrations in catalogues with such clarity that it was impossible to tell that I had not photographed the actual objects.

The French system which erected a barrier against foreign auction houses also encouraged the privileged members of the Paris market to adopt an indifference, amounting virtually to contempt, as to what went on in other countries. Most of the time they did not know what was on offer in the rest of Europe, and many of them could not have cared less. In addition, French dealers were handicapped by the restrictions of the Banque de France: they had to get specific permission to send money outside the country and that could take a long time. Often they did not speak a foreign language and felt lost abroad, and they were limited to taking three thousand francs when they did venture out. Consequently the Paris market was so isolated that prices bore no relationship to those in other capitals.

We would select something which was to be auctioned abroad and would appeal to French buyers. For instance a fine eighteenth-century French commode coming up for auction at Bukovsky's in Stockholm and illustrated in their catalogue. We took the photograph to an expert and he gave a provisional estimate several times that published in Stockholm. So I put in a bid, subject to the piece being as described, and succeeded in buying it.

'Please consign it to Paris,' I told Bukovsky's. 'I regret that I cannot pay you until the commode has been delivered;

you understand I am tied down by rules of the Banque de France.'

Meanwhile I contacted a *commissaire-priseur* who worked with the expert and we all went to the warehouse which was behind customs. If the expert had given an unfavourable opinion, I would have refused to accept it on the grounds that it had not matched up to the description, and as it had not formally entered France it would have been sent back without any problem. In fact it was fine, so I handed it over immediately to the *commissaire-priseur* against a fifty percent cash advance from which I was able to pay Bukovsky. The auctioneer was happy; the piece had been legally imported and he was able to get his money out of the country. I earned a good profit without having to put up my own money, having turned the French restrictions to my advantage in buying as well as in selling.

My contacts in Japan, too, were rather out of contact with most European centres. We now had a secretary who would go through the catalogues, photographing the most attractive pieces. Thus we produced our own catalogue, and the Japanese could not tell that we did not have the items illustrated in our own warehouse. As we were able to select objects from many foreign catalogues, our own gave the impression that we carried an enormous stock which was always changing, and our turnover appeared to be colossal. I was also able to offer things coming up for auction in France, basing my price on a modest profit over the expert's estimate since it was to my advantage to build up turnover and thus become established in the market rather than copy the majority of French dealers who tried to go for the fattest possible profit margin. If there was no feedback from a client, I knew that there was no interest. However when a client was prepared to buy at my price, I would bid at the auction and if not successful, would tell him that unfortunately the object had been sold before his offer was received. Sometimes a dealer who had bought the object at auction later offered it to my client. This also worked out well, since he would assume that the dealer, who would be quoting a far higher price than mine, had bought from me. My price would appear to have been very competitive and the client would be all the keener to deal with me next time.

As my relationship with the *commissaires-priseurs* matured, many of them were prepared to disclose reserve prices. This was very useful since, if it was clear that something was not going to reach its reserve, there was no need to bid against the reserve. After a piece had failed to sell, I was often able to buy at a far lower price.

For instance, because of being given inside information by one of the largest and most prestigious firms of *commissaires-priseurs*, I was able to buy an oil painting by Toulouse-Lautrec, one of his most famous subjects, *The Jockey*, which had failed to reach its reserve, for three hundred thousand French francs. A lithograph of the same subject would have been worth that, but there are many reasons why a painting might not realize its reserve if the auctioneer so decides. I had already had an offer from a Japanese house so the painting was virtually presold but they never knew about the failure of the auction, and I sold for many times what it cost me.

One day, Paul went to an auction organized by Ader, Picard et Tajan. The auctioneer was the young Maître Picard and we were especially interested in a Renoir for which Gekkoso were prepared to pay one-and-a-quarter million francs. The price ran up quickly to five hundred thousand and then slowed down as bidders fell out. Each time Paul bid, his bid was accepted by the auctioneer, and at seven hundred thousand no other bid was forthcoming. Three times, Picard offered the lot, then knocked it down. One of his assistants approached Paul, who was very happy at the profit we would make. To his amazement, the assistant walked straight past him to a man at the back of the room.

'That was my bid,' Paul appealed to Picard.

'No, sir, I knocked it down to the gentleman at the back,' said the auctioneer.

Paul had a shrewd suspicion that the 'buyer' was a stooge of the auctioneer and there were rumours that Ader, Picard and Tajan resorted to this practice to ensure that a piece did not go outside the charmed circle, and he was not the only one. After we had been cheated several times, I resolved to give the auctioneers a taste of their own medicine.

At that time, there was little or no control over telephone bidding in Paris, or even in Sotheby's and Christie's. So, when Ader, Picard et Tajan advertized a canvas by Foujita which I knew would interest Gekkoso, I called their office on the morning of the viewing and introduced myself as a Mr Forster.

'I am interested in bidding for the Foujita tomorrow,' I said. 'Unfortunately, I shall not be able to attend the auction as I have an important meeting in London.'

'Would you care to leave a bid with us?'

'I would much rather bid myself,' I replied. 'I enjoy the excitement. Would it be possible for you to call me at the Dorchester and accept my bids by telephone?'

Maître Picard was quite prepared to allow this. The fact that they would be calling me helped to reassure them, as did the use of a first-class hotel. Many auctioneers favoured telephone bidders since they could push the absent bidder up above possibly non-existent bids in the room.

Next day, Paul flew to London and went to the Dorchester.

'My name is Forster,' he told the concierge. 'I am expecting an urgent call from Paris. Would you mind having it put through to me here?'

He gave the concierge a twenty-pound note and settled in an armchair to await the call from the Drouot. Picard's assistant got through to the Dorchester and asked for Mr Forster; Paul was called to the phone and bid with such persistence that the painting was knocked down to him.

'I shall be back in Paris tomorrow and will come round to your offices to settle,' he said.

But as the days passed and Forster failed to appear, the auctioneers became concerned. A call to the Dorchester confirmed their fears – they were landed with the painting. I let a couple of weeks elapse before dropping in on the *commissaire-priseur* for a chat during which I enquired if he had any interesting items which had failed to make their reserve.

'There is a Foujita which we sold but where the buyer has not claimed the picture.' Since he had made an advance against the painting, he was anxious to get it off his hands. So I bought it from him much cheaper than at auction and without being obliged to pay the official commission. It was a game which one could not play too often with the same auctioneer, but luckily there were plenty of them.

Incidentally, the phone technique worked also for sales outside France. For instance, a painting by Manet, a charming harbour scene, was advertized to be auctioned by de Vuyst in Belgium. The provenance could not have been better, the Musée des Beaux-Arts, but I was cautious since Manet's output was very small. It was my intention to sell the painting in Paris where it would need to be certified by a French expert; the obvious course would have been to bring the expert with me to view the painting before I bid for it. However, this would risk drawing the attention of the Paris crowd to the sale; left to their own devices, they would probably not notice an important painting being offered outside, even in Belgium, their own backyard. And since so many Paris dealers made secret deals with each other, I could not be sure that the expert would not come to some arrangement with one of his cronies and cut me out, but I was dependent on his approving the work. So again I installed Paul, this time in Amsterdam, with instructions to buy the painting at any reasonable price in the knowledge that if it were certified as genuine, we would make a big profit over whatever it would cost at auction.

Only after the painting had been bought and left on the hands of the auctioneer did I invite Henri Martin, a noted expert and a very kind person, together with one of his colleagues, to view a Manet in Belgium. It was an enjoyable outing for them, staying overnight at the Amigo and dining at the Villa

Lorraine. When we went to de Vuyst, however, I made a point of inspecting first a number of other paintings coming up at the next auction. Only then did I ask to see the Manet, so it was never made clear to Martin that the Manet had already been auctioned. This way I hoped to get a more favourable opinion from him. As it happened, he did not approve the painting and I had a perfect justification for not taking it. If it had been OK, I would have done a deal as a disappointed under-bidder who had chanced to hear that the painting had not been taken by the phone – or phoney! – buyer.

As the business grew, we moved out of the George V to the Lancaster. It was smaller, but had more class. The George V had become patronized by a new, brash clientèle, often oil-rich Arabs, and was haunted by prostitutes, but it had served its purpose. Now things were going well, I remembered to repay one debt of honour. I presented the woman who watched over the toilets in the Hôtel Drouot with a thousand francs. Since the going rate was one franc, she was mystified until I explained how she had unknowingly been my banker. At first she was suspicious. Although long past the first bloom of youth, maybe this guy was some weirdo who was into older women, but the money was real enough and she eventually decided that I was either a joker or had just pulled off a coup in the saleroom. Anyway, she insisted that I give her a kiss on each cheek, and from that time on I had free access to the loos of the Hôtel Drouot.

By now I had attracted attention for bringing new, high quality merchandise to Paris, and some *commissaires-priseurs*, respecting the wealth of my Japanese clientèle, would warn me whenever they got hold of something exceptional. My secretary would photograph the object, we would multiply the expert's estimate by a suitable factor and offer it to clients. However, I informed them that another, purely fictitious, client was also interested. If their offer was sufficient to ensure a substantial profit, they would be successful but if, because they did not offer enough or the competition in the actual auction was stiffer than had been expected and the price went too high, I said that unfortunately the other client had already bought the object, or advised them against it on the grounds that almost certainly it would not be possible to get an export licence, which made them feel pleased at their skill in selection.

Our relations with the Paris dealers were highly ambivalent. I had kept on the table at La Grange-Batalière, and occasionally would allow favoured dealers or auctioneers like Henri Gros to take it. They would compete for our business and were affable and obliging, even obsequious when they were looking for a favour, but for many dealers we were outsiders until they came to appreciate that we could be useful. Our tactics were to keep them guessing and to play up my enormous wealth, especially in the early days when we were broke.

Provincial sales were usually quiet affairs. My brother Guy and I went to one at Enghien-les-Bains, attended by the local worthies. These sales were in striking contrast to the chaos of the Drouot; social occasions, for which people dress formally and reserve seats in advance. This sale however was important enough to attract a gaggle of Parisian dealers who wore anything that came to hand, and we turned up in our jogging suits since we had been running. The locals were shocked at this invasion but it was the Parisians we had to watch. Some formed a ring to squeeze us out of the bidding or force us to pay usurious prices. We soon tumbled to it and decided to give them a run for their money. There were some things I wanted, and I bid keenly for them. The provincials watched in amazement as the prices mounted and first one of the Paris gang then another took over the bidding against me. One important item was a Modigliani which they were sure I coveted. I encouraged them by starting to bid briskly. The pack from Paris pushed the price higher and higher; they were in a delirium of delight because they knew that if I really wanted something, I would persist. The tension was terrific and everything was going according to plan until I abruptly stopped bidding. The auctioneer shot a pleading glance at me, but I shook my head. I never wanted the thing in the first place, and neither did the furious dealer who was landed with it. There was a shocked pause as the ring realized they had been taken. Guy broke the stunned silence.

'Is the next picture square?' he called out to the auctioneer.

The auctioneer gazed at him in utter bewilderment.

'Because if it is,' Guy continued, a benevolent smile on his lips, 'my brother will buy it. He loves square pictures.'

## III

As I became better known among the fraternity, another source of revenue was fronting for French dealers. This appealed to them since they were obliged by law to settle any transaction for more than five thousand francs by cheque. But cheques are messy things, leaving a trail of records, whereas cash is anonymous and untraceable. Although Axel Hammerschmidt, which had been formed as a successor to Cerbino, was a French company and required to comply with this requirement, we were not French residents, and so, as individuals, we were able to deal for cash; for a modest five percent commission, we extended this service to our less favoured French friends.

The very first transaction with Henri Gros had demonstrated one way in which an enterprising *commissaire-priseur* could switch money out of the country, and there were countless variations on two basic operations. In the first, money or paintings would be moved physically outside France and the paintings could then be imported legally and declared at customs so that, when sold in France, the proceeds could be paid abroad and there would be no need for an export licence.

Of course all regular border crossings were watched, particularly those into Switzerland. Quite by chance, I found a way through the chain of customs posts. I was in Amsterdam, celebrating a good sale. I was in high spirits when I left the restaurant and decided to buy a present for my girlfriend, something a bit out of the ordinary. Suzuki jeeps had recently appeared, so I bought a shining bright red one. Then I drove it to the flower market and had the astonished florist fill it with earth in which I planted trees, shrubs and flowers. So I brought her a mobile garden which I intended driving back to Paris with the plants for my apartment.

I took off in the jeep, a Garden of Eden on wheels. There are no formalities on the Netherlands-Belgium border, but crossing into France was a different story. The French *douaniers* did not find my floral offering at all funny. Their disapproval was reinforced by my appearance. Having had a few days on the town, I was unshaven and dressed in jeans. Since I was carrying most of the three hundred thousand guilders with me, they were very suspicious and searched the jeep thoroughly but could find nothing wrong, so they told me sternly that the importation of unauthorized plants into France was prohibited and ordered me to get rid of them before presenting myself again at the border.

I drove back several kilometres into Belgium and looked for another border crossing where the guards might be a bit more easygoing. I drove quite a long way, passing a Novotel hotel before I realized that I was in France and had not seen any customs post. The road crossed the border unobstructed by any sort of control. Here was the simplest way of turning a French-owned painting into one legally imported from abroad.

But there was an even more open way of penetrating the screen of French security. When they built Charles de Gaulle airport at Roissy, to the north of Paris, the French boasted that it was the most advanced in Europe. A great, drum-shaped building, with travellators enclosed in plastic, like giant, transparent toothpaste tubes, it looked as if it were from another planet or century. But while legions of customs men attempted to seal the remote borders of the country, the great gap in security was here, in this airport of the future.

It was Paul who stumbled on the first hole in the security

system; eventually we were to come across so many it might have been made of Swiss cheese. Somebody flying into Paris goes through immigration and passport control and proceeds to a large space where he passes customs. Once beyond, he is confronted by the toothpaste tubes which lead down to street level. In case he has heavy baggage, a lift is provided. The entrance to the lift, however, is actually behind customs. Whoever designed the system was confident that nobody would come into the airport from the street and attempt to proceed up the travellators which are running downwards. But what was overlooked was that the lift, which takes passengers down, also goes up.

A dealer had a painting for which he knew he would be unable to obtain an export licence. I drove with him to the airport. While he waited in his car, I went up in the lift with the painting. Then I walked back to customs, said that I had just arrived in Paris and wanted to leave the painting in an *entrepôt douane*, a customs-free depot, since I would be leaving again soon and did not wish to bring the painting into France. It was checked to make sure it was not some sort of bomb and I was given a receipt; it was not even necessary to show a ticket. Anybody flying out of Paris, on producing the receipt, would be given the painting. Of course the painting had never officially entered France. I handed the ticket to the dealer who could now import it legally and would have no problem getting an export licence. To be on the safe side, we could even meet somebody at this level who had travelled into Paris and borrow his ticket just in case we were challenged. The French customs made no charge for the use of the *entrepôt douane*.

Exactly the same procedure could be used for smuggling money out of the country, although since we declared the contents of a suitcase as being currency, we would be asked to show our foreign passports. So we were able to deposit a suitcase of cash and hand it over to a Frenchman behind customs. One pitfall for the unwary smuggler to avoid was flying from Paris to Geneva, since the French regard that as a domestic flight and a Frenchman with illicit cash or a black painting which he had picked up behind customs in Paris would be faced by French customs again on arrival at Geneva. It meant a longer flight, but he would be better advised to go to Zurich.

When we wanted to bring paintings into France without having to declare them, the facilities of Charles de Gaulle extended this privilege also. Before an incoming passenger reached customs, the corridor forked, in one direction for international arrivals and customs control, the other for national arrivals – and no customs. It was quite comic to watch passengers off the early morning flight from Amsterdam, trotting gaily through the national arrival channel. It might have been a scene in a Jacques Tati movie! But many were probably involved in more sinister business than smuggling works of art. Because Charles de Gaulle was so wide open, it became the entry point for drugs distributed not only throughout France but into Belgium and Holland as well.

I gradually built up a select list of wealthy Japanese clients, and the Japanese connection really brought us respect. In no time, we were treated like VIPs. Our apparent uncouthness was regarded as the loveable eccentricity which accompanied wealth. We gave Dutch soirées, serving herrings and genever, with models as waitresses in traditional cheese-girl costumes. The dealers and auctioneers appreciated the hearty un-French informality and everybody had a good time.

As business prospered, I needed a proper French-registered company, at least for some deals, and to keep the Japanese happy, which was why Cerbino was replaced by Axel Hammerschmidt. The Japanese preferred to deal with an established gallery with formal secretarial administration and a telex on the spot. It was time to move out of hotel suites.

# 17

# GRIMM'S FAIRY TALE

Paul Petrides had come to Paris from his native Cyprus and set up as a tailor at the dawn of the epoch of the *rive gauche*, the Paris of Cocteau and Sartre, of Utrillo and Picasso. He had befriended penniless artists and swapped clothes for paintings. He would pay for their food, settle their debts or dry them out when the booze got to them. He genuinely loved art and had a sincere affection for artists; eventually he set up as an agent. Throughout the years, he collected and eventually built up a fabulous collection of such artists as Utrillo, Foujita, Vlaminck and Marie Laurencin.

Although in his eighties, he played golf to a handicap of twelve, was a top dealer and a recognized expert, as sharp as a needle and up to all the tricks. He had been condemned in 1980 for dealing in stolen paintings and deprived of his right to issue certificates but because of his age, his four-year prison term was commuted to house arrest. Certainly, dealing in stolen paintings was not his style, and although his son Gil has the right to issue certificates, Paul Petrides remained the acknowledged expert and continued to issue certificates for a fee ranging from one to ten thousand francs but styling himself *expert pour les douanes* instead of *expert pour le cour d'appel*. This, together with the allegation that he added touches to some paintings by Utrillo, led to fresh charges being brought against him for 'false certificates and dealing in fakes' and 'misuse of the title of expert'.

I had a weakness for him although there were rumours about his wartime activities: he had something in common with Patrikiades. Each could get up to all sorts of devilry, but they had panache and never stooped to pettiness; robber barons, not pickpockets.

Petrides had become the acknowledged expert on Utrillo and remained the agent for his paintings after the artist's death in 1955. But Utrillo's widow, Lucie, shortly before her own death ten years later, revoked his contract. Her confidence in Petrides had been seduced away by her former secretary, Jean Fabris; she willed her entire estate to Fabris and the daughter, but to Fabris alone, most importantly, the *droit morale* over Utrillo's works.

This caused great outrage. Fabris, still a young man, was rumoured to have been Lucie's lover and he certainly knew how to charm older women. If she chose to leave him her goods, that was her affair, but how did his flattering attention to an elderly widow qualify him to exercise authority over the paintings of her dead husband? Three times this was challenged in court, but the Supreme Court confirmed Fabris's claim.

The *droit morale* requires Fabris to protect Utrillo's reputation. Instead his behaviour has wrought havoc. Rather than approaching gallery owners privately for the discreet withdrawal of a suspect painting, Fabris has repeatedly stationed himself in the street outside a gallery, screaming that a picture is a fake, gathered a crowd around him, then called the police and had the picture seized and subsequently burnt. So virulent have been his denunciations that gallery owners have hidden away fine Utrillo paintings and only shown them covertly to trusted clients as if they were pornography. That is how Fabris has protected the artist's reputation! There is a great deal of confusion over the authenticity of many Utrillos. When his work began to gain popularity, it attracted forgers and sometimes he would sign works of other artists as a favour. On other occasions, his wife and his mother, both talented artists, painted canvases which he signed with his name because Utrillos were selling well.

Petrides cared for Utrillo through the poverty of his early years, and fought for his genius to be honoured; due to his efforts Utrillo received the freedom of the city of Paris.

Petrides has never issued certificates for badly executed fakes and when seven paintings authenticated by him were offered for auction in London in April 1988, and Fabris shouted that they were fakes, Sotheby's preferred to accept Petrides' opinion. Fabris repeated his Paris antics in the auction room, shouting like a fishwife, 'Ze paintings fakes. Sotheby not good, no gentlemen: me *droit morale*!' He was shown the door, but went on making a nuisance of himself on the pavement. He was ignored; the sale went ahead and prices were more than double the estimates. In countries where the *droit morale* is not enforceable, Fabris has luckily neither legal authority nor professional reputation.

He once offered me ten 'Utrillo' drawings, complete with his certificates, if I would set him up in a proper office. I told him to fuck off, but first took photocopies of the drawings. When I showed them to Petrides, they were such bad fakes that he burst out laughing. And Fabris has the final say over any work which purports to be by Utrillo – at least in France!

Petrides had been living since the 1930s in a fabulous penthouse in the Avenue Delcasse across the street from the Avenue Matignon and round the corner from his gallery in the Rue de la Boetie. But now he had bought premises over the Drugstore at the Rond Point in the middle of the Champs-Elysées. He had leased the penthouse from a man called Xavier Rey who owned the building which runs the entire length of Avenue Delcasse. Petrides said it would be simple for him to assign me the lease for a cash consideration of a million francs; in other words, if I paid him key money which he could justify because the monthly rent was nominal. I said I would like to see the place, so Petrides called the Count and arranged that I should go straight round there.

'This fellow is an awkward customer,' Petrides warned me. 'His wife was a princess and he is a Polish count but he does not use his title. His family must have got a lot of money out when they quit Poland since he owns a great chunk of the eighth arrondissement as well as a whole village outside Paris. But one word out of place and you will be out on your ear. However, I know how to handle him so you just look at the apartment and come straight back here. If you like it, don't discuss details with him: leave me to tie up the deal.'

Xavier Rey lived in the flat below the penthouse; a cheerful, sprightly man of about forty-five who retained a trace of the swagger of a Polish aristocrat and cavalry officer, complete with bushy whiskers. He welcomed me with open arms and a bottle of very special vodka. The apartment was lovely and I complimented him on it. Rey glowed with pleasure and we went back to his flat where I learned that Petrides' account of the situation was somewhat at variance with the facts. He did not hold a lease which he could sell on: the original lease had long expired, but he had continued with the tenancy. Now, he was quitting as soon as he could move into his new place. A lease was available so I signed an agreement. I had my penthouse without paying a franc of key money.

The ink on the contract was barely dry when the phone rang. It was Petrides, calling to make sure that his key money did not slip through his fingers. When he discovered that he was too late, he howled with rage and frustration. Although incredibly rich, he would begrudge the loss of any potential profit. But his fit of foul temper was shortlived.

'A million francs is too much,' I told him, 'But we do business together, so let's come to some sensible arrangment by which I buy some of the fittings, and things like the pictures, for a hundred thousand francs?'

'Why not?' he laughed. 'They are a unique collection.'

That was undoubtedly true: not one was genuine. Some time ago, the apartment had been burgled and Petrides had lost two paintings – genuine Renoirs. He had shipped the remaining canvases off to a Swiss bank, but first he had the paintings photographed, using a sophisticated technique to ensure that the copies, mounted on linen and of the same dimensions, were as close as possible to the originals. I found it incredible that a man of such wealth in daily contact with fine art should be content to live surrounded by copies: he could have bought originals of less important but agreeable works. But in accepting my offer, he had overlooked the beautiful, handcarved antique frames which had graced the originals and in which the reproductions were mounted.

The next important sale at the Hôtel Drouot was of antique picture frames, and I received far more for his seventeenth-century frames than I had paid for the framed photographs. Petrides was not used to somebody scoring off him, but he is not malicious, and respected me for seizing the opportunity.

Living in the penthouse was very pleasant, but for one drawback. Whenever the jovial count felt the urge to reminisce about life in the old Poland, he would materialize on my doorstep a bottle of that special vodka, distilled on the former family estate. I did not object to these sessions, his stories were often amusing, but they were not always convenient.

However, one day quite unexpectedly Xavier Rey started to talk about the wonderful paintings which had belonged to his family. 'I still have many of them,' he confided. 'There's one in particular which is absolutely first-rate. It's by Frans Hals. I thought that, being Dutch, you might be interested so I brought this book; there's an illustration of my painting inside.'

He produced a heavy tome, and showed me the portrait of a seated man. It certainly looked like a Hals.

'And would you consider selling it?' I asked, knowing full well that the old fox would not have approached me if that had not been his intention.

'If the price is right, and on certain conditions.'

'Such as the transaction taking place outside France?' I enquired

'You do understand these things,' Rey assented.

I understood very well. Although Rey retained Polish nationality, he was legally resident in France and consequently not permitted to hold any asset outside the country unless it was declared to the authorities. I was pretty sure that this seated man was lodged somewhere unknown to the French customs or tax collectors. And, if and when the painting were sold, provided it was handed over and paid for in some other country, there would be no hassle from the Banque de France either.

'I would of course pay you a commission if you arrange the sale, but there would be no need for formal receipts or other unnecessary paper.' Rey made the situation quite clear. 'The painting is in Germany under the control of Professor Claus Grimm, the Hals expert who wrote that book, and I will give you a letter of introduction.

'I had sent the painting to Zurich for some restoration in the Swiss Institute,' he continued, 'and Grimm saw it and contacted me. He made a big fuss about how much he liked it, and he wanted to include it in his book, which would authenticate it as a Hals. Obviously I was not going to bring it into France, and since he was an acknowledged expert I was happy to accept when he offered to take charge of it for me.'

Rey wanted a million deutschmarks for the painting and agreed to pay me from his side of the transaction a hundred thousand marks commission, which he confirmed in a contract. I called Grimm to make an appointment. I thought of approaching the Japanese, but there were some eager buyers closer to home.

A couple of orthodontists, specializing in children, wanted to acquire some valuable works of art. It turned out that they were running virtually a couple of factory production lines, one in Amsterdam the other in a prosperous little town nearby. There were half-a-dozen chairs in each surgery, and they would operate simultaneously on all the patients, passing from one chair to the next. The kids were treated like bits of a machine being assembled in a factory and to make sure that no bond of sympathy grew up, each dentist would alternate every week between Amsterdam and the small town. I was sickened by their indifference, particularly since I remembered how my father, when he was still practising dentistry, would treat his child patients; buying small toys and going to endless trouble to make friends with them and help them conquer their nervousness. But the orthodontists had a very useful sideline to protect a substantial segment of their earnings from the taxman. They had set up a Swiss company which sold them dental equipment at inflated prices, thus creating a pool of money in Switzerland. It was not surprising that they were looking for investment opportunities!

They agreed to buy the painting for a total consideration of DM 2,400,000, payable in instalments, provided they were satisfied as to its provenance and authenticity. This was a lot more than Rey would receive but I was able to make an arrangement which would have greatly enhanced its value. Dr Levie, the director of the Rijksmuseum, whose authority had been so important in the sale of the Rembrandt to the MOA, enthusiastically agreed to my suggestion that if the sale went ahead, the Hals should be lent to the Rijksmuseum for five years. There could be no finer provenance for any Dutch painting than to have been accepted by the museum.

Professor Grimm lived in a little town outside Munich called Grafelfing. He is one of those faceless men who would pass unnoticed in company. I explained that I had clients interested in the painting and he was very friendly. When I called him, I asked him to prepare a signed statement confirming his opinion as stated in the book that the work was a genuine Hals. At our meeting he handed me a typed declaration that he had first seen the painting in 1973 when it was being restored at the Swiss Institute for Art Studies in Zurich and had recorded it as a genuine Hals in two publications, Grimm-Montagni, printed in Milan in 1974, and in another catalogue under his sole name in 1980. The report from the restorer showed the owner of the picture as the Countess Rey and it was illustrated in a book on Hals published in 1921 in Stuttgart and Berlin.

Grimm told me that the painting was lodged with a Munich notary, called Novak. I had brought my own photographer, on the pretext that I wanted some good transparencies, but really so that I could spend a couple of hours in the company of Grimm and Novak and have a chance to assess them. Grimm's affability was beginning to get on my nerves. It was artificial, positively slimy.

'I wish you luck in selling the painting,' he said with a smile. 'And when you do, you will pay me half a million deutschmarks of course.'

I stared at him but he nodded. 'I have this understanding with Monsieur Rey that I would control the picture, including of course the conditions under which it may be sold. I am sure you appreciate that its inclusion in my book was what established it as a Hals. Without that, what would it be worth?'

'Who owns the painting?' I demanded.

'Why, Rey of course.'

'But you see, Professor Grimm, I have a valid contract with Monsieur Rey. The painting has been authenticated by you in print. I am prepared to pay you for the written confirmation which is now in my briefcase. A reasonable fee would be fifteen hundred marks. As for your commission, you can get stuffed!'

Grimm's good humour vanished. I pulled some hundred mark notes from my wallet and counted out fifteen which I placed on the notary's desk. I wondered whether Grimm would have the guts to throw them in my face but he pushed them into his pocket.

From then on, Grimm became an implacable enemy. He had ambitions to sell the Hals himself and his first objective was to cut me out of the deal. Depositing the painting with Novak was a cover. It would never do for the respected professor to be exposed as a dealer with a stake in the sale.

Meanwhile, I had my buyers to contend with. Armed with Grimm's published opinion and the possibility of having the painting exhibited in the Rijksmuseum, I insisted that they would have to pay me a substantial deposit before we could go further. Eventually they came across with payments which totalled 750,000 guilders. From this I made an initial down payment to Rey of some $25,000. It was all very well the Dutch orthodontists financing the sale, but I was not prepared to pass everything on to Rey: the later instalments would cover the balance of what was due to him.

Rey was not very happy at my taking money up front, but he was receiving money outside the country, was covered by a contract, and still kept possession of the painting. He ought to have been well pleased, but later I found out the reason for his unease. Grimm, furious at the prospect of not receiving his cut, had called Rey and accused me of practically every crime in the book short of genocide. I was a crook who was planning to swindle the legitimate owner out of the Hals.

And now Rey really had something to worry about. The Dutch buyers, overdue with their next instalment, became very evasive. I extended the deadline, but they still did not come up with the money, and this meant that the Count was also kept waiting. I warned them that unless they honoured their commitment they would forfeit the deal and lose the deposit already paid. They confessed that they had become involved in other business deals and had overstretched themselves, so they had no more cash readily available. I was unsympathetic. Find the money or the deal is off, I told them.

What made me take so uncompromising a line was not only my disgust at their behaviour towards their young patients but also the fact that I had become aware of the nature of some of their other ventures.

The source of my information was Alain, a French police inspector. Paul and I had been at lunch one day with a great friend who was terminally ill with cancer of the liver. Each meal we had together was special; it might be the last. Beneath the high spirits there was agonizing tension. So, when we emerged from the restaurant, we were very drunk but Paul insisted on driving. He hit quite a few cars before we were stopped by the police. They made Paul drive back, although he was in no fit state, to check on how much damage he had done. Two inspectors escorted me to the station but outside I shook my head and pointed to a café opposite. 'Why don't I make my statement in there?' I suggested.

I was more than half drunk and they were amused, so they agreed. One of the inspectors, called Alain, was a Moroccan which did not endear him to the French. I ordered couscous for everybody which went down well with him. After a few beers and some wine, the atmosphere became quite cordial and they soon lost interest in any traffic offence. Having learned that I was an art dealer, Alain proposed that I buy some paintings from the police depot.

'There are plenty there,' he told me, 'and some have been there so long they will never be claimed. I can make the necessary arrangements.'

I did not deal on those paintings, but Alain became quite a good contact and would invite me home for a tagine or a couscous. From time to time I would buy pictures which he offered, minor works for which I paid exaggerated prices. He delivered useful information, such as a copy of a letter exposing a drug ring and naming the orthodontists.

This was proof that they had advanced money to one of the biggest importers of drugs into Holland and were unable to collect from him. That was their problem: I had no intention of letting it become mine. I did not want to have anything further to do with them.

So time passed and Professor Grimm continued to cast wild aspersions on my character. Rey, while holding on to the painting, argued that I had failed to meet my obligations and was not entitled to go on with the sale. He was jumping the gun, since my formal option had not expired and I had the right to find other clients in place of the dentists. So Rey was insisting that I was out of the deal and I was arguing that I was still in. But did I want to go on with the Hals? I felt it would be prudent to obtain a second opinion on the work's authenticity.

The most respected international expert on the works of Hals is Seymour Slive, Gleason Professor of Fine Arts at Harvard's Fogg Art Museum. I found that he had given a negative opinion on the painting in a book he had written in 1974 so I got in touch with him. He wrote back that he saw no reason to modify his unfavourable view. I showed his letter to Paul.

'If Grimm is such an expert on Hals, he must have read Slive's book,' he said. 'Yet when he gave you his opinion, he never mentioned Slive, or explained why he disagreed with a leading scholar.'

So with the collapse of the Dutch syndicate, I resolved to extricate myself from the deal: Given Slive's opinion, I could not feel confident offering the painting as a Hals, and Grimm would be delighted to get me out. So, if his complaints could be believed, would Rey. But I had invested a lot of time and paid money to Rey: if he wanted to cancel our deal, he should repay it. The noble count, who had received these sums in his wife's account in England and had of course not given receipts, dug his heels in. So our agreement stood, but now I was the one wanting out. And all the time, the barrage of abuse and slander continued from Grimm.

One fine afternoon I took my telephone out on to my terrace. Rey was in the apartment below, but could not overhear me. I dialled his number. 'Please, I wish to speak with Count Xavier Rey.' I spoke hesitantly and with an atrocious Scandinavian accent.

I told Rey that my name was Svensson and that I was speaking from Stockholm where the National Museum had learned from a Professor Grimm that Monsieur Rey was the owner of an important painting by Frans Hals. I could hear the excitement in his voice as he confirmed this. I informed him that the museum would be very eager to acquire the work and were prepared to pay in the region of two million dollars. Rey said he was considering selling and would deal with the matter personally.

'I am participating in an international symposium,' I continued, 'so I am afraid that it would be difficult for you to reach me. Would you permit me therefore to call you again at the same hour in two days' time? Good. Until then.' I hung up before he could ask any questions and sat down to wait.

Five minutes later my landlord arrived, clutching the habitual bottle. It was high time we got rid of any misunderstandings which might be fouling up our friendship. He toasted me, I toasted him, we toasted ourselves.

Having completed what he considered to be the softening-up process, he got down to business; putting on a casual air he enquired how I was getting on with the Hals.

'Fine,' I said happily. 'Everything is going well. In fact, I am just about to prepare a contract. You ought to have all your money a year from now.'

'Really,' he said with a smile, but I could discern his dissatisfaction. So we had another drink. Gradually, and hesitantly, he got round to suggesting that maybe, with my being a very busy man, it would be better for both of us if I discontinued my efforts to sell his painting.

'Obviously,' I said, 'it is your property and you can dispose of it however you please. But we do have an agreement, and I have invested a lot of time and money in the operation.'

He fully understood; he would not countenance my losing out. The only course would be for him to buy back his contract at a price which would compensate me for my work. So eventually I allowed myself to be persuaded into accepting DM 150,000 and the Hals deal was back with him. So Xavier Rey alone had the right to the proceeds of his sale to Svensson of Stockholm. As far as I was concerned, I was well out of the affair and had made a satisfactory profit on a sale that never was.

But that was not the end of the matter. The orthodontists had the nerve to complain to the Dutch police that I had swindled them. The police made a thorough investigation, but when it came to light that the dentists could not fulfil their contract they quietly allowed the case against me to lapse.

Rey made a statement at the request of the police while I was living in Paris and I was curious about it, so it was time for another couscous with Alain. I asked if he could get me a copy of Rey's deposition. The next day I read the *procès-verbal*, in which Rey told how he had left the painting with Grimm but had not signed any paper. He agreed it was very likely that it had been deposited with the notary. Grimm had the right to sell it, provided he first informed Rey and the price was agreeable. Rey then stated that Grimm had sold the painting for DM 1,500,000 and had deducted a commission of DM 200,000. The buyer was an American but Rey did not know his identity.

By now, Grimm's trickery was crystal clear. By interposing Novak he had masked his role as a dealer and his extortion of DM 200,000 from Rey. But Rey had only Grimm's word for price and had never been told who had bought the picture so God knows what Grimm actually got for it and how much he also squeezed out of the buyer. A dealer who had placed a work with a respectable institution or private collector would normally be proud to tell the seller. The fact that Grimm made sure that Rey did not find out, together with his underhand arrangement with Rey, point to yet more deceit. Rey, on the other hand, retained an aristocratic aloofness from skullduggery. For him, a handshake would be as binding as a contract and he would have accepted Grimm as a gentleman and a scholar.

I have no idea if the buyer was ever informed of the opinion of Seymour Slive. I rather doubt it, especially as there are a number of other paintings which Grimm has included in his book as by Hals which are disclaimed by Slive. Xavier Rey may not have been the only owner of a dubious painting to be assured that if it were put under Grimm's control its authenticity would be vouched for in his book. The care with which he covered his position suggested that Grimm was an experienced operator, not just some small-town professor.

As for Xavier Rey, he did not long enjoy what Grimm let him have from the sale. The vodka took its toll, and he died a few years later, in his early fifties.

# 18

# THE CHALLENGE

## I

I started my Paris operation early in 1982. By the end of the year, my company was well established and I was enjoying life in my new and beautiful apartment when I received an unexpected visitor.

'There's a call for you, Monsieur van Rijn,' said my secretary, as I walked into the office one afternoon. 'A Mr Otto Burchard.'

It was fantastic. I had once spent months chasing this fabled man all over the Middle East; always he had just left, or else turned up out of the blue after I had gone. Now, when I had all but abandoned the quest, here he was, calling me.

'Mr van Rijn?' The voice was soft but firm. 'I have heard your name a lot and our paths have crossed but I have never had the pleasure of meeting you. I am coming to Paris tomorrow morning for a couple of days, and wondered whether you would have some time free?'

I would have put off any appointment, deferred any travel plans, for the opportunity of meeting Burchard.

'Please, do be my guest,' I urged. 'I shall have you met at the airport, and my secretary will fix accommodation and make any other arrangements to suit you.'

He gave me the time of his flight but asked me not to go to any trouble: he could deal with everything when he arrived.

Nevertheless, next morning Paul reserved a suite for him at the Bristol, just a few minutes' walk from my apartment, and was at Charles de Gaulle.

Burchard was in his late seventies; tall and slim, he made an instant impression of a gentle yet strong character. His smile was friendly but Paul seemed a bit ill-at-ease. I greeted Burchard and asked if he was comfortable in the Bristol.

'Thank you very much for taking the trouble but I am afraid I might have embarrassed Mr Polak,' he said with a laugh. 'I have my own very special hotel in Paris. A small place – you would not even have noticed it.'

'And can you guess how much they charge Mr Burchard?' Paul asked. 'One bottle of whisky and a carton of cigarettes.'

Burchard laughed. 'You see, during the war I needed to make a number of trips to Paris. You appreciate that this was dangerous for me, being Jewish, and also for anybody caught helping me. The owner of this hotel not only sheltered me, but refused payment. Well, I was able to lay my hands on cigarettes and whisky, as rare as gold dust in wartime France, so I made him a present of a carton and a bottle. We became firm friends and that is where I stay whenever I come to Paris, and always the tariff is the same.'

To me, Burchard was almost a legendary figure. I knew he had been there when the state of Israel had been proclaimed and had been obliged to fight for its existence. He had brought magnificent things out of Egypt and museums throughout the world had been enriched because of this man's vision. I would have loved to hear his stories, but he kept steering the conversation back to my own career.

'You know, you have been quite a nuisance at times,' Burchard told me with a smile. 'Something really good would turn up, but by the time I got to it, this young Mr van Rijn had snapped it up. Or I would find that I was having to pay more than I had reckoned because you had expressed an interest. So I decided I would have to meet this man.'

I was not sure quite how to take this, but we talked easily and he admired a small Cézanne landscape I had recently acquired. As soon as I had moved into the apartment, I had started buying works of art and antiques and it was a pleasure to show them to Burchard who appreciated and loved these things without affectation. In one corner stood a display cabinet containing antiques; Burchard commented on them with the perception of a connoisseur. Suddenly, he pulled an object from his pocket.

'And what do you think of that, Mr van Rijn?' he asked.

What nestled in my hand was a small ivory male figure which I thought was Assyrian, a very rare object which should command a price of at least half a million dollars. Was this some sort of test? I expressed admiration and asked whether it was for sale.

Burchard chuckled. 'If that is how you conduct your business, you won't get far. Do you think an old man would risk walking about with something so valuable in his pocket? I had a copy made. Look at it carefully: wouldn't you say it is a fake?'

Was this a bluff, or maybe a double bluff? 'Never mind,' I answered, 'I am still interested.'

He shook his head with a smile and took it back. To this day, I do not know whether the ivory was a fake.

He had the genuine warmth of a great and knowledgeable man. Rather than go to a restaurant, I made a simple lunch which we took in the kitchen; I felt that this would be more to his taste.

'Now,' he said, after the meal, 'I have something here which you may find intriguing.' From his wallet, he drew out a photograph of a sketch of the head of a girl, looking down with a pensive expression.

I gazed at it. 'Could it be by Leonardo or one of his circle?' I asked.

'Yes,' he said, 'but what and where is it? Just think, maybe hidden away somewhere there is a Leonardo which you could bring to the market. Wouldn't that be of interest to you, Mr van Rijn?'

'Please tell me about it?'

Burchard shook his head. 'Not now. You have been a very kind host and I have satisfied my curiosity but I have things to attend to before I leave Paris. Why don't you come and discuss this drawing over lunch on Tuesday in Zurich. Shall we say at one, at the Kronenhalle?'

He did not wait for my answer: he knew I would be there.

## II

It was a cold, wintry day when I pushed my way through the heavy curtain which protected the Kronenhalle from the icy wind blowing across the lake and raking the Limatquai. The Kronenhalle is a very special restaurant; the food is splendid, but the most amazing feature is the decor. Many museums and galleries would be proud to own the paintings which glow down on the diners. I said I was with Mr Burchard, and was shown at once to a table in the centre, overlooked by a magnificent Matisse still life.

Burchard arrived with his other guest whom he introduced as Teddy Horowitz. I had met him before and knew him to be the world's most influential jeweller, with such customers as the Sultan of Brunei. He could only have been a couple of years younger than Burchard and they had been through dangerous times together in Egypt during and after the war. Yet, after a friendship of fifty years, the younger man always addressed him as Mr Burchard, while Burchard called him Teddy.

'Teddy is getting older so he is taking things a bit easier,' Burchard told me. 'He still receives customers in his office in Geneva, but he displays the worst things he can find in his window so as not to attract passers by.'

Inside, a visitor regarding the extraordinary office equipment might have thought he had entered the headquarters of IBM, rather than that of a jeweller possessing some of the world's most fantastic stones. The owner did not appear to be a man who was taking things easy. Like Burchard, he had the aura of someone who had not merely witnessed history, but had helped to create it. It was a privilege to be with them and to hear them reminisce.

Burchard talked to Horowitz about several weeks when the latter had disappeared.

'I went to Zambia,' he told us. 'I got interested in their emeralds.'

'He became the country's emerald expert,' Burchard explained.

While they were deep in conversation, the wine waiter arrived and rather than interrupt them, I chose one of the very fine vintages from their cellar. He returned with a bottle of the house wine.

'No,' I said, 'that is not what I ordered.'

The wine waiter retreated, but the maître d'hotel came to the table and whispered in my ear. 'Excuse me, sir, but that is the wine that Mr Burchard always takes.'

Naturally, I let the wine waiter pour and I must admit that it was excellent. There was the same lack of pretension to Burchard's choice of food. He started with a *matjes* herring, served on a great block of ice, accompanied by a glass of aquavit.

Burchard and Horowitz are immensely wealthy, and both had handled and were still involved in deals much bigger than anything I had experienced, yet they talked to me as if they had accepted me as one of them. Whereas some older men I have met resented me and did their best to put me down, these two went out of their way to give me opportunities to make good.

Burchard produced the photograph he had shown me in Paris. 'As you said, Mr van Rijn, this could be a Leonardo; look at the broad, round face, the way the hair is swept back and that sweet yet serious enigmatic expression. It is only a sketch, and judging from the photograph, it could be in poor condition. Even so, if it turns out to be a genuine Leonardo, it could cause quite a stir, don't you think?' There was a twinkle in his eye, but this was no joke. 'Now I don't know whether it is a Leonardo, nor do I know where it is. In fact, it may no longer even exist.

'If I were younger,' he continued, 'I would drop everything to try and track down the drawing. Of course, it might have got lost or destroyed during the war, but I would have enjoyed the chase. Do you think you can find it?'

'If it has not perished, I think so.'

Burchard nodded again. 'I have been quite impressed by the way you have chased around, spotted good things and snapped them up. Don't think me arrogant, but you remind me of myself in my younger days. But you need a real challenge, with money on the line. All I can tell you is that the drawing was last heard of in Italy. Can you find it? I doubt it. Even if you succeed, and buy it, since the Italians would not allow a Leonardo to be exported, how would you sell it and for the right price? So, what do you say, Mr van Rijn: will you take up the challenge of the missing Leonardo?'

I had not the remotest idea how to solve these problems, but I felt that if I succeeded, I would have shown myself worthy of being accepted by these men I admired so much. And I knew that if I could only get hold of the drawing, the Japanese would go crazy for it.

I recalled a conversation with Sogi, the husband of Hiroko, Madam Nakamura's virtuoso pianist daughter. He enjoyed the modern, materialistic values of Japan, playing golf and driving his Lamborghini Countach, and had been a very successful author before his marriage but Hiroko, like her mother, seems to dominate and drain others and he was never able to write another word. Both he and his wife were wealthy, but he also earned big money as a calligrapher, painting those characters which, far more than simple letters, are symbols, the gateways through which the Japanese enters the world of his unconscious.

When Sogi executed the graceful brush strokes of the word 'dream', for example, he had not spelt it, he had conjured up the essence of dreaming. A lover of calligraphy could lose himself in the simple contemplation of the character, and would not see Sogi's vision but would read his own fantasies into the symbol. The Leonardo drawing had the same evocative quality. Whereas a Western collector might object to the unfinished look of the sketch, that same vagueness would enchant and intrigue his oriental counterpart. It would cease to be a mere sketch, becoming instead the screen on which each would project his own vision of Leonardo. And from a purely commercial point of view, the Japanese museums, companies and collectors had the money and were beginning to assemble fine collections of Western art. To the best of my knowledge they did not yet possess any work by Leonardo . . .

'I accept your challenge,' I said.

Burchard smiled. 'And are you prepared to back up your confidence with something definite? I suggest you pay me a commission if you do find the drawing and sell it. If you buy shrewdly, you can make millions. How about paying me a couple of hundred thousand dollars?'

'When I find the drawing?'

'If you find the drawing.'

'I think that I shall somehow locate it, and then be able to sell it, and at a good price,' I replied. 'So why don't I pay you a hundred thousand dollars now and another fifty thousand when I locate the piece? If you are not sure that I shall succeed, it must make more sense for you to take a certain hundred thousand, while, as I am prepared to pay you that much up front, win or lose, then it is fair that I only pay you a further fifty thousand, and even that will be before I bring off the deal.'

Burchard laughed. 'It's a deal.'

Find the drawing, buy it, get it authenticated, find some way around the export licence impasse and sell it at a good profit. That was the challenge Burchard had issued. It was a hell of a tall order, and I was actually paying him for the privilege!

'Perhaps when you are next in Geneva, you might find the time to call on me, Mr van Rijn?' said Horowitz. 'There are a couple of propositions which might interest you. One is the casino at Divonne which can be bought together with its golf course, the biggest in Europe. Maybe you can find a buyer or put together a consortium for all the different activities. The other is the Petit Palais Museum in Geneva. You can buy both the building and the collection.' That was the scale of business for these extraordinary men.

## III

A few days later, I called on Teddy Horowitz who gave me dossiers on the two projects.

'The museum is owned entirely by a man called Dr Oscar Ghez,' he told me, 'who built up a rubber processing business in Italy and made a great deal of money during the war. Afterwards, he took up residence in Switzerland. He was only allowed to take out part of his money, but he managed to transfer his incredibly valuable patents from Italy to Switzerland. When he was established in Geneva, he started to collect paintings. But what made him very rich was his foresight. He invested heavily in the common stock of IBM many years ago, before its price went into the stratosphere.'

'And what sort of art did he collect?' I asked.

'He has always been very careful with his money and is not the sort of person to buy great and expensive paintings,' Horowitz answered, 'so he has accumulated a vast number of works, mostly by secondary artists. There is no real distinction between works owned by the museum and those which are his private property; that is a matter for negotiation with a buyer. Ghez is in his late seventies and would like to sell building and contents, but it is essential that everything is done with the utmost discretion. Geneva society is a small clique, very bourgeois and riddled with hypocrisy. Ghez has been granted Swiss nationality, a rare privilege; he has become a respected member of the Geneva establishment, and is expected to behave accordingly. He has been well treated here because it is believed that he will leave his museum to the canton, and Ghez plays them along. There would be a terrible scandal if it got out that he was planning to sell out to the Japanese.'

'Does he have any heirs?' I asked.

'Yes, a son in the United States with a thriving medical practice; he has even been spoken of as a candidate for a Nobel prize for his work in neurology. He has already inherited from his mother a larger fortune than that of his father so it is most unlikely that he would want to continue with custody of the museum. The cantonal government in Geneva are so confident that the museum will be bequeathed to them that they look upon it as part of their national heritage, so you can see how delicately the sale would have to be handled.'

'What sort of price is Dr Ghez looking for?' I asked.

'Something in the region of fifty to seventy-five million dollars, but I am confident that if you find a buyer for the whole thing, you will be able to deal for less than fifty million.'

Teddy Horowitz went on to tell me that the Divonne project also had to be treated with considerable tact since the owners were members of the Rothschild family who did not wish their name to be involved.

I took the two dossiers and told Horowitz I would come back to him once I had spoken to my Japanese contacts. I was deeply moved that so much trust should be put in me by a man who inspired in me such respect and admiration.

## IV

'And how exactly do you think we can hunt down this drawing?' asked Paul.

We were in the bar of the Hotel Duca di Milano, having just driven into Milan.

'It ought to be listed,' I replied. 'A law passed in 1939 laid down that any object of artistic or historic importance should be listed as a protected work. The owner has to declare it to the Ministero de Beni Culturali and it is then entered in a register. Once listed, the owner is obliged to declare where it is kept. He can sell it but it may not be sent out of the country except for short periods and then only with permission. Our drawing might have changed hands several times and consequently there could be a number of references to it in the register.'

'But from what Burchard told you, it sounds as if it were last registered a long time before 1939.'

'Even so, it ought to show up. The 1939 statute only confirmed earlier legislation.'

'So what's the problem? We simply look at the register and find the name of the last recorded owner.'

'The problem, Paul, is that there is no single register. What appears to be a simple task is made incredibly complicated by the chaos of Italian administration. You see, it should be registered with the Sovraintendenza per i Beni Artistici e Storici, but each province has its own goddammed Sovraintendenza, and they do not coordinate their records.'

'So we go to each provincial capital,' Paul proposed, 'and examine the records.'

'We may have to, but there are other problems also. The entry could be under owner rather than artist. However, in the case of Leonardo, I guess the drawing should be under his name. If we only knew in which city to look! And, of course, provided it was registered in the first place.'

'And assuming that it was ascribed to Leonardo.'

Touring would be no hardship; both of us loved the Italian countryside, Italian food and wine, and were not averse to Italian women. As it looked as if we might be scouring the records for a long time, we took a whole floor in the hotel, setting up part as an office, and took on a full-time staff.

With my brother Guy (*left*) as children in Holland.

The wondrous icon of St Peter, the star item in the icon exhibition which I organized in Delft.

Franz Hals' portrait of a man seated, a contentious subject of authenticity and art dealing.
(*Schweiz. Institut für Kunstwissenschaft Zürich*)

A painting by Rembrandt van Rijn (no relation of the author), perhaps the first authentic one of its kind to be brought into Japan.
(*Schweiz. Institut für Kunstwissenschaft Zürich*)

Patrikiades' silver dish from the Kumlucu treasure,
a marvellous example of Byzantine art.

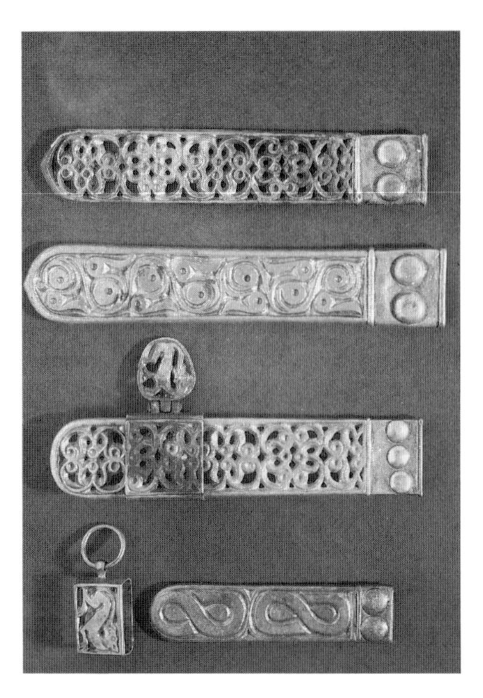

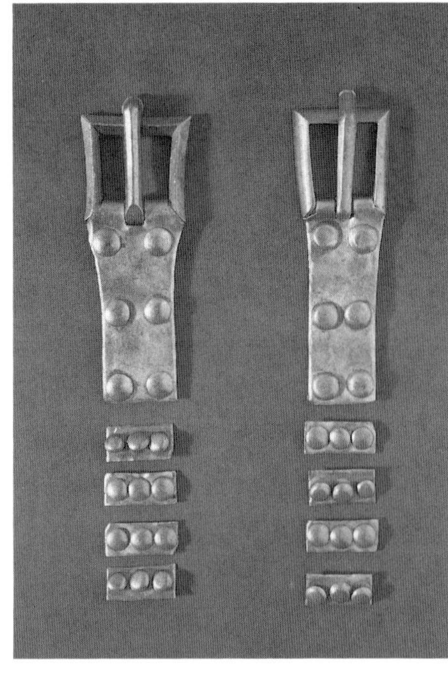

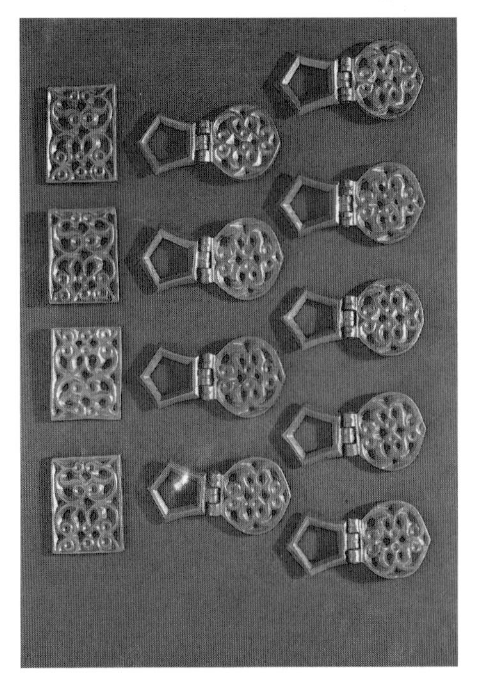

Part of the Avar treasure, a great hoard discovered in what is now Albania, more than ninety years ago.

The Leonardo sketch of the head of a girl that set off my chase
for the original in Paris in 1982.

With Professor Carlo Pedretti, generally accepted as the greatest living authority on Leonardo, and (*slightly behind, left to right*) Madam Nakamura, Mr Sasaki and Rosanna Pedretti, in front of the MOA in Japan.

With Paul Petrides (*right*), acknowledged expert on Utrillo and as shrewd as they come, in front of a painting of a woman.

'The Menil Christ'.
The actual segments are indicated, and were removed by Aydin, whose drawing this is.

Peg Goldberg and Stewart Bick visiting Holland, both here in Dutch national dress.

The missing 'Feet of Christ' mosaic. Holding the box containing the mosaic section.

The actual mosaic section in its box.

I telexed a hundred thousand dollars to Burchard's account. It let him know that the search had commenced. Even from the indistinct photograph, I had been moved by the delicacy and fleeting beauty of the sketch. Surely it could not have been ignored or unnoticed for centuries? There had to be a record of it somewhere.

'Let's start in Rome,' I said to Paul, when we had got ourselves organized. 'Perhaps I'll get a clue from Massimo's archives.'

Massimo was an official in the Ministero di Beni Culturali whom I had met casually one day when consulting records in the building. Whenever I turned up in Rome he was pleased to see me, and for my part he was a very useful contact. He was in charge of archives which are not open to the public, but Massimo let me have access to them, which meant access to the records of registered works, and a starting point for tracking them down. Massimo had told me that he was a bachelor and lived alone, but every now and then we would have dinner and I would bring him a small diamond from Amsterdam as a present for his non-existent wife. It would be a great advantage if we could locate the drawing with his help, without personally having to search local registers. Despite heavy penalties for illegally exporting 'national treasures', there is a constant flow of antiquities and works of art over the frontiers, so a couple of foreign art dealers combing registers are likely to attract attention.

This smuggling is encouraged by the sheer stupidity of the regulations supposed to prevent it, and by the philosophy of letting sleeping dogs lie which is the basis of the Italian system. Once a work has been registered, nobody takes any further notice of it unless there is some scandal. Then, of course, all hell is let loose as officials make a great show of energy and public spirit. So, if the owner decides to take a painting off the wall and substitute a copy, nobody is any the wiser. And the ultimate idiocy is that in the unlikely event that it comes to light that the painting now on the wall is a copy, the owner merely looks shocked and declares that this is the picture he acquired or inherited and he is merely an innocent victim. He protests it must have been the copy which was registered with the Sovraintendenza in the first place and nobody can prove him wrong. So the system protects absolutely nothing, except the jobs of the bureaucrats who administer it. I was fully aware that even if I were able to trace the drawing, it might have been replaced by a copy.

Paul brought me back to the work in hand. 'If we find the drawing and buy it, how are we going to make money out of it? Sure, we can sell it in Italy, but without an export licence, nobody is going to offer more than a fraction of its true worth.'

'In this country,' I told him, 'nothing is completely impossible.'

In Rome we checked into the Hassler, and I started the enormous task of searching the records for works of Leonardo. With Massimo's help I was able to locate several, but there was no trace of our drawing.

'Where next?' Paul asked. 'Florence, Venice, Naples, Bologna?'

But I had a hunch that the answer lay here in Rome. A chance remark by Massimo set me thinking on fresh lines. We had been discussing a work's authentification by a world famous authority.

'Don't talk to me about experts,' he growled. 'They change their opinions nearly as often as we get a new government.'

Of course, modern scientific techniques might modify or reverse some earlier opinion on authenticity, but maybe there was something more subtle, a different way of looking at objects from one generation to another – could that affect the views of experts? Was it possible that a scholar fifty or more years ago would be more or less in harmony with the style of the drawing than an expert today, and consequently rate it higher or lower? It was an idea worth pursuing, so back I went to the archives.

I started by searching all the works listed as being executed by 'followers' or 'pupils' of Leonardo, but again drew a blank. There was another category, listed as 'attributed' to Leonardo, and suddenly I recognized the lady. It was an exultant moment as I stared at those gentle features in an old, faded photograph. From this entry, I learned that the drawing had been registered in 1929 and again in 1932 in the office of the Sovraintendenza in Milan, ironically our starting point.

So back to Milan and the Duca de Milano. With what I had culled from the Ministry of Culture, I was able to track down the references in the office of the Sovraintendenza. There was even a copy of a postcard made of the sketch in 1901. The registrations in 1929 and 1932 under the provisions of a law passed in 1909 showed the owner as Ermanno Albasini Socrasati who lived in the Via Besana in Milan.

'You've found it. That's great!' Paul enthused.

'Not so fast,' I warned. 'There has been no new entry for fifty years although every change of ownership or location ought to be reported. Is it likely that Signor Albasini Socrasati is still alive and that he never sold or even moved the drawing in all that time? This is just the beginning of the trail.'

I went to the Brera Institute, responsible for examining works and deciding whether they should be listed, but all they had was a copy of the same registrations. We had to start searching from scratch and to proceed very discreetly. If I were to sell the drawing to the Japanese, at some time we would have to try to persuade the Italians to grant an export licence. It was important not to make a lot of fuss. As long as we did not make enquiries, the Italian bureaucrats could not give a damn where the drawing was, so I needed to find the owners without alerting the authorities.

As it happened, Burchard received his fifty thousand dollars very soon afterwards. The first place I looked for the name of the family was in the phone directory and it paid off at once. They had never moved out of the Milan area!

The next problem was how to approach them. I could hardly

phone them and ask, 'Do you have a Leonardo drawing that you might sell, or has it disappeared?' I needed somebody who moved in Milan society and might be acquainted with the family.

I had been introduced by Burchard to another of his contemporaries, and was in touch with his son, Johnny Eskenazi. As the family was rich and well respected in Milan, I explained how I was hoping to hunt down a Leonardo drawing and asked if he happened to know any of the Albasini Socrasatis.

'Yes, I see the son of one of them from time to time. Would you like me to introduce you?'

'That will be great,' I said. 'Johnny, let's make this happen. I'll give you twenty-five thousand dollars, cash, if we locate the drawing.'

I knew Johnny did not need the money, but somehow injecting a business element made the whole thing come to life. And sure enough, two days later the three of us were lunching together.

The good news was that the drawing was still in their possession. The snag was that its ownership was divided between two sisters and a brother, all in their eighties, the original registered owners, and I feared that it might be difficult to get them to reach a unanimous decision to sell. An even greater worry was that once they were approached and it became obvious that the drawing was a thing of value, how many other putative heirs might emerge?

But the young man was eager to be my ally.

'If this drawing is what you hope, how much are you willing to pay for it?' he demanded.

'That depends on a lot of things,' I said, but he interrupted.

'Listen, Mr van Rijn. I can get the old fools to agree to anything. First, I tell them that they need one person to speak for all of them, and that person is me. Then I sell you the drawing, but first I want half a million dollars, cash.'

'What I was going to say,' I continued, 'was that I had in

mind a hundred or maybe two hundred thousand dollars. It doesn't make a lot of sense, does it, to pay you half a million if the price is a couple of hundred thousand?'

'You pay me five hundred thousand and I guarantee that I can get it for you for less than two hundred thousand. How about it?'

'All right, let's see if you can perform. But I am certainly not going to hand you half a million dollars before you deliver.'

'And I am certainly not going to get you a deal on the drawing without the money in my hand,' he retorted.

'I tell you what I shall do. I will give you post-dated bills of exchange which you can hold. When the deal is done, they can be exchanged for cash.'

'Bills on an Italian bank?' he queried.

'Of course not. Bills on my bank in Geneva.'

I insisted on seeing the drawing and he brought it to my hotel. I could see that it was the real thing – not that it was necessarily by Leonardo himself, but if it turned out to be a copy by one of his followers, as I explained to Paul, it was the original copy and not a copy of a copy! I gave the family fixer the go-ahead. It was easy to dislike the guy who did not give a damn for the rest of the family, but I needed to string him along, so I drew a couple of bills on the Algemene Bank Nederland in Geneva, headed them Milan and made them payable to him by name, and that satisfied him.

However, before negotiating the purchase, I wanted an authoritative opinion on the strength of which I could seek a commitment from Gekkoso.

## V

I called Carlo Pedretti in Los Angeles, generally accepted as the greatest living authority on Leonardo. Pedretti, already well known for his erudite work on Leonardo's manuscripts rather than on his pictures, had been appointed by Christie's to write the scientific analysis for their catalogue when the Codex Leicester, perhaps the finest surviving Leonardo document then in private hands, came up for sale. Pedretti advised Armand Hammer to buy it, reckoning that since the Italian government was concentrating on coping with the devastation caused by a recent earthquake, the politicians would argue that they could not possibly spend money on acquiring some ancient document while victims were crying out for relief. In the London sale, Hammer bought the Codex for a mere five million dollars.

Hammer was one of the outstanding humanists of the age. Revered in the Soviet Union for his personal generosity and for organizing aid in the early days after the Revolution when people were starving, he was equally respected in the West where he had been the emissary extraordinary for several American presidents. Hammer was a scholar, connoisseur and very knowledgeable collector, but also a trained doctor with a sense of vocation which inspired his life.

Unlike the French, who will announce before an auction if no export licence will be given and thus deprive an object of much of its market value, the British allow any sale to go ahead while reserving the right for one of the national collections to match the final bid and thus save the work from going abroad without unfairly knocking its price. Such was Hammer's standing that, as he foresaw, the authorities ensured that no attempt was made to prevent him from exporting this unique treasure. The manuscript is now known as the Codex Hammer. Pedretti was appointed to the Armand Hammer Professorship of Leonardo Studies at the University of California in Los Angeles, a chair specially created for him as a tribute and a token of Hammer's gratitude.

Pedretti's knowledge is encyclopedic, his enthusiasm unbounded. He identified the work when I called him; it had been described in a book on Leonardo a mere eighty years ago. He believed it to be genuine but of course was eager to examine it.

'It is a wonderful drawing, related to one of Christ in Milan,' he told me cheerfully, 'and recorded as belonging to a priest called Mussi.'

'When was that?' I asked.

'In 1804. You'll find it in a little book by a nineteenth-century scholar, Carlo Amoretti.'

That was sufficient for me to get in touch with Gekkoso and, as I had foreseen, the prospect of acquiring a Leonardo met with an enthusiastic response. Western opinion of a damaged sketch of dubious authenticity, as opposed to the Japanese vision of the subtle essence of Leonardo, was expressed in valuations from Christie's and Sotheby's of £1,500 and £1,000 respectively, but I had confidence in my assessment of the Japanese response and was prepared to back my judgement with money.

I flew into Tokyo for a meeting with Madam Nakamura, Hashimoto and Kaneko in Gekkoso's Cercle de Crillon. Standing there in the club, wiping the clay off his hands, was Yasuhiro Nakasone, then prime minister of Japan, and a close friend of Madam Nakamura. He was very much at ease in this setting and I dutifully admired a ceramic mask he had created. The atmosphere in the club where political and business leaders exchanged formal suits for artists' smocks was just right for sounding out projects and fixing enormous deals, and Gekkoso were right there.

Nakasone left, but another man remained for our meeting: Mr Sasaki, introduced to me as the *homme de confiance* of Mr Shigeo Nagano, chairman of Nippon Steel and of the Japanese Chamber of Commerce, who had formed the Japanese consortium to construct the second Panama Canal. Nagano was a man of great vision, and operated on a colossal scale. He was now an old man and living in a hospital but he continued to work with vigour and was as powerful as ever.

'Mr Nagano is a very good friend of Mr Nakasone,' explained Madam Nakamura. 'They mounted an operation, masterminded by Mr Nagano, to rescue the Mazda motor car company which got into bad financial trouble. It is felt appropriate that Mr Nagano should receive recognition, a matter for which I am responsible. I am most happy Gekkoso should be in a position to acquire some substantial asset which could provide a reward for Nagano. Not just a single painting but something which will produce a surplus over its cost of fifty to seventy-five million dollars. Do you happen to be in touch with any project on this scale?'

'There is the possibility of buying a casino complex in France or an entire museum in Switzerland,' I told them, and outlined the propositions.

They listened attentively and questioned me on details.

'We are very grateful for these suggestions,' said Madam Nakamura, 'and shall talk to you about them when we have had an opportunity to discuss them. Now, what is the situation on the Leonardo? We wish to sell the drawing to the Museum MOA, owned by the SKK, so of course we shall need an expert opinion on its authenticity.'

'Professor Pedretti is positive it is a Leonardo,' I assured her. 'I shall arrange for him to see it and ask him for a certificate of authenticity. But you must explain to your clients that it will be necessary for us to buy the drawing in Italy and then to arrange for an export licence.'

'And is that likely to prove difficult?'

'I think that with the political contacts we both have, we should be able to overcome any problems. But the SKK will have to be very patient,' I replied. 'Once they have acquired the drawing, being a well-known religious organization, they will be in a good position to ask for a temporary licence, let's say for six months, in order to put the drawing on show.'

'Can we be certain that it would be given?'

'With support from powerful politicians and some money spent to win over the bureaucrats, it is very likely. I have the ear of Signor Fanfani, a former premier and now President of the Senate. Or more precisely, I have the ear of his wife, Maria Pia. He is a highly cultured man and a talented painter;

he would be the ideal person to invite to officiate when the drawing goes on display in the musuem. And why not organize an exhibition of Fanfani's own works in your gallery at the same time? In addition, I am sure that a Japanese contribution to help preserve some worthy example of the Italian artistic heritage would carry weight with him.

'But above all, we must do nothing to upset the bureaucrats in the Brera, the Ministry of Culture in Rome, the office of the Sovraintendenza in Milan, even local art critics and experts; they all get very worked up if they think some foreigner is trying to run off with part of their national heritage, and the more petty-minded they are, the louder they will howl insults and accusations. So, once the first licence is obtained, make sure the drawing is brought back to Italy and let some time go by before application is made for a fresh licence. It may be convenient if the MOA is requested to loan it for another exhibition. The second time it ought to be easier to get through, and after a while you can ask for a longer period. It may take years, but eventually the drawing will no longer be topical. The bureaucrats will get bored and you will be able to keep it out of the country. That is the only way to play it.'

'Very well,' said Madam Nakamura, 'but my clients will want to examine the drawing before they decide to buy it, and to be sure everything is in order. There has been a big scandal about the SKK – corruption, extravagance – as you surely remember. The president even had to flee to Brazil. It was splashed all over *Time* and *Newsweek*, so you understand that everything now must be absolutely correct; they cannot allow the slightest suspicion of irregularity.'

When we discussed price, I proposed two and a half million dollars, but we settled on two million, subject to Pedretti's authentification.

'As for payment,' Madam Nakamura said, 'you remember the icons you sold us for five million dollars shortly after we completed the purchase of the Rembrandt?'

I remembered very clearly. At their request, I had shipped a batch of icons worth a few thousand dollars for which they had paid me five million. No customs official or inspector enforcing exchange control would have had the slightest idea of the true value of the pieces. Part of the money had then been remitted to a numbered account in Luxembourg and the balance collected and distributed by Fujiwara and I had declined to make any charge.

'We propose making a similar arrangement to transfer the two million dollars to you,' Madam Nakamura continued. 'When you leave, we shall give you some paintings from our stock which are not recorded in our books. You can sell them back to us against letters of credit.'

I had plenty of experience of money laundering for the French, and I was ready to work with Gekkoso, but at first I was a bit surprised and embarrassed that this important concern should make such an approach. I expected them to be better organized than to call upon the services of an outsider.

'We have a Buffet and a Rouault immediately available,' Kaneko said. 'We could buy them back for $50,000 and $100,000.'

When they added a couple of fake Millets to make up the first instalment of $350,000 which they arranged to buy back through credits opened by the Kyowa, Sanwa and Mitsui Banks, I revised my opinion: they were very well organized indeed.

'And, in addition to the Leonardo,' said Madam Nakamura, 'the SKK is very keen to buy some important paintings for the MOA. It is their dream to have a collection of splendid Old Masters. Can you find some major works we can propose to them? A Raphael or a Velázquez, artists of that renown.'

I told her that I would be able to offer some works of interest, but this request did set me a problem. The MOA were so important that normally I would have scoured Europe for suitable works, but I simply did not have the time, and there was no way I could depute Paul or anybody else to undertake the task, so I decided to apply to some of the leading galleries, among them Wildenstein, whose gallery in Paris was just round the corner from my apartment.

Some days after our meeting at the de Crillon, I met Madam Nakamura in the gallery.

'We have decided against Divonne,' she announced. 'A casino would not be a suitable investment in view of the involvement of prominent political personalities. Maybe we can come back to it in the future. For this business with Mr Nagano, we much prefer something in Switzerland. Owning a museum in Geneva is very attractive, provided, of course, we can negotiate the right terms. That is what Mr Nagano would like.'

So I was given the green light to approach Oscar Ghez, and Yoko Nakamura set out her policy quite openly to me. She had already negotiated with Mazda for them to buy the building and selected pictures for seventy-five million dollars.

'Now, Michel, you go back to Dr Ghez and get him to agree to a deal at twenty-five million. You can provide us with an invoice showing a consideration of seventy-five million which we need for Mazda.'

Gekkoso would kick back half of the fifty million dollar surplus to Nagano and, after further substantial pay-offs, what was left would be their profit. But, in what would be a fantastic deal for Gekkoso, they would assure Ghez that they would reinvest their profit by taking the rest of the twelve thousand or so works from him, spread over a period of ten years, but on the basis of an agreed current valuation. So Ghez would be able to realize a great deal more than twenty-five million dollars, provided the valuations matched his expectations, and he would be guaranteed that the entire collection would eventually be taken off his hands. But Gekkoso would obtain what amounted to free stock and stood to make a huge profit over a period as the contents of the museum came up for sale. They would benefit from the higher values in Japan than those prevailing in Europe and from their enormously efficient publicity machine which could turn little known artists into cult figures. They could promote exhibitions, plugging the theme of peace, and other pictures could be added to the collection to cash in on the publicity. Since they would be paying Ghez over a period, they would be able to pay him out of profits they would already have realized on sales. In fact, they would not have to put up any capital; the whole operation would be self-financing and, once again, the great variability of art prices would be used to cover up what was being taken out of the deal. We agreed that Madam Nakamura would lead a group to come to Europe in a month or two and I would arrange for them to meet Ghez and thrash out the details of a working scheme.

Before I left, Madam Nakamura expressed her satisfaction at the way our business was developing and referred to their banking operation, Luna Trading.

'We shall be very pleased if you will agree to act as an adviser to the company,' she said.

'I shall be honoured,' I answered.

# 19

# THE MADONNA TAKES WINGS

As soon as I got back to Italy, the family fixer was anxious to tie up the purchase of the drawing but I allowed the talks to drag on for months until the details with Gekkoso had been finalized before buying the drawing for $175,000. This, in addition to the $150,000 I had paid Burchard, was a lot of money for a sketch in indifferent condition and of doubtful authenticity but I hoped to turn its shortcomings to my own advantage. The sense of incompleteness which fascinated the Japanese displeased some Western experts, so if the bureaucrats of the Brera regarded it as an inferior work, perhaps they would not raise objections to an export licence.

As soon as the deal was sewn up, the young creep was round, demanding his half a million dollars. After the way he had screwed his own family, I told him what I thought of him and to fuck off.

'I still have your bills,' he countered. 'I shall present them to your bank in Geneva. They will have to honour them.'

'Do that,' I invited, 'and with your name on them and an Italian domicile, you will go straight to jail.'

He swore and ranted, but there was nothing he could do. My own dealings had been strictly in accordance with Italian regulations. I had acquired the drawing legally, having paid for it and taken delivery in Italy. The authorities had been promptly advised of the change of ownership and informed that the drawing was now lodged in the vault of the Algemene Bank Nederland in Milan.

One of the reasons why it took a couple of years to complete the sale of the drawing to Gekkoso was that not everyone was convinced that the drawing was by Leonardo or that it was worth the $10.5 million which Madam Nakamura was demanding, a figure inflated by the various kickbacks she was promising in order to swing the deal. Takaoki Nakano, chairman of the MOA board, vehemently opposed the purchase but the power to decide whether the sketch should be bought rested with the board of the MOA's parent, the SKK, and so Yoko Nakamura persuaded the president, Chikara Nakamura, no relation of hers. All the time I was negotiating with Gekkoso, she was bringing pressure to bear upon Chikara Nakamura, and finally extracted from him in November 1983 a firm promise to buy the drawing, although there was nothing in writing and he never consulted the board.

Chikara Nakamura received from Gekkoso land and a house valued at about $630,000, and this was eventually denounced in the Japanese weekly, *Shukan Bunshun*, in February 1986; but long before that, Chikara Nakamura had been obliged to give an explanation to those outraged members of his board who were not in on the deal.

He had given his word that the drawing would be bought by the SKK, but the money had to be borrowed, Chikara Nakamura told them. He took the land and house in order to enhance his credit with the bank. He was also given by Gekkoso a ten-year contract as consultant to the gallery for Y1,000,000 a month, which presumably looked after the bank interest.

Other people said that Chikara Nakamura needed the money urgently because of unwise stock market speculation, and that he had helped himself to the organization's money for his own use, such as the $420,000 he spent to have his son educated in England.

As early as February 1983, Kaneko came under fire. I had given him a copy ot the postcard of the drawing, which stated that it was by Leonardo. However it described it as a preliminary sketch for the *Virgin of the Rocks* in the Affori Church in Milan and, wailed Kaneko, modern scholars had dismissed that as a mere copy of the famous painting in the Louvre. Logically then, if the Affori painting was a copy, the preliminary sketch for it could not be by Leonardo, in flat contradition to a memorandum I had signed. He referred me to a definitive work on Leonardo by Chiesa, published in 1967, and offered to send me a book by a Japanese scholar named Tanaka which repeated Chiesa's attribution.

Professor Tanaka, the leading Japanese Leonardo scholar, was something of an enfant terrible. He was truculent and provocative but he had been invited by the Wildensteins to participate in an international symposium which they organized in Italy on a great painting, *The Madonna of the Yarn Winder*. During the sessions, the consensus was that the probability of the work being by Leonardo was two to one in favour, but Tanaka became a laughing stock in the West when he interpreted that as meaning that 66.6% of the picture was by Leonardo. However, Tanaka insisted that the press attention was a tribute to his scholarship, so he remained a force to be reckoned with in Japan.

'There are several versions of *The Virgin of the Rocks*,' I explained, 'and this postcard was not produced by a scholar, so it simply referred to that version which would have been familiar to the Milanese. It does not mean that the Affori painting was executed from this sketch. Since 1901, there have been lots of changes in critical opinion on the various versions of the painting, but that has nothing to do with the authenticity of the sketch.'

Kaneko was still unhappy, and suggested I get confirmation from other Italian scholars; but what would really clinch it and 'help us to deny the postcard', would be a certificate by Professor Pedretti and a statement that it would be included in his forthcoming book on Leonardo.

Pedretti treated the connection with the Affori painting as nonsense. 'It looks as if it has been touched up a bit but whatever may have been said when the sketch was declared to the Sovraintendenza, it was always accepted as a sketch for *The Virgin of the Rocks* when Mussi owned it.'

I pointed out to Kaneko that no other scholar would have the temerity to contradict Pedretti so, on the strength of an eventual certificate from Pedretti, he dropped his demand for other Italian opinions.

Nevertheless, because of his reputation in Japan, I resolved to win over Tanaka when I next visited Japan, but first I wanted other world authorities to declare the sketch to be the work of Leonardo. The problem was that it was tucked away in a bank vault and could not be exported. How could I persuade these scholars to call the sketch a Leonardo without their having seen it?

My solution was to get the very prestigious law firm, Bisconti of Milan, to write to a selection of the most famous museums, on behalf of the owner, offering to lend them the drawing for display for two years and enclosing a photograph. I knew it would not be worth their while to go to all the trouble for so short a period and for a drawing of indifferent quality, but they would be bound to send a polite refusal. I purposely used one of the firm's more junior partners, Dr Paolo Grondona, who was prepared to be helpful.

The drawing was described as a preliminary sketch by Leonardo da Vinci, for his painting, *The Virgin of the Rocks*, and I counted on at least some of the replies referring to the work as a drawing by Leonardo. These letters could be produced as additional weighty evidence of the work's authenticity.

Replies flooded in from such institutions as the Louvre and the Victoria and Albert Museum, several of which regretted being unable to accept the kind offer of our Leonardo. Professor Kemp of the Department of Art History of the University of St Andrews, another noted expert on Leonardo, was most sympathetic, suggesting the Louvre or the National Gallery in London as 'the most relevant' of a number of galleries which he imagined 'would be pleased to show it for two years'. He gave a list of stipulations which we should impose on the galleries on lighting, type of glass and frame, temperature and humidity, all of which was evidence for the MOA of the value and importance of the work. But the real prize was the response from the Royal Library at Windsor Castle. Both the Honourable Mrs Roberts, Curator of the Print Room, who urged us to get in touch with the British Museum, and Sir Robin Mackworth-Young, the Librarian, thanked Dr Grondona for his letter, 'concerning the Leonardo drawing belonging to your client'. There it was in black and white, a reference to a Leonardo drawing, not a drawing attributed to, or by a follower of, or a copy of, or any other circumlocution for a dubious Leonardo. They should know at Windsor, they have enough unchallenged Leonardos of their own. And the Windsor collection is the personal property of the monarch; surely even the men at the MOA would not suspect the Queen of England of giving false attributions!

And since a favourable valuation of the drawing might also provide useful ammunition, I obtained a handwritten letter from Henri Gros, that most obliging of *commissaires-priseurs*, stating that he had examined the drawing and indicating a value of three and a half million dollars. So Gekkoso were already sitting on a big profit, if they believed a Paris auctioneer who did not specialize in the period.

On 1st March, Kaneko tabulated their requirements on authenticity. First, a document from the Italian government saying clearly that the drawing was by Leonard da Vinci, although God alone knows how they were supposed to know! Then there should be a stamped and signed declaration on the back of the photograph that this was the picture referred to in the first statement. There should be an X-ray photograph and a scientific report which would prove that the drawing, or at least the paper, was from the period of Leonardo. And the key condition, a certificate signed by Professor Pedretti.

I had already put the scientific analysis in hand. Next to the Brera Institute, which is an organ of the Ministry of Culture, stands the Atelier Brera, a private body which undertakes restoration and conservation of works of art and which has absolutely no official connection with its distinguished namesake. I knew well and respected greatly its director, Giorgio Cavacuti, and arranged that the drawing be entrusted to him; the Atelier Brera was well equipped to carry out infra-red, ultra-violet and X-ray analysis. A shred of the paper was sent by them to Dr Hermann Kuhn, of the Deutsches Museum in Munich, a specialist on dating and classifying paper. His name was known in Japan and his report could have a tranquillizing effect although all that it could prove was that the drawing, whenever and by whomever it had been made, was on paper manufactured in the period of Leonardo.

A week after Kaneko sent his list, he asked me to bring the drawing to Tokyo. So should my next move be to have the drawing inspected by Pedretti and vouched for as a genuine Leonardo in order to help Gekkoso sell it for a high price – or should I first negotiate with the Brera for a temporary export licence while it was still of dubious authenticity? The Italian state, which in practice meant the Brera, had the right to acquire the drawing for a period of two months from the official date of my purchase.

Pedretti told me that he would not be able to get away from Los Angeles for about six months so I decided to approach the Brera for permission to bring the drawing to him.

My reception was less than sympathetic. I had punctiliously observed all legal requirements; the purchase had been recorded before a notary, properly reported and tax on the transaction paid in full and promptly. But although I had not courted publicity, the registration of the change of ownership attracted the attention of the people at the Brera who ordered that the work should be inspected. Nobody had seen it for half a century so they were understandably curious to see what sort of state it was in and possibly to reconsider attribution. Ideas on authentiticy might have changed over the years and that would clearly have a bearing on the value of the work and on whether it was sufficiently important for its export to be prohibited and perhaps for it to be compulsorily acquired.

It would obviously suit me if the Brera were to find the picture uninteresting and I was encouraged when their expert arrived at my hotel where I had deposited the drawing in the safe. He was two hours late and scarcely glanced at the work. He remarked on its poor condition and furthermore pronounced that it was clearly not by Leonardo, nor one of his pupils.

'So it is not an important work?' I asked hopefully.

'By no means.'

'God, that's terrible,' I exclaimed. 'When I bought it I hoped that it was a genuine Leonardo. But perhaps the Brera will want to buy it back?'

His scornful grin assured me that I had cleared that obstacle. He thought I had been taken, and that made the bureaucrat happy.

Next day I presented myself at the Brera and was received by another expert, an assistant to the Superintendent of Cultural Resources, Rosalba Tardito. He had been informed of the negative report which had been accepted and for which I now had to pay.

'So there should be no difficulty in my obtaining an export licence?' I asked.

I was rewarded by a hostile stare. It was easy enough for the first expert to declare that the drawing was a poor thing. But opinions might change and what if he and Tardito were held responsible for the loss of one more national treasure? Suddenly the full force of bureaucratic inertia was brought into play.

'What about a temporary licence, just for a few weeks,

to have the work examined by your great Leonardo expert, Professor Pedretti?'

That was not a popular move. After all, hadn't I just been given an expert opinion?

I pleaded with him. If the drawing was such a poor thing and the Brera had no intention of acquiring it, why should I not be permitted to ship it overseas? But my persistence only hardened his attitude.

'The drawing cost me $175,000,' I reminded him. 'I am devoted to the great cultural heritage of your country and I am prepared to contribute a considerable amount to the fund to save Venice or to some comparable appeal.'

He was unmoved. It was not money in his pocket; why should a senior official at the Brera be interested in Italian culture?

'Where are you keeping the drawing, Mr van Rijn?'

'It is in the safe of my hotel.'

'But when you registered the purchase, you stated that it would be held in the vault of the Algemene Bank Nederland branch in Milan.'

I repressed my irritation. 'I brought it to the hotel for your colleague to inspect it.'

'It must be returned to the bank without delay. However, the bank will be closed now.' They were good at the Brera: they could spot a phoney Leonardo, and tell the time. 'For tonight you may keep it in the hotel safe. But tomorrow morning it must be taken back to the bank. I shall accompany you personally.'

The arrogance and stupidity of this functionary infuriated me, and I was in no mood to submit to his ridiculous ruling. Back in my hotel, I put through a call to Pedretti. He would be delighted to see me in Los Angeles and was very excited at the prospect of handling the long-lost Leonardo.

Next morning, the hostile, pompous official presented himself. I had summoned my lawyer and we bestowed on the occasion a completely spurious solemnity. The expert was impressed. He was more at his ease when my secretary, a sparkling and vivacious girl, offered him an espresso.

Prior to his coming, I had prepared two identical manila envelopes. Into one I had slipped a piece of blank cardboard the same size as the drawing. I sealed it and dropped it into one compartment of my briefcase. Then I collected my assistant, my lawyer and the man from the ministry, Superintendent Tardito's bloodhound. We trooped down to the hotel safe. The drawing was produced with great ceremony.

Up to that moment, the bureaucrat had been enjoying his day out of the office. His coffee had been served by a beautiful girl, not squirted out of an automatic dispenser. Then he had been allowed to show off his importance. Now I spoiled things by handing him this precious object. Never mind that the first expert had been so lukewarm about it: thrust into his hands, it seemed to become unbelievably valuable, and if something happened to it now, he would be the one to lose his pension.

'In view of the importance of this work, I presume that you wish to carry it personally to the bank since I have not been able to arrange insurance for its transportation,' I stated.

I had counted on the fact that no civil servant takes easily to responsibility. He looked worried. 'No, I would rather you carry it,' he replied. 'But I shall come with you.'

'As you wish,' I answered.

I put the drawing in the other envelope and sealed it. I placed this second envelope in my briefcase, in a different compartment from the first. Even if the guy had plucked up the courage to carry the briefcase, both envelopes were concealed in closed compartments so that he could not have been aware of the presence of the other envelope, but I would have known which to produce at the bank.

We took a taxi, me holding the briefcase and the man from the Brera dutifully watching me. The bank manager had been forewarned and led us directly to the vault. I produced the first envelope, signed the back of it and indicated that the bureaucrat should sign also. He solemnly did so. We shook hands and left the building, he to return to the routine of his desk and to report that the command of Superintendent

Tardito's representative had been obeyed to the letter. As for me, with the drawing snug in my briefcase, I dropped into the café next door for a campari to celebrate.

Next morning I flew to Los Angeles via London. I bought only one ticket but I was accompanied by a lady. However, she stayed inside my briefcase.

# 20

# MADONNA AT THE DISCO

## I

The flight from London to Los Angeles was not uneventful. I found myself sitting next to a charming and attractive girl. In no time, we were on friendly terms and I was resolved to be unfaithful to the virgin in my briefcase. Alas, there was an outbreak of salmonella on the aircraft. I felt dreadfully ill and had to stop the taxi repeatedly on the way from the airport and dash into cafés to use their toilets. By the time I hobbled into The Beverly Wilshire hotel, sex was far from my mind. Somehow, I had to keep my appointments but my journeys were punctuated by frequent emergency stops. I needed all my strength for my rendezvous with Pedretti; my frequent dashes to the lavatory must have detracted from my dignity.

I was given an exuberant reception by Pedretti and his wife. Entering their house was entering Italy. They are sunny, emotional people who do not hide their feelings. Carlo Pedretti has the fresh-faced look of a spoiled schoolboy, Rosanna Pedretti is a kindly, forceful woman who retains the directness of a simple housewife, makes her own pasta and runs the household. She was convinced that everybody took advantage of her husband's good nature and was quick to defend his interests.

'Do you have the drawing with you?' Pedretti demanded eagerly.

I shook my head. 'It is in the hotel. Since I have brought it out of Italy illegally, I did not want to risk embarrassing you by bringing it here. I shall be delighted if you will both come to lunch and examine it.'

Pedretti appreciated my consideration and Rosanna was concerned about my health. We chatted about Italy, but I knew that Carlo was itching to see the sketch.

We went to the hotel where they were my guests in the Saddle Room, but first I led them to the vault. Pedretti took the drawing in his hands. 'It is exactly as I hoped,' he cried ecstatically. 'You see, it is the sister to the Christ in the Brera. You have made me so happy. I have longed to set eyes on it.'

'So you have no doubts that it is a Leonardo?'

'It is certain.'

'I am most grateful to you, Professor,' I said. 'Now allow me to give you a remuneration for your opinion.'

'No, that is not necessary. Being allowed to see it and hold it has been a privilege.'

'Don't be a fool, Carlo,' snapped his wife. 'You always let people walk all over you. Why shouldn't you accept some money? It is your opinion which will make the drawing valuable.'

Pedretti shrugged, his scruples were overcome without too much resistance and I handed him fifteen thousand dollars in cash.

Next day, I left for Tokyo, bringing the drawing and an impressive certificate from Pedretti stating that the drawing was by Leonardo although there were some later additions by his pupil, Francisco Melzi. I emphasized to Madam Nakamura that the removal of the drawing had not been noticed in Italy and that I would have to take it back before its absence was discovered. The longer the lady played truant the greater the risk that some officious civil servant might demand another inspection to ensure that the drawing was still safe. I did not know that Gekkoso had not been frank with the MOA people about the complications of getting an export permit.

And not long after my arrival, a new obstacle arose.

'The certificate from Professor Pedretti,' Yoko Nakamura told me, 'is not worded exactly as our clients would desire.'

'But he says categorically that it is the work of Leonardo.'

'Yes, but he goes on to state that it seems to have been touched up by Franciso Melzi.'

'That's hardly surprising. Melzi was more than a pupil, he was trusted by Leonardo and it was usual for artists in those times to leave details to their apprentices.'

'Even so, our clients are unhappy. If the work by Melzi is as unimportant as you claim, it should not need to be mentioned in the certificate.'

Madam Nakamura was being devious. She wanted to strengthen her position against the opposition in the SKK and the Museum, so did not want to show them a certificate which she felt might not command the utmost respect. She wished me to obtain a more wholehearted testimonial from Pedretti, but was not prepared to admit that the request came from her, placing the responsibility on the MOA and implying that I had not been able to obtain a sufficiently convincing document. I was unhappy about asking a man with Pedretti's reputation to modify his written opinion, but Gekkoso still owed me money so back I went to Los Angeles.

Madam Nakamura had already sized up Pedretti as a man whose opinions she felt she could manipulate. This was the result of an earlier encounter with one of Pedretti's 'Leonardos'. My friend Roy, from the Galerie Nikolenko in Paris, had offered me a Madonna and Child which had been testified as a genuine Leonardo by Pedretti and which I bought for $2,000,000. The photographs were magnificent, the certificate even better; it was a pity, in retrospect, that neither Roy nor I had a chance of seeing the actual picture. I sold it, unseen, to Gekkoso for $4.5 million. When the painting was eventually unwrapped in Tokyo, I was mortified to find myself gazing at a seventeenth- or eighteenth-century copy of an earlier panel, and poorly executed. However I had to take it to Gekkoso, and even with their limited experience they could see it was a fake. I lost face and was out of pocket for travel expenses and for option money. This work was so bad that Pedretti later wrote to many museums and institutions, stating that his endorsement had not been a certificate but merely a private opinion, which he now renounced. I never undertstood the logic of how his written opinion would be altered according to whether it was in the form of a letter or a certificate.

This had caused the first doubts about Pedretti to arise among the Japanese, and it now encouraged Madam Nakamura to attempt to get amended certificates from Pedretti. She understood that what mattered was not who painted the picture but which name was on a certificate.

And so I found the learned professor very understanding. Of course, he had not changed his mind about the involvement of Melzi, but it was not such a vital piece of information and could be glossed over. He produced a new certificate, stressing the typical Leonardo treatment of the eyes.

'There is another little problem,' Madam Nakamura announced a few days later. 'It concerns the certificate of Professor Pedretti.'

What? The new certificate?'

'I am afraid so. Our clients feel the professor is not exactly enthusiastic about the drawing.'

I was furious. 'Look,' I exlaimed, 'here you have a statement by the world's leading authority that the drawing is the work of Leonardo da Vinci. There are no ifs or buts, no other name is included. What more can they want?'

'Perhaps if the professor could be persuaded to write with more passion on the significance of this unique work of the master?'

I shook my head. Madam Nakamura looked stern. She was not accustomed to being refused: her requests were commands.

'It would be extremely discourteous,' I told her.

'Without a stronger certificate, you are making it more difficult for us to finalize our sale.'

The truth was that she needed Pedretti to come out strongly in favour of the drawing because it was vital to win over Japanese scholars.

'If you want Professor Pedretti to write a new certificate, invite him to Tokyo,' I said. 'He will have to obtain leave of absence from his academic post, so arrange that he be requested to give a lecture on Leonardo at the MOA. Treat him with the respect which is his due – and make sure to invite Signora Pedretti.'

Madam Nakamura got the point. The Pedrettis were given the best suite in the Okura, were the guests of honour at dinners and receptions, and received lots of presents. Madam Nakamura knew that Carlo Pedretti could always explain it was impossible to refuse to accept them at a formal dinner.

Rosanna Pedretti later complained to me. She had been presented with pearls, worth perhaps fifteen thousand dollars. She made it clear to the Japanese that she believed that her husband merited every possible honour and she accepted the pearls. 'But what do I care about pearls! Why didn't they give me the money instead?' She grumbled like a child who had been given a toy, but would have preferred something else.

The schedule proposed by Madam Nakamura was truly impressive. I have never met anybody more adept at fixing things. Chauffered limousines brought the party to Atami and Pedretti was photographed at the museum by respectful crowds. Such deference might have dazzled any scholar. However, the Japanese with whom the Pedrettis mingled were not from the museum but were Gekkoso people. Madam Nakamura was taking no chances until she was sure of Pedretti. He had prepared his lecture for the MOA, but nobody asked him to deliver it. That was simply a pretext; what Madam Nakamura wanted was a new certificate.

Pedretti, however, was eager to please and he wrote another

revised certificate. More dinners, more receptions, more presents, more flowers – and a courteous request from his hostess for yet a further amendment. Pedretti restrained his irritation and complied.

Yoko Nakamura always worked through others, so it was I who had to ask Pedretti for yet a further revision to his continuously upgraded certificate. He turned to me and announced, 'I am tired of all this nonsense and am going to bed.'

But in the end we had a panegyric so glowing that a reader might have concluded that the painting in the Louvre was a mere student copy of the really important work, our drawing. I was surprised nobody objected to its being too partisan, but we heard nothing further.

## II

With Pedretti in Tokyo, it was the right moment to win the support of Professor Tanaka. He was a vociferous critic and Pedretti was very nervous at the damage he could cause. So I invited Tanaka to a breakfast meeting in the Okura.

Professor Tanaka was a man of very forthright views. The Japanese are a courteous people but they do not consider it impolite to speak with a directness many Westerners find disconcerting. Tanaka expressed absolute certainty in his own judgement. He did not defer to Pedretti and came out with his verbal guns blazing.

'I am the most qualified person at this table,' he informed us, 'to appreciate the work of Leonardo since I come from another culture and can look at his works objectively.'

Pedretti looked uncomfortable but, although not habitually modest about his own accomplishments, he kept quiet. Tanaka, as if to prove his competence, insisted on talking to me in Italian which he spoke moderately well. As might be expected from a scholar with so exalted an opinion of his own abilities, he was an embittered man. He complained that his stipend was not sufficient for him to pursue research in Europe.

'Why, that is shameful,' I exclaimed. 'My organization will be making arrangements for an important exhibition of Italian works of art to be shown in Japan and I hope that you will participate. And your research is of such importance that my company would like to offer you a grant for you to spend time in Europe. We would extend the invitation to your wife and will, of course, pay hotels, travel, and make you a living allowance.'

He accepted like a shot and, now that the preliminaries had been completed, he examined the drawing.

'I see no reason to differ from the opinion of Professor Pedretti,' he announced solemnly and from then on never uttered a word against the sketch.

For two months, Professor and Mrs Tanaka were my guests and he carried on his academic research on beaches and in shops in Italy and France. Although I gave them twenty thousand dollars spending money as well as paying for their hired car, air and train tickets and hotel bills, Tanaka saved the checks from every restaurant, and presented them for reimbursement. But we had removed a serious obstacle to the drawing being accepted.

Meanwhile, the sketch was still in Japan and I was responsible for its unauthorized absence. But Gekkoso, even though they had agreed to purchase it, kept raising new points for discussion and showed no inclination to give it back. I wanted to delay informing the Brera of Gekkoso's acquisition until the drawing was back in Italy; all hell would break out if they demanded to inspect it again and we were not able to produce it. I later discovered that Gekkoso had borrowed money from the SKK and had deposited the drawing as collateral and, since Chikara Nakamura had promised to buy the drawing from Gekkoso, the SKK naturally wished to be able to display their prized possession. My insistence to Madam Nakamura to proceed by slow stages to get approval for export from Italy had either not been passed on to the museum or ignored in the blazing power struggle going on in the SKK boardroom.

*Shukan Bunshun* ran a story that Chikara Nakamura took money from Gekkoso for eleven months. There was such a furious row among board members that he was sacked, although he went on using the president's office. With his defeat, Madam Nakamura switched tactics. It was no longer politic to back the dismissed president; her vice-president, Hyakuso Hashimoto, announced he was suing Chikara Nakamura for fraud: Chikara Nakamura replied by suing Hashimoto for libel.

The pro and contra Chikara Nakamura factions struggled over whether the SKK should buy the drawing. Another former president stated that the purpose of pressing on with the purchase was merely to divert attention from the scandals surrounding Chikara Nakamura. Madam Nakamura's champions argued that Gekkoso had spent a lot of money on the drawing; she had certainly spent a lot in buying support. If the SKK went back on their word, they argued, the gallery would be hard pressed and might sue the SKK. Chikara Nakamura's former secretary, Hiroshi Nakadomari, hit back. If Gekkoso were to win a case against the SKK, that would be a personal defeat for his old boss. Too bad. 'Now we have kicked him out, why should we buy it?'

## III

Late one evening, we were in Madam Nakamura's office. My temper was frayed; although all the conditions of the sale had been finalized months ago, the Gekkoso team were attempting to alter the conditions of payment. I could only claim final payment from Gekkoso when I had fulfilled conditions which required my taking the Leonardo back to Italy, but Gekkoso, under pressure from the SKK, were raising difficulties about releasing it. I was confident that the deal would stand. Gekkoso were crazy to have the sketch as long as Madam Nakamura believed that she had the SKK on the hook, but I had to get my hands on the drawing. So I made the excuse that I would need to see it because they had insisted that I have some minor restoration work done. I made out that unless I were able to inspect it, I would not be able to instruct my restorer and Gekkoso gladly used the same excuse to persuade the MOA to let them have it for examination. The drawing now lay on Madam Nakamura's desk. Hours passed, and I knew that they hoped to wear us down until we accepted more onerous terms. Then they could start all over again, demanding fresh concessions. I picked up the drawing casually as if to glance at it, then turned and galloped out of the room, closely followed by Paul.

The Japanese were stunned and took a moment to recover but then they followed in hot pursuit. We immediately picked up a cab. 'We are going to dinner at Serina,' I shouted to the Gekkoso contingent. 'See you in the morning.'

The restaurant was one habitually used by Madam Nakamura for entertaining. It had seats around big horseshoe-shaped *teppanyaki* tables. As I expected, shortly after our arrival we were joined by Madam Nakamura and her entourage. She peremptorily ordered all the seats of our table to be vacated so that we were flanked by her people as we ate. She demanded that we give her back her drawing at once, but I pointed out that as Gekkoso had not yet fully complied with the payment conditions, the drawing was still legally mine. We argued throughout the meal. It was quite late when we finished, but Leonardo's lady had spent so much time in a bank vault, it would have been churlish not to take her to the trendiest disco.

So the chase continued into the Neo-Japonesque discotheque, Paul, me with the drawing in my arms, and a highly agitated battalion from Gekkoso running to keep up.

The Neo-Japonesque was the in-place. Punk had hit Japan and they had taken it up with the same obsessive mania as they had taken up making cars and cameras. Schoolgirls in prim uniforms would run into the bushes in Yoyogi Park, and emerge with razor blades and other weird decorations stuck all over them. The same spirit pervaded the Neo-Japonesque. A huge rear projection screen and wildly flashing lights accompanied the crashing of heavy metal and hard rock. The music was deafening but that did not prevent the Japanese from shouting to me to be reasonable. We drank champagne, the Japanese stuck to mineral water. The sad-faced madonna sat back in her chair while her fate was debated. Paul and I took turns dancing and mounting guard over her.

It was a shrewd choice of location. The place was full of relaxed people, many of whom chatted to Paul and me. I had frequented the disco and sponsored a Miss Neo-Japonesque competition which had gone down well, so we were in our element, while the middle-age contingent from Gekkoso in their formal suits felt out of place. Even those who might have patronized a disco were caught off balance. Madam Nakamura had lost control of the situation, and shortly before dawn she capitulated. The balance of the purchase price would be paid promptly and Gekkoso undertook that the drawing would be taken back to Italy. What they arranged with the MOA was their affair but I did explain to Madam Nakamura how she could stick the sketch inside the inner cover of a book. She could tell the MOA it had been sent to Europe for the restoration work.

I was anxious to get back to Paris to get moving in my search for other Old Masters for the MOA. Then I would return to Italy and press ahead to obtain a temporary export permit and win support for exhibitions, promising good Japanese money for deserving Italian causes, political as well as cultural.

As soon as Madam Nakamura had been satisfied with his final certificate, her concern for Pedretti had evaporated. Carlo felt he had been used and resented it. Rosanna was furious. I argued that we would need all the support we could get in Italy to obtain that vital export licence and that since Pedretti was respected in official circles, his backing would be a tremendous advantage. When she realized that she still needed him, Madam Nakamura was once more full of charm and attention. He was fêted and humoured and wooed all over again. Eventually, Pedretti agreed to join me in Italy and use his considerable influence to help promote an exhibition of great Italian works of art in Japan as a way of easing the way for the export licence.

'That will mean travelling around the country,' Signora Pedretti pointed out, 'so you must buy us a car.'

The day they arrived, her wish was fulfilled.

# 21

# MUSEUM PIECE

## I

The conflict over the Leonardo in the SKK boardroom intensified during the summer: it was the issue over which the attack on the president, Chikara Nakamura, for bribery, corruption, extravagance and scandals going back long before the proposed purchase of the sketch, was now concentrated. With his fall, MOA chairman Nakano stepped up his attack, but he was reckoning without Yoko Nakamura. She worked unceasingly on Yasushi Matsumoto, the new president of SKK, whom she persuaded to buy the drawing, and in August announced that she was ready to come to Europe to deal with outstanding business.

Yoko Nakamura joined me in Geneva in September, 1983, inspected the premises of the Petit Palais Museum and we held initial discussions with Dr Ghez, following which she drew up a memorandum as the basis of a formal agreement. Gekkoso would buy the museum and selected works for a total price not to exceed $25,000,000 and would pay me a ten percent commission on completion. A great deal of work had to be done in listing and valuing the thousands of works, as well as the routine investigation of Ghez's title to building and contents. A first list was promised for the end of the following month and in November, Yoko Nakamura, with Kaneko and Sasaki in tow, met me again in Geneva.

The encounter with Ghez was tricky; he was a difficult man, quick to take offence, she was a dominating personality and her arrogance was not altogether obscured by her diplomacy. However, the deal survived this second meeting; then came the practical problems.

Madam Nakamura had impressed on me the need for absolute secrecy on the Japanese end of the sale. I had to explain to her that the Swiss side also required extremely careful handling because of the expectation in Geneva that Dr Ghez would leave the museum to the city. Also there was a legal obstacle to the acquisition of real estate by any foreign person or corporation and even a disposal of the collection to an outsider would be resented, unless presented in a manner which obscured the issue.

It was necessary to employ a lawyer who not only knew the ropes, but more important, knew all the right people and how they should be handled. Gekkoso were persuaded to enlist the services of Dr Ariel Bernheim, a friend of Ghez and of the most influential members of the cantonal administration. Bernheim did not endear himself to Yoko Nakamura by promptly demanding a cash retainer of ten thousand Swiss francs and her irritation was heightened when after a few days he required a further ten thousand francs; she liked to have every transaction properly recorded. However, Bernheim played a crucial role in the presentation of the deal to the authorities.

Bernheim reminded them of Ghez's age and the probability that his son would not be interested in the continued existence of the museum. Suppose Dr Ghez were to die without having bequeathed the museum to the city or the canton, it was likely that his heir would simply sell off the collection. Would it not be safer if the museum and its contents were sold to a major international company which would assure its continued existence in Geneva? A snag arose when the name of Toyo Kogyo was mentioned which the Swiss did not recognize until it was pointed out that this was the holding company of Mazda, and that was the best hope for the museum being retained in Geneva. And what made the deal even more alluring was that the Japanese would set up a sister museum in Hiroshima. Both establishments would be dedicated to the cause of world peace. Works of art would move freely from one to the other for exhibition. So, instead of disappearing, the Petit Palais Museum would achieve a new significance.

What was not pointed out to the authorities was the role of Gekkoso and its intention to sell off the contents of the museum when they had been shown in Japan. Furthermore, because the inventory of the museum was not public knowledge, they would be able to slip in all sorts of other things as part of the Petit Palais collection; there was great scope for what has become known as creative accounting.

The Petit Palais was owned by a company called Centonia. Bernheim confirmed that Ghez was the sole owner of Centonia and that since the shares of the Swiss company were in bearer form, when the company was bought the certificates could simply be handed over without any authorities having to be notified or any transfer being recorded. But the Japanese wanted more formal documentation, a registered transcript of Centonia's ownership of the land and building, even a copy of the national registration of Centonia to prove that the company legally existed. A suggestion by Ghez that the Japanese purchaser rent the building from Centonia and thus get round the prohibition of foreigners buying real estate in Switzerland was rejected by Nakamura since it would have removed one of the attractions of the deal. Bernheim was unwilling to do anything which might draw attention to Centonia and any possible change of ownership, so he delayed and Nakamura fumed in frustration.

More important were the questions of just what the Japanese

were buying and at what price. The building was straightforward; a three-storey structure with three additional basement floors occupying 440 square metres on the Terrasse Saint Victor in the old city of Geneva. Ghez demanded ten million Swiss francs and this was not contended. Madam Nakamura concentrated on the overall cost of the deal and it was the inventory of the museum which was fraught with problems because Ghez owned literally thousands of pictures and there was no division between the contents of the museum and his private collection.

In fact, the Petit Palais collection consisted largely of second-rate works with a fair sprinkling of doubtful paintings. Ghez had bought cheap, but sometimes this had paid off. For example, he became interested in works by Jewish artists, and consequently had collected canvases by Chagall and dozens of Kislings which were now highly regarded.

On the basis of the catalogue which was produced by November, Gekkoso chose a number of paintings for which they arrived at a price of fifteen million dollars. Ghez stood out for eighteen million. The Japanese concept was that prices should be based on what would be paid at auction, but Ghez, who had an exalted view of the value of his collection, regarded the prices set by the London auction houses as an insult. He wanted a valuation as if the works were being offered in a gallery. Since gallery owners buy at auctions, their prices are usually higher, but Ghez was prepared to accept a reduction in the region of ten or fifteen percent. An expert, Monsieur Yves Hemin, from the Galerie Bernheim in Paris, was appointed by mutual consent to provide a market valuation.

Hemin had been chosen and paid by Oscar Ghez, but I found him pliant since he was already borrowing money from my company in Paris and I bought a favourable estimate for Gekkoso from this impartial judge. Although he was promised a percentage on the valuation by Ghez, so the higher his estimate the more he would be paid, Hemin was a realist who wanted the deal to go through and he knew that the prices Ghez proposed were wildly exaggerated. When she had received the list of paintings and sculptures, Madam Nakamura had excluded inferior works, which reduced the inventory from several thousand pictures to 515 and Dr Ghez excluded some things he wanted to keep but at last, in December, a new memorandum was agreed. Yoko Nakamura would take 520 paintings; there were Chagalls, Picassos and Kislings, for example, but a Modigliani and a Cézanne were excluded when I warned her that they were fakes.

Rather than accept a lower figure, Ghez threw in a couple of thousand works by unknown artists. This suited Gekkoso since it helped to justify their sale to Mazda for $75 million but also because they had the right propaganda machine to build up the reputation of such artists. After much ritual breastbeating, the Japanese increased their offer to $17 million and invited Dr and Mrs Ghez to be Gekkoso's guests over Christmas in Tokyo – in order, as they put it, to ensure a favourable psychological climate in which to work out the details. But Ghez flatly refused to be placed under any obligation. Eventually Gekkoso grudgingly edged up their bids until they conceded the $18 million and my own commission was increased to eight percent on the total selling price on completion of the sales.

## II

Back in Italy, Pedretti had enlisted the support of Contessa Maria Guida, to whom I had been introduced by Ghez, together with her close friend, Maria Pia, the wife of Ettore Fanfani, the elder statesman of the Christian Democrats and one of the most influential men in Italy, to press our case for authorization of the export of the drawing. Maria Guida reported optimistically. She is a remarkable woman, charming and accomplished, and must have been an outstanding beauty when she married a wealthy banker. As a widow in her fifties, her social contacts were unsurpassed. She was a competent painter with a delicate, feminine style, and exhibited annually with considerable success at the Petit Palais Museum. The two women were a formidable combination. I was confident that if the full weight of Fanfani's authority were brought to bear on the recalcitrant Rosalba Tardito, the Superintendent at the Brera, she would either toe the line or be overruled.

However, nothing could be achieved before the drawing was back in Italy; and it was still with the MOA who, having made some payments to Gekkoso, continued to hold the drawing as collateral.

Pedretti came up with a suggestion. 'Why don't you propose something to Gekkoso which they can offer the MOA in place of the Leonardo?'

'Such as what?' I asked.

'Such as another Leonardo,' Pedretti answered.

'I don't have another Leonardo,' I pointed out patiently.

'I do,' grinned Pedretti. 'That is to say, I know where there is another drawing, and a very fine one too, which can be bought.'

'And how do we get the export licence for that one?'

'We don't need one. It is in Switzerland. It can be shipped anywhere with no problem. Even if you bring it into Italy, it would come in as a temporary import and you could take it out again whenever you wished.'

Pedretti showed me the drawing in a catalogue. I needed his goodwill, so I proposed that he open negotiations with the owner. After discussions, Pedretti quoted me a price of $500,000 and I made a down payment of $50,000. Pedretti estimated that the drawing, St Anne, could be sold for four to five million dollars so Paul took it to Tokyo. He was kept waiting several days for Gekkoso's decision.

'I am afraid our clients do not favour this drawing,' Madam Nakamura told him eventually. 'So they are not prepared to release the original picture and accept this one as alternative collateral.'

Their objection was the clarity and definition of the St Anne. It did not possess that dreamlike quality which endeared the sketch of the Madonna to them. So Paul brought it back to Zurich.

I called the Hôtel du Théâtre to see if Burchard was in town. My luck was in.

'And how are you getting on with the Leonardo drawing?' he enquired.

I told him of our progress, and of my now having a second Leonardo drawing to sell.

'That's very interesting,' he said. 'You know, a friend of mine, Julien Stock, Sotheby's expert, is in Zurich. Why don't you show the work to him?'

I agreed. He called Stock and we arranged to meet at the Baur au Lac.

I was struck by the enormous respect Stock showed for Burchard. I showed him the drawing.

'It is an old friend.' he said. 'Indeed, I could introduce you to the artist. He might be a Leonardo, but certainly not a da Vinci. It is a very good fake.'

When I asked Pedretti to refund my money he was reluctant but eventually complied.

All through my career, I had kept in touch with a dealer my father had known, an outrageous man named Bob Fitzgerald. I called him Indiana Jones long before the Spielberg movies; he really did come from Indiana, and his name had been Jones before the CIA provided him with a new identity. His original occupation, prior to the murky world of the intelligence services, had been that of animal catcher in the South American forests, and he looked the part: heavily built and ponderous, he exuded brute strength. Perhaps it was while stalking prey in the Andean jungle that he came across the ruined temples and artefacts of the Incas. He graduated from exporting live animals to smuggling out works of art. I never enquired into when he was recruited into the CIA or what little jobs he undertook for them in South America. But when he retired into private life, he retained his contacts and his taste for activities which blithely ignored the distinction between legality and illegality.

Now I invited him to Milan where I introduced him to the Pedrettis. The concept of mounting a great exhibition of Italian pictures in Japan as a way of influencing opinion to grant an export licence was taking shape, and Bob could approach American museums for the loan of works.

'Bob, do me a favour,' I urged. 'Say fuck a hundred times now and get it out of your system.'

'Why, for fuck's sake?'

'So that you don't have to say it when we are with the Pedrettis.'

With Bob a Midwest cowboy, every other word has four letters, and he divides people into good cocksuckers and bad cocksuckers.

'You can rely on me,' he replied with a hurt expression.

Like fuck I can, I thought, but hoped for the best.

I had reserved a table at Biffis, the historic restaurant nextdoor to La Scala. There had been a gala performance and the place was buzzing. The Pedrettis had taken their places and Bob was settled between them.

Suddenly he slapped his cheek with a resounding thwack. Heads turned. With a bellow like an enraged bull, he shouted, 'Goddammit! The cocksucker bit me!'

I felt like sinking through my chair, anticipating the scandalized Pedrettis stalking out of the restaurant. There was a momentary hush, then, absolutely unperturbed, Professor Pedretti leaned forward and gazed at Bob's face.

'Indeed? I can't see anything,' he stated in his beautiful English accent.

We burst out laughing, and from then on our conversation was unrestrained. At the end of the evening, Bob said he thought that he could sell the fucking St Anne in New York and I told him that he could take the fucking drawing with him to the States.

In fact it was bought later by Slava Dvorsky, Christie's

Russian expert in New York, who sold it for a fortune and retired shortly afterwards.

Pedretti worked tirelessly at winning support for the proposed exhibition, and with his mounting enthusiasm, having written extensively about Leonardo and issued certificates of authenticity, he seemed to think that the time had come for him actually to discover some of the master's works. There was a flood of Pedretti Leonardos and even a Michelangelo, a little *cupido dormiente*, for which Pedretti arranged that a colleague, Professor Paronghi, should take credit. Pedretti reckoned that his credibility was strengthened by his being the undisputed authority on Leonardo: to sponsor a Michelangelo might dilute it.

I do not think that Pedretti deliberately issued false certificates, but he did take a sanguine view of some works brought to him. His house was at Vinci where Leonardo made his first drawings. He ate, drank and lived Leonardo and even his handwriting was similar to that of his master. And he never paused in his output of books and articles. He would carry pen and paper into the lavatory. He had already three hundred published works to his name, his first publication when he was sixteen.

## IV

Among the works discussed for the exhibition were the Royal Academy's sculpture *Tondo Taddei* by Michelangelo, a Leonardo painting, two Raphaels – *La Velata*, whose renown is comparable with the *Mona Lisa*, and *Cardinal Babini* from the Pitti Museum in Florence – together with a number of works from the Uffizi and from Armand Hammer's private collection as well as the fantastic, full-size reproduction of the Leonardo *Last Supper* and the photographs of the details of the stages of the restoration work which had been made by Polaroid.

He rushed around the country with me and introduced me to directors and curators of some of the world's most important artistic institutions. Paolo Galuzzi, the director of the Science Museum in Florence, told us that the museum was due to be closed for work to be done on the building and we planned to display in Japan some of its outstanding collection of antique scientific instruments.

One privilege which I enjoyed due to the esteem in which Carlo Pedretti was held was when I visited Santa Maria delle Grazie, the convent church in Milan, where I was allowed to mount the platform in front of Leonardo's *Last Supper* which was under urgent restoration. I stood alone, face to face with the sublime visage of Christ. It was a moment so profoundly moving that I find it difficult to express the emotions I felt. The artist has captured the innermost character of each disciple. They are living men, not a mere supporting cast for the central figure which, although not looking at them, appears to embrace all of them with his radiance. And that calm gaze takes in the viewer also. From my vantage point it was as though I had entered into the painting.

We were not yet ready to approach the Brera for an export licence but Gekkoso were coming under increasing pressure from members of the MOA who did not want to buy the drawing, and although this hostility had not yet become public knowledge, Madam Nakamura wanted to get the deal through before there was more serious opposition, so she decided to send a delegation to Italy to hurry along the granting of the licence. The first we knew about this was a telex stating that Kaneko and Tochira Kikawa, the legal expert from Gekkoso, were on their way. They were obviously a disaster looking for somewhere to happen. Despite all my warnings, they had no concept of how delicately they would have to tread to avoid upsetting the bureaucrats and politicians.

'They insist on going to the Brera,' I said to Paul, 'so we will have to make an appointment for them.'

'Couldn't you persuade them it is too soon?'

'They are already on their way,' I replied. 'And before you suggest that we take them somewhere else like the Atelier Brera, you can bet your life they will come with their cameras and where they go will be recorded on film. No, we have to take them to the Brera but make sure that they don't say anything to upset the Italians – or if they do, that nobody understands them.'

The moment they passed out of the airport, Paul hurried them away to ensure they had as little contact with responsible Italians as possible. Fortunately neither of them spoke any Italian and they were shepherded to the Brera before they could catch their breath. They were received with great courtesy and a total lack of comprehension. Paul, in the interests of international misunderstanding, acted as interpreter.

Kaneko announced in atrocious English that they had acquired the drawing by Leonardo. The mystified Italians awaited illumination; Paul obligingly translated into Italian: 'Mr Kaneko would like you to know how much the great works of Italian artists are admired in Japan.'

'Will you grant an export licence for the drawing by Leonardo?' Kaneko enquired.

'Mr Kaneko asks whether you often give export licences for works by Leonardo?' Paul translated.

'By no means,' replied the Italian.

'It is quite possible,' Paul translated.

We are very much looking forward to having the drawing on view in Japan,' Kaneko continued.

'Mr Kaneko ways that it was a long flight from Tokyo and they are very tired.'

The men from the Brera nodded sympathetically and got to their feet. The Italians were flattered at the consideration the Japanese had shown by consulting them before committing themselves to buying works of art and their visitors were satisfied at the progress they had made. However, when I met them, they kept reverting to the question of the export licence. They needed written confirmation from the Italian state.

We took them to Rome and Paul and I presented ourselves at the Ministero di Beni Culturali with the excuse that we had some business to discuss. We timed our visit to coincide with the lunch hour. Carrying heavy folders and files, we hurried up to the entrance where we were faced by a security guard. I put on an unconcerned smile and prayed.

'*Buon giorno*,' I called.

The guard nodded, and we strode past him unchallenged. With every step along the corridors, the tension grew. We stopped outside the door of the director. I tapped on the door and waited. Nothing happened. I rapped again louder. Nobody was in sight. Very gently, I turned the door handle and peeped inside. I gasped with relief: the room was empty.

There was not a moment to lose. If somebody were to discover us now, God knows whether they would believe that we had lost our way and wandered into the office. We ignored the papers on the desk, but I grabbed some impressive-looking rubber stamps and Paul tore down a notice from the wall, printed on official paper.

Another glance to make sure the coast was clear, and we scampered out of the office. Minutes later, after passing the guard with a cheerful '*arrivederci*', we hit the first bar to down a couple of Fernet Brancas.

A few days later, I received from the Dutch printer to whom I had sent the notice, several sheets of notepaper with the heading of the ministry beautifully reproduced. We concocted a letter promising absolutely nothing, but in an officialese which confirmed that the possibility of an export licence could be under consideration. We affixed the rubber stamp bearing the man's rank over which I made a completely illegible scrawl.

I explained to the Japanese that the production of such a document was highly irregular, and was only possible due to my standing with the men in authority. I arranged with my friend Massimo that we should be able to use one of the more impressive meeting rooms in the ministry building, and the delegation were shown in as if for a conference. Then, at the psychological moment, Massimo arrived. As far as the men from Gekkoso were concerned, he might have been the director himself. Very solemnly, he handed me an envelope for which I thanked him effusively.

'No, no, for you it is a pleasure,' he replied. Then, with a courteous bow towards the Japanese, he withdrew.

I gave the letter to Kaneko. It brought some happiness into their lives.

So far, the fact that the drawing had been smuggled out of Italy had not yet leaked but some rumblings had been heard in the Japanese press and the feuding factions on the MOA board insisted that they must be confident that the licence would be granted before going ahead. So shortly after the Gekkoso team had returned with their letter, a visit by another delegation, this time including senior members of the MOA and their lawyers, was announced.

I consulted Pedretti. 'We have to make sure they get the red carpet treatment but don't have the chance to say anything to arouse the Italians' suspicions.'

The first thing was to impress upon this new contingent the immense authority of Professor Pedretti who had stated so definitely that the drawing was a genuine Leonardo. As soon as they arrived, they were escorted to the private jet we had hired, flown to Pisa airport, then driven to Florence.

The party were ushered into a dignified, panelled room, the conference room at Giunti, Pedretti's publishers. All around were copies of his works, many of them enormous, beautifully bound in rich leather and so specialized that the limited imprints sold for thousands of dollars. There were copies of manuscripts, facsimiles, reprints from learned journals – it was a breathtaking display. I had spent the previous day staging it. And there, amid this veritable library, they were presented to the professor himself. Pedretti was very nervous because of the doubts being expressed in Japan and his own profligacy in handing out certificates, but the meeting went well.

But it was not all plain sailing. The Japanese were delighted by their reception but they wanted to deal with their request for an export licence. I had arranged that the formal business would be dealt with at once in this most favourable setting. They intended not only to check on Pedretti but to control every single document, and then to my horror one of them produced the letter we had fabricated.

I felt poised on the verge of exposure. Pedretti, who of course had not been implicated, took the letter and glanced at the indecipherable scrawl with which it was signed, but he recognized the rubber stamp.

'The director who signed this letter was a great friend of mine,' he exclaimed. 'He died three months ago,' he explained as he handed the letter back.

I felt a great surge of relief. It was an unbelievable stroke of luck that the director had been a friend of Pedretti and that, by his remark, he had unknowingly made sure that the letter was accepted without question. Everybody expressed their condolences, nobody else even glanced at the letter and the topic of the export licence was laid to rest for the time being.

That evening, I laid on a cocktail party on the Piazza Pomadoro with its fantastic panorama of Florence. We went on to a reception I had organized at the Excelsior Hotel, complete with the directors of the Uffizi and the Museum of Science.

In Rome there was another reception in honour of the Japanese at the Ministero di Beni Culturali; in Milan they were presented with the medallion of the city. Pedretti scurried about. His influence and reputation were all the greater now that he was about to be appointed cultural adviser to the Italian government, and he ensured that our guests were treated handsomely. Rumours were rife: they had come to support the Save Venice fund. Wasn't it Sony who had put up the big money to preserve the Leonardo *Last Supper*, although Polaroid scooped the publicity? And as long as the Italians were convinced that the Japanese had come as benefactors, they went on fêting them and asking no questions. The Japanese returned, certain that the problem of getting an export licence was a triviality.

Soon after this delegation got back to Tokyo, the Petit Palais negotiations came to a premature conclusion. A scheme had been devized by which the Japanese would form a charitable foundation in Switzerland to purchase the building and the agreed paintings. Maître Bernheim was confident he could obtain official authorization as long as the ultimate purchaser was Mazda, whom they believed would protect and even expand the collection. It was proposed that some gaps could be filled by purchases from private collectors. The Japanese would then found the parallel museum in Hiroshima, owned by the same foundation. Negotiations dragged on, complications mounted and tempers became frayed. In August, Madam Nakamura complained that she and Dr Ghez had agreed that 550 paintings of her choice would be transferred but only 518 had been confirmed. As with the Leonardo negotiations, she hid behind her client who, she averred, had objected to the discrepancy. There were differences in the catalogue which had been prepared for works from Geneva to be shown in a Petit Palais exhibition in Japan between the list of paintings which were to be bought and those to be shipped for the exhibition.

Then quite suddenly the whole project came to a halt. Most inconsiderately, in September 1984, Nagano, the intended beneficiary, did what all retired tycoons eventually do. He died, and Madam Nakamura's design for the museum was shelved. Gekkoso was later the target of so much bad publicity that it was never revived.

If Ghez had donated the museum to the canton of Geneva it could have been transformed into a foundation which would have constituted a worthy tribute to him and his family. He was wealthy far beyond his requirements so did not need this deal. Madam Nakamura was only too happy for the inflated price, concocted to conceal all the kickbacks, to be publicized. It exaggerated the importance of the museum and its collection. With the Mazda name and the dedication to world peace, the scheme would have brought her great prestige, profit and, above all, power.

# 22

# VENI, VIDI, VINCI?

## I

In spite of everything, Yoko Nakamura persevered with the sale of the Leonardo to the MOA. She was blessed with extraordinary ability, but the fatal flaw in her character was an intolerance which shaded into outright arrogance, and that made her many enemies.

Even after the triumphant return from Italy of the MOA delegation, Takaoki Nakano, chairman of the MOA board, remained bitterly opposed to the purchase and Pedretti was beginning to regret the fulsomeness of his endorsement; he was embarrassed by this mounting controversy while his appointment as adviser to the Italian government was still under consideration. When he disclaimed his opinion on the painting which we had brought from Paris, Pedretti said he did not issue certificates. That could have undermined the drawing's credibility. Madam Nakamura responded by offering it for $7.5 million to Armand Hammer, enclosing of course Pedretti's latest and most glowing certificate. It was an astute move. Hammer could have paid for it out of petty cash, and of course Pedretti could not simply disown the sketch to his patron. But Hammer did not want it, nor did

Madam Nakamura want to sell it to him; she had the MOA on the hook for a higher price, but she brought Pedretti back into line.

At a meeting of the MOA board on 12th August 1985, Nakano expressed his opposition to SKK President Matsumoto's decision. He did not believe the drawing to be an original Leonardo, he was sceptical about getting permission to have it permanently in Japan, and felt that ten and a half million dollars was wildly excessive. The board voted to advise against buying, but the decision rested with the SKK, whose president Madam Nakamura was clearly able to manipulate.

Still, the MOA people did represent the art professionals and had to be taken seriously. The SKK board met on 24th August, and Matsumoto revealed that they were morally committed to honour the verbal undertaking given by his predecessor of which at least some of the board claimed to be unaware. No decision was taken, but the SKK was scared of yet more scandal, so they agreed to extend a series of loans to the gallery, against works of art as collateral. Meanwhile Nakano and his supporters launched a press campaign against the drawing and the people at the Brera flipped when they read in a Japanese newspaper in August 1985 that it was in the Japanese museum.

So, in September, Angelo di Palermo, a canny lawyer from Milan retained by Madam Nakamura, informed the Brera that the drawing was now the property of Gekkoso and would be deposited in Barclays Bank in Milan. At his request, a new purchase agreement was drawn up with me, showing the price not as $2 million, which was what Gekkoso actually paid, but $500,000, since they thought this would improve their chance of getting an export licence.

After the formal declaration that Gekkoso had bought the drawing, there was a celebratory dinner in Milan. The Japanese were present in force, and of course the Pedrettis. Rosanna Pedretti was outraged when she heard that the drawing was being sold for ten and a half million dollars. She was indignant that the world did not reward her husband adequately for his enormous industry and scholarship.

The report that the drawing was in the vaults of the MOA was strenuously denied but Di Tardito had her doubts and called on Gekkoso to produce it. But by now, the Madonna was a seasoned jetsetter and she popped up on 6th November at the Brera, escorted by SKK's lawyers, Tochira Kikawa, Bakoto Sakaoka and Haruki Iwamori.

One thing was sure. If the MOA were to be bullied or persuaded into taking the Leonardo, they would want it hanging in their museum in Atami, and the complexities of obtaining an export permit had not been properly presented to them. The situation was too serious. So after it had been inspected by the Brera, the sketch was extracted from the safe and a reproduction substituted. Yoko Nakamura denied taking it out of the country, but being a prudent woman, insured it with the Tokyo Marine Insurance Company. And in her own name!

On his return to Japan, Sakaoka gave a very indiscreet lecture in which he bragged of having brought the drawing back to its rightful owners after having substituted the copy. A student in the audience taped his remarks and they later filtered through to journalists.

## II

Nakano's supporters leaked to the press that the MOA had started paying Gekkoso; this alarmed the bank, which called in the loan it had made to Gekkoso to acquire the drawing, so the gallery pressed the SKK for further support. In October, SKK's lawyer, Tochira Kikawa, advised that they buy the drawing but despite his position as president, Matsumoto was unable to push the purchase through and a compromise was reached by which further loans were extended, enabling Gekkoso to repay the bank.

Yoko Nakamura waged her own propaganda campaign: if the museum did not buy the sketch, it would be relegated to a second-rate institution, said Gekkoso's lawyers, and quoted Pedretti's endorsement. Nakano retaliated by trying to discredit Pedretti. Jinji Kubo, Professor of Italian Renaissance Art at Nigata University, said he had never heard of a sketch for the head of the Madonna and could not believe it authentic. Professor Kazuhiro Susowake, a friend of Pedretti, suggested apologetically that he was surprised that Pedretti should have spoken out because he was really an expert on Leonardo manuscripts, not his paintings. The learned professor, at least as reported in the Japanese press, apparently did not know that the work in question was a drawing, not a painting.

# 23

# WHITEWASH AND BLACK MONEY

Throughout 1984, I was virtually commuting between Italy and Japan in our attempt to clinch the Leonardo deal, with frequent visits to Geneva for the Petit Palais Museum negotiations and occasional trips to London or New York. But the centre of my activity remained Paris. From the French dealers, galleries and auctioneers I was able to get material for Japanese clients while they, in addition to regular deals, were only too pleased to have a ready channel for bleaching their black money white.

We had regular customers for this service among the most distinguished members of the *Compagnie des Commissaires-Priseurs de Paris*. Many people preferred to deal with me rather than through the auctioneers, which would leave an official record. For an important work, they knew they were unlikely to get an export licence and this would be reflected in the price they would obtain, but I would pay them considerably more since our system turned the French-owned painting into a foreign import. These pictures would be bought by the *commissaires-priseurs*, absorbing their black money which was perfectly acceptable to me since I could use it for buying more black paintings. Then the paintings were brought by me to the *entrepôt douanier* at Charles dc Gaulle airport, where they were deposited and declared as entering France from abroad.

The paintings were collected by the *commissaire-priseur* as legal imports which he would then sell, and since the paintings had come in from a foreign country 'legally', remit the proceeds of the sale which ended up in his Swiss bank account.

One important client who benefited from our overseas connections was the Galerie Aimé Maeght. They had large stocks of works by such artists as Chagall, for whom they had acted as exclusive agent, but as Monsieur Maeght grew old, the driving force in the firm was the manager, Daniel Lelong, and when Maeght died, a power struggle broke out between his son and Lelong. Lelong quit the gallery and set up his own, which he called Galerie Maeght Lelong. The rivals squabbled over the allocation of works in the inventory and the younger Maeght took legal action to force Lelong to drop the name of Maeght from his firm. However, while I was active in Paris there was both a Galerie Maeght and a Galerie Maeght Lelong and I had dealings with both.

I bought a lot of unsigned etchings by Chagall, from the original Galerie Aimé Maeght and, when I started a collection for my daughter, I purchased some interesting works for her, such as etchings and lithographs by Chagall, Picasso and Léger, from the successor gallery Daniel Lelong. I was such a good client of Lelong that he offered me first option of buying ten complete series of *Vue sur Paris*, the last suite of lithographs made by Chagall, which was limited to fifty sets, and each set worth a small fortune.

I bought a lot of works from Galerie Aimé Maeght and paid in instalments by depositing bills of exchange drawn on Paris for several million francs with the gallery.

I had a somewhat different arrangement with Lelong. With the division of the original gallery's inventory, he had managed to get some works which he had never disclosed, so although I took them from him in France, it suited him to take bills of exchange drawn on Geneva, where I paid him, thus leaving no record in France.

Henk Slis, an old contact, brought me a gouache bearing

the signature of Joan Mirò. I wanted to sell it to a Japanese collector, but first to have it examined and pronounced geniune or fake. In his will, Mirò had empowered a compatriot, Luis Juncosa Iglesias, with the supervision and protection of his works, and he had passed on the power to adjudicate in Paris to a director of the Galerie Maeght Lelong, Jacques Dupin, so I sent it to the gallery for adjudication.

Daniel Lelong called me. 'This gouache, Michel, Dupin says it is a fake. It has to be destroyed, you understand. But, my friend, I have managed to keep your name out of it.'

At that time I did not suspect Slis but thought that the fake had been passed off on to him. With the order for its destruction, I thought I had heard the last of the 'Mirò'. I was to be proved mistaken on both counts.

In January, 1985, I took a portfolio of works by Foujita, Marie Laurencin and Chagall to Zurich. I was accompanied by Slis and two friends, Peter and Richard, and the three of them made the rounds of the galleries, offering some Chagall etchings, bought from the Galerie Aimé Maeght. The owner of one gallery which had been visited by Henk Slis called me.

'I would like to keep these Chagalls overnight and show them to Lelong's office here. Do you have any objection?'

'None at all,' I answered. 'Go ahead.'

I was certain that the etchings were genuine as I had bought them from the Galerie Aimé Maeght, and I was sure that this would be confirmed from Lelong's records. It would have been the height of folly for me to allow them to be examined by the one gallery where they would be denounced if I had the slighest suspicion there was anything wrong with them.

The next day I made a trip to Geneva, leaving my stock in the hotel room which the boys were free to use. Slis had returned to Paris, but I called from Geneva to check on what was going on. I asked for Richard but was put through to the manager.

'Monsieur van Rijn, there has been a great scandal here. I am afraid that your friends are in police custody.'

He told me how Richard and Peter had been in the hotel

when a horde of police had descended and arrested them. 'They were dragged through the lobby in handcuffs in front of everyone,' he told me in a shocked voice. 'And the police have taken everything from your room. I guess that they will be looking for you, too,' he added apologetically.

I immediately called a lawyer I knew in Geneva and he agreed to see me at once. I explained that I wanted him to act for my friends and to obtain their release.

'But why have they been detained?' he asked.

'I would very much like you to find out,' I answered.

He put through a few calls and informed me that there had been a complaint from Lelong's gallery about some Chagall etchings which had been shown to them and which it was alleged were my property.

'I don't understand. The etchings were genuine,' I said.

'Precisely, Monsieur van Rijn. But the artist's signature on them was not.'

'They were unsigned,' I protested.

'If you say so, but it appears that by the time they arrived at the gallery they had been signed by somebody.'

I was in a difficult situation. The Swiss were clearly going to prosecute and it would be impossible for me to prove that I had not forged the signature since I had a shrewd idea that Slis would swear that I had, and it would be his word against mine. Since the complaint was lodged in Switzerland, it would be a fair assumption that the offence was committed there also, so it seemed sensible for me to get the hell out of the country. So, having made arrangements for the lawyer to get my friends out of prison, I drove into France.

But this was only the beginning of my troubles. The Swiss police eventually returned the works they had seized to the Galerie Aimé Maeght and I phoned them to enquire how much I owed them on my account. They insisted that the balance due to them was 1,400,000 francs. I knew this was impossible, but they steadfastly refused to credit me with the works which had been returned. A case was brought against me although the bill was drawn by the Paris-based company Axel Hammerschmidt where I only had an authorized signature. But I was heavily engaged in following up the Leonardo proceedings. This was not the time to get further involved in denunciations and counter denunciations in Paris, so I quit my apartment and moved out of France.

As for Lelong, he promised to return to me in Paris the bill maturing in February which I had paid in Zurich but he came under official investigation for suspect currency offences and did not dare admit that he had been paid in Switzerland for the bills, so denounced me for failing to honour the bill when it matured.

Police investigations and accusations of fraud sent shivers of fear down the spines of the gallery owners and *commissaires-priseurs* with whom I had dealt and for whom I had shipped money out of France.

A case was cobbled together against me, accusing me of defaulting on the bill. In France, drawing a cheque or a bill without sufficient provision in the bank is a criminal offence, so now I had a problem in France as well as Switzerland. But since the bill was drawn on Geneva in favour of Galerie Maeght Lelong in Zurich, it is still a mystery to me how the French could have the nerve to claim jurisdiction. It was their policy to get a judgement against me, so they rushed the case to court without making any attempt to contact me and give me the opportunity to defend myself. I was condemned to four years' imprisonment, in absentia, and an Interpol warrant issued for my arrest.

On the warrant, my address in Marbella where I was by then living was quoted; it was known all the time to the authorities, so it had to be an act of deliberate policy that they concealed from me that they were bringing an action against me. To boost up the warrant, every possible wild allegation was included. They accused me of driving my Rolls-Royce and my Bentley in order to give a false impression of wealth. No charge was too ridiculous for the French to include.

Their aim, of course, was to obtain information of the number accounts in Switzerland of the art dealers and later, as soon as they thought they had me in their power with the threat of extradition, they proposed a deal, which I, of course, declined.

Their perusal of my records yielded no incriminating documents. But I did have, and still do possess, the statements from Mitsui for pictures stating that cheques were made out in settlement to Galerie Maeght Lelong and the covering letters indicating that the same cheques, drawn on the Banque Française du Commerce Extérieur, had been delivered. Any auditor searching for the receipt of such cheques in Lelong's Paris books would never be able to trace them, but he would have more luck if he were able to gain access to the records of their Swiss bank account.

# 24

# ¡BIENVENIDO A ESPAÑA!

## I

Back home in Holland, I reviewed my situation. In Switzerland, I was wanted by the police and with the threat of Lelong's using my bill of exchange against me and the unravelling of our money laundering activities, it would only be a very short time before I would have trouble in France also, while the Italians were intent on prosecuting me for the illegal exportation of the Leonardo. The obvious base for me in Europe was my own country, but the Dutch police were also looking for me, following the complaints lodged by the drug-running dentists.

'Why don't you go to live in Spain?' suggested Gino, my Italian secretary and assistant in Paris; Gino was trustworthy and loyal. He knew a lot of people and it was because of his contacts that he recommended my moving to Marbella.

Gino had already spoken of me to Felice, a fellow Sicilian, a man of great wealth, with a lot of interests in many countries. He was the head of a group which owned casinos throughout the Caribbean and elsewhere and his activities were widespread. He was a warm, direct man and, as I was to discover, whenever he promised something, he delivered. Once he had accepted a person, his loyalty was unwavering.

'There is a whole group of important people in Marbella who know and respect Felice and who work together,' Gino urged. 'It is like a private club. They dine or sail or play golf together, but they do serious business as well. You would be accepted at once with Felice as your sponsor.'

I had already acquired one useful asset thanks to Gino. He had introduced me to an organization known as the Knights of Malta and I had become a member. Influential people had formed the order which acted as a network rather in the manner of the Freemasons; the name invoked the image of the crusading order of St John of Malta, with which it was frequently confused. I acquired a diplomatic passport as a member of the Knights of Malta and was appointed minister plenipotentiary to Japan. I had no difficulty in flying out of Schiphol on this absolutely unofficial 'passport' and was given VIP treatment despite the police enquiry and there actually being a warrant for my arrest.

Gino was right about the Marbella group: they were like the kernel within the juicy nut of Marbella society. They knew everybody and could fix virtually everything. Among the Italians were members of the most powerful masonic lodge, the legendary P24, which embraced the top ministers, clerics and bankers. Their influence permeated the Vatican where they were able to hide Roberto Calvi after the collapse of his Banco Ambrosiano for three years, and Ruiz Matteos, whose Rumasa empire in Spain had been seized by the Socialist government, was given shelter. I knew that I would need protection once the French tried to get their hands on me. Because of the threat of ETA terrorism with its claim for Basque independence, France and Spain had done a deal by which extradition between the two countries was almost automatic and I was not yet ready to face the charges which would be brought against me in France.

Felice certainly got things moving. I was met at Malaga airport and driven to the house which had been taken for me, a magnificent villa beside a lake, nestling among trees on the hills overlooking Marbella and the sea. A fine golf course was conveniently close, my Rolls Corniche and Bentley Turbo had been driven from Paris, and a staff of South Americans had been enrolled, together with a superb Italian chef.

The evening of my arrival, I called the majordomo.

'I am going out for dinner,' I told him. 'I want you to take care of this suitcase.'

I had not travelled with much luggage, but I did bring more than a million dollars in cash which I now entrusted to him. I knew it would be reported to Felice, and it was my way of sending a signal that I trusted him and his men a hundred percent.

That night, I invited Felice to dine with me and he arrived with his aides. I approved of the way they were not dismissed to an inferior table and found that Felice was not impressed by rank or status. He was regarded with respect and real affection by those who worked for him, a man who had not lost his roots. He still had his bread flown in from Sicily. He was a handsome, soft-spoken man in his fifties. However, he did not beat about the bush. His answer to any request was immediate and direct. 'Yes' meant that he would perform without qualification, while if he did not wish to do something, he would say so straight out. Clearly, he had immense power. Everybody of importance passed through his house, received with the same frankness and seriousness. But he liked to go out early to market and choose his own food and often cook it himself, preferring this to eating in restaurants or living it up at Marbella's endless round of all-night parties. We talked easily through the meal and after the usual toasts, Felice rose, took my glass in his hand and saluted me: '*A nostra amisticia*!' Then he drank from my glass and handed it back. As I raised it to my lips, everybody stood and drank to our friendship. I had been accepted into a true band of brothers.

Life in Marbella was totally unreal, a sort of Hollywood setting for the rich, the famous, the glamorous, as well of course as for a ravening horde of hangers-on. The pages of the *Marbella Times* and *¡Hola!* were packed with descriptions of parties and the same list of names. You might see Jackie Collins in Regine's in Puento Romano or Sean Connery teeing up on the Aloha golf course. There would be a millionaire's cocktail party on Kashoggi's yacht, while suddenly the road might be blocked by police because the King of Morocco had dropped in for dinner at Club 31. Professional hostesses were in demand, and the likes of Gunilla von Bismarck were virtually professional guests. German princes and barons were being eclipsed by oil sheiks but men like the brothers Flick who had sold out Daimler Benz were still worth the odd hundred million dollars.

It was impossible for the passer-by not to notice King Fahd's enormous villa in the hills with his guest house, a replica of the White House. He had built a splendid modern mosque on the other side of the highway, so he constructed a bridge for himself and his guests.

The so-called Golden Mile comprised the five miles from Marbella to Puerto Jose Banus and was lined with beaches with their casual *chiringuitas* where the rich could pursue the simple life, eating barbecued fish and absorbing sunshine and the golden Esmeralda wine from Catalonia. Standing out like jewels were the Marbella Club and Puento Romano, among the most sumptuous hotel complexes in Europe, both bought by the Arab financier, Asmai. Days would be whiled away by their pools or on the golf courses or paddle tennis courts. In the evenings one could dance at Regine's or Olivier's in Puerto Banus or at Jimmy's in the Marbella Club. The casinos did a roaring business and young girls would come aboard any expensive yacht lying at anchor, uninvited but on offer to anybody who could afford such a boat. Indeed, the opulence had a seedy side, turning simple girls into prostitutes.

For the aficionado, as I am, there was the chance to see the most celebrated bull fighters in Spain.

One could enjoy the most fabulous cuisine from Roger Verger, while for those who preferred the customs of the country, there were flamenco joints, sometimes quite authentic

Andalusian tavernas where the music and the wine were rough and full-blooded. Of course, there were others with stamping men and flaunting women where you could buy a glass of water for the price of whisky! For the rich and overweight, there was the Buchinger Clinic, where the same glass of water was even more expensive.

## II

But there was a serious side to my life in Spain. I was busy with sales all over the country and there were big auction houses in Madrid and Barcelona where there were also important art fairs. I was still working on winning an export licence for the Leonardo and had become Felice's expert in art. In his open manner, he had suggested we go to Japan together.

'You know the country and have good connections there, Michel. The place appeals to me for business, but it is not part of my customary territory. Would you show me around and introduce me to people?' I was pleased to be of service, and he got to know Yoko Nakamura and the Gekkoso set-up.

Meanwhile, I had stayed in contact with Bob Fitzgerald and he came to visit me. Although not involved in the sale of the Leonardo drawing, he watched developments carefully. If Japanese investors would pay more than ten million dollars for such a sketch, Bob reckoned they should be cultivated. And, despite his failure with 'the fucking St Anne', he believed that the name of Pedretti on a certificate would command the respect in Japan which would enable us to sell more Leonardos there.

'Look, Michel,' he proposed. 'I know that if you show your face outside Spain you can be thrown into the fucking slammer, so why don't I go to Tokyo and handle that end of our business? There are a whole series of Leonardo drawings being offered in London. Let's get Felice to put up the finance and I'll sell to your goddammed Japanese. What do you say?'

I looked at the photographs and shook my head. 'It won't work, Bob. The Madonna was a sweet, pretty girl: it had a sort of mysterious charm which the Japanese adore. What you have here are caricatures of ugly old men. For the Japanese, they are like wicked demons. They simply will not sell in Japan.'

'But with Pedretti?'

'Forget it.'

'It's still the same cocksucking Leonardo, isn't it?'

'That's not the way they'll look at it.'

Bob looked unconvinced but dropped the subject. He disappeared, but a few days later Felice called me from Switzerland.

'This guy Fitzgerald, is he your partner?'

'We're buddies and we share certain deals, you understand. But also we each have our own business.'

'Well, he has suggested that he and I do business together with Japan. He wants me to put up the money to buy a statue supposed to be by Leonardo – at any rate it has a Pedretti certificate to say so.'

Felice had learned not to put too much confidence in such certificates.

'You will forgive me for not talking to you sooner, but Fitzgerald asked me not to say anything to you. I wanted to find out what he was up to, so I agreed for the time being. Fitzgerald has an associate in the deal, a man called Nickerson.'

'I know him,' I said. 'He owns the Mallett Gallery in London.'

'I met them at my bank in Lugano,' continued Felice. 'They have a scheme to sell the statue to Japan, but first to use it as a mould. Fitzgerald seems to think they can sell plenty of copies this way. I do not approve of the way he has tried to go behind your back. As far as I'm concerned, Michel, you are my man in art. The piece is in my bank and is at your disposal. If you wish to sell it, the only condition I would expect you to observe is that the owner should be paid what is due to him. Otherwise, you are free to keep whatever you can make on it.'

'I would regard you as my associate, Felice,' I assured him.

'No, this would be your deal. If Fitzgerald wants to sell the statue, he has to do it through you. You had better explain to him that he made a big mistake if he thought I would go behind the back of my friends.'

I am sure that if Bob had pulled off the deal without me he would have been delighted but would have handed me some money afterwards, not a full share, and have refused to talk about the operation. It was not possible to explain our relationship to Felice, whose loyalty was absolute. We could work together and we understood each other but with Bob, you always had to watch your back. And this was fine with me since it gave me a certain latitude even when we were co-operating.

Bob had discovered that what I had told him about the old men sketches was true. Gekkoso simply were not interested. But he was not discouraged and so he came up with this even more outrageous 'Leonardo'.

I think that this model of an equestrian statue was perhaps Pedretti's most optimistic venture. We showed it to Gekkoso and, if it had been genuine, it would have been a sensational piece, worth almost any price. But the Japanese now regarded the spate of certificates with mistrust.

But Bob was undeterred. He brought in an associate from the States to have gold and silver copies made. He would sell a whole stable of Leonardo horses and by using the statue as a mould, each would be an original. But disaster struck. The statue was made of wax and instead of using a computer to sense the configuration of the model and make perfect replicas, Bob, in a hurry, used the soft wax model as a mould. At the end of the operation, he had a horse whose body appeared to writhe in agony. As part of our attempt to win favour for the export licence, I arranged for a bronze model to be presented on behalf of Gekkoso to the museum in Vinci, who accepted it gratefully. But Pedretti must have had a shock when he saw Leonardo's horse with its head facing to the east, presumably to the Japanese market, while the rest of its body pointed west!

## III

When Gekkoso's attorney, Angelo di Palermo, informed the Brera that they had bought the Leonardo drawing, Madam Nakamura needed to press ahead with the sale of the sketch in the face of mounting opposition from Nakano and his allies in the MOA. She could not wait for the campaign by Pedretti and myself for an export licence to bear fruit.

For more than a year, Gekkoso had been pressing me to wheedle an export licence by any means from charm to corruption. Now there was an abrupt reversal. All hell would break out if, as a result of my pestering Rosalba Tardito, the Brera insisted on inspecting the drawing and found that the Madonna had only paid a fleeting visit to Milan and was once more off on her travels.

So di Palermo visited me in Marbella and paid me $330,000 on condition that I leave the gaining of the export licence to him. Some years later, he is still waiting.

A few weeks afterwards, Madam Nakamura asked me to meet her in Madrid. She was charming, as suave as ever, but I knew her well enough to sense that she wanted a favour.

'Mr van Rijn, you must have seen some of the bad publicity which I and Gekkoso have been getting, and the Japanese press is running a vicious campaign against us. Of course, they attack you as well, but we are their prime target. I expect you will be approached by journalists eager to unearth scandal and I want your assurance that you will not disclose anything about the business we have done together or give them any information about Gekkoso.'

'You have my word that I won't talk,' I said.

'I never had a moment's doubt,' she said with a smile. 'But

there are people who have been involved in our business who needed reassuring.'

I understood that many men who had been involved with Gekkoso would be feeling nervous and she wanted to have my word in order to calm them down.

What the hell, I thought, the business is finished, so we shook hands and parted, and that was the last time I saw that amazing woman.

# 25

# WELCOME HOME, LEONARDO

## I

Kikawa's advice to the board of SKK at a meeting on 4th February 1986 was that they were committed to buy the Leonardo drawing and should set up a branch in Italy, just as I had urged Yoko Nakamura to do more than two years before. The next day, the board decided by six votes to five to go ahead with the purchase. They did not stipulate a definite price but agreed a range within which they were prepared to deal. Madam Nakamura now exhibited a hastily fabricated third contract, showing the price at which I had sold as $6.5 million, and stated to the press that in addition she had incurred expenses of another $1 million.

Gekkoso's expenses, real or fictitious, could not forestall criticism by Nakano. He knew that Matsumoto's position was weak and a whiff of scandal over the drawing or about Gekkoso could easily swing the waverers on the SKK board. So a couple of weeks after the SKK meeting, *Shukan Bunshun* repeated that the drawing was in Japan. Di Palermo threatened to sue them, but Rosalba Tardito was alarmed. As long as there was no fuss, nobody in the Brera could have cared less what had happened to an unimportant sketch. But the Italian papers picking up the story from Japan made it a different matter. Just as at the first whiff of political scandal in Italy, the government falls, the Brera was vulnerable to any suspicion that the drawing had been illegally exported.

So she had to give the impression of tough, decisive action. On 7th March, she ordered di Palermo to explain the whereabouts of the drawing, and on 12th March the ministry gave him one week to produce it. To make sure that nobody removed the sketch, the next day Dr Tardito ordered that the safe in Barclays Bank be impounded. 'The courts investigate the Rape of the Virgin of the Rocks,' proclaimed *Chronache Italiana*. The next day, *Corriere della Sera* suggested that it might have been the work of Luini or Gianpietro, respectable minor artists, but not men whose works would command the price of a Leonardo. *La Stampa* meanwhile were tracking down Pedretti, claiming that what he had said about the sketch 'was ambiguous', which it certainly was not. In Tokyo *Sankei* ran a headline, 'Several Billion Yen Painting is a Fake'.

This emanated from an interview with the head of the art department of the ministry suggesting that the work, not being a true Leonardo, was worth about twenty million lira whereas SKK were supposed to be paying in the region of eighteen billion! This was manna from heaven for the sensational press. Any story would do: it was a fake, it was a swindle, it was smuggled, it was in Japan. In its issue of 27th April, *La Repubblica* reported that the SKK would give the drawing back but that Tardito was outraged not only by the shuttling of the sketch but by the 'criminal act' by the new owners of having it restored.

Nakano's plan paid off. Another meeting of the SKK board decided to reverse the former decision. The Leonardo was to be returned to Gekkoso and the gallery ordered to refund the purchase price. On 26th March, Dr Tardito applied to the magistrate for action to be taken, as a result of which judicial notices were issued against Angelo di Palermo, Yoko Nakamura – and me. At least, so I read in the *International Herald Tribune*; no notice ever reached me.

The two forceful women were now faced with problems. Madam Nakamura encouraged the belief that she did not have the money because of all the kickbacks she had disbursed, and Dr Tardito did not have the drawing. There was a farce played out at the bank when she demanded that they open the safe deposit. No one could find a key, at least not in Italy, and nobody put in an appearance from Japan. The furious Superintendent ordered that the safe door be blown, but it was pointed out that if the drawing were inside, it would be reduced to ashes. It was stalemate. Dr Tardito did not dare take the risk that the drawing was in the safe, and if it weren't Madam Nakamura was not going to come to Italy where she would be put in prison for up to three years.

But now it had become an affair between the governments of Italy and Japan. In a statement to the paper, Antonio Gulloti, Minister of Cultural Resources, announced that the matter was being taken up with the Japanese government and vowed that 'we shall get it back'. Premier Craxi raised the matter during an official visit to Japan. All this over a damaged sketch of uncertain origin!

Yoko Nakamura persuaded the board of SKK to accept other paintings in place of the Leonardo as security for a loan to repay them what they had paid Gekkoso for the drawing. But one of the conditions imposed on Gekkoso by the SKK and the MOA was that the drawing had to go back to Milan. There followed a bout of confidential bargaining between the two Amazons. If Dr Tardito wanted her sketch brought back by Madam Nakamura, she must grant her Japanese benefactress safe conduct. It would have suited the Japanese for the return of the Madonna to be accomplished with as little fuss as possible, but the Italians put on a fantastic show. When the plane landed, Milan airport was sealed off by armed *carabinieri*. One might have thought there was imminent danger of a terrorist attack by Briganti Rossi or that Mussolini was returning from some infernal Elba rather than the arrival of one woman gallery owner, her lawyer and a drawing.

There was complete hysteria, with national television coverage, the press berserk and formal government statements. As for the actual drawing, if it were, as Dr Tardito alleged, a poor thing of little worth, what was all the fuss about? She had waded into the smear campaign with gusto, declaring that the $10.5 million price 'was simply absurd, the work had been the instrument of a swindle'. The Brera had been notified that the work was 'attributable to the school of da Vinci: value a few dozen millions (lira)'. And with an unsubtle thrust at Pedretti, 'someone else might think otherwise, but the sketch is not a unique work, not very rare'. Did she mean to imply that Pedretti, on the brink of being appointed cultural adviser to the government, was a party to this swindle?

But if the work was so unimportant, why move heaven and earth to get it back? Dr Tardito said it was a matter of principle. Actually it was about the disruption of bureaucratic status quo; jobs could be on the line.

So there had to be a lot of behind-the-scenes negotiations before Yoko Nakamura flew in and, with di Palermo in close attendance, formally handed over the sketch. Then she graciously granted an interview to the Italian press and cast a spell over them. On 15th July, the *Corriere della Sera* carried a scoop, a complete whitewash: 'Extremely elegant in a sea-green dress embellished with an antique pearl necklace [Yoko Nakamura] seemed to have the same smile as the *Virgin of the Rocks* . . . which she had just brought back to Italy.'

She dismissed the notion that Gekkoso had intended to retain the Leonardo in Japan in defiance of the Italian authorities. Far from being the villains in a plot to subvert the law, Gekkoso had 'made an effort to convince the SKK' to return the drawing. So although the outcry against the drawing had been launched by the chairman of the MOA, it was his own masters, the SKK, who had refused to follow Madam Nakamura's entreaties to respect the law and return it to Italy. It was a masterly piece of buck-passing.

But the awkward question remained: who had brought the

drawing illegally out of Italy? Madam Nakamura said she had no idea. It certainly was not Gekkoso, who had heroically brought it back again 'at considerable financial sacrifice' and with the ardent desire to strengthen cultural links between the two countries. The financial sacrifice consisted of swapping other paintings, she mentioned a Renoir, for the Leonardo. But since she had been paid for the drawing and now substituted paintings, valued at Gekkoso's selling prices, she was actually making a good profit on the transactions, while completely winning over the reporters.

On two things Nakamura and di Palermo were adamant. The sketch was the legal property of Gekkoso, and it was a genuine Leonardo. But while Yoko Nakamura charmed the press, Rosalba Tardito had been humiliated by the way the drawing had been brought in and out of Italy and she instituted a vendetta against everybody concerned.

Yoko Nakamura was far from out of the wood. Charges were brought against ten people but in April 1988, those against Nakano and Sakaoka were dropped.

I was indicted for exporting the drawing, once together with my alleged confederates, Vittorio, Aurelia and Maria Albasini Socrasati who were 85, 79 and 90 years old respectively and who had parted with the sketch for $175,000, and a second time with Paolo Grondona, my lawyer. On the Japanese side, charges stood against Madam Nakamura and, from the SKK, Matsumoto and Iwamori, for taking the sketch to Japan on 8th November 1985, presumably directly after Kikawa and his colleagues had exhibited it at the Brera, but no case was brought before the courts until 1989. Not surprisingly, no mention was made of my voluntarily bringing the drawing back to Italy.

Of far more immediate importance for Gekkoso and the SKK was what was happening in Japan. The feuding on the SKK board grew more intense and led to Matsumoto being dismissed as president in February 1988, four years after Chikara Nakamura had got the sack. He refused to accept the decision but since his term of office expired a month later, the question soon became academic. An independent enquiry was set up and it has submitted an interim report but it is still dredging through the mud. Yoko Nakamura was constrained to write an apology to the SKK for having misrepresented some views of Pedretti, and she and Hashimoto resigned from the board.

The Gekkoso connection had brought to a head the fierce conflicts on the SKK board and the extent to which intimate dealings had degenerated into outright corruption, in stark contrast to the ethical and religious background and professed aims of the foundation. The bitterness spilled over into actual violence.

In September 1986, supporters of the two factions came to blows. A pitched battle was fought in the headquarters of the organization dedicated to peace and enlightenment and ten people were injured. A boardroom squabble had mushroomed into a national scandal. It was vital to prevent things getting even more out of hand and a few days later, the MOA was closed to the public 'on a temporary basis' as more than a thousand zealots prepared to do battle in the idyllic gardens. A year passed before officials felt it was safe to reopen the building to the public.

The conflict over the Leonardo revealed the rottenness in the management of both Gekkoso and the SKK and, so it was alleged, reduced the institutions to severe financial straits.

# 26

# Michelangelo

## I

Michel de Bry has described himself as an archaeologist, but he is something far rarer – a maker and marketer of myths. And the most dazzling myth he sells is himself. De Bry has cultivated the image of a patron of the arts, a collector of ancient and beautiful objects, a friend of the cultural elite. Even more he purports to be a man with a message, for he has a theory that will change the world's perception of Hebraic history of biblical times – only just what that theory is has never been stated.

Undoubtedly, de Bry has a good eye for the potential in an object. He will find something promising – such as the marble head of Achilles he famously sold to the Getty Museum for $2.5 million as the work of the fourth century BC sculptor Skopas – and create around it a mystique, an aura.

The tiny statuette with which de Bry was again to shake the artistic world was a thing of great beauty, clearly connected with the Michelangelo statue of David, perhaps a copy made by one of the master's talented apprentices. But having been touched by the de Bry magic, the little figure in his laboratory was not *just* a David, it was the *first* David, indescribably rare and precious, the model Michelangelo had created and used.

But to persuade the world of this, it would be necessary to create a provenance and to have the work proclaimed by some outstanding scholar.

So, with patience and artfulness, de Bry set about enticing a respected academic to be part of his project. There was an obvious choice, Sir John Pope-Hennessy, the renowned Renaissance scholar and Michelangelo specialist. Having been director of New York's Metropolitan Museum and both the British and Victoria and Albert Museums, his credentials were unassailable. Like de Bry, Pope-Hennessy had the power to make a work authentic by a nod of his head, only in his case, this was due to honest scholarship, not the creation of an illusion. Nobody has ever accused Pope-Hennessy of exploiting his reputation to put money in his own pocket. Inevitably, people called him 'the Pope', but it is more than an obvious play on his name. His authority is supreme and unchallengeable.

But so is his integrity, and that could be a problem. Michel de Bry knew that if Sir John did not believe that the statuette was genuine, no amount of de Bry magic could persuade him to say otherwise. Of course, it might very well be the real thing, but calling on Pope-Hennessy was a risk. There had to be another scholar with a worldwide reputation who would be more malleable, who would succumb to the de Bry charm.

De Bry singled out Frederick Hartt, Emeritus Professor of the History of Art in the University of Virginia, after carefully studying his victim's life and career. On 22nd May 1986, the first silken threads of the spider's web had been cast so lightly that the poor fly, sitting in his home in Charlottesville, suspected nothing.

Hartt's phone rang, and an unknown person with a charming French voice wished him happy birthday. It was a brilliant stroke. The caller then said he was in New York and had a Michelangelo document which he wished to show Hartt for an opinion. The professor stated his conditions: 'the policy I have had to establish out of self-protection and to discourage frivolous questions'. No problem, assured the caller, and next day de Bry's emissary and his wife were on Hartt's doorstep. But the approach was so contrived, some unknown Frenchman searching out his birth date to bring him the promise of something magical, it should have put Hartt on his guard.

He was brought not a document but some very fine black and white photographs of the stucco figurine. They were enough to fire the professor's enthusiasm: if the object was what it appeared to be, he was on the verge of the most fantastic discovery of the century. He had preparations to make, books to consult, facts to check. First he called Paris.

The conversation was the beginning of a love affair, at least on Hartt's side. He stated that, being arthritic, travelling was not easy, but de Bry was as anxious to please as a starry-eyed youth wooing the love of his life, or that is how it must have struck Hartt when he accepted a reservation on the Concorde flight.

'Sleep well,' de Bry concluded. 'That is, if you are able to sleep now.'

Such sweetness, such consideration. The professor was peculiarly vulnerable. A scholar of great distinction, he had studied at Princeton, but although he had been invited to deliver lectures at Yale and Harvard, had ended his career at Virginia. Was there not a twinge of discontent that he had never been offered a professorship at an Ivy League college? He claimed to be perhaps the only man alive to have handled all the Michelangelo manuscripts, and at the end of the war, as a lieutenant in the American army, had carried priceless paintings to safety in a jeep bumping over ruined roads. He had been physically close to greatness in Italy and then it had passed him by. And so with his career: it had lacked some triumphant climax.

And now, when it seemed that it was all over and his final niche was Charlottesville, this stranger had brought magic back into his life. For what he had provisionally identified from the photographs was the long lost modello Michelangelo had made for his statue of David.

Hartt spent the next week consulting records. There was some documentary evidence that Michelangelo had used a tiny modello for his David, and it stood to reason that he would have needed one. Vasari had spoken of a wax model, but there is a record of a stucco model being stored in the Guardaroba Secreta of the Palazzo Vecchio in Florence, a part of the palace which was destroyed by a fire in 1690. Clearly, a wax model would have perished, but the photograph was of a figurine which had been badly scorched, and Hartt argued that there was not necessarily any contradiction with Vasari's testimony, since Michelangelo might have first made a wax model and gone on to make the stucco figure.

At last, on Sunday, 9th June, Hartt was in Paris and was driven to a hotel room close to the Etoile which had been carefully prepared, filled with books and flowers and with a colour photograph of the figurine, beautifully mounted in a sixteenth-century wooden frame. And de Bry was so attentive. The professor should spend the day quietly in order to get over jet lag. He would see the Michelangelo the following day. One might have expected the impatient scholar to say, 'To hell with jet lag! Let me get to this wonderful piece.' But no, he was already under the spell of the master magician.

Next day, Hartt was in the magician's chosen setting, surrounded by his wondrous works of art. He was invited to admire letters from famous museums, thanking de Bry for some work he had donated. He would give some minor work, and the museum was obliged to write a courteous letter acknowledging the gift.

Certainly, Hartt was impressed by the tributes to this Maecenas, a man who must have given lavishly and yet so discreetly that his renown had not reached the professor in Virginia. Then, at last, the bewitched academic was privileged to hold in reverently gloved hands what he had already convinced himself was the long lost modello.

Hartt was highly susceptible to de Bry's taste and charm, but even without that conditioning, could not have failed to be impressed by the beauty of the tiny stucco torso. It was only a fragment and it had been severely damaged by fire, but that was what Hartt's scholarship would have led him to expect and he was even able to conjecture how it must have fallen forwards to be burned in that specific manner. Studying it and comparing it with photographs of the finished statue, and even with one of a study in the Louvre which Michelangelo had made of a muscular youth whom Hartt thought might well have served as a model for the David, he was convinced that the piece was genuine.

And when he was not working on the modello, Hartt chatted with his delightful host, of other objects in de Bry's treasure house and of the wonderful book Hartt would write about the modello and how he would get the famous art photographer David Finn to illustrate it. Then there would be the triumphant moment when he, Emeritus Professor Frederick Hartt, would present the news of its discovery to the world. The charming collector who had found the work was so modest he did not even want his name mentioned. Well, not at that time. De Bry's wish for anonymity was intimately connected with considerations of French tax law and restrictions on the export of valuable works of art. But that was not the sort of thing which should worry Hartt who was deliriously happy.

Michel de Bry is a contagion, infecting everybody he involves in his activity. It was essential that Hartt be more than a disinterested consultant; he had to be an accomplice. Between them, they could mount the most flamboyant selling operation the art world had ever witnessed.

It was their duty to bring the Michelangelo back to the world. So, at the appropriate time, de Bry said sadly, it would have to be sold. 'And you must be part of that,' he purred.

And so the conversation glided away from art and into money. What percentage of the proceeds of a sale did Hartt want? What sort of price did he expect the modello would make?

How can one put a price on something unique? But Hartt was prepared to put a price tag on it of $45 to $50 million, perhaps more. His friend Carter Brown, at the National Gallery of Washington, would be ready to pay that sort of money. De Bry was to talk of double that figure, but he wanted Hartt to feel that he would be able to place the work with Carter Brown. Hartt would feel relaxed; de Bry could make his own plans for realizing the work, while retaining the backing of Hartt's scholarship. As for what he ought to receive, Hartt had no experience. Maybe five percent?

Back in the United States, a sudden thought struck Hartt. Michel de Bry was such a generous man, perhaps he would give the modello away as he had given so many wonderful things? Then where would Hartt stand? And although, as de Bry himself had told him, it would remove the benefit of competition, he had spoken of the possibility of a private sale. Hartt was busy with his book and had already planned simultaneous publication in Paris, London and New York. The great publicity value to the book would be negated if there were no public auction. And what would happen to his five percent?

'If the price falls below $20 million, my percentage will have to be increased proportionally to maintain the level which I would have received from a public sale,' Hartt wrote to de Bry, a claim which he illogically justified by his probable liability to federal taxation of perhaps thirty percent. As Hartt regretfully wrote, 'There is no way of escaping this; tax evasion is heavily punishable.' He did not suggest that it might be unethical.

The method by which Hartt arrived at a figure of five percent is illuminating. He explained in this letter to de Bry of 26th June that he was willing to settle for half of what Berenson took from Duveen. It was only after he had got back home that he checked and found that Berenson had gouged not ten but twenty-five percent out of his deals. However Hartt was a gentleman: he had shaken hands on five percent, so be it. The Berenson-Duveen arrangement has been universally condemned as corrupt; it was a highly questionable basis to adopt. 'I like to be methodical and precise,' he continued. 'I must therefore insist on a detailed contract in all these respects, including heirs, which is viable both in France and America. The problem of an international contract should not be insurmountable; a local businessman often handles these.'

The retired professor appears to have been quite knowledgeable on commercial matters. But de Bry had already spoken about selling the David through a Swiss foundation, so would it not have been 'methodical and precise' to have ensured that the contract was 'viable' also in Switzerland?

On 22nd November 1986, the business was finalized in a delightful letter from de Bry to Hartt. He is full of praise for David Finn's photographs and for the superb erudition of Hartt's work. Of course, the professor is proud of what he claims will be the crowning achievement of his career, but de Bry insists that Hartt must accept some material reward for his efforts. The fact that Hartt had already put in his claim in writing is tactfully disregarded: de Bry presses him to accept five percent with a minimum of $2.5 million.

Considering Hartt would receive royalties from his book, this appears a wildly inflated payment for an authentification, even allowing for the importance of the work. The letter is a strictly business document, signed by de Bry's son and daughter as well as himself and a copy was returned, signed by Hartt and formally acknowledged in the French manner, *lu et approuvé* (read and approved), indicating that it was legally binding. It was just one more symptom of the de Bry contagion that, having enticed Hartt into a sordid financial transaction which was to cast doubt on his objective scholarship, he now involved his children in his scheming.

Then it was de Bry's turn to ask a little favour. He had received a copy of Hartt's book in draft which he acknowledged.

'There is a problem, *cher ami*,' he explained. For the work to have been in a Swiss foundation with no awkward questions being raised by the French, it would have been necessary for the figurine to have been in Switzerland when Hartt first saw it. Hartt's book was sacrosanct, not one word of his analysis of the statuette should be altered. But maybe the venue of their meeting could be changed?

Such a harmless request! But it was to prove disastrous for Hartt. In this formal letter de Bry had specifically talked of their arrangement applying if the sale was effected through a 'Davos or Honegger foundation' so there is no doubt that they had discussed Swiss foundations and Davos had been mentioned by de Bry. Davoust was the name of de Bry's ex-wife and de Bry was to affirm on oath before the Queen's Bench Division of the High Court of Justice that: 'Professor Hartt misheard Davoust and in his dealings with the press indicated that the owner of the Modello was the Davos Foundation.' De Bry lied on oath, and Hartt was persuaded to lie in print.

## II

De Bry had promised Hartt that the modello would not be offered for sale until after the launch of Hartt's book, but the growing furore surrounding the attribution of the Skopas Head which he had sold to the Getty forced him to change his plans. He had to protect his credibility, at least until the David had been sold. Afterwards, there would be no problem. The staggering price which it would command would dumbfound the critics, and de Bry would be vindicated. This time, the water would stay wine forever, there would be no need for another miracle.

But that meant buying off the Getty, taking back the Skopas Head, so he had better raise three million dollars; two and a half would be required to refund the museum, and interest would absorb the rest. Although it was premature, this meant moving in to find a buyer or a partner for the David. He would not get such a high price as if he had waited to cash in on the publicity from the book, but he hoped to be able to deal without the detailed investigation which a public sale would provoke. And he could always explain his secretiveness by saying that he had promised Hartt no sale would take place before publication, and alleging that Hartt would be so upset if he knew that the work was being offered before it had even been seen by the National Gallery in Washington that he might withdraw his support. In fact, he had expressly raised the possibility of a private sale in his letter when he promised Hartt his minimum $2.5 million.

Just as carefully as he had marked down Hartt to authenticate the piece, de Bry considered who should be his instrument for marketing it, and selected Richard Camber. Camber had a name for being eager to get into deals both for Sotheby's and privately. He heard everything that was going on and loved to talk. De Bry knew that by feeding him the story about Hartt being kept in the dark about a private sale, he could implicate Camber also, and so he would be able to stay on top in their relationship.

But before he showed the statuette to Sotheby's, he needed to perfect its provenance and to elaborate a story to explain why he wanted money urgently. He had already outlined to Hartt a history of the figurine, saying it had belonged to Arthur Honegger, the Swiss composer, and that he had acquired it from his children. De Bry had been a friend of Honegger and when he had died, de Bry had laid on an official funeral. This gesture had won him the undying affection of Pascale Honegger, Arthur's daughter, so when he spoke in grandiose, though vague terms about setting up some foundation to commemorate Honegger, he was assured that she and her brother would go along with anything he proposed. They became two more flies enmeshed in his web.

And he had another fable prepared which he was convinced would win Camber's sympathy. Camber had set up special sales for Sotheby's in Israel and de Bry told him how he was collecting strange and wonderful artefacts from biblical times which would change the way the world interpreted Hebraic history. He had bought them from Bedouin Arabs in Lebanon, so he said; they had been of such apocalyptic importance, it had been essential that he buy them. Now the Bedouins were camping in the Parc Monceau and would kill him if he did not pay them. If Camber and others thought him a bit eccentric with this fixation, so much the better; they would be inclined to accept him as a harmless old intellectual, not interested in money but dedicated to scholarship. And he was cunning enough to profit from the widespread instinctive sympathy with Jewish history.

With the benefit of hindsight, I think that Richard Camber believed de Bry's story, even if the Bedouins had not literally pitched their tents in central Paris. Later, Camber told me that he became convinced that these Hebraic artefacts were made to order for de Bry, but at first he drew the wrong conclusion – that it was de Bry who was being exploited.

# 27

# The Giant in the Shoebox

## I

Meanwhile I had decided to move temporarily to the United States. Since I was still on the Interpol list, I assumed the name of Davis and installed myself in the Palm Beach Polo and Country Club. Prince Charles plays polo there, it caters for a rich clientèle and, as a foreigner, it was a highly acceptable business address. I was there primarily for relaxation but I needed something more serious to occupy me. My Japanese business had faded out and I needed new activity.

I had virtually lost contact with Pedretti, but now with time on my hands in Florida, I remembered conversations we had had in Tuscany, when he had announced that he had come up with what he said was a work by Michelangelo. Why not follow it up? After all, even though I had heard about it from Pedretti, it might be genuine.

In fact, it was by then well documented, a small statue of a sleeping cupid, *cupido dormiente*, the work which Pedretti's friend and associate, Professor A. Parronghi of Florence, had excused as being an early work of Michelangelo. I bought

Parronghi's book and did my homework. Then I set about planning an operation.

First, I checked out Paronghi and was assured that he was a serious scholar. Since the Italian authorities wanted to interview a Michel van Rijn who, they alleged, had smuggled a valuable Leonardo out of the country, I announced myself as Mr Davis, adviser to a small but richly endowed American cultural foundation. We were interested in this rare work by Michelangelo. I would be grateful if he could put me in touch with the owner. Paronghi was delighted to oblige.

I approached my old friend Bob Fitzgerald who was always ready to take a chance on me.

'How about it, Bob?' I challenged. 'Do you want to be part of a deal on a Michelangelo?'

Fitzgerald squinted but I knew very well that it was the sort of gamble that would appeal to him. For a share in the final deal he could stake me for expenses. He went through his routine grumble and agreed.

The owner of the statue, Paolo Millin, lived at Budrio, a tiny village near Bologna, and after speaking to him I sent an impressive little party from the non-existent foundation to visit him, led by a genuine German baron. Millin was a mild-tempered, elderly man, retiring and intellectually inclined. When the obviously well connected Mr Davis got round to discussing the possibility of buying the *cupido dormiente*, Millin confirmed that he had the sole right to sell and was prepared to do a deal, provided the terms were right and he did not get into difficulties with the Italian authorities. He must have been delighted by the ease with which Mr Davis disposed of these difficulties.

There was no chance of an export licence, so he would be given a paper showing that the statue was sold in Italy which would clear him of any problem if it turned up later somewhere else. Further the buyer, whose name I would provide, would be an Italian. We agreed a price of $1.5 million. I explained that it would take a month to complete the formalities. My intention was, of course, to arrange the sale of the piece and be in funds at the same time as I would need to pay Millin.

Since I ought to be able to sell it for several times that price, I put out feelers and consulted Sotheby's in New York. They referred me to one of their people in London, somebody I did not know, and I left my name and number for their specialist to call me back.

'This is the Davis residence,' I announced when the phone rang.

'Well, hello, Michel,' said Richard Camber who recognized my voice at once. 'What a surprise. Are you involved with this Mr Davis?'

There was no point in continuing the charade, so I told him what I had found.

'Michel, this is fantastic. You must come to London. I have something phenomenal for you. Yes, I know from our New York people what you have to offer, but wait until you have heard what I am in touch with.'

I was intrigued by Camber's excitement. What could he have got wind of which would be more important than a Michelangelo?

A couple of days later, I walked into his office. I have always marvelled at this exercise in English understatement by which top directors of Sotheby's are housed in rooms not much larger than closets where they handle merchandise worth God knows how many millions.

I entered with some trepidation. Maybe after the fiasco of the Avar treasure he had found out that the French were seeking me through Interpol and I would be greeted by a posse of police? Actually the first things I saw were a pair of Ibedjis, Nigerian twin carvings I had presented to him on the birth of his twins. This gave me some reassurance: it was a sort of gesture that we were friends again and as we talked my confidence grew. But, I wondered, what could he possibly have to outclass my Michelangelo? Incredibly, he had a Michelangelo too. It was a case of, I'll show you mine if you show me yours.

'But, Michel, this one might sell for tens of millions of dollars. The owner is talking of a hundred million and that could be realistic, especially as it is being backed by Hartt who is writing an entire volume on it. Look at these.'

I knew Professor Hartt's reputation as the world authority on Michelangelo. Camber passed me photographs of a fragment of a male torso. It was a monumental piece and gave the impression that it was enormous, yet in one photograph it was held between two fingers of a man's hand. I said that although it had been damaged, it was clearly a lovely thing, reminiscent of the huge statue of David, with its finely sculpted muscles.

'But that is precisely the point,' beamed Camber. 'What has come to light is the actual modello Michelangelo made for his most celebrated statue!'

His enthusiasm was infectious and the importance of such a modello certainly put the *cupido dormiente* back to sleep.

'So where did this modello turn up?' I asked.

'In a shoebox. Honest to God! In a shoebox in Geneva to be precise. Do you know much about Arthur Honegger?'

'Only that he was one of those composers who worked in Paris between the wars. *Les six*, weren't they?'

'That's right. But while the other five were French, Honegger was Swiss and his son and daughter live in Geneva although they have kept his apartment in Paris. He wrote an oratorio called King David, and an admirer presented him with this broken copy of the Michelangelo statue as a tribute. Or at least that is what the Honegger family thought it was, a nice little thing of no great value, and when the old man died it was packed away in a shoebox and forgotten.'

'So how has it come to light now?'

'It was found by a man called Michel de Bry, a collector and a bit of a dealer who has done business with us. He lives in Paris and is nearly eighty and was a friend of Honegger. When he was in Geneva recently, the subject of King David came up in conversation, and Pascale, Honegger's daughter, showed de Bry the giant in the shoebox, and he recognized its importance.'

'So it belongs to the Honegger family?'

'No,' smiled Camber. 'De Bry did a deal with them and he is now the sole owner.'

'He bought it?'

'Not exactly. He told Pascale and her brother, Jean-Claude, what he believed the piece to be. They are devoted to their father's memory and were prepared to swap the modello for a bronze death mask which de Bry had made of him. But since even a damaged Michelangelo statuette is worth rather more than a perfect de Bry bronze, he has also set up a Honegger Foundation, and he will endow it with some part of what he gets for the modello.'

'So if there are no problems, why not sell it by auction if it is that important?'

'We probably will when the time is right. But here is an opportunity for you to get in on the deal, Michel. As I told you, an important book is being prepared by Hartt, the great old man himself. It is being illustrated by David Finn. Have a look at these.' He pushed over some more photographs, works of art in themselves.

He went on to tell me of the plans for simultaneous publication of Hartt's book in London, New York and Paris with a great blaze of publicity, but how de Bry was besieged by Bedouins to pay for his 'Hebraic artefacts' and was looking to raise some six million dollars.

'Bedouins in the Parc Monceau? He must be joking!'

'He puts on a bit of melodrama, Michel. One has to make allowances, but the fact is he needs the money and so has resigned himself to selling the Michelangelo.'

'Are you saying that he intended to keep it for himself?'

'No, not at all. His problem is that he has promised Hartt that he will not do anything until after the book appears, and that won't be before October or November. He tells me Hartt has also arranged for the statuette to go on a tour of the great museums, and would be so shocked if he thought the modello was being sold off now that he might abandon the whole project. So de Bry wants to do everything secretly, without his name appearing anywhere.'

'Wouldn't Sotheby's give him an advance on the modello?'

'Well, we would rather wait until the book has been published also,' Camber said with a smile. 'Let's say, if de Bry is short of money that gives you the chance to arrange something with him.'

I could see how that could be to the advantage of Richard Camber also. 'So what do you want out of the deal, Richard?' I asked.

'My dear fellow, let's talk about that afterwards. The first thing is for you to see de Bry. I have already mentioned your name to him as a very active dealer, someone with extremely good connections, especially in Japan. Let me call him now and arrange for you to see him in Paris.'

'Not Paris.'

Richard Camber was probably unaware of the disputes in the City of Light over the laundering of money for the French dealers but, with an Interpol warrant out, I was ultra-cautious just in case I was being set up. What is more, I have a policy of meeting my adversary off his home ground.

'Give him a call,' I said to Richard, 'and explain that I am in London with an official delegation from Zaire. They are setting up a national museum and I have been asked to act as adviser. They are going on to Brussels and I can see him there in a few days' time.'

Since I was staying in a London hotel under an assumed name, I had told Richard I was living in the Zairean embassy. It was a useful address. People would never try to call me there. I would be able to contact de Bry whenever it suited me, but would remain inaccessible to him.

'He won't be pleased,' Camber warned. 'He is a touchy little chap.'

Richard was right. When he got through, there was an explosion at the other end of the line. It was an insult, an outrage, to expect him to be so inconvenienced. I could hear him squeaking in great excitement. '*Mais c'est incroyable . . . je ne bouge pas pour ce petit gamin . . . non, non, absolument non.*' However, when he had been promised that he would be collected by my chauffeur and flown to Brussels in my private jet, driven from the airport, invited for lunch at the Villa Lorraine, as fine a restaurant as any in France, flown back to Paris and deposited at his house by my car, he was sufficiently appeased and convinced of my immense wealth to agree to our rendezvous.

Whenever I undertake an operation such as this, I make a detailed strategic plan. I moved into the Hotel Amigo in Brussels from where I contacted dealers and friends in Paris and enquired what was known of de Bry. They confirmed that he was a collector and at times a dealer. He was reputed to have good taste, but a lot of my dealers had no first-hand experience of him. I probed deeper and gathered that he was a fussy little man, very proud of his Legion d'Honneur, a member of a number of cultural societies, and tinged with that sense of the superiority of all things French which so many Parisians affect. What intrigued me was the absence of feedback. Nobody brought up his name as someone they would contact if they had something important to offer. He never bought outstanding things, so he was not regarded as an important client. Assuredly, de Bry was not one of the big spenders with a famous collection. He sounded an insufferable, narcissistic snob. I knew that such men, despite their pretensions, are very impressionable.

I lunched at the Villa Lorraine the day before our meeting with a group of distinguished-looking black men. I had a great time assembling our guest list. I found a most impressive gentleman from Zambia, a hotel porter, on whom we bestowed the temporary rank of ambassador. A more portly Ghanaian waiter ranked as financial attaché while two genuine Zaireans, both chauffeurs, also became instant diplomats. They ate and drank well and were treated with every courtesy. The restaurant staff were enormously impressed by the dignified party, the bustle of security guards, urgent telephone messages, and the motorcade in which the guests departed.

I let it be known that I would be meeting the same group the following day in the restaurant for a drink, although I would be lunching with another party. Before they left, I informed our 'diplomats' that this was merely a rehearsal. They were to come back next day, either in formal European clothes or in magnificent African dress; wives welcome, as long as they wore brilliant plumage and native jewellery.

Michel de Bry was escorted from Paris by Sonia, my fiancée, a charming and beautiful woman, and he was flattered. In the Villa Lorraine, she accompanied him to the bar while Mr van Rijn wound up an important meeting with representatives of several African nations. He saw a succession of well-dressed black men and women take their leave of me and file out of the restaurant to where chauffeurs and bodyguards were waiting. Their official cars, complete with national flags, whisked them away. Just as they were about to depart, I introduced them to him and got the impression that while he would not admit to being a racist, he was not truly at ease with them. But since each was presented as a senior member of the diplomatic corps, he was obliged to show the deference due to their status. They looked perfect diplomats; it was a pity they had to go back to being hotel servants. They had no idea why they had been hired, but were delighted to get dressed up, be well fed and earn some money.

'But this is delightful,' beamed my visitor. 'Now, let us enjoy our lunch and get to know each other a little. I shall share some of my secrets, but this is not the time to talk about selling the Michelangelo, no?'

I recognized that he wanted to make me impatient and frustrated. After all, why the hell should I have brought him there if we were only going to discuss the weather? So I resolutely kept off the subject. My opponent was the one put psychologically off balance, being made to meet me outside his home ground, and then being the one who had to propose that we get down to business as the time for his departure was approaching. For, despite all his show of indifference, I could sense his eagerness. I played along until at last he started to talk about the modello.

He was the one who eventually mentioned price. After a long rigmarole about how Hartt had suggested it should make forty to fifty million dollars since his friend at the National Gallery would willingly pay that, de Bry said he would put double that value on it. But to obtain that would mean waiting and Richard Camber, his very good friend, had quoted to him that English saying about a bird in the hand being worth two in the bush.

'But you know,' he said with great fervour, 'this is not simply a matter of money. I am privileged to have something of great value to give to the world, a new concept of history, but this is not the time to discuss that. Let us restrict ourselves now to how we can present this miraculous work of Michelangelo, a creation from the hand of the master rescued from fire and neglect. It is a revelation, the first David. Already, the Italians want to show it in Florence, they have begged me to let them display it next to *il gigante*. That will be something marvellous, won't it? But I have refused until I am satisfied they will protect it properly; it is fragile and must be cherished, so they will have to construct a bullet-proof enclosure for it. Of course, it will go to the Louvre and the Royal Academy in London. But, *mon cher ami*, Professor Hartt, has asked me to let it be displayed at the National Gallery in Washington, and he would like them to have the first opportunity to buy it, so you understand why I have to be discreet. The Washington show will be opened by President Reagan himself, a fitting tribute, don't you think?

'And you, Mr van Rijn, I have been told such good things about you by Mr Camber, he says you are a brilliant dealer.'

'No, I just try hard,' I said, but de Bry waved aside my modesty.

'You have feelings, you understand these things,' he enthused. 'You have handled wonderful things, but it is not just a matter of buying and selling, not with you. If something has beauty, real quality, you are a man who sees this, so you deserve to be involved with the very finest works and nowhere in the world will you find anything as miraculous as my Michelangelo.

'So, a man with your sensitivity must know the pride I feel in bringing this masterpiece back to the world, and the honour it will bestow upon me. I have children, but they have no deep interest in art, so it is not something I can share with them. But it is altogether too great an undertaking for one man alone, and from what I have heard about you, Mr van Rijn, as an able businessman as well as a lover of the arts, I feel that you are the one person whom I should permit to share in this triumph.'

I interrupted his rhetoric. 'If this were a matter of investing up to, say, ten million dollars, I would buy the piece immediately for my own collection. But since we are talking of tens of millions, it has to be sold, and for that sort of money, I shall offer it directly to the museum.'

De Bry nodded understandingly and I was sure that Camber had told him there was one particular Japanese museum with whom I could place the work.

'I would want your assurance that you would do nothing to interfere with the proposed exhibitions.' His voice was anxious. 'Indeed, there is a further condition I would insist on' – that the David should be shown in what was his own city, Jerusalem. 'Promise me you will offer it to the museum there on loan.'

'It stands to reason that publicity given to exhibitions in the greatest museums in the world will increase interest and be a help in selling,' I said. 'It would be silly of me to disrupt your arrangements.'

He smiled encouragingly. 'Richard Camber was right. You are an able man, I can sense that. I will enjoy our association. And when you have succeeded with this, my David – no, our David – that will only be a start. I would have loved to leave my collection to my children, but they do not appreciate its beauty and the loving care with which it has been assembled. And if they were to sell it, they do not have the knowledge and are sure not to obtain its true value. It is better that you should sell it and protect them. You will see, it will fetch hundreds of millions.'

I disliked the way he condemned his own children to a total stranger. Even if what he said turned out to be true, I felt he was exploiting them to win me over. De Bry was always ready to use people; Hartt, Camber, even Ronald Reagan's name. If he planned to use me also, I was quite prepared to play along to see where the game might lead.

Despite his protestations, I judged already that beneath the cultural show he was in the business for the money, especially when after describing in detail the magnificent illustrations for Hartt's book by David Finn, an outstanding artist who had been photographing works by Michelangelo for twenty years, he went on to tell me that Finn's firm, Ruder, Finn and Rotman Inc of New York, had been retained to stage the exhibitions. The announcement of the discovery and of Hartt's book would be made on Michelangelo's birthday, with the world's press and television in attendance. This went beyond the natural excitement of the scholar and art lover: it was pure Madison Avenue razzmatazz.

The best strategy is the simplest. We went through the motions of a serious discussion of price, but basically it was immaterial if we agreed on his hundred million, Hartt's fifty million or the twenty-seven million we later arrived at, since I did not have the money anyway. I needed to get de Bry to sign something so that he would be committed and I would be involved. Then I could play for time while I checked his story and found an institution to buy the piece. He too, for reasons which were to become clear, was anxious to tie the business up with the minimum of formalities and had been led to believe by Camber's remarks that one particular Japanese museum was an excellent prospect for a sale. Since he assured me that he alone had the right to sell, we quickly reached agreement. I drafted a note which he signed to the effect that he was granting me an option and that the terms would be properly drawn up on my return to London. Then, leaving with me some of the photographs, he accompanied Sonia back to the airport. She told me that he kept muttering, '*Qu'est-ce que j'ai fait?*' It was as if he were in two minds, gratified that he had found somebody to finance his sting and doubtful because, after all his elaborate preparations, the whole thing had happened so quickly. It seemed too easy.

I had to placate my partner as soon as they had left. Bob was waiting outside the restaurant, hopping mad at having to pay for our meal while not being allowed to eat there himself as I wanted to keep him out of sight of de Bry at that time. When he saw the bill, he exploded.

'Holy shit! You paid that for one bottle of wine? And why in the name of Jesus did we have to hire the Harlem Globetrotters and a private jet for this little creep?'

'Because this little creep is going to make us rich. Come on, Bob, we're not in some crap game for a couple of bucks. He has to think I'm loaded.' Although he continued to moan, Bob knew I was right. While de Bry thought that I was rich beyond compare, we could start looking for a buyer and real money.

When I called Richard, he asked me what I had made of de Bry. Too bloody full of self-importance and as phoney as hell, that was my private opinion, but I kept it to myself.

'We got along fine,' I told him. If Richard was up to something, it would make sense to play along, at least until I had a better idea of what was going on between him and de Bry. In fact, although de Bry had consulted Sotheby's by bringing me in Camber was effectively backing two horses since he would be paid off by me if I brought off a private sale and the alternative of public auction remained open. When I told him of my having got de Bry to sign up, he instructed Sotheby's legal department to draft a proper option for me which they did in the form of a letter of offer from de Bry and which Richard Camber took personally to de Bry.

My option on the modello would run until the middle of October, and for it to become effective I would be obliged to pay a million dollars on counter-signature of an agreement, and a further five million twenty-eight days thereafter. Of course, it was pure fantasy that I was going to pay six million dollars for the right to buy an object I had not even seen and which had been vouched for over lunch!

But what would happen if I had not sold the piece by the expiration of the option? I would not be able to reclaim the money which had been paid, but de Bry assured me that I would be granted a further option on other works 'from de Bry's collection'. He claimed to possess great treasures, but this raised once more the question I had put to Camber. While Sotheby's may, for reasons of their own or to suit Camber's private arrangements, have declined to advance money on the modello, surely de Bry could have raised what he needed on the collateral of his collection? The excuse was that this would mean shipping valuable goods to London, arranging insurance and legal formalities, and that he could not bear being parted from these beloved treasures, 'his children'.

Much later I learned the truth from Camber. He and several of Sotheby's experts had inspected this stupendous collection and judged that two-thirds of the pieces were fakes and the remainder of such poor quality that the whole lot were probably not worth a hundred thousand dollars.

## II

No sooner had the option been framed in a letter, than de Bry began to express second thoughts. Would he not be better off if he were guaranteed the full twenty-seven million dollars, regardless of whether I was able to sell the modello, rather than the option money, a bagatelle of seven million? He was conscious that he had made a mistake in signing the first letter of intent in Brussels.

He told Camber he was not satisfied and wanted to settle for an outright sale. The drafting of a new agreement suited me also. I needed time and was ready to string de Bry along with demands for more specific information which he either did not come up with or took a long time to provide.

So we arrived at a new arrangement by which Fitzgerald and I would buy the piece outright for twenty-seven million dollars, of which a million would become payable on agreement and the balance would be covered by notes guaranteed by a leading Swiss bank due on 15th March 1988. As far as de Bry was concerned, he would get the same down payment, but if for some reason the work became unsaleable, he would have been paid in full instead of only the option monies. What mattered to him was that the Swiss bank notes could be discounted, so that he would not be obliged to wait until March 1988 for the balance of the purchase price. Thus, only a couple of weeks after telling me that the statuette could realize anything up to a hundred million dollars, de Bry was eager to sell for less than twenty-seven million, allowing for the cost of discounting the notes. This new agreement was as totally unreal and ridiculous as the option!

I had returned to Palm Beach and kept in touch with de Bry, mainly through Camber. By the end of January, our new agreement was completed and Bob Fitzgerald and I signed it on 1st February, actually at West Palm Beach airport, where we had been joined by John de Bry, Michel's son, a friendly man in his forties, without any of his father's pretentiousness.

I had great sympathy with John de Bry. He showed absolute loyalty to his father, but he was so different in character that he must have been under a lot of stress. He had lived in Florida for twenty years and was thoroughly American. His father wrote to him in French, but John always replied in English. He had formed a company which brought up treasure from the sea bed. John could have sat behind a desk being the big executive, but he went diving each day, putting his own life on the line. He was a genuine guy, and if it had been up to the two of us, we would have come to a deal on the Michelangelo by which everybody would have made good money.

We handed him the signed agreement and he flew with it to Paris where his father signed it on the following day and then delivered it to Richard Camber.

Despite all his bullshit, de Bry was unequivocal on one point. He had undisputed ownership and the sole right to sell. He was to claim that his transaction with the Honeggers had been completed in February 1986, a year ago, and I wanted formal confirmation from the Honeggers, but for a long time de Bry was unable to produce anything in writing. And in conversation he became more and more vague, sometimes talking as if the Michelangelo were his, at other times as if it were owned by an entity called the Honegger Foundation. So I had a genuine worry that if the piece were sold for some astronomical figure, the Honeggers would at once slap in a claim.

For the whole week following the signing of the purchase agreement, de Bry continually pestered Richard Camber for the money. As we had no proof that he owned the piece, or that it even existed, apart from the photographs, this was a ridiculous piece of theatre. Finally, Bob flew into Geneva and met Michel de Bry in Grindlay's Bank.

John de Bry accompanied his father and the three duly inspected the modello which was in a small case. Bob gathered that Michel de Bry had brought it with him, but before they left it was put in a safe deposit box in the bank, there to remain in joint names until such time as it would be brought to London. Richard Camber was due to attend the meeting also, but was unable to at the last minute. We still only had Professor Hartt's opinion that it was a work of Michelangelo, but at least we now knew that there was indeed a modello as described.

Geneva seemed the logical place for it. De Bry had told Camber that it was there he had first seen it, in the Honeggers' home, and it was there also that Professor Hartt stated in the revised version of his book that he had first set eyes on it.

Bob pointed out that we needed documentation for any buyer and although we were assured that the work had been in the Honeggers' possession since 1921, we would want a formal statement from the Italian government that they had no claim on the work. After all, it must have originated in Florence, so it was important that we establish that it had left Italy long enough ago for there to be no basis for a claim. The Italian Law of Antiquities only covers the exporting of works of art after 1936.

When Bob called me and said that de Bry had been at the bank and had made all the arrangements for opening a safe deposit before he arrived, I was instantly suspicious.

'It's OK, Michel,' he assured me. 'I signed a paper there. The piece is in our joint names.'

'Get back to the bank as fast as you can,' I told him. 'Say you are checking that everything is in order.'

As I had guessed, when Bob walked into Grindlay's, nobody wanted to know him. A bank official agreed that his name had been added that morning to the authorization for access to the safe deposit, but after the gentlemen had placed the object in the safe, Monsieur de Bry had returned and removed Mr Fitzgerald's name from the authorization.

I knew this aspect of Swiss banking practice and had heard of cases where crooked dealers had swindled owners out of entire collections, since it was possible to hire a whole room in certain banks. The dealer would discuss acquiring a collection and propose that the owner deposit it in their joint names in the bank. Proper contracts could be drawn up, but before the owner came to the bank and signed, the dealer would have dealt with the formality of opening the safe deposit account. He was then able to remove the other name, just as de Bry had removed Bob's. If, for example, the dealer had agreed to buy the collection for cash, he could otain from the owner a note to the effect that, on receipt of the money, the collection would be released to the dealer. He might say that he needed such a paper to show his own bank when he went to withdraw the money. The dealer could then take the money out of his own bank and remove the owner's name from the safe deposit account. When the owner went to take back his collection, he would be refused access. If he complained, the dealer could produce his conditional receipt and a notice of withdrawal of funds from his own bank as evidence that the owner had been paid.

The fact that Michel de Bry was conversant with this loophole made me certain that he was not the dedicated antiquarian he claimed to be but had experience of the scams and tricks practised in the underworld of the art market.

I had been put on warning that I was dealing with a professional, but I resolved that I would be his match. However, before leaving the bank, de Bry had agreed to come to London for a further meeting with Bob and me the next day at the Marriott Hotel and to bring his files in the hope of bringing negotiations to a conclusion.

Bob came to my hotel and told me how de Bry had related the way he had purchased the modello.

'You mean how he had exchanged it for a bronze mask,' I corrected him.

Bob shook his head. 'He definitely used the word purchased and never mentioned masks or any kind of swap. And he went into how he had put it in the name of a Swiss foundation in order to avoid paying French taxes. That is why he does not want his name to appear.'

That at least was the same story he had told me, but we would obviously need proof that, as he claimed, the Swiss foundation and he were essentially the same, when it came to a question of ownership.

'And I also made it clear that we want a second opinion on authenticity,' Bob continued. 'Of course we respect Hartt, but if this statuette is really worth so much, we ought to have independent confirmation of his opinion.'

'What did he say?'

'No problem. I suggested a letter from Christie's or Sotheby's and he went along with that.'

'What about the Honeggers?'

'Well, there could be a little delay since they are out of town, but de Bry told me that he is like a father to Pascale and she will provide a statement under oath if he asks.'

I was to recall those words a year later when his account of how he had bought the modello from the family was denounced as a pack of lies and it became clear that he had used his influence over them to implicate them in attempted fraud.

At the London Marriott, John de Bry was present with his father, and Richard Camber arrived a little later. I insisted we get down to serious business and finally de Bry allowed me to photocopy documents from his briefcase, which he carefully selected. I had particularly wanted a copy of a letter to him from Professor Hartt in which he confirmed that he believed the work to be the actual modello by Michelangelo. At our first meeting he had given me an incomplete copy.

I was again denied a chance to see the whole letter. 'The rest of it is personal, and has no bearing on the modello,' de Bry said. 'But I shall give you the papers you can have copied, the ones you really need.'

Everybody went to lunch, while I stayed behind to take the photocopies. I learned later that the missing page had been in his briefcase, since he accused me of rifling his case and copying the forbidden letter. By the time he made that allegation, I had indeed a copy of the letter, which I had obtained in quite a different manner. I have been given another incomplete letter from de Bry's censored file, a letter from Hartt to Lewis Douglas, Curator of Sculpture at the National Gallery in Washington, of which the first page, just as in the case of the Hartt letter to de Bry, had been withheld by de Bry. Despite his claim that the National Gallery were wild about the modello, Douglas, at least initially, had reservations about its authenticity. Hartt's letter to him defended his judgement but although de Bry said that Douglas was now convinced by Hartt, I never saw any written confirmation that he had revised his opinion.

I knew that de Bry had sent a copy of Hartt's letter to Douglas to Richard Camber, and in his office I asked if I might look at it. Camber had actually also received the letter from Hartt to de Bry and thought I was asking to see that one. He had therefore passed it to me, complete with first page, on which Hartt claimed his stake.

From the papers I was able to copy in the Marriott, I gleaned one important fact: namely that Hartt was prepared to lie in print. Among the papers which de Bry, perhaps inadvertently, had passed to me, was a first draft of Hartt's book. I had been told that he had seen the modello in Geneva and indeed when the book appeared, the chapter was entitled 'A Summons to Geneva'. In the draft, it read 'A Summons to Paris'. I scanned the pages. So de Bry had had it in France. That threw a completely new light on the matter. As a Frenchman, not only would he have tax to reckon with but if the work were genuine would have to apply for permission to export it, and I could not imagine the French allowing it to go out of the country legally.

But why did Hartt connive at this deceit? It was not until I saw the missing pages of that other letter which Camber 'leaked' that I understood the true relationship between them.

De Bry had never concealed that a fee would be paid to Hartt for his authentification. Hartt's letter to him of 26th June 1986 confirmed that Hartt had negotiated a five percent share of the ultimate price. This hardly seemed a 'disinterested' opinion.

When subsequently I exposed Hartt's interest, he came out with an even more incredible statement. This payment, he told the press, was not for his opinion, for which he had received a perfectly reasonable $1,000, but as a reward for writing his book. It must be the first time in history that an art historian claimed not only to receive royalties when he wrote about an object but also a share in whatever the object could be sold for!

By the time I was aware of all this correspondence, it was clear that Hartt and de Bry had entered into a conspiracy. Hartt was not de Bry's consultant, but his partner.

## III

As soon as I had de Bry's signature on that first paper, I had swung into action to locate a buyer. Bob had got to know Maes Nouveldt, an important film producer in touch with institutional investors. When Bob told him we were looking for somebody to buy a unique work of art for tens of millions of dollars, he gave him an introduction to Robert Armao, who controlled vast funds. I remembered how, during the presidency of Jimmy Carter, Armao had been the US government's spokesman in its dealings with the Shah of Iran whose personal fortune he managed. He drives everywhere in a bullet-proof Mercedes because he still handles the Pahlavi-family wealth.

Bob and I went to New York and visited Armao in his office in the Rockefeller Centre. He was pleasant, friendly and very open. He had the intelligence and ability to remain at the top of his profession, but although he handled billions of dollars, he remained a nice, unpretentious guy. He invited us to lunch; we told him what we had to offer and he was interested and asked for details. Since we would have to appoint lawyers to act for us, it was convenient to use the same firm as Armao and he gladly introduced us to Finley, Kumble. I worked with one of their partners in their London office, a very talented lady called Lisa Spry-Leverton. She understood immediately the game we were playing and knew when to hustle things along and when to go slow. By keeping de Bry running around for one paper after another, she played her part to keep de Bry hanging on until we had the sale tied up. As de Bry conceded one point, I would raise another, and with each delay he grew more desperate for money. He had planned the greatest sting in art history, yet day by day he was the one being stung.

Meanwhile, de Bry kept calling Camber, claiming payment of the first million dollars. He had been told that we must have satisfactory documentation. He was perfectly aware that he had not yet performed; he never once offered to hand over the modello against the first payment and it was obvious that any investor we found would insist on the official papers. Everything was promised: nothing was produced.

The tone of his calls to Sotheby's became more strident. What did Camber think he was doing? He felt he had Richard at a disadvantage. And, as he constantly explained, it was the fault of those Bedouins, besieging him in his own house and threatening his life. Something had to be done to keep them at bay; he could not wait until the formalities of the purchase agreement had been completed.

Camber reported these hysterical outbursts to me and so, while the approach to Armao was being followed up, we drafted yet another agreement to give de Bry some relief. He had stated that he did not need a great deal of money but if he could show the Bedouins a cheque, even post-dated, they would retire to their tents, at least for a while. By 23rd February, terms had been agreed under which we now only bought a half share in the modello and we would pay de Bry a hundred thousand dollars on signature and provide him with a guaranteed three million dollars within thirty banking days of the execution of the agreement.

Of course there were obligations on the part of de Bry, notably that the statuette should be deposited in a mutually agreed bank and that we should have access to it since we accepted the responsibility and cost of insuring it. In addition, we still required proof that de Bry was the owner and had good title, that he provide us with a notarized and sworn statement from the Honeggers that they had no claim outstanding, and that the modello had been continually in their possession since prior to 1921. These documents were required by 2nd March.

I phoned Camber to make final arrangements. 'What's the latest from de Bry?' I enquired.

'Well, he's still going on about his Bedouins so the sooner we get this tied up the better.'

'And the agreement?'

'Oh, he's perfectly happy. Are you sending it to him today?'

'Paul is going to Paris to deal with him. Lisa has the

agreement in her office. Bob and I shall sign it there and they will fax it to their Paris office. Paul can take it to de Bry.'

'Sounds fine. Will Paul pay him anything?'

'Sure, a hundred thousand dollars. In notes, as will be stated in the contract.'

'I don't know if that will be enough to keep his Bedouins off his back.'

'Come on, Richard, do you believe in these bloody Bedouins?'

'Well, you know the way he is. But he does owe some money and is being pressed. I even had the bank manager call me directly.'

From the first moment when Camber had brought the deal to me, I had been studying de Bry, trying to get inside his head. I lived de Bry; there was no detail of what de Bry said or did that I did not try to follow up.

Once Richard had let slip that he was using banks in London, strictly against French law, I set to work to get information out of them. The first step was to locate the bank. I asked Paul to phone all the likely banks around Sotheby's. He is very good at getting information out of people. He claimed to be speaking from a branch of the Algemene Bank Nederland which had an order to pay money into the account of Michel de Bry, but the instruction was not clear, and he wanted to make sure that the bank he called could 'apply the funds'. Several banks replied that they had no such account in their books, but then we struck lucky. The Bank Leumi in Woodstock Street confirmed that they could credit his account. We might have guessed that he would hit them with his 'Hebraic artefacts' story. But how to find out if he had taken money from them, and if so how much?

A couple of days later, I called the bank, assuming a French accent. To the clerk on the line, one French voice was much like any other, and I exploited this lapse of judgement. 'This is Monsieur de Bry. I am expecting to receive a remittance and

I would like to clear up my overdraft. Please let me know how much I need to send you.'

The supposed call from the Dutch bank would have prepared them to expect money for de Bry. This call confirmed what they expected. It was quite a considerable sum, borrowed illegally by the Frenchman. But why had the bank been willing to lend him money?

I confronted Richard Camber, and he was acutely embarrassed. De Bry had got him to arrange the introduction to the bank, playing on Camber's interest in Israel in his choice of the Israeli bank. So, not only had de Bry taken the bank, but he had also manipulated Camber.

I wanted to get the modello into a London bank of my choice, but de Bry was screaming for three million dollars, guaranteed by a bank within thirty banking days. I had no intention of seeking such a guarantee, especially as I was not obliged to do so under the conditions of the contract, so I worked out a plan to string him along, playing on his greed and his character.

Bob and I decided to give him a cheque for three million dollars, just to show the Bedouins! It was one of those cheques which are strictly for looking at, not for encashing. We purposely used an American bank since that would entail several days' delay in it being presented; moreover, we knew that in the United States, a cheque could be stopped without any legal complications. Bob has a savings account jointly with his wife in a local bank, the Fidelity Federal Savings Bank of Florida, which they used for their weekly shopping, or paying the bill at the gas station. So he wrote a cheque, post-dated to 7th April. He even wrote on the counterfoil that it was 'for Michelangelo'. It made a change; the previous stub was in favour of the local supermarket.

However, de Bry had to be persuaded to deliver the modello, and for that I wanted his signature on the contract. Bob's cheque would be my weapon. It was a sort of super-chess. I was playing for control of the modello which would ensure me a share of whatever it was sold for; my opponent was out to nail me down for real money to keep the Getty sweet. But mine were the white pieces, I made the first move and would be able to keep the initiative. Once the piece was in the London bank, I would have de Bry cornered, and that after laying out hardly any money. And I was prepared to play it tough because I had found that he had no respect or consideration for anybody, living or dead. Even the memory of Arthur Honegger was exploited by this hypocrite.

On 23rd February, Paul flew off to Paris, collected the fax from Finley, Kumble's office and presented himself to Michel de Bry. John was also there, but his father did not allow him to take any part. I was in Camber's office, from where I called Paul.

'He is demanding the bank guarantee for the three million dollars before he will sign,' Paul told me.

'Of course he is,' I replied. 'Now listen. You tell him to call Richard Camber who will be able to satisfy him. Don't say anything about cheques or guarantees, let Richard do the talking. And if he wants to delay things, remind him you have urgent business here in Amsterdam. Your private jet is standing by and its flight plan has been fixed.'

A few minutes later an enraged Michel de Bry called Camber. Richard is proud of his command of languages and speaks reasonably good French, but not fluently enough to keep up with the torrent which poured across the line. I was able to prompt him, but he was dead scared that de Bry would hear me.

'We have something better,' he explained. 'Instead of a promise of money thirty banking days after the contract, I have here a cheque dated 7th April.'

De Bry was not convinced. 'Yes, Michel, I give you my word, there is a cheque,' Camber said. 'I am holding it in my hand. It is post-dated but perfectly in order, signed, drawn on an American bank and for three million dollars. Why is it post-dated? Well, that is normal. It is to give you the couple of weeks necessary to get the documents demanded in the contract and to hand them over to Mr van Rijn and to deposit the modello in a bank where both you and they can have access to it.'

There were more squeaks and splutters at the other end.

'But I tell you I already have the cheque,' Richard repeated. 'And you have my solemn promise that I shall hold it until I hear from you that you are satisfied and have signed the contract. Then I shall take it myself to the post office and have it sent to you by special delivery so it will be with you tomorrow.'

'*Mais, est-ce que c'est guaranti?*' insisted de Bry.

I understood of course that he was demanding whether the cheque was guaranteed by a bank. Richard thought de Bry was asking for him to guarantee that he had the cheque and that it would be delivered.

'*Oui, oui, bien sûr*,' I prompted Richard loudly.

He signalled to me to be quiet. '*Oui, c'est guaranti*,' he told de Bry.

Richard's solemn assurance appeared to satisfy de Bry, but a short while afterwards, when I called Paul again, there was another explosion.

'Now what's the matter?' I asked Paul.

'The old prick is going bananas.' He spoke in Dutch, and that is a free translation, but the violence of de Bry's outburst had so rattled him that he forgot to watch what he said in case de Bry was taping the conversation. 'He swears you promised him a hundred thousand dollars in cash and what I am offering him is only a hundred thousand Swiss francs.'

'Put him on to me,' I said. This was the moment to get to the point and tie up the deal. 'Monsieur de Bry,' I said, 'we have come a long way, so let's not spoil things now. I am sorry about the misunderstanding about the hundred thousand francs, but what you are getting is not a hundred thousand dollars but three million. And once we have an agreement, that is only the beginning. There is all the rest to come, tens of millions more. Now, let's get something done. Take the money and sign the contract so that we can get on with the sale and let Paul go for his plane.'

Ever since de Bry had signed at the Villa Lorraine, he had been showing more and more signs of impatience and annoyance. He was in a corner and his wild stories about Bedouins made me surer than ever that the longer he was left with the promise of money dangling in front of his nose, the more readily he would accept tougher conditions. And each time I asked for some fresh document, it had been a reasonable request and he had been forced to agree to provide it in order to retain his credibility with Sotheby's and his lawyers.

There were more calls, but with Paul stressing that his plane was waiting, eventually de Bry pocketed the hundred thousand francs and signed. As I had reckoned, tempted by ready cash, his greed overcame every other consideration. A minute or two later, de Bry himself called to confirm to Richard that the contract had been signed.

When Paul got back, I learned that the meeting had not been quite as straightforward as he had led me to believe. De Bry had played a couple of cunning moves. As soon as Paul had handed him the document, de Bry had protested, 'But this is only a carbon copy. I should have the original.'

'It is not a copy, it is a fax of the document in London,' Paul corrected him.

'Even so, it is not the same thing. You see, there are the signatures of Mr van Rijn and Mr Fitzgerald, but their real signatures are on the paper in London.'

He sent his son to find a sheet of carbon paper, then, turning his back so that Paul could not see, he affixed his signature through the carbon, so that it would appear on the fax as a copy. He thought he could claim he had never signed an original document. De Bry also added the words, 'Agreed, dependent on receipt of $3 million (by cheque)'. That seemed perfectly reasonable, since the cheque was only to be mailed to him when Paul confirmed that the agreement had been signed.

The cheque duly arrived. I imagined de Bry waving it from

his window as hordes of Bedouins galloped past. He presented it straight away to his bank in Paris. The bank naturally refused to discount it. It was a personal cheque, not bank guaranteed; they could send it to the States for presentation, but that would mean waiting for his money. But de Bry was convinced that the cheque was the weapon he could turn against us because, in his arrogant certainty that other countries must have the same legal requirements as France, he thought that Bob had committed a crime, since post-dated cheques are illegal in France. And issuing a cheque without the money being in the bank to meet it when it is written, even if the funds arrive before it is presented, is an offence serious enough to warrant a prison sentence in France. This was why he could not believe that Bob would have written it without it being covered. And he had extracted the statement from Richard Camber that it was 'guaranteed' as additional security. His daughter, who worked in a bank in the United States, enquired at the Fidelity Federal Savings Bank. An official very improperly disclosed that they were not holding anything like three million dollars in that account and burst out laughing that anyone should be so crazy as to think large sums of money would be held in a savings account.

I happened to be with Camber when de Bry called, beside himself with rage. He had been tricked, given worthless paper which he had taken solely on Camber's word. But, as I told Richard, the fact that funds were not in the bank was irrelevant. If we wished to settle with him using the cheque, there would be ample time to move in funds. As his daughter had told him, nobody would keep millions of dollars in a savings account for any length of time. What was more, we had never promised that the payment would ultimately be made by the cheque. It was open to us to substitute another form of payment. The cheque had been given solely because he had claimed that he needed something to show his Bedouins. If that had honestly been its purpose, it was perfectly satisfactory.

Nor could he claim that we had failed to pay him. He was only entitled to his three million dollars after thirty banking days, and then only if he had performed under the contract. He was shifty and cunning, but despite his little game with the carbon paper, he had signed and was committed. The modello had to be delivered to London.

## IV

Once Paul had brought back the contract from Paris with de Bry's signature, the operation was under control. Whatever de Bry's fantasies over the status of cheques in French law, or signatures through carbon paper, any failure to deliver would render him liable for breach of contract and, at least as important, destroy his credibility, something impossible for such a megalomaniac to contemplate.

I thought even de Bry would have enough common sense to recognize at this stage that I also had qualities and if we stopped cutting each other's throats and worked together on the modello, the prospects were terrific. Finding the piece, hypnotizing Hartt, ensnaring Camber, these were his achievements. But now that I had manoeuvred myself into the act, I knew that I could deliver on the selling. Working with Fitzgerald, I had Bob Armao who had a ready client, but I wanted alternatives. There was already the possibility of using Sotheby's and I now got in touch with Dr Charles Avery, a director of Christie's and an expert on Renaissance art, and Dr Geza von Habsburg.

Geza had also been a director of Christie's before establishing his own auction house in Geneva. He was a strong personality with a good eye for art and for business and, with his family name and plenty of money behind him, he was going places. He had opened a branch in New York and I knew he was looking for works which would make a dramatic impact. He went crazy at the chance of handling the Michelangelo. So I proposed that he fly to London and view the figurine as soon as it had been delivered from Geneva. I therefore had four potential bidders lined up, Armao, Geza, Sotheby's and Christie's.

On Thursday, 5th February, John de Bry met Paul in Geneva at Grindlay's Bank. John withdrew the modello from the safe and put it in an aluminium camera case. The tiny object had been placed in a stocking.

'My father is a romantic,' John told Paul. 'This is real silk, the same stocking in which it was wrapped when he first saw it. Nylon had not been invented then.'

Who was de Bry kidding? Was this meant to persuade us of how many years the modello had lain like the sleeping princess, waiting for Prince de Bry to awaken it with a kiss?

Next, the package was swathed in rust-red velvet and a pair of white silk gloves were put in the case so that when the statuette was handled it would not be stained by sweat or dirt. The case had been lined with layers of foam rubber in which a space exactly large enough to accommodate the wrapped modello had been hollowed out. Together they went to the airport, John always carrying the case.

The two of them met up with Lisa and me at a Lebanese restaurant in Shepherds Market, and the whole party were in high spirits. John de Bry had once been an official US adviser in Saudi Arabia and the Emirates and was a fluent Arabic speaker, which went down well in the restaurant. It came as a surprise when Lisa, my Jewish-American lawyer, turned out also to speak the language! There was none of the tension which had marked my negotiations with Michel de Bry. The food was good, the conversation sparkled, the place was alive, and, as a climax, we took David out of his case. People at neighbouring tables peered curiously. It was the first time Lisa or I had seen the tiny, beautiful thing. Everybody gathered around our table and wanted to look at this marvel which had materialized from another age into so incongruous a setting.

After the meal, we went to Finley, Kumble's office, where I had arranged for Geza and Avery to see the statuette.

Avery, wearing the white gloves, carefully examined the

scorched, broken fragment but feared committing himself. At last, he spoke. 'It's very interesting. I cannot say that I can see anything which would make me wish to contradict the findings of Professor Hartt.'

'Do you think then that it is the actual modello for the David?'

Avery squirmed. 'It certainly warrants further study. But before I could commit myself to a firm opinion it ought to be seen by other experts.'

Geza was much more forthright. He loved the piece, and was eager to do a deal. As for authentification, Hartt's opinion was good, but he wanted something more. He was quite definite: bring over Sir John Pope-Hennessy. In his own way, Pope-Hennessy was as temperamental as Hartt, and each enjoyed scoring points off his rival. But he was not a petty-minded person who would debunk the piece simply for the pleasure of blowing Hartt to pieces. However, he had the reputation of being a bit of a prima donna, so he would have to be handled tactfully. And of course if the modello were given the thumbs up by both Hartt and Pope-Hennessy, nobody in the world would go against them.

'What about Avery?' I asked.

'I don't care what Avery says,' Geza said dismissively. 'Pope-Hennessy is the man. If he says it is authentic, I want it and I would offer you on the spot an advance of $5 million.'

'I would want a minimum sale price of $25 million,' I said.

'Agreed,' Geza answered.

That was good news, and I was quite prepared that the first $3 million should go to de Bry. I told this to John, so I knew that his father was made fully aware of the situation. John had been in another room during the negotiations and I had not informed him of the identity of my visitors. However, he is a resourceful man. Finley, Kumble's office was in Leconfield House, which also housed MI6. This of course was a top secret location, but everybody seemed to know it. Anyway, to get into the building, visitors had to sign a book in the lobby and

John went downstairs and simply read the names of the two gentlemen who visited Finley, Kumble. I must concede that he scored a point off me there. If Geza auctioned the work, that would be tough on Sotheby's and Christie's, but neither de Bry nor I were tied to them, and Richard would be taken care of.

Finley, Kumble banked with Coutts, and we had made arrangements that the David would be deposited at their head office in the Strand. I liked the elegant style of this, the Queen's bank, and it had the right atmosphere. There were some complications since the Finley, Kumble account was with another branch and anyway it was too late to put it in the bank that day, so we consigned it to the safe in the Intercontinental Hotel where I was staying, in the joint names of John de Bry and Paul. Both here and later at the bank, Paul signed in place of me because I was still using assumed names while I remained on the Interpol list.

Next morning, I found John de Bry waiting in the lobby, holding the metal case containing the modello. He wanted me to see that despite our instructions to the hotel only to hand over the case to the two of us together, when he signed for its withdrawal alone, they had given it to him without hesitation. He did not say that, had he behaved as his father had in Grindlay's, he could have been on a plane to anywhere with the piece and that would have enabled him and his father to adopt a different negotiating position.

We went to Coutts where we met Lisa who deposited the case in the name of her firm. The handing over was quite a solemn affair and Lisa then gave a formal undertaking that access to the modello would only be given with the consent of both parties, de Bry and ourselves.

The same day that the stucco David was consigned to the vault, its discovery was announced. In America, the tiny figure was seen on coast-to-coast television. Throughout the world it was headline news. Front pages carried pictures of great blow-ups of photographs of the shoebox model and of *il gigante*, the huge statue in Florence, with Hartt standing in between in a suitably didactic pose. 'Happy Birthday, Mike!' proclaimed the *New York Post*. 'Plaster Model Called a Lost Michelangelo' announced the *New York Times*. The chorus was taken up by the *Corriere della Sera* and *La Repubblica*. *Time* magazine ran an article, as did the colour supplement of *Le Figaro* – '*On a retrouvé un Michelange*!'

But it was the dailies and the TV commentaries which got across the breathless excitement when Hartt made the announcement in a press conference in New York, and was overwhelmed by the deluge of questions. Who owned it? How was it discovered? How did Hartt come to hear of it? He was prepared to explain why he thought the piece was authentic, but these questions threw him into confusion. He remembered that he was supposed to have seen it first in Geneva and that Michel de Bry had insisted that his name not be mentioned. So he floundered, coming up with the romantic story of the gift to Arthur Honegger and his wonder when he realized what had come to light.

'Do the family of Honegger own the piece now?'

'No,' Hartt admitted.

'So who does?'

'It has been acquired by a Swiss foundation,' he answered.

Pressed for a name, he remembered what de Bry had written to him.

'It is the Davos Foundation,' he affirmed.

The journalists sought out Pascale Honegger. She had not been briefed either. She had no idea she was going to be at the centre of a sensational news story, so while Hartt stated that the model had been bought more than a year previously by the Davos Foundation from the Honeggers but refused to name his contact in that foundation, in the same article, in the *New York Times* of 6th March, Pascale Honegger said openly that it had been exchanged for 'a bust' of her father (not a bronze mask) with Michel de Bry, a friend of the composer, not years but only 'several weeks ago'.

So Michel de Bry's name was revealed on the very day the discovery was announced and the first jarring note sounded on Monday, 9th March, when the correspondent of the London *Times* wrote that the confidence with which the announcement of the discovery of the Michelangelo had been greeted had been 'undermined' when it became known that the source of the work was none other than Michel de Bry.

Confusion spread around the globe. *Il Messagero* was also positive that it was owned by the Davos Foundation. *Die Weltwoche*, a Swiss journal, waited until Tuesday, 10th March when its account reverted to the death mask. In the same article, de Bry's Bedouins also made a fleeting appearance with the suggestion that he had been offered in the Near East a stone menorah, dating back to the time of Herod. It was too expensive for him, so the article reported, but rich friends of his had bought it and given it to him in exchange for the David, so they now owned the piece.

The journalist from *Weltwoche* who visited de Bry in Paris the day after Hartt's bombshell was charmed by his modesty and other-worldliness. 'We are wearing the same watch,' said the self-styled archaeologist, 'but we live in different worlds.'

The modello is even more beautiful than the finished statue, de Bry claimed, because of its wonderful arse. It would be a star attraction in the San Francisco homosexual magazines, whereas the buttocks of the statue 'were like coffee beans'.

'I believe it to be a Michelangelo,' he had told Pascale Honegger. 'Will you sell it to me?'

De Bry said she had not wanted to sell it, but went on to state that he did not own it. But Hartt's rash announcement that the work was owned by the Davos Foundation in Switzerland put him on the spot. He admitted that the Davos Foundation did not exist, but stated that the work was being put into the Honegger Foundation which had been registered in Geneva.

The account which Pascale Honegger gave the paper was different. She did not recall how the figurine came to be in her father's study in Paris. He did not like to receive visitors there; even his family were not permitted to disturb him. As for the death mask, she could not recall how this 'informal exchange' took place, she only knew that her brother had agreed. Considering that de Bry claimed that he had told her this was a work of Michelangelo, was it not strange that her recollection should be so hazy? Pascale explained that her father owned a fake van Gogh and she was sceptical about the authenticity of the modello. The first she knew about the great sensation was when she was phoned by a reporter. That was why, she said, in her confusion, she had talked of the statuette being exchanged for a bust instead of a bronze mask.

But the inconsistencies between Hartt's version and Pascale's in the same *New York Times* report led to further enquiries and on 30th March, the paper ran a story headed 'David Model Mystery: Who is the Owner?' They had searched for a Davos Foundation and had come to the conclusion that there was no such institution. In his clarification, de Bry stated that he had never said that it was the owner of the work.

'No, no that is absurd, a misunderstanding. I have never said anything about any Davos Foundation. The story is all wrong. The owner is an organization in Switzerland known as the Honegger Foundation.' De Bry never wrote to the paper to disclaim this statement.

But the reporter persisted. Had de Bry owned the statue? Yes, but it had been exchanged for those 'Hebraic antiquities'. So were these objects more valuable than the Michelangelo? No, but they meant more to him personally. But the man from the *New York Times* was not satisfied.

'Do you own the modello either fully or in partnership with others?'

The reply was a classic piece of de Bry evasion. 'If I tell you no, you will think I'm lying and if I tell you I can't tell you, you'll deduce the answer is yes. Let's just say that one is not obliged to tell everything to everyone.'

With the modello in London and, as we believed, accessible to us, we were able to set up a formal meeting with Armao.

Lisa, Bob and I turned up with the two de Brys and Richard Camber at Armao's suite in Claridge's. Armao was not the sort of person to be taken in by Michel de Bry's affectations. Confronted by him, de Bry relapsed into vague statements but he reaffirmed that the David was now owned by the Honegger Foundation, a Swiss organization, and that he could speak for it. Armao said he was interested and asked for a copy of the statutes of the Honegger Foundation. We had spoken to him of a price of eighty million dollars; he could command that sort of money and act speedily, without a lot of red tape, once he was satisfied. He was surprised and irritated that de Bry had not brought the most basic documents with him. He had flown Concorde specially for this meeting and naturally expected that we would be fully prepared. Nevertheless, he said that as soon as de Bry came up with the necessary papers, the money was ready.

The meeting broke up but as we were about to leave the hotel, one of the bell boys ran after us, waving a piece of paper.

He handed back to Michel de Bry Bob's cheque for $3 million which had fallen out of his pocket. Bob and I burst out laughing, the treatment accorded with what the cheque was really worth. Even in Claridge's, people are not usually that careless with cheques for millions, but de Bry did not even give the boy a tip!

However, as soon as the modello had been delivered to Coutts, a drastic change came over Michel de Bry. At first he had tried to flatter and charm me. Then, as he got more and more frustrated at his failure to grab money from me, he began to act meanly, but when he appreciated that he had lost control of the modello and still had not got his three million dollars, he became insanely vindictive.

# 28

# WHOSE MODELLO?

At the end of the month, I was invited to dine with de Bry in his Paris club. He referred to it simply as le Cercle, but when we arrived, I found that its full name was Le Cercle de l'Industrie et du Commerce, and despite its serious sounding name, it turned out also to be a casino.

The place was packed but de Bry was an habitué and we were shown to a table. The waiter said we had been invited to join two men at another table for a glass of wine. De Bry presented me and told me they were the president of the club and his cousin. He whispered that the place was owned and run by men with 'underground connections'. I was already rather suspicious: the whole scene was so deliberately set up. As soon as we were sitting with our hosts, de Bry suggested that we renegotiate our agreement.

'I think it is better if we discuss business somewhere private,' I told him.

'No, no,' he insisted, with a meaningful nod at the men opposite. 'We are all friends here, *n'est-ce pas*?'

These were his terms. We were to give him back the modello immediately and he was to get his $3 million but we were not to have our fifty percent stake in the work. If it were sold, we could receive perhaps $13 or $14 million but we had lost the right to control the sale. I wondered whether de Bry had been taking lessons from his Bedouins, but I found his performance as underworld big shot unconvincing. It was plain that he wanted to terrorize me into relinquishing the modello. I guessed that if it were once back in France, we could go and fuck ourselves for our money.

By talking heavy money, I could see that he was also hoping to impress the other men, but they seemed embarrassed. They did not give me the impression that they were really involved in his clumsy blackmail and in fact his plot misfired badly.

Because of the problems which had arisen in Italy, I had to take de Bry's implied menace seriously. I called Felice in Marbella; he immediately flew to Paris and I went back to the club with him. The men who ran the place were Corsicans who knew that the worst thing that could happen to a casino owner was to have his name linked to organized crime. They were outraged when they learned that de Bry had tried to use them as a threat to me. They said that they would have 'a serious talk' with him, but I told them to forget it, I could deal with the matter myself.

The Corsicans thought him a mean son of a bitch. Casinos habitually offer good meals at low prices as an inducement to gamblers. De Bry exploited this, treating the place as his private club and eating there each day, but never once wagering a franc. They tolerated him because, with his name dropping and big talk, they believed he had influence in high places and it would pay to keep on good terms with him.

During the first week in April, de Bry wanted assurances that he would receive his $3 million and we were adamant that he would not get another cent until he had provided the documentation. As he showed no sign of performing by 6th April, we told him the cheque would not be honoured.

All our dealings from that time onwards were marked by a new bitterness in de Bry. Gone was the other-worldly visionary who treated me as the young man destined to share in the fulfilment of his dreams. I had not fallen for it, and now de

Bry was trapped by his own deviousness, for once the modello had been deposited in Coutts, he could not touch it without mutual agreement. He was a highly intelligent man, a sort of evil genius, and ought to have recognized that the game was over. If he wanted us to negotiate the sale, he would have to take us into consideration. If, on the other hand, he wanted to handle the thing himself, then he should buy us out since we were partners in the deal, but he was so embittered he could not bring himself to do either.

Since the use of menace had proved ineffectual, de Bry turned to Scotland Yard. Had it transpired then that I was wanted by Interpol, things could have been difficult, but he could not have made a very convincing case, since the British did not even bother to check with Interpol. Still, it was a near thing: de Bry had by sheer chance come close to making trouble for me.

Meanwhile I had moved into a house in Hampstead and found a new investor. I had decided that I ought to live in London for a while to be on top of the deal and to stay in close contact with Richard Camber. His wife was an estate agent, and she found me an elegant house directly opposite theirs. I loved that part of London with its little shops and charming houses with the broad sweep of the Heath on one side and the panoramic view of the city on the other, a village perched above a metropolis.

I used to go into town every day on a mountain bike, perfect for dealing with the steep hill up to Hampstead. It was bright yellow and fitted with a telephone. It was convenient and a lot of fun. In Amsterdam, everybody rides some sort of bike, so to arrive at a meeting in a Rolls-Royce was smart. In London, nobody would be impressed by yet one more Rolls, but this eccentric Dutchman on his very special bike, that was something else. I would leave it with the porter at Sotheby's or the concierge in the Westbury who loved it. He would answer the phone with the words, 'This is Mr van Rijn's bicycle speaking.'

Around this time I met Jean-Pierre Schick, whose wife was a childhood friend of my fiancée. He had a fine country mansion in Kent, and we were invited there as house guests. I found him as fanatical in his belief in the innate superiority of all things French as Michel de Bry. He was young, had inherited a lot of money, and was looking for investment opportunities and interesting speculations. Being hot news, the modello came up in conversation, and when he learned of my part ownership he got very excited. How could he get a slice of the action? he wanted to know. He had no desire to get involved in the actual work, but was quite ready to take a stake in this adventure. He was meticulous about how his money was spent, but entertained us with great hospitality. I had not been looking for an investor, his eagerness came out of the blue, but I agreed an arrangement which would suit us both, since my new house and running expenses required finance.

My house was near Hampstead golf course, so most days I had time for a round before riding to Sotheby's or Christie's. In the spring evenings, I would walk across Hampstead Heath with Richard. From the moment de Bry had approached Sotheby's, he had dealt through Richard who had brought me in.

It was a good time. I was doing something I understood and enjoyed, and I was living well. De Bry and Camber, Bob and Schick, Geza and Armao, each had his part to play. And I, who had started from the outside, had got myself into the middle of things, spending little of my own money, but getting a great deal of fun and pleasure.

Our attention was now focused on the approach to Armao, which could have submerged our differences with de Bry in a flood of dollars. Armao, still waiting for the statutes of the Honegger Foundation and other papers, got in touch with John de Bry. When that approach did not bring results, he became concerned and set up a proper investigation.

He called Lisa and told her there was no trace of any Honegger Foundation in Switzerland. What the hell was going on? Immediately, I flew with Lisa and Paul to Paris and met with Armao.

'I have been provided with a document of title which is factually incorrect,' he stated. 'According to this, title has been conveyed to a non-existent foundation.'

We explained our role, but he was quite clear. 'The fault lies entirely with Mr de Bry, since he, and he alone, is in a position to say where the figurine came from and who owns it. No matter what explanation he might offer, it is impossible for me to go ahead with a deal where the facts have been blatantly misrepresented. I am advising my clients accordingly.'

We could say or do nothing to repair the damage de Bry's deceit had caused. As far as Armao was concerned, the deal was dead.

'But I am sorry for you, Michel,' he said, as the meeting broke up. 'You must have put a lot of work into this thing and de Bry has let you down.'

'Would you mind writing a letter explaining the reason for your pulling out?' I asked.

'It will be a pleasure,' he answered. 'And I shall make it very strong and very formal.'

De Bry could pretend that this was a misunderstanding. But he could not claim that the work was owned by the Davos Foundation instead, because he had already disclaimed that, and people might have wondered what this pillar of the French establishment, so proud of his Legion d'Honneur, was doing owning a Swiss foundation in contravention of French law.

And what had the Honeggers to say? There ought to be some trace of this mysterious foundation. Pascale had mentioned the modello being in her father's study in Paris, so how was it supposed to have got to Switzerland without any formal declaration to the French authorities? But she was forced to back up de Bry.

A formal document was at last produced by Michel de Bry, assigning to the Honegger Foundation the modello and signed by the two Honeggers and Michel de Bry, dated 2nd February

1986. But the copy was only certified before the Commissioner of Police in Paris on 28th February 1987. According to de Bry, he had been busy and there had not been any reason to hurry with forming the foundation, which hardly accords with the reverence he claims to have for his friend's memory.

On another paper, dated 10th April 1987, the Honeggers do state that de Bry is the sole owner of the modello and they refer to him as the 'instigator' of the Fondation Honegger, '*in the process of being formally established*', but that document was not attested before the Commissioner of Police until 29th May 1987.

On 21st July 1987, the Fondation Arthur Honegger was at last registered, domiciled not in Switzerland but in Paris. De Bry had been forced to abandon the whole tissue of lies, and obliged at last to create the foundation of which he had spoken so often; but of course it had to be based in France, now that the conspiracy to locate the discovery of the modello in Switzerland had come to light.

And where did this leave Pascale and Jean-Claude Honegger, who had been prevailed upon to make false or misleading statements, some under oath? In yet another sworn statement on 12th October 1987, Pascale admitted that she had known there was no Honegger Foundation when she had sworn of it being the owner of the piece. But she stated, 'I had no doubt that Michel de Bry would see to it.' She also went on record that de Bry had seen the statuette for the first time in her Geneva flat and that it had never previously been regarded as a thing of any great value or historical interest and that she had no further claim to it. In which case, why did it take more than two years to drag the story out of de Bry?

A year later, the very basis of the story, that de Bry acquired the modello from their father, was to be challenged in the French courts and exposed as a lie.

# 29

# ENTER THE LAWYERS

Armao's walking out had been a setback, but not necessarily a disaster. If it had convinced de Bry to come clean about who owned the piece, his own title to it and where it had been all those years, then something positive could have emerged.

But just as de Bry could not get to the statuette without my say so, neither could I if he refused. He had not got his $3 million, so he was not going to co-operate. Instead, since threats had not worked, he retained lawyers to take us to court. He argued that as we had not handed him the money, we had lost all rights over the modello, and must give it back to him. Our case was clear. The contract was still binding: he had not been paid because he had not complied with its conditions. The lawyers had a wonderful time with long-winded letters flying between them; they at any rate were going to make money out of the modello.

In spite of all the legal charges and counter-charges being hurled about, I believed that I could still pull off a sale, but the first thing was to get a favourable opinion from Sir John Pope-Hennessy. With de Bry trying to squeeze me out of the deal, there was no point in talking to him again directly about selling through Geza von Habsburg. Our problem then was how to have the figurine shown to Pope-Hennessy in the presence of Geza von Habsburg against the wishes of Michel de Bry.

We had a valid reason for Pope-Hennessy seeing the modello. Under the terms of the last contract, we were bound to have the work insured, so I contacted Lloyds to obtain cover for $50 million. But quite independently, Finley, Kumble had spoken with their insurance brokers, and suggested temporary cover of only $5 million, an absurd figure, simply because it had been in their office after it had arrived from Paris and they had anticipated that it might have to stay there overnight. The underwriters had enquired which expert had seen the work and found that Hartt's name was quoted in both cases. They of course wanted the work examined before they would issue a certificate of insurance, and now stated that they needed more than one opinion. The obvious man to invite was Pope-Hennessy.

So Lisa wrote to de Bry's lawyer, Mr J.S.S. Smyth, and told him about the inspection for insurance due to take place on 7th May, and, as an act of courtesy, invited him to send a representative.

This put Smyth on the spot. He had written us a list of complaints, claiming that we had not fulfilled the terms of the agreement, and one of the points he specifically stressed was that we had neglected to have the modello insured. Lisa had replied that we were in touch with the insurance market. She also mentioned that, under the terms of our agreement, both de Bry and ourselves were allowed to view the object on the spot. Permission was only required if either party wanted to remove it.

As late as the evening of 5th May, when Lisa phoned Smyth, he approved our insuring the modello and, in principle, of an expert being given access for this purpose. Smyth, on de Bry's instruction, enquired the identity of the expert, and in her letter of 6th May Lisa put forward the name of Pope-Hennessy.

De Bry immediately told Smith that under no circumstances was Sir John to be allowed to see the modello. So, just when we were complying with his demand over insurance, Smyth was obliged to write urgently that his client had refused permission for us even to have access to the modello. The agreement was no longer in force, he wrote, and the David would be perfectly safe in the bank where it did not need insuring, until we handed it back to its rightful owner, his client! It was pompous legal bullshit and certainly did not impress Keith Schilling of Schilling and Lom, the British lawyer I had retained to represent Bob and myself.

One clause in Smyth's letter was very revealing. Having said that de Bry would not allow us to see the statuette, nor allow it to be removed for any purpose, Mr Smyth went on to say that his client objected to the piece being displayed before Hartt's book appeared, 'particularly to those claiming expert knowledge'. That was some description to apply to a man of Pope-Hennessy's standing! But if it were not going to be displayed, that applied to everybody, so why put that in? Was de Bry scared Pope-Hennessy would say it was a fake? Anyway, Pope-Hennessy was already halfway across the Atlantic, making a stopover on his journey to Italy just to view the work, and Geza was also on his way.

When he heard that Smyth had told Coutts nobody was to be allowed access, Bob tried to get John de Bry to persuade his father to be sensible. Michel de Bry hated Michel van Rijn, so Bob tried to turn this to our advantage.

'Listen, I want to settle this when all the fire dies down,' he told John. 'I don't give a shit what Michel van Rijn thinks: your father deserves a better deal. Now John Pope-Hennessy is in London tomorrow to see the piece and if he is not allowed to see it, the piece is dead. The piece will be destroyed and no one will make any money out of it.'

Bob is not very strong on tact and he was just getting into his stride. What is more he was pretty sure that his calls were being taped. John de Bry denied this, but the practically verbatim reports he gave Smyth look very much as if they were taken from tape transcripts. Bob made sure they got good value.

'If Pope-Hennessy doesn't see it tomorrow, he will go against the piece, the press will get hold of the story and we shall all have had it. These fucking attornies don't give a shit and don't understand the situation.'

Having dealt with Mr James Spence Sealy Smyth of Smyth and Co, Bob turned back to his prime objective, Pope-Hennessy.

'The Pope wants to do a catalogue on the piece so he can come out equal with Hartt but if he does not see it tomorrow, well, just read between the lines. If the Pope does not give a positive decision, it will be like an atomic bomb. Afterwards, just take the piece back, it's finished.'

The seriousness of the situation got through to John de Bry and he did try to call his father, but he reported back to Bob that Michel could never be contacted.

Bob must have thought the time had come for strong language.

'I am going to call Geza von Habsburg and the Pope, but believe me this is no bullshit. If your father does not stop it, the whole story will be all over the *New York Times* and the London *Times*. If you slap the Pope in the face, he will go to the press. So please contact your father and convince him, even if you have to stay up all night. It is in your best interests.'

John de Bry kept calling his father, but without success, and finally Bob suggested putting the inspection off until midday to give John more time to find and persuade Michel de Bry.

It all came to nothing. Coutts had received warning letters from Smyth and very politely declined to grant access to Pope-Hennessy or Habsburg who were left standing on the pavement! When finally John did talk to his father, he was told that he should contact Smyth and that Michel de Bry had no intention of talking to von Habsburg, Fitzgerald or van Rijn, nor of allowing Pope-Hennessy to examine the piece.

A few weeks later, Hartt needed to confirm weight and measurements of the modello for his book. As a 'dedicated scholar', one might have expected him to have recorded them the moment he commenced his study. He repeatedly phoned de Bry to arrange this and on 30th May, was writing of it as a matter of urgency. The officious Mr Smyth then had to plead with us to allow the access his client had denied us. Our reply was the legal paraphrase of 'fuck off'!

It was a pity Pope-Hennessy never got to see the figurine, for despite the references in the inventories of the Guardaroba Secreta to stucco figures of the David (they never stated that they referred to a modello), he had said he would have expected such a modello to have been made from red clay rather than marble chips. Nor was it the gesso which Hartt had anticipated. Indeed, he was in so great a hurry to get into print that he had finished the draft before he received the technical report from Professor Max Schvoerer of the University of Bordeaux. The little figure was made of a kind of plaster, so Hartt was obliged to consult his scientific colleagues and revise his book to explain that an alabaster had been used, which was why the piece did not have the dead look of a plaster model. Schvoerer had been unable to date the piece since it had been burned and calcium sulphate, of which it was made, as opposed to the calcium carbonate of stucco, is highly susceptible to heat hence in his opinion thermoluminescence analysis was not reliable.

But while Hartt was busy reconciling his book with the facts, de Bry was fighting to get the courts to order us to restore the modello to him, and that needed money. I learned from Camber that he was desperately trying to raise funds from his collection. He had a stroke of good fortune when he was able to sell a harp around which he had woven one of his myths. The buyer brought it to Sotheby's who told him it was worth only a fraction of what he had paid; he then said he had bought it from a man called de Bry in Paris. But then that money ran out, and, rather than do a deal with us, he sold a share in the work to his lawyer, Harry Donckers, to look after his mounting legal costs.

Throughout the summer of 1987, there was a stalemate with neither side allowing access to the other and no sign of the case coming to court. But there was a growing exposure of the extent to which de Bry had distorted or exaggerated his earlier claims. Ruder, Finn and Rotman had not yet agreed to manage the exhibitions; only in May did they write with proposals. De Bry refused to meet any of the costs of mounting the exhibitions. Rather, he pointed out that he should be one of the parties to benefit and made a sickening gesture, announcing his intention of donating some part of the profits which he did not have to the campaign against AIDS. In fact, none of the museums had agreed at that time even to show the modello. But that was quite irrelevant while it remained in the bank vault.

# 30

# COUPE DE CARABANCHEL

I enjoyed living in Hampstead, but Marbella was now my home. For me, it was not merely a rich man's playground, but also an ideal environment for business.

One of the most amusing of the Marbella set was a Dutch woman called Janneke. She had made the grade by marrying a man called de Monschy who owned oil storage tank farms throughout the world and was fabulously rich. He had installed Janneke in a villa and she proceeded to bleed him white until his children by an earlier marriage threatened to take legal action. So she divorced him, having acquired sufficient wealth to live her own life. What singled her out from the other rich divorcees in Marbella was her frankness. Lots of them sold their bodies to obtain wealth but unlike the others, Janneke could not break with her old habits. She was constantly introducing pretty girls, and I met a lot of them, but was never tempted into a long-term commitment.

Then one day, Janneke told me about a girl who was different. 'You ought to meet her, Michel. She is beautiful and has style. She is not some silly kid, a woman in her thirties who had a short unhappy marriage. A lot of guys have tried to make her, but she has refused them all. You would find her quite a challenge.'

That was how I met Sonia and I found her as intriguing as Janneke had promised although, as I was to learn later, she had not been the unapproachable beauty Janneke had depicted.

Sonia loved the opulent boutiques and restaurants she could patronize through living with me. She came from a small town in Germany and her rigid, bigoted upbringing had left her superstitious and basically uneducated. But she was intelligent enough to see what she was missing and so I gave her something more than the rich life – I was her liberation.

We enjoyed a great sex life and I found her a loyal and efficient person to run the house and assist in my business arrangements. I never have been able to stick to one woman, but when Sonia bore me a son, I really began to think that maybe this time I was going to settle down.

My relationship with Felice was based on mutual respect. I recognized that it was due to his special protection that French requests for my extradition were being frustrated. For my part, he would always seek my advice when he was approached with offers of works of art.

'Michel,' he said one day, 'I hope you will not be annoyed but I have given your name to this woman, Hilda de Pinnapar. She says she can get hold of works of art confiscated during the war from Jews and others, which remain unclaimed. She will call you and explain the details.'

Of course I agreed to talk to her to oblige Felice, but I did not like the sound of the business; there was something unclean about trafficking in works stolen from war victims. I knew her, a charming woman from Argentina, now about fifty, a baroness who lived by her wits and exploiting her title. Not long before, she had approached me with a Sorolla, backed by a document signed by one of the painter's family. I knew that the only acknowledged expert from the family was Pons Sorolla but the baroness had a paper from some other member, hoping to impress a buyer without my background knowledge.

So I was suspicious of the baroness and I was not impressed by the story she told me. A lot of Nazis had fled to Spain at the end of the war, bringing their loot. While Franco lived, they had been undisturbed, but they felt vulnerable now their protector was dead. She repeated that she could lay her hands on fine works which had not been claimed by their previous owners or their heirs, if Felice would provide the finance. For now she could offer a lot of Impressionist paintings which she said had been stolen during the war.

'I have very important contacts in the various ministries who make this business possible,' she told me over the phone, and went on to talk very openly about how she could fix things.

'She told me that she can get certificates for whatever she offers when she first called me,' Felice said.

'Certificates are not the problem,' I warned him. 'Faking certificates is big business. You can choose dead experts and use old photographic paper and make copies of rubber stamps. It is specially easy to get away with it in Spain where there are no proper records.'

'Then if the certificates are fakes, so are the paintings.'

I agreed. 'And if the lady is bringing in fakes, the war loot story is just a cover. My advice is not to have anything to do with her.'

I am always very careful what I say on the phone, but I was convinced she was not on the level and I was not the only one. Her phone had been tapped and shortly afterwards the baroness was arrested for trafficking in fake works of art.

But that phone tap led to a lot of trouble for me. Interpol agents in Madrid heard my name in the conversation and checked on me. They found that the French had issued an Interpol warrant for my arrest in 1985. The French had known that I had a house in Marbella; so why, the Interpol men wanted to know, was I enjoying liberty on the Costa del Sol? Of course the answer was Felice, and normally the request for my detention would have been suppressed in Madrid. But telexes demanding immediate action were despatched both to Madrid and to Malaga. So the demand for my arrest slipped through the net; two Interpol agents from Madrid met up with some local men, led by the police chief, and they swooped on my house.

I was sitting quietly on my terrace when they caught me totally unprepared. I was bundled into a car and driven to the police station in Marbella.

I had been in the police station for precisely ten minutes when I was taken into a small room and Gianni, Felice's *consigliere*, entered. He nodded to the policeman, who went out leaving us alone.

'Felice regrets that he has not come in person but thinks it is wiser not to be seen with you while he makes enquiries. But he wants you to know that you have his complete support and will not be extradited. The French are pushing hard, and we have to play this carefully,' Gianni continued. 'You will be moved to Malaga and then they will take you to Madrid where all demands for extradition are decided. The conditions in Malaga are bad, but be patient. Things can be arranged in Madrid for you to be more comfortable and no effort will be spared to make sure your stay is as short as possible.'

The sound of the cell door clanging shut and the dreadful feeling of being penned in is a shattering experience. I was locked in the communal day cell. The prisoners, mostly kids picked up for minor offences, were fairly relaxed. Visitors were allowed to come to the bars and pass in food and there was a constant smell of hash. Two days later, I was taken, handcuffed, to Malaga.

The prison in Malaga was big and overcrowded. We slept in dormitories of more than forty prisoners. Most were involved in dope, or else they were gypsies, vagrant robbers. From them came the maddening, incessant clashing of guitars and raucous singing accompanied with clapping. To this day, for me flamenco music is the sound of prison.

In contrast to Marbella, many of the prisoners here were serving long sentences and there was an elaborate system of graft which was necessary for conditions to be bearable. Inside such a prison, you were in a different world with its own rules, its bosses and barons. The first person to come to terms with was the leader of the dormitory. Once you were accepted, he would sell you a mattress. Everything could be bought, if you had money. If not, you could work for other prisoners who would pay. But if you were not accepted, you would be banished to another dormitory, the cesspit, infested by the worst drug addicts and AIDS cases. In Madrid the evil dormitory was known as the Bronx.

Old hands in for ten or fifteen years ran the kitchen and controlled the supply of official food. The guards would buy things from outside and ran their own racket, charging whatever they felt like. The food was served up by the extensive gay community, the *chico-chicas*, as they liked to be called, who defiantly proclaimed their sexual ambivalence in their clothes and painted faces. There were transvestites, transsexuals, male prostitutes, even pimps running strings of whores who for money would share your cell for the night. But life is tough in jail, and many of the gays were raped.

Yet, despite the jungle law and violence, the Spanish system is more humane than, for example, the French, who lock up prisoners all day. In Spain, men can walk in the open air in the patios most of the day, and are only locked in for the night. After the evening meal at seven, the cell doors are left open and everyone can wander as he pleases inside the gallery. Men visit friends and the space in front of the cells is transformed into a veritable street market. At ten the cigarette vendors or hash or coke sellers go back to their cells and only then everyone is locked in. Wives and girlfriends are allowed to visit usually once a month and there are rooms set aside where the prisoner can enjoy sex in privacy with his visitor. But often men away for long stretches find themselves slowly forgotten; wives stop coming and frequently men will take up with a *chico-chica* out of frustration and loneliness.

My arrest was widely reported, even splashed on TV. I was described as dangerous, *peligroso*, a French criminal. Although

I found this publicity unwelcome, it did assure wholehearted acceptance among my fellow prisoners.

I now found myself a lawyer and, by pretending that I did not speak foreign languages with any fluency, had Sonia appointed his official translator. Since lawyers are allowed access at any time, this meant we could meet whenever we pleased, and that I could keep track of my business. I learned that my transfer to Madrid's Carabanchel jail was pending and that better arrangements could be made for me there. Escape from Malaga would not have been difficult. I was even offered the official plan of the prison's plumbing system which would have enabled me to escape through the sewers. But that would have led to my being constantly on the run and I had already decided I was going to stand and fight against extradition, no matter how ghastly conditions might be in Carabanchel.

Carabanchel has a reputation as one of the toughest prisons in Europe, even worse than the notorious Turkish jails where at least foreigners are kept apart. Around fifty prisoners are murdered every year and nobody has bothered to reckon how many non-fatal stabbings and beatings take place; seven guards have been killed and even a former director of the prison is now serving a sentence for murder. Knives are everywhere, men file away the backs of spoons to make daggers. For a hundred dollars, a man serving a twenty- or thirty-year sentence will kill. What difference does it make if he is ordered to serve a few years more?

Some of the men serving a life sentence, which means what it says, remain solitary and withdrawn. Convicted ETA members are given special treatment for their own safety. If they stood in line for meals someone would slip a knife through their ribs.

I was taken to Galeria 6, where most of the foreigners were lodged. A man without money or influence in Carabanchel will kill to survive: I was fortunate in having both.

'Your case will have to come before the *audiencia nacional*,' my lawyer Miguel Ibañez told me.

Next morning I was brought before Ramon, the head of

the Guardia Civil in the *audiencia nacional*. He had the rank of colonel and an impressive office. All cases for extradition passed over his desk. He rose to greet me and motioned me to take a chair.

'I do hope that you will be comfortable, Señor van Rijn,' he said. 'Just say the word, and we can have you moved to another prison more to your liking or you could be lodged in a hospital with your own private suite. I am sure you are aware that it is highly irregular for anyone being held on a demand for extradition to be released on bail, and it is almost unheard of when the request comes from the French, who usually obtain extradition within twenty-four hours. We have to maintain good relations with them to make sure they do not give asylum to Basque terrorists. However, yours is a very special case and I personally will make representations to the Ministry of Justice. But these things do take time.'

'I think I shall stay here until my release can be negotiated,' I replied.

'I quite understand. However, if you feel like a change, send me a message.'

I was prepared to buy things for my business, and certain luxuries, but I refused ever to have a pillow or a blanket since I felt this would mean that I was coming to terms with prison and I was determined to fight with everything I had for my freedom. I knew that Felice, who felt particularly concerned about me since my arrest had resulted from the baroness's indiscretion, would do whatever he could.

I had been there a few days when I was called to see a visitor, and found a stranger waiting for me. 'My name is of no importance,' he said in French, 'and my visit is strictly unofficial but I am here to make you a proposition. Give us the names and account numbers of the people for whom you have moved money out of France, and tell us how it was done, and demands for your extradition will be dropped.'

'Nice of you to come,' I replied, 'but I am busy cooking

spaghetti, and I hate it if it is not *al dente*, so unless you have anything else to say, please excuse me.'

That was the last I heard about the proposed deal.

To make life tolerable, I needed real money and this was brought in by my lawyer Miguel, folded in a newspaper. We should have been separated by a partition, but the 'trusties', suitably paid, turned a blind eye.

Then I set about bargaining with the guards and their bosses. I acquired a large cell, had it decorated, installed a mobile phone (we took an apartment opposite the prison to relay signals), TV and hi-fi. I realized everything was available to the man who ran the prison shop, so I got him to sell it to me. I was fortunate in making friends with Stephan, a Frenchman who was a great cook. I have always enjoyed cooking, so our friendship grew as we prepared our favourite dishes.

There were good wines, every kind of booze and excellent cigarettes or cigars, all for the buying. So were the women who were brought in, but that was not a matter I discussed with Sonia. Carabanchel was the most expensive hotel in which I have ever stayed.

I invited some of the more interesting people to dine with us and they welcomed the chance of a few hours' distraction for prison is a form of death. Incidents which would attract a few minutes' comment outside became matters of absorbing interest. Prison life is humiliating and the hardest thing was the sense of helplessness. Men would despair of keeping their wives or girlfriends.

Stephan stood out from the gypsies, petty crooks and coarse, hardened criminals. He was awaiting extradition to France where he was accused of being the leader of one of the most audacious bank robberies ever, that of the Credit Lyonnais in Marseilles. He never admitted the charge to me: 'That is for a judge to decide,' he commented, but told me in detail how the robbery was carried out.

'The guys who did it dug a tunnel right up to the wall of the bank vault,' he recounted. 'It took months of hard, cautious work. Then one morning, they burst through the front door of the bank just as it was opening for business. They wore masks and waved guns about to give the impression that they were ferocious killers and took the staff and the few early customers as hostages. Then they closed the bank, and in no time the *flics* were everywhere.

'The inspector who took charge of the operation was the head of the special anti-gang squad, a man called Broussard. He had a real macho reputation, the killer Mesrines, you remember?'

I remembered very well the sense of outrage and disgust when Mesrines, a gangster with something of a Robin Hood image, who was regarded with respect even admiration by the public, was savagely gunned down by Broussard's men. An ambush was set for him on the motorway which circles Paris. There was no warning, no demand that he surrender. The police fired volley after volley into the car, killing Mesrines and his girlfriend. The man was not resisting arrest, it was simply a brutal judicial murder; that was Broussard's style.

'You can be sure that Broussard was looking forward to shooting holes in the gang in the bank,' Stephan went on. 'He flew in from Paris in a private jet and swaggered before the TV cameras. He was sure he had them bottled up inside the bank so sooner or later they would have to surrender and release the hostages. He had eight hundred men there, armed to the teeth, and helicopters circled the place incessantly. It was virtually a siege carried out live before the TV cameras and Broussard put on a great show as the tough cop who always got his men, dead or alive. He loved every minute of it.'

The guys in the bank played him along, demanding a ransom of forty million francs, a getaway car and a plane. Broussard carried on the negotiations over television, he loved the publicity. He ordered the gang to come out and not to harm the hostages. They never had any intention of doing so; once the vault was open, they were made to help smash open the safe deposit boxes. Even the manager had to assist in robbing his own bank. Sack after sack was filled with bank notes and jewellery. Then the hostages were told to continue working, while the robbers opened more safe deposits in another vault. 'You are not to leave this vault till we tell you,' they were told. 'But there is no reason why you should not share in what we have got here. So, fill your pockets.'

While the hostages went on breaking open boxes, the robbers broke open the wall to the tunnel. Broussard, tiring of negotiating, issued an ultimatum – surrender by the deadline or we come in and get you. Meanwhile, the gang had slipped away through the tunnel, taking their spoils.

Outside, Broussard prepared to storm in through the front of the bank. The hostages were nice and quiet, working away as ordered. After an hour or two, they began timidly to venture out of their vault and they eventually realized they were on their own.

All France watched as the door of the bank was pushed open and the bank manager emerged. Broussard was triumphant: the gangsters knew they were beaten.

'Where are they? Are they coming out?' he demanded.

'But they have gone,' replied the bewildered manager.

'Impossible! The place has been surrounded for hours.'

I remembered how the French public had laughed at the discomfiture of the big-mouthed cop. And people had admired and been amused by the audacity of the robbers, except for those who banked with the Credit Lyonnais in Marseilles.

'But since everyone got clean away, how did you end up here?' I asked. Stephan was intelligent, not the sort to blunder into the hands of the police.

'This friend of mine invited me to his house. I knew he handled stolen goods, so I told him I would only come if the house was clean. He swore there was nothing inside, but in fact it was stuffed full of hot jewellery and was being watched by the cops. They busted the place when I was there.'

Despite the comforts and conveniences I had installed, there was always the feeling of being enclosed. During the day, we walked in the patio and those hours were precious. But I wanted to make more of them and to bring a bit of fun into the grimness of prison life. That was what inspired me to organize the Coupe de Carabanchel and donate the prize.

With a little persuasion, some whitewash and brushes were brought in and volunteers marked out our tournament tennis court. Rackets, balls, the net, all were bought and the lists opened for competitors. All of a sudden, there was something to break the monotony. Everybody went tennis crazy. Men who did not know the first thing about the game asked more experienced players to teach them to play. The actual games went on for weeks, so many people entered. And there were not only the singles to be played. There were men's doubles and, once the *chico-chicas* joined in, taking such names as Martina or Chrissie, ladies' matches and even mixed doubles.

There were competitors from every continent; some of the strongest players were South Americans. However, Stephan and I managed to fight through to the finals. Then I was called once more to the *audiencia nacional*. The colonel rose to greet me.

'I am pleased to tell you that your friends have been successful and the courts have decided to allow you to go out on bail.'

'That's terrific! How much do I have to put up?'

'They were talking about a million dollars but I urged them to be reasonable. The sum agreed is a hundred and fifty thousand pounds. I am sorry but you understand that it is necessary to show something. We have been under a lot of pressure from the French.'

'I am very grateful for all you have done,' I answered.

I was escorted back to prison to await notification of my impending release; my interview with Ramon was strictly unofficial. Every evening between seven and eight, there is a sense of brooding tension in the jail. That is when the names of the men who are to be set free the following day are announced.

There is no earlier warning so every man waits, praying that his name will be called. Even men with years to serve wait and listen, in case the impossible has happened. Afterwards there are celebrations for some and disappointment, jealousy and black anger for others. My name was not called, so I was not the target of envy, but early in the morning the guards came for me.

I walked out with just the clothes I was wearing, determined never to set foot again in that stinking jail. I was happy to leave behind everything I had for those less fortunate than me. The only man to express regret at my leaving was Stephan.

'Pity you could not have waited for the final,' he said. 'I suppose I'm awarded the match now as a walk-over but that's not the same as winning.'

'I was looking forward to our game as well,' I answered, 'but I wouldn't let anything in the world delay me for one minute from walking through that gate. But I'll send you in some special food so that you can celebrate in style.'

The formalities were completed and I walked to freedom. The pavement outside was packed with people in fiesta mood. All I wanted was to walk for miles, putting Carabanchel further and further behind me, so I dodged the reception. I had not wanted even Sonia to be outside that gate: I walked halfway across Madrid to join her.

Back home in Marbella, I was able to relax. Sonia was overjoyed to have me back, and friends came round to celebrate. Then one night, I was sitting in the gardens savouring the sweet, calm air and the simple feeling of freedom. I did not hear a car approaching the house, but suddenly there rang out the almost simultaneous crashes of four doors being violently slammed.

In a flash, I was on my feet and running. Only cops would have made that racket outside my house at that time of night. I sprinted across the lawns and threw myself into the bushes at the end of the garden; then I ran across gardens and clawed through bushes to reach the road leading to the highway. Once the squad passed word back that I had got away, patrols would be sent out and the highway would become a trap. But I had to follow the road.

The instant I hit the highway, I threw myself into the ditch and started crawling towards the town. I tensed at every approaching car. Several times, police patrol cars raced by me, but they passed without stopping. What the hell had gone wrong? I had Felice's word that once in Marbella I was under his protection, and what Felice promised, he delivered.

After twenty minutes' crawling, I sprinted up the hill to Gianni's villa and hammered on his door. He hurried me inside.

'I know what has happened,' he said before I could say anything. 'Sonia called me the moment they had finished going over your house and the grounds. You will be safe here.' Gianni's house, like Felice's, was inviolate from the police.

'I have already been in touch with Felice,' Gianni told me. 'He is shocked and is checking to find out what has gone wrong. He knew you would make for here and told me to let you know how badly he feels about this and to assure you he would do everything to keep you safe.'

I took a shower and changed into some of Gianni's clothes.

The following morning, Felice came to the house.

'The news is not good, Michel,' he told me. 'The French are hammering away to have you extradited. Up to now, one of my men has always been able to intercept their demands for you to be picked up and make sure they got lost or filed away. But yesterday, he had to be away from the office and just on that day another urgent demand hit the office.

'You know how closely the Spaniards are co-operating with the French. When the news got back to Paris that you were out on bail, they knew somebody was protecting you. They have stepped up the pressure and divided their complaints into two separate demands for your extradition. They reckon two demands look more serious than one, and if you can evade them on one, they can get you on the other. Anyway, they pushed the guys in Madrid who checked up and found that you were living openly in Marbella. Then they went crazy: they did not want to look incompetent or stupid to their buddies in Paris, so they sent a squad from Madrid to pick you up immediately. That is why they moved so fast.'

'But is your man back at his desk now?' I asked.

'Sure. What I have told you is from his report.'

'Then things are back to normal?' I asked, but I knew the answer.

'I am afraid not, Michel. The order is out from Madrid for you to be taken. It is too late to stop it, but the situation is under control.' He paused and looked straight at me. 'You know what I think you ought to do? You should go back to Madrid and surrender to your bail. Ramon will arrange for you to be made as comfortble as possible. It will only take a few days to get you out on bail again. But if you stick around here and that squad take you, they will put you in jail in Marbella and there will be days or weeks while they have you transferred to Malaga. Then more delay before you are conducted to Madrid. That way, you will be in one prison or another for a month or more.'

The idea of going back through that gate, even for one day, filled me with loathing but I knew he was right.

So the next day, I was formally ushered into Ramon's spacious office. He rose, kissed me and motioned to the guard to leave.

'Señor van Rijn, I am so sorry that you have been subjected to this annoyance but you will receive the best treatment possible. Before we get down to tiresome formalities, you will do me the honour of accepting my invitation to lunch.'

We drove off in his official limousine with military escort on motorbikes to Horcher's, still the most elegant restaurant in Madrid. There we sat, the colonel and his 'prisoner', enjoying smoked salmon, *boeuf en croûte* and a choice Burgundy while Ramon invited me to choose to which jail I would like to be delivered.

'If you wish, we can arrange for you to be housed in a suite in a hospital,' he suggested.

I shook my head. 'I am most grateful, Colonel, but I wish to return to Carabanchel.'

He stared at me in disbelief.

'Any prison, no matter how comfortable you might make it, is still a prison,' I explained. 'I need my freedom as I need air to breathe but if I must go inside for a few days, then let it be where I have found friends. And there is another reason.' I told him about the Coupe de Carabanchel. 'So isn't it the sporting thing to see if I can win the final?' I asked.

Ramon burst out laughing. 'You must be the first man in the history of Spain to have volunteered to go to Carabanchel.'

Nobody expected to see me back in that stinking jail and I was greeted with astonishment and mostly with sympathy, although some, envious of the position I had enjoyed during my earlier stay, were quite happy at my return.

'How long do you think you will be staying this time?' asked Stephan.

'Extradition hearings can drag on for years, or they can move like greased lightning,' I replied. 'So let's get on with the final of the Coupe de Carabanchel.'

So here I was, apparently settling in for a protracted stay, taking back my room, laying in the best food and wine, and Stephan was offering to cook a special meal. He had just received the food I had promised to send him when I was released, so ironically I was able to share it with him.

The next day a big crowd assembled to watch the Match of the Year. I had been in training and was in good shape but Stephan was quick on his feet and had an uncanny ability to tuck his shots just out of reach. Although he was the better player, I made him fight every inch of the way before he finally scraped through. I suppose that it did look better, since I had donated the cup, that it should be given to somebody else.

Two days later, I was released on renewed bail. Once more back to Marbella. Felice's greeting was typically Sicilian and emotional. Although he was in no way to blame for my arrest, he felt responsible for me. I only enjoyed the good life on the coast for a short time.

'Michel,' Felice told me one day, 'things are getting very serious. The French are furious that you have slipped away again. Ramon has warned me that questions will be asked and they will go on pressing to have you extradited. I cannot promise that I shall be able to keep the case against you stalled indefinitely. You cannot count on being safe if you remain in Spain.'

The French had now added a charge that I had attempted to pass a fake Mirò gouache, the one I had sent to Lelong for adjudication. It should have been destroyed, but now I was informed that a stranger, claiming to represent me, had stated that it was the property of a gallery in Tokyo which disclaimed knowledge of either me or the painting. It transpired that the stranger was Henk Slik, seeking to take advantage of my absence. I was sure that if I could have fought all the charges in court, they would have been exposed, but the way the French work they could keep me in jail indefinitely without a chance to clear my name. My life could have been ruined simply waiting to come to trial, so I determined to deal with them in my own country. The Dutch police too were being pushed to take action against me but I was not prepared to run to some third world country to avoid extradition.

I still had my American passport, so I flew to Amsterdam. Then I reported to the Dutch police.

'Here I am,' I said, 'the supposed dangerous criminal. I know that here I shall not be tried and condemned in my absence in the French manner. So tell me what I am accused of and give me a fair chance to respond.'

I sat down with inspectors for three days, at the end of which all complaints against me in Holland were dropped and there was no way that the Dutch would agree to the extradition of one of their nationals.

At last, I had a base from which I could fight back.

# 31

# GANGSTERS

I set about making a home in Amsterdam for Sonia and our son. Although little Michel was only a few months old, I got tremendous pleasure out of planning his nursery and finding antique toys which he could enjoy when he was older. I found a fine old house, spacious and with a lot of character but very run down, which I began to restore. It was close to the three museums and concert hall around the Museumplein and almost next door to Christie's offices and saleroom. It could not have been more convenient.

I wanted to bring over the things from my Paris apartment; fine furniture and my collection of art and antiques, which I had in store there. Not being able to go to France myself, I thought it a stroke of luck when an old acquaintance, Max, told me that he frequently moved containers of goods for his business and offered to handle my things along with a consignment he would be sending from Paris. I did not know that since I had last met him, Max had gone into the drug trade; he was only too pleased to use my legitimate goods as a screen.

My relations with the Dutch police were normalized after my return to Holland, and they requested professional assistance in tracking down the perpetrator of a series of fake paintings and lithographs of such artists as Joan Mirò and Karel Appel, an investigation which had occupied them for two years. I had a personal interest since the culprit was Henk Slik, who, using my name and that of Axel Hammerschmidt to obtain expert certificates for his works, had brought both the gallery and myself into discredit. So I agreed to help and their competence and integrity persuaded me to take them into my confidence.

One of my Armenian contacts in Paris had recently told me that the system we had used to obtain United States passports to smuggle people out of the Soviet Union had been discovered by terrorist groups in Lebanon, but the authorities were apparently unaware of what was going on. This preyed on my conscience. I had taken advantage of it myself, but how could I stand by while innocent people were slaughtered?

So I told Inspectors Simon de Waal and Will Snyder of the squad devoted to anti-terrorist and drug activities how it worked and that it was now well known in Beirut. Remembering Dergazarian's alleged source, I said I suspected that the most violent terrorists might be using American passports obtained in this manner.

'So how did you get your passport then?' asked de Waal.

'It was ridiculously easy,' I answered. 'I filled in a form in a post office: names of parents, date of birth and of marriage, etc. This application had to be supported by proof of identity, such as a driver's licence, but I knew from previous experience that a voter's registration certificate would be sufficient, so obtaining that was the crucial step. This is outrageously simple, but as an extra precaution I applied from Miami where there are so many people with every sort of ethnic and national background that an American citizen speaking with a marked "foreign" accent is quite usual. I simply had to present myself to the relevant government office, put my hand on a bible and solemnly swear my new identity. I had then become a registered American voter and automatically eligible for a passport.

'The ease with which anybody could become to all intents a US citizen amazed me when I first saw the system at work,' I told them. 'People make fun of bureaucratic incompetence, but this was no laughing matter. With a valid US passport, any man or woman can travel freely throughout the civilized world, certainly into every country which presents a terrorist with a desirable target. How can it be that the United States, which prides itself on being the world's leader of the struggle against organized terror, itself provides such a loophole?'

'What about the people your group got into the States?' Snyder asked.

'The immigrants Dergazarian and I smuggled in from the Soviet Union were peaceful, law-abiding folk. But that certainly is not true of other people who may have infiltrated the States and perhaps other countries from Lebanon,' I told them. 'All that is needed is the swearing of an oath. Even finding an American willing to co-operate is not essential: official records can be consulted for names of citizens virtually certain never to have left the country. The swearing of an oath on the bible is still taken seriously by people who live by traditional values but do you honestly believe today that a committed terrorist, often a fanatic for whom the bible has no significance, is going to be deterred from making a false declaration under oath?'

They listened attentively and subsequently, working with the Americans, obtained vital leads which enabled them to penetrate one of the most important drug-smuggling operations. The ring had contacts with a number of terrorist organizations, such as the IRA. It was a great breakthrough and a framed certificate acknowledging their gratitude was presented to de Waal by the US Drug Enforcement Agency.

But the Dutch force was being pestered by the French who now suspected me of being the fence disposing of the things which had been stolen in the Marseilles bank robbery. I knew that Chantal, Stephan's wife, and their children were having a hard time. Stephan had become my friend, so I invited her from time to time to Amsterdam to get away from her village, where all the neighbours knew her husband was in jail, and I had wired her some money, to help the family over a difficult period. The French police followed her everywhere. Chantal stopped flying into Holland, driving instead, but they spotted the car and followed it also.

But Chantal did not drive alone. She was escorted by Jacky Lebreq, who had been an admirer and follower of her husband but who was also under observation, and this was sufficient for the cops to swoop. They had Stephan locked up in Spain. So vengeful were they after the humiliation of the Marseilles robbery that they informed the Spaniards that he might break out given the chance, so he was moved to a high security prison where he was put into solitary confinement. Now, in order to break his spirit completely, they arrested his wife, alleging that she was living off the proceeds of the robbery, although they had not yet proved his guilt.

As for the money I had given her, they assumed that this was part of the money resulting from the robbery and they requested the Dutch to let them come and interview me.

The accusation was ridiculous but as my rebuttal could conceivably help Stephan and take the pressure off Chantal, I agreed to receive them. They suggested that we meet halfway, in Brussels, but this trick was too transparent. I insisted on holding the meeting over dinner in Amsterdam.

After the arrogant behaviour of the French towards me, I was gratified that they now had to ask humbly for the right to interrogate me on Dutch soil and were able to see the good terms I was on with the Dutch police. The restaurant I chose was Thai where the diners knelt on cushions. The big, bold cops who, if the interview had been in France would have had me in jail and bullied me with their questions, were obliged to kneel before me and behave with courtesy while they ate the delicate food I gave them.

I explained why I had given Chantal money. They wanted information on Jacky Lebreq but I am not a grass. Whatever I knew about Jacky was my own business.

# 32

# THE INTEGRITY OF DANIEL WILDENSTEIN

Almost a hundred years before I set up Axel Hammerschmidt, another picture dealer had opened his gallery in the Rue du Faubourg St Honore. Nathaniel Wildenstein already had a reputation for astuteness. He was heavily involved in the Duveen family plots. Before Joe Duveen started seriously trafficking in paintings, he took heavy, gilded furniture from Wildenstein: his aristocratic clients offered such items in exchange for paintings. Duveen sold these antique pieces in London; they were not fashionable enough for refined Paris taste. But when Joe Duveen entered the market, Nathaniel Wildenstein included him in the syndicate formed to carve up the famous Kann collection with finance from J.P. Morgan who secured first choice of the pickings. He was also a moving spirit in the unsuccessful attempt by the Duveen brothers to oust their father from the business. The relationship survived this; old Joel Duveen was dying and soon Joe Duveen was in command. As one of the Duveen partners, Joe's uncle Henry, put it, they wanted the best pictures and Wildenstein had them.

That was precisely what I felt when Madam Nakamura told me Gekkoso were on the look out for top-class Old Masters. Wildenstein had an enormous stock of paintings; maybe I could do business with them. With galleries in New York, Buenos Aires and London as well as Paris, they would hardly resent me as a rival. However, they did have a jointly-owned company in Tokyo, trading under the Wildenstein name, and I suspected that it had dealt with the MOA, so it seemed prudent to approach Daniel Wildenstein, the head of the firm and of the family, to explain frankly for whom I would be dealing and ensure that there would not be any conflict of interest. I had never met him, nor had I any formal introduction, so taking my courage in both hands, I phoned him out of the blue.

Since the buccaneering days of grandfather Nathaniel, Wildenstein had acquired an impressive patina of respectability. Daniel was very accessible and received me cordially in the Paris premises which Wildenstein claim is not a gallery but a centre for research and for their publications. I did not know it at the time, but Daniel Wildenstein had reason to pay attention to his relations with the French tax authorities. They objected to his claiming to live in Lausanne since he spent so much time in France and they put him in prison to show that they meant business.

However, Daniel, then in his sixties, was the doyen of the Paris art world. Not only was he the only dealer to be a member of the Academie des Beaux Arts, the highest academic distinction the French Republic can bestow, he was also an acknowledged leader of Paris society. The owner of a great stable, his horses had twice won the Prix de l'Arc de Triomphe; Daniel, with his carefully dyed red hair and escorted by beautiful young ladies, cut quite a dashing figure at Longchamps. He embodied the self-assured arrogance of the family, 'our dynasty' as his son, Guy, expressed it to me.

I was very open with him, reminding him that I had already sold the Rembrandt self-portrait to the MOA, and said that they would be my ultimate client. I made no attempt to conceal my contacts: with the extraordinary intelligence network which Wildenstein possessed it would have been futile; moreover, I had complete confidence in the integrity of the Wildenstein name.

Daniel indicated that they could help me, and mentioned several works they could offer, including an outstanding El Greco. Then he asked whether such a painting would be exhibited soon after its purchase. I told him that several years had elapsed before the Rembrandt went on show.

'More than five years?' he enquired.

I said that would probably be the case and he seemed satisfied.

Daniel made two conditions: first, the name of Wildenstein should not appear anywhere in the transaction. Later he was to allege that it was I who imposed this condition, to conceal the name of Wildenstein from my client in case they went direct and cut me out of the deal. This was patently absurd. Wildenstein's name was so renowned that to quote it would have been an enormous advantage. I supposed then that the benevolent old gentleman thought he was helping to boost my reputation by suggesting that I could offer this important painting without an intermediary.

His second condition was that future meetings should be with his son, Guy, who was based in New York. Subsequently, I asked whether my business could be handled out of Europe rather than New York, to which Daniel replied that this was no problem. I suppose that the Paris establishment could have got itself into hot water with those troublesome tax people if it was used too brazenly for buying or selling, but for whatever reason Guy repeated to me that, irrespective of where we met, the business must be channelled through the American gallery.

Subsequently, Daniel denied on oath in his deposition that this conversation ever took place, stating that my first meeting was not with him, but with Guy. This was a blunder, since in his evidence Guy contradicted his father and bore out my account. Under cross-examination, Daniel repeatedly answered awkward questions by stating that he did not remember. After this forgotten meeting, Daniel contacted Guy and instructed him to make available to me photographs and information on certain paintings.

I found Guy congenial, good-humoured and easy to get on with. He was a keen sportsman and an adept polo player. He was tough and plucky; he once finished a game with a broken foot. At our first meeting, I convinced him that I was serious and was not simply trying to spy out which paintings Wildenstein had in stock and were prepared to offer. I confirmed to him that it was for the MOA Museum that Gekkoso were on the lookout for Old Masters. It was a logical policy for the museum for, although they had an extensive collection of oriental art, Western art was still very under-represented.

Guy consulted his father and proposed a group of works from which I selected two canvases by Velázquez, a Gauguin and the painting of Saint Sebastian by El Greco. I forwarded material to Gekkoso who showed interest in the El Greco and in a Botticelli which Wildenstein also offered. Since their Tokyo company had done business with the MOA, they could have gone direct to the museum with these paintings. I presumed that they were letting me have a crack at selling them as a way of giving a helping hand to a young dealer trying to make a name in a market they had dominated for nearly a century.

Madam Nakamura was delighted, and on 28th March 1983, I asked Guy to reserve the Botticelli and the El Greco. Next day, Gekkoso wrote that they 'will handle' the El Greco *St Sebastian* for $3,200,000 and *Profile Portrait of a Woman* by Botticelli for $2,000,000. As usual, they stipulated a possible discount of about fifteen per cent, a common enough practice in Japan, but not regarded as proper in the genteel European art market. My asking price for the El Greco which Wildenstein offered to me for $2,400,000 had been in the range $3,400,000–3,500,000.

In August, I was back in Japan and Wildenstein had consigned the paintings from New York to their shipping agents in Tokyo. A typically Japanese problem arose. The head of the SKK wished to see the pictures before they finalized a deal with Gekkoso but it was unthinkable for a man who was treated with the awe due to divinity to be dragged into a warehouse. The paintings had to be shown in the gallery but, since they had not yet been paid for, the agents were not authorized to release them. So I sent a telex to Guy explaining the situation, naming Gekkoso. I did not mention the MOA for reasons of security, since I was sending my telexes from the Okura Hotel. Daniel tried to use this omission later to claim that he had never been aware that the MOA were my client. Guy agreed, under certain conditions, to allow the paintings to be temporarily removed. I collected them and presented myself at the office of Gekkoso.

It was nine o'clock in the morning, the streets were thronged and the rush-hour traffic was as dense as ever. However, nobody had yet turned up at Gekkoso. The gallery was locked, so there I was on the pavement with an El Greco under one arm and a Botticelli under the other. There is absolutely nothing to stop me walking off with them, I thought with a grin. A few months later, I almost wished I had!

Both works met with the approval of the MOA, so Gekkoso confirmed their purchase but, true to form, they knocked down the price, and we settled for a total of $4,350,000 for the two. However, I was able to extract a non-returnable deposit of $50,000 and then negotiated a concession from Wildenstein to compensate for about half of the rapid rise in the yen which was reflected in the lower dollar price now offered by Gekkoso. We agreed that I would pay $2,900,000 for the two.

It had been my intention to make payment to Wildenstein after receiving a first instalment from Gekkoso but they were holding back until they were paid by the MOA. Guy Wildenstein was friendly, helpful and encouraging. Far from indicating any conflict of interests, he suggested that we might cooperate in the Japanese market, which meant primarily in selling to the MOA.

The prospect of becoming Wildenstein's partner in such deals was fantastic. Japan was the up-and-coming market, and Wildenstein the ideal source of important works. In September, I flew to New York to sign a contract with Guy and met him at Kennedy airport. Because of Gekkoso's delay in settlement, I increased my purchase price to $3,000,000 to show my good faith and my appreciation of his sympathetic approach. We signed an amended contract to which Guy added in his own handwriting that the El Greco was 'the property of Dr Hinderling'. I never even left the airport but flew straight back to Paris. A short time afterward, I remitted $150,000 to Wildenstein as a first payment.

Daniel stated during the trial that a month before that meeting, Guy had told him that I hoped to sell the El Greco to the MOA. I had met Guy three or four times previously, and Daniel had been present on each occasion. There cannot be the slightest doubt that he knew that the MOA were the ultimate buyers and that they were demanding certain reassurances on both paintings. Yet he testified in court that if he had known that I was going to approach the MOA, he would never have offered me the painting, hence his denial of our first meeting. However, for the whole of the next year, he did nothing to dissuade me from the sale, and on a number of occasions when questioned, he assured me that there was absolutely no problem with the painting.

Gekkoso proceeded cautiously with the purchase of the two Old Masters. Everybody in the firm from Yoko Nakamura downwards was prepared to take infinite pains to allay any doubts which the museum officials might express. But at the same time, Madam Nakamura was willing to use all the political muscle she could command or cajole to bring pressure to bear on her very demanding client. And that was where the intimate circle of her Cercle de Crillon were so helpful.

Prime Minister Nakasone laid aside his modelling clay and paid a visit to the MOA Museum at Atami. The party moved slowly, pausing to admire the treasures. Nakasone walked purposefully to where the Rembrandt self-portrait had recently been hung. He looked at it carefully and with an approving nod remarked to his hosts, 'I hear that your beautiful Rembrandt is soon to be joined by a brother and a sister.'

There were polite smiles all round, but the message was clear. The men of the MOA should stop dallying: the Botticelli girl and the El Greco man ought to be hanging beside the Rembrandt.

The factions within the SKK and the MOA were fighting over the Leonardo and now there were questions over these paintings. But Yoko Nakamura was resolved to push the deals through and once again she had outmanoeuvred the opposition. Nobody wanted to defy so powerful a political boss, despite genuine doubts about all the pictures. Yoko Nakamura stood close to Nakasone, her face a mask. She was the inscrutable Sphinx of the Ginza, marvelled at for her enormous ability, envied for her success and feared for her influence.

While Madam Nakamura was working on the Petit Palais deal and persuading the SKK board to buy the Leonardo for the MOA, that group was raising objections to the two Old Masters I had taken from Wildenstein.

The problem with the Botticelli was, were they getting the picture described in the literature? A few years earlier, Marubeni, one of the big trading houses, had brought in a fine Botticelli which had been bought by the Japanese National Museum in Tokyo. It was customary for institutions, unused to the technicalities of dealing overseas, to channel such operations through the leading trading houses, whose reputations also reassured sellers unfamiliar with Japanese business. But when museum officials compared the painting with photographs in art books, they spotted significant differences. During the war, the painting had been hidden in a cave. How could they be sure they were getting the painting which had been taken into the cave so many years ago? Alarm bells sounded; unscrupulous Western dealers were attempting to palm off an inferior painting in place of the Botticelli.

A team of experts, led by Peter Wilson, was sent out to Tokyo, inspected the painting and explained that it was the same picture but that the books used photographs taken years before and that subsequently the painting had been restored and later additions removed. What the museum now had was more authentic than the painting as photographed. But how could he prove it? Wilson insisted it was the same painting but each time he was asked to prove the unprovable. Eventually he had to laugh, but then he was denounced as hiding behind the deceitful smile. The Japanese press wrote of a clique of deceitful foreigners telling this story in smoke-filled rooms to dupe the honest Japanese. The museum took fright and backed out of the deal. Marubeni's good name was at stake, so they completed the purchase. The painting now graces the office of the president of Marubeni who is unwilling to sell it in case it revives memories of the scandal. Meanwhile the company is content to hold on to a tremendously profitable investment.

Wildenstein's Botticelli also differed from pre-war photographs and for the same reason: it had been restored, and eighteenth- or nineteenth-century additions removed. Look at the provenance, protested Wildenstein. The painting was from the collection of Lord Rothermere and had been authenticated by Bernard Berenson himself. That was a few years before the publication of a book, *The Artful Partners*, which revealed the extent to which Berenson had a financial stake in the paintings he approved for Duveen and how closely they worked with Wildenstein, so his name was still highly respected in Japan. But is this the painting Berenson saw, demanded Gekkoso? Pedretti, who did not confine his activities to Leonardo studies, certified that the painting was genuine, but they wanted more proof. Because of the sensitivity the Marubeni affair had caused, they could not afford the merest trace of suspicion, so the panel was subjected to rigorous analyses.

There were X-ray and infra-red studies by the Swiss Institute for Art Research in Zurich and samples of paint and wood were sent to Dr Hermann Kuhn in Munich. These bore out that the materials were consistent with the painting being of the right period. But the restoration work had been so heavy handed, with a lot of infilling, that when Dr Bosshard, then a member of the Department of Technology at the Swiss Institute, now conservator of the Thyssen-Bornemisza collection in Lugano, examined the panel, he complained that it was difficult finding sufficient spots of the original work for him to take pigment samples for analysis. The picture was also examined at the Courtauld Institute, but Mr Headley, who had gone to the National Conservator Center in Ottawa, was not prepared to declare unreservedly that this was the same painting. The ruinous state of the picture and the lingering doubts that maybe it was not the original were partly responsible for my spending two years seeking technical reports and dealing with the points raised by the Japanese, but the purchase was finally dropped because of the scandal which arose over the El Greco.

The *St Sebastian* was a genuine El Greco, exactly as in the illustrations. It also had an impressive provenance, having for something like seventy years been in the Romanian royal collection, then acquired in Switzerland by a Dr Hinderling, or so I was assured by Daniel Wildenstein, who said there had never been any question over title to the picture. Then in May 1984, the MOA informed Gekkoso that while the painting had been on loan to an exhibition at the Prado, it had been claimed, together with another El Greco, *Canon Bosio*, with the same provenance, by 'alleged descendants of King Carol' – that is, royal bastards as they were later described by Daniel Wildenstein – and that fearful of a big scandal, 'the organizer of the exhibition, Mr William B. Jordan, sent these two works back to the USA in great haste'.

Yoko Nakamura was furious. This revelation was a terrible humiliation. She rounded on me. Was I trying to deceive her when I said that there was no question over ownership, or was I so inefficient that I had not checked the provenance?

I was thunderstruck. Nobody at Wildenstein had said a word about the incident and I immediately flew back to Paris and met Daniel and Guy. The MOA demanded a certificate, guaranteeing them against any similar 'problems or litigation in either foreign countries or Japan'. What I got from Daniel was a declaration that the Prado incident was a lot of nonsense and there had been no claim against the *St Sebastian*. He also gave me a written statement that the painting had been bought in Switzerland from King Michael through the intermediacy of Princess Marie-Gabrielle de Savoie and that the painting had been in Switzerland for about thirty years.

Since this had nothing to do with the MOA's request, they continued to press Gekkoso who pressed me. Their original assertion was incorrect: the claim at the Prado was not on behalf of the 'royal bastards' but of the Romanian Government, and when this became clear they demanded a guarantee that there was no claim by the government and that none would be made.

Daniel continued to maintain that there was no claim to the painting. I repeated his assurances, but the Japanese wanted something more substantial than a bald statement. Daniel Wildenstein finally gave me a guarantee, offering to refund $2,000,000 should any claim succeed in a Swiss court, which also sidestepped the questions put by the MOA – was there ever any claim on the painting and, in particular, had there been an attempt to seize it at the Prado in May 1982?

The Romanian case was that the paintings had been stolen when King Michael, who abdicated in 1945, had taken them out of the country. They did not belong to him, they argued, but to the 'crown of Romania' and furthermore their permanent removal from the country was expressly forbidden in the will of King Carol I who had originally bought them in 1878. The Romanian government was attempting to recover property from ex-Queen Elena, Michael's mother, and her heirs through the Portuguese courts, since she had taken up residence in Cascais, near Lisbon. Their lawyer, Galvao Teles, knew he was unlikely to get any response from the authorities in such countries as Switzerland or the United States, but the shipment of the paintings to Spain presented an opportunity to take effective action, or so he thought.

The Portuguese judge, in response to an application by Teles, requested the Spanish Ministry of Justice to order that the paintings should not be removed from Spain pending the outcome of the case to determine their ownership before the Portuguese court. The Spanish tribunal agreed, and an order was issued, freezing the paintings.

But before agreeing to let the paintings leave the country, Wildenstein had persuaded the American organizers of the exhibition to obtain from the director-general of Bellas Artes, a section of the Spanish Ministerio de Cultura, a guarantee that their paintings would be granted immunity from any claims while on loan in Spain and would be returned to the United States. Of course, if no claim was made at so well-publicized an exhibition, it would look ridiculous if the Romanian government were to try to make a claim subsequently. And, since the exhibition was for a limited period, he could take a chance on the 'communistic government', to use his phrase, being sufficiently well organized to launch a claim in a foreign country. He could then show that the painting had been displayed at an important exhibition and thus add credibility to its provenance. But if, contrary to his expectations, the Romanians did succeed in lodging a claim, he could count on it being towards the end of the exhibition which would reflect badly on the Romanians, and anyway he was covered by the guarantee of the Bellas Artes.

The men at the Prado were in a quandary. Should they honour the undertaking given by the ministry or obey the law? The Americans were not willing to wait and Alfredo Perez, the director general of the Bellas Artes, who was personally involved in the exhibition, agreed to honour his undertaking in defiance of the court. The moment the exhibition closed the paintings were removed by Jesus Macarron, a well-known specialist in framing and shipping, and moved to the United States embassy. Perez signed a paper, transferring responsibility for the pictures to Roger Mandle, the curator of the museum in Toledo, Ohio, who had originated the exhibition. The two El Grecos were flown to New York the following day.

A couple of days earlier, the Toledo museum had been informed that the Spaniards had refused to grant an export permit for the *Canon Bosio*, and presumably also for the *St Sebastian*. Macarron persuaded the Spanish customs that the export permit, given when the temporary import licence was issued, was still valid.

Trouble had been anticipated. As early as 1st February, the US government had acted to foreclose any official action by American courts with respect to the Spanish paintings when the exhibition reached the United States.

I resolved to get a statement from the man who must have known what had happened, Dr William Jordan, assistant director of the Kimbell Museum in Fort Worth which had bought the Canon Bosio, and organizer of the exhibition at the Prado.

I called the Kimbell and was told that Dr Jordan was in Washington. I put in a call to his hotel, explained who I was and why it was vital for me to obtain an accurate account of what had happened at the Prado. We agreed that I should call on him when he returned to Fort Worth, which would be after he had made a short visit to New York.

Bill Jordan at once called Alec Wildenstein. He had just learned that the Romanian government were filing a suit in a Texan court for the return of the *Canon Bosio* but although he phoned to check on who I was and whether I had bought the other painting, he swore on oath that he never mentioned the Prado incident in that conversation.

But with the Japanese insisting there had been a claim and Daniel Wildenstein repeating that there was no problem, I was impatient for independent confirmation and I could not afford to wait for Jordan's return to Forth Worth. Learning that he was to stay at the Westbury Hotel in New York, I despatched

Paul Polak who was waiting in the lobby when he arrived on 28th July.

Jordan seemed embarrassed by the unexpected intrusion. Paul explained that he was my assistant and Jordan told him that the Romanians had attempted to prevent the *Canon Bosio* from being shipped out of Spain and that they had filed a complaint in May against the Kimbell.

'What about the *St Sebastian?*' Paul asked. 'Did they try to have that held in Spain also?'

Jordan shook his head. 'No, it was just our painting.'

'Would you object to confirming that in writing?'

Jordan considered for a moment. 'Well, sure, as soon as I get back to Fort Worth, I'll send a note to Mr van Rijn.'

'Why not now?' Paul pressed. 'It really is urgent that we calm down our clients.'

'I haven't brought any headed stationery with me,' Jordan pointed out.

'That doesn't matter. Here, let me get some hotel paper. All we need is a brief note, nothing formal; it can be handwritten.'

Jordan wrote:

> July 26th 1984
>
> To: Mr Michel van Rijn
> As we discussed recently, the Kimbell Art Museum's in concert with the Prado Museum and the owners of both the *Bosio* and the El Greco portrait of *St Sebastian* (which had the same provenance but was not named in the Romanian suit), removed the two paintings from the exhibition and transported them to the National Gallery of Art in Washington, which was the next venue of the exhibition. The Romanians have since filed suit in the US federal court in Forth Worth, Texas for the 'recovery' of the Bosio. We fully expect to win this suit.
>
> W.M. Jordan.

Paul thanked Jordan and left. As soon as I heard from him, I called Kaneko.

'I have Dr Jordan's written statement that, just as I told you, the St Sebastian was not claimed by the Romanians at the Prado,' I said. 'I am sending you the note in Dr Jordan's own handwriting.'

Kaneko was delighted but Daniel Wildenstein called me and was furious. He shouted that I should not have approached Jordan and must not speak to him again. I could not understand why he should have been so upset: Jordan had merely confirmed Wildenstein's story.

Shortly afterwards, Kaneko asked whether I could get Jordan to rewrite his note on Kimbell headed stationery, but when I called him his attitude was completely changed.

'No, Mr van Rijn, there is no way I will write that statement on Kimbell paper. In fact, I deeply regret having written the note and I would be obliged if you will return it to me.'

'But why?' I demanded.

'My lawyer, John Johndroe, warns me that I should not have made any sort of statement about the attempt to seize the *Canon Bosio* while the case is before the courts.'

'But I am interested in the *St Sebastian*,' I pointed out.

'Even so, I have acted imprudently, so please send me back my letter and do not call me again.'

But the people at MOA were still not convinced and Jordan's anxiety to retrieve his letter persuaded me that I should speak with Johndroe, whom I called on 16th August. The lawyer added nothing to the version that the *St Sebastian* had not been involved but in his evidence before the court he swore that he had actually admitted that the yarn Wildenstein and Jordan had told me was untrue and that the Romanians had tried to seize both paintings at the Prado. As if to bolster up his fabrication, he produced a memorandum which he said he had made of our conversation. Is it your practice to record all telephone conversations, even when imparting no information, at such length? he was asked, but the Texan was impervious to irony.

Daniel had carefully avoided committing himself in writing, but I had Jordan's note and Jordan had been in contact with Alec Wildenstein and with Daniel, who had been so annoyed at my having talked with Jordan, yet Jordan testified that he could not recall whether he had spoken to Daniel.

During the summer there was something of a lull, but Jordan still wanted his letter back and he agreed to see me. I visited him in the Kimbell, where I recognized a number of paintings which had at one time been offered by Wildenstein. This strengthened my conviction that the relationship betwen Jordan and the Wildensteins was particularly close.

Jordan, although surrounded by his files, still made no attempt to amend his story: all that concerned him was retrieving his damaging letter.

'The problem is', I told him sympathetically, 'that I have sent it to my Japanese clients.'

'Could you persuade them to return it?' he asked.

I refrained from observing that as they were howling for him to confirm the letter on Kimbell stationery, they were hardly likely to give up the only document they had. However, I offered to approach them if he would request the return of the letter in writing. He must have been a very worried man because he instantly dictated the following on Kimbell headed paper, dated 29th October:

> Dear Mr van Rijn,
> Some months ago, I wrote you a letter on stationery from the Westbury Hotel in New York concerning a painting by El Greco. As we are currently involved in a lawsuit with the government of Romania over a painting by this artist which we own, I would very much appreciate it if you would return this letter to me.
> Thank you very much,
>
> Sincerely yours,
> William B. Jordan
> Deputy Director

I perused this letter with interest. For the life of me, I could not see how my possession of Jordan's letter had any bearing on the action against the Kimbell. I detected the hand of Johndroe, who knew that Jordan's statement was untrue and could be damaging for his client. I was very content to have Jordan's formal request for its return since that acknowledged that he had written the original letter. It would now be impossible for him to disavow it.

Incredibly, Jordan persisted in his story that the *St Sebastian* was not involved in the Prado incident, even at the end of October; but to satisfy the Japanese I decided to clear the matter up once and for all. I called Jordan yet again. This time, he admitted that his version had not been true. He was apologetic and agreed to receive me, so on 13th November I went to Fort Worth, listened to Jordan's excuses and waited while he dictated yet another letter which I took back with me. In this letter, at last he came out into the open.

> Dear Mr van Rijn,
> As you will recall, some months ago, following several transatlantic telephone calls you made concerning El Greco's *St Sebastian*, formerly owned by Wildenstein, you sent a colleague of yours to meet with me at my hotel in New York [the Westbury]. At your urging, I wrote by hand a letter on the hotel stationery stating that, to the best of my recollection, the said painting had not been part of an attempted seizure by the Romanian Government, through the Spanish courts, of this museum's El Greco portrait of Giacomo Bosio during the El Greco exhibition in Madrid in 1982. I am afraid that, being away from my files and not being prepared to deal with this matter, my recollection was faulty. The Spanish court action did attempt to seize both El Grecos which had previously belonged to the kings of Romania. We have since been sued by the Romanian Government in the US federal courts, and this suit is now pending. It is my understanding

that they intend to pursue the *St Sebastian* in the same manner.

I am concerned that I mislead [sic] you or your client, and I would like to retrieve the letter that I wrote from New York and to correct the record. We are confident that we can win this suit, but the matter may be in litigation for some time.

Thank you very much,
Sincerely yours,
William B. Jordan
Deputy Director

I noted the insertion of the phrase, 'to the best of my recollection'. When he met Paul, Jordan had not found it necessary to qualify his answer, so slipping in this reservation seems, since he had no copy of his original letter before him, another case of defective memory. What I found more bewildering was how a man in so responsible a position could have forgotten the attempted seizure of our El Greco only a couple of years earlier. Such an incident should have been indelibly imprinted in the memory of an official who had organized an exhibition. And what a strange coincidence that this lapse of memory corresponded excactly with the version I was given by Daniel Wildenstein!

Bill Jordan strenuously denied this. It was an honest misunderstanding, he protested. If only he had been able to consult his files that day in the Westbury, he would have realized that he was confusing two quite separate issues. Paul had asked if the *St Sebastian* had been involved in the Prado incident: his reply had been to a different question – were the Romanians claiming the *St Sebastian* in the same suit as the Bosio? Of course not, since the paintings were owned by different people. An honest error? An error Dr Jordan did not notice for four months. He was busy with other things, but with litigation pending over the *Canon Bosio*, it is remarkable that he did not find the time to consult those crucial files in which his memory was apparently entombed, even when I visited him at Fort Worth.

Now that there was no shadow of doubt, I had to telex Kaneko and admit that, misled by Daniel Wildenstein backed up by Bill Jordan, my rebuttal of MOA's account was wrong.

Whether the Kimbell or Wildenstein would win their cases was not the point. The Japanese had been assured there was no case outstanding against the *St Sebastian* whereas it was common knowledge, at least in Fort Worth, that such a case was in preparation. They had also been informed that the painting had not been involved in the Prado incident. This was completely untrue. And since these pieces of misinformation had been channelled through me, their confidence in me as well as in these deals had been shattered.

The Prado incident occurred in May 1982. Mandle drafted a memorandum setting out the attempt by the Spanish court to seize both paintings. 'In 1978 (or earlier)' he wrote, 'the Romanian government tried to get Wildenstein (or some other owners) to return the paintings to Romania which says it has legal claim to these works, their having been sold without the proper authority and ownership by the former royal family.'

On 7th November 1984, Daniel Wildenstein sent me the following telex:

> I WISH TO STATE THAT NO CLAIM WAS MADE AT THIS DATE BY THE ROMNIAN GOVERNMENT OR ANY OTHER PARTY FOR THE GRECO PAINTING *ST SEBASTIAN*.

On 15th November, Kaneko informed me that the MOA had cancelled the contracts for both the El Greco and the Botticelli. The effect on my business in Japan was catastrophic and I sought redress in the courts from Wildenstein. But the fracas over the Old Masters was also the fuse which exploded the relationship between Gekkoso and MOA. After this loss of face by Gekkoso, their opponents within the MOA switched their attack to Madam Nakamura's conduct in the matter of the Leonardo.

> A very short time before our client was going to take delivery of the paintings he got absolute proof that the ownership of the El Greco was insecure since the Romanian government had taken action to try and seize the painting in Spain. This was contrary to what Mr van Rijn had told us.
>
> It is because of the fact that this claim had been raised against the painting that we have been forced to cancel the agreement with Mr van Rijn and because of his fake information we will cancel all our business and stop eventual future business.

Those were the concluding paragraphs of a telex from Kaneko to Cameron Clark, a New York lawyer I retained to prosecute my case against Wildenstein. And in the three years from the cancellation of the contracts until the case came to trial, not one piece of business materialized with Gekkoso.

When Gekkoso informed me that their purchase of the El Greco and the Botticelli had been 'irrevocably cancelled', I immediately telexed Wildenstein, reclaiming the money which I had already paid. Daniel received the telex on 15th November 1984, communicated its contents to Guy in New York, and payment was made the same day, less $33,000 which Wildenstein claimed was the cost of shipping, insuring and storing the paintings in Japan. Of course, if the deal had collapsed because of some capricious change of mind on my part, this would have been justifiable, but why should I be penalized for Daniel Wildenstein's inconsistency? I had spent a great deal more than that. Shouldn't *they* be liable for *my* expenses? And what about my loss of profits as the bad news spread like a disease and business with my other Japanese clients died?

When I approached the Wildensteins, Guy was sympathetic but Daniel denied responsibility and refused any compensation. So, I had no alternative but to do the unthinkable, to take legal action against the most powerful gallery owner in the world, to accuse the most respected of dealers of fraudulent misrepresentation. When I briefed my lawyer, I never expected that Daniel would fight the action. He might challenge my assessment of damages, that was to be expected; but dragging the Wildenstein name through the courts and disclosing such things as the way they hid their ownership of the painting behind their Swiss lawyer or their readiness to acquire works of dubious provenance and hold them in Switzerland long enough to acquire good title, surely they would not allow this to come out into the open? Even if they were to win the action, the unwelcome publicity, I reckoned, must persuade them to settle out of court, and it might very well have proved cheaper. But I did not know just how obstinate Daniel was or with what tenacity he and his lawyer, Jeremy Epstein, were prepared to fight.

My case was straightforward. By first concealing the Prado incident, Daniel Wildenstein had caused the MOA and Gekkoso to cancel their purchases and gravely damaged my business. Daniel and Epstein relied on three tactics to defeat this argument. First, to present Daniel in a sympathetic light. Secondly, to argue that he had good title and that was all that mattered. Thirdly, to throw as much mud as possible at me to confuse the jury and obscure the issue.

Daniel at first tried to give the impression that he was a rather nice old man, aloof from the business to such an extent that he did not even know his own official status. He was questioned by Janet Hoffman, my junior counsel.

*Hoffman*: Mr Wildenstein, what is your occupation?
*Daniel*: I'm a retired art dealer.
*Hoffman*: Are you still in business?
*Daniel*: Yes. Off and on, yes.

*Hoffman*: What is your position with the company?
*Daniel*: I'm one of the directors, I think. I'm not any more.
*Hoffman*: You are not currently a director?
*Epstein*: I think Mr Wildenstein said he is a director.
*Daniel*: I am one of the – I own –
*Epstein*: You are chairman.

He was just as dismissive and vague about his sons, appearing unsure as to whether they were officers of the company, whether they were stockholders, what Guy's responsibilities were, and so on.

Daniel argued that when I found myself in difficulties with my client, he went out of his way to be helpful. He even gave me that guarantee, promising to refund $2 million should there be a successful action to reclaim the painting within two years before a Swiss court. My counsel argued that this was 'a pretty worthless guarantee', depending as it did on a Japanese company being sued by the Romanians before a Swiss court (they had already started proceedings in Portugal and then in the United States). Daniel replied that they could sue anywhere else if they wanted, but that of course was not covered by his guarantee.

*Daniel*: . . . And don't forget, Mr van Rijn had not paid one cent at the time I gave him that.
*Clark*: Are you certain of that, Mr Wildenstein?
*Daniel*: What?
*Clark*: Are you very certain of that?
*Daniel*: No. He paid a few, he sent a few, ten or twenty or thirty, or $40,000.
*Clark*: How about $165,000?
*Daniel*: That's possible.

But soon more important inconsistencies began to emerge in his testimony. Had he known I was going to offer the painting to the MOA Museum, he would not have allowed me to have it, he declared. Yet, Guy Wildenstein stated that he had known a month before they concluded a contract selling the picture to me. But Daniel's evidence was not only in conflict with his son's; he was prepared to contradict himself. He told the court that it was I who had requested that Wildenstein's name did not appear and to assist me, he had shown Dr Hinderling, his lawyer, as the owner of the painting. But in his deposition, he had declared that I wanted him to be named and he had answered that he was a resident of Switzerland, 'but as I am not in Switzerland a lot of times . . . therefore I put my lawyer. Lawyers are made for that, no?'

Questioned about his failure to disclose the Prado incident, however, Daniel revealed quite a different character. He claimed that he had told me about it in 1984, prior to the lawsuit for the recovery of the *St Sebastian* coming before a court in New York in 1985, and hadn't spoken to me about it before because 'there was no claim whatsoever by anyone whatsoever'.

So how did Daniel square this statement with the undisputed attempt by the Romanians to seize the painting in 1982 at the Prado when a case was before the Portuguese court? He simply affirmed that no claim would succeed, therefore there was no claim. When it was pointed out that what was at issue was not the result in some hypothetical case but quite simply the concealment of the Romanian attempt to seize the painting, he dismissed the incident as irrelevant.

Daniel's assertion that there had never been any case brought for the recovery of the paintings was of course challenged by my attorney who produced telexes sent to the company and in one case personally to Daniel by the Portuguese lawyer representing the Romanian government. Daniel tried to deny ever seeing the telex. When cornered by Clark, he retreated and insisted that he did not remember. He repeated this act throughout the trial, when faced with facts that could not be denied.

Jeremy Epstein, a quick-witted, combative protagonist, presented Daniel as the soul of integrity, a pillar of the artistic establishment; by implication, I was a mere adventurer. How could a jury take my word against his!

To demonstrate the awesome respectability of the Wildenstein name, Epstein called Thomas Hoving, a former director of the Metropolitan Museum of Art in New York and currently editor of *Connoisseur*.

Hoving proclaimed his belief in Wildenstein's integrity. A concern with branches in New York, London, Paris, Buenos Aires and Tokyo, that had been in the business 'from the beginning' inspired confidence. But under cross-examination, Hoving's ebullience got out of control. When he ran the Met, he claimed, he would check the history of every item offered by a dealer. Even if its provenance was produced by the dealer? he was asked. Especially then, he asserted. In a short time, he would know more about the piece than the dealer himself. So he would never rely on the word of the dealer. And would that apply to the Wildenstein crew? Sure, he would thank them for their research and then do the checking all over again with his own uncommitted museum team. The jury might have concluded that the integrity of the Wildenstein name was no more to be taken for granted than that of any lesser mortal.

But Tom Hoving was faced by a dilemma. I was convinced that there was a cosy coterie of leading dealers, critics and museum directors. Hoving insisted that he was not being paid by Epstein or Wildenstein, but if one of his circle was in a spot of bother, would it not be only natural for him to give support, just as paintings offered by Wildenstein would be looked at more sympathetically than those from somebody outside his charmed circle?

This was vigorously denied by Hoving who pointed out that he could recall that while at the Met, he once paid more for a Caravaggio from another source than he had spent on any single purchase from Wildenstein. He had been summoned to sing Wildenstein's praises but was now obliged to soft pedal.

If he were to admit that he would give more credence to a Wildenstein provenance than to one from another dealer, that might be taken as evidence of an over-friendly relationship.

But this chumminess became obvious when Hoving described how he had been briefed on the case over lunch by Epstein. He had checked with the legal adviser to the Metropolitan Museum about the litigation over the El Grecos, but had he been told about the case in the Portuguese courts? No, and he had not asked about it. Did he know anything about a catalogue by a Leo Bachelin? No, nor had he been told anything about the will of King Carol I; he had never seen the document and had no idea of its provisions. All he knew about the case was what he had been fed by Epstein. He was not being called to testify as to facts. His job was to proclaim what jolly decent fellows they all were at Wildenstein. The Prado incident had not been important: he had been told so by Carter Brown, Director of the National Gallery in Washington, and also one of the inner circle, so that settled the matter!

At the end of his deposition, he petulantly pointed out that he was Dr Hoving, not Mr Hoving as he had been addressed throughout. Whatever might have been made of his somewhat guarded defence of Wildenstein's integrity, it was clear that not one word of his testimony had any bearing on whether the details of the Prado incident had been deliberately suppressed, which was what the case was about.

'So what's so important about this catalogue by Leo Bachelin?' asked Paul. The court had recessed while the judge considered arguments put forward by Epstein opposing the introduction of the Bachelin catalogue as evidence.

'According to the will of King Carol I, it is the paintings which were included in this catalogue which must stay permanently in Romania. Wildenstein and his lawyer know that the St Sebastian is included,' I replied.

'Can you prove that Wildenstein knows?'

'Goddammit, Paul, have a look at the provenance he gave me. The very first reference is to the Bachelin catalogue. Of course he knew, but if they can disallow the book as evidence, we won't be able to make the point to the jury.'

'So what is Epstein's objection?'

'The Bachelin catalogue has been put forward as evidence by the Romanian government in their case against Wildenstein and Epstein says he is not prepared to accept a document coming from a "communistic" government in case they have tampered with it.'

'Wait a minute,' Paul protested. 'When was this catalogue published?'

'In 1898,' I told him. 'It was OK for the provenance when it suited Wildenstein: it becomes communist misinformation when it is used to nail them. And do you know where we got the copy we are submitting as evidence?'

Paul shook his head. 'From Wildenstein themselves. They wanted to withhold it: my lawyer had to order them to produce it.'

'Hold it,' Paul objected. 'Even if the court allows the catalogue as evidence, can you produce King Carol's will or prove that it states specifically the paintings to remain permanently are the ones listed by Bachelin?'

'That is stated in another book, produced for an exhibition in Paris in 1937 for which the El Grecos were lent. Epstein is objecting to the inclusion of that book also. The book is unpublished.'

'So maybe Daniel didn't know about it?'

'It was produced by his father's publishing firm for the exhibition which was organized by him, assisted by Daniel.'

'As Daniel knew all this, that means the Romanians have a case that the paintings were taken illegally out of the country.'

'It means that they were stolen by King Michael in 1945, or rather by his mother, since he was technically a minor, and Daniel Wildenstein possibly knew that when he bought them thirty years later. Swiss law allows a buyer title if he has held something for five years and he bought it in good faith, even if it turns out that it was stolen. It explains why he was so concerned when I first met him that the painting would not be displayed for five years after he sold it to me and also why when he bought it the buyer was shown as his lawyer. We can show that Daniel Wildenstein must have known all about the doubtful title to the painting, but we cannot prove that Dr Hinderling did.'

Paul was right. The crucial question was whether Daniel was aware of any doubt as to ex-King Michael being the legal owner of the pictures and his mother having the legal right to dispose of them when he bought them in 1976. If so, he could hardly claim to have been a *bona fide* buyer and the fact that he had held the *St Sebastian* for more than five years would no longer give him undisputed title.

Daniel fudged and dodged, saying that, 'Things that belong to the crown belong to the King', and that the unpublished book meant nothing, as its author might have intended to correct it.

Eventually, he was asked by Janet Hoffman whether 'you or any Wildenstein' were aware of statements 'to the effect that the Bachelin catalogue El Grecos had been left to the crown of Romania forever and wholly to remain in Romania?'

*Daniel*: Maybe that they were left to the crown of Romania, but certainly not to remain in Romania, because the pictures were allowed to get out of Romania with King Michael. Therefore they belonged to him.

But of course the whole basis of the Romanian case was that the pictures were not allowed to go out. All Daniel's answer meant was that if they had been removed illegally, the former king and his mother had got away with it.

Epstein attempted to justify Daniel's contempt for the Romanian government's claim by pointing out that when they came before the courts in Texas for the *Bosio* and in

New York for the *St Sebastian*, both cases failed. The jury might well have been led to believe that the courts had heard the Romanian arguments and decided against them. In fact, their case was never presented: they simply declined to instruct counsel and produce documents which had been demanded. The cases were dismissed because the Romanians did not go to the expense and trouble of pursuing them before courts in the United States.

By now, the outcry over the Leonardo scandal in the Italian and Japanese press had been picked up by papers all over the world. Epstein argued that it was the fiasco over the Leonardo which had led the MOA and Gekkoso to break with me; my complaint about the El Greco was just a smokescreen. This was to fly in the face of the facts. What aroused the Japanese was how Madam Nakamura could justify a price of $10.5 million for a drawing which was not accepted by some scholars as being by Leonardo while the Italians were incensed by its unauthorized exportation, neither of which could possibly explain Gekkoso breaking with me. Kaneko had stated quite definitely that the true reason was the deception over the Prado incident and nothing Epstein could say or hint could alter that fact.

Not suprisingly, Bill Jordan's memory proved even more defective than Daniel's. He had obviously been instructed by Epstein and his own lawyer, John Johndroe, to say as little as possible. That was a pity; Jordan was a chatty individual. But he had this problem remembering facts.

Asked whether he had been told that I had purchased the El Greco from Wildenstein, he could not remember.

*Hoffman*: How did he me get your name?
*Jordan*: I don't remember . . .
*Hoffman*: Did he tell you how he knew there was such an exhibition [The El Greco exhibition at the Prado]?
*Jordan*: . . . He didn't that I recall.

*Hoffman*: Did he tell you that your name was suggested by anybody else as a person to call?
*Jordan*: Not that I remember, no.

And so on. When the questioning turned to the meeting at the Westbury Hotel, his memory showed no improvement.

*Hoffman*: Did you tell Mr van Rijn on the telephone . . . that you were going to the Westburv?
*Jordan*: I don't remember. I must have. Perhaps I did.
*Hoffman*: So you have no recollection of having told Mr van Rijn that you were going to New York after Washington?
*Jordan*: I don't. But I don't remember conversations that vividly.

And so his testimony continued. He remembered nothing that had happened at any stage of our dealings. Eventually the court heard the rigmarole of his having only discovered that he had not told the truth in the Westbury letter when he finally consulted his files – that was the point of his repeated apologies for lapses of memory.

The judge summed up William Jordan: 'He has a very high level of forgettability.'

My impression that Jordan and the people at the Kimbell had a particularly close relationship with the Wildensteins was strenuously denied by both sides. I had recognized quite a lot of exhibits in the museum as having been in Wildenstein's gallery, although, of course, I could not be certain that they had all been purchased directly from the firm. Yet they had not been the first potential buyer Wildenstein approached for the El Grecos. The *Canon Bosio* was offered to the National Gallery in Washington and the Chicago Art Institute without success. The Bavarian State collection in Munich were also approached but Wildenstein got a more interested response in Dallas.

The Southern Methodist University were the proud possessors of the Meadows Museum whose patron, Algur Meadows, paid for its acquisitions, and only works approved by him were bought. Mr Meadows had a long and colourful experience as an art collector. A Texan oil millionaire who had started as a car salesman, he had made a collection for his first wife during the fifties of Spanish paintings and eighteenth-century Italian works. All possessed impressive certificates of authenticity, and every one was a fake. Since Meadows had paid an average of $30,000 for works which should have been worth millions, he might have had some doubts on their authenticity but when he transferred them to a Meadows Foundation, seven Goyas, three El Grecos, a brace of Rubens, a Murillo, four Riberas and a Gauguin, Millet and Corot which had somehow strayed into the Spanish school, they were valued for millions for insurance – and for Mr Meadows' tax deduction! For his second wife, a new collection was formed, glorious array of fake Impressionists and post-Impressionists, supported by certificates from Pacitti and letters from bemused widows of Derain and Vlaminck and from Jeanne Modigliani. The whole lot cost $540,000 and were valued at seven million. The fame of the Meadows collection spread, but with a visit from the American Art Dealers Association the ugly truth emerged. Meadows needed to get his hands on some genuine pictures, and fast. He called in the most important dealer in New York who was not a member of the AADA, Daniel Wildenstein.

So a cordial relationship grew up and Meadows bought other paintings for his private collection and later for the museum. He, and the director of the Meadows Museum, would visit the New York gallery where the president of Wildenstein & Co, Louis Goldenberg, offered them the *Canon Bosio* for two and a half million dollars. But Goldenberg was a sick man and when Daniel's son, Alec, took over the deal the price was inexplicably hiked to three million. Meadows, annoyed by what he construed as a crude attempt to screw him, refused to buy.

The disappointed director of the Meadows Museum was Dr William Jordan. He was already friendly with the people at the Kimbell Art Museum, and it was to that museum that Alec Wildenstein then sold the *Canon Bosio* for the full three million dollars. In 1981, Bill Jordan joined the Kimbell as deputy director. Daniel Wildenstein testified that, after the death of Louis Goldenberg, Alec did a lot of business with the Kimbell.

When Daniel Wildenstein bought the paintings from ex-Queen Elena, he paid $1,575,000 for the two, 'an unprecedented amount' for El Greco, he claimed. Yet, within a year, he had sold the *Bosio* alone for $3,000,000, a profit margin which he indicated was not exceptional in his business.

At the end of the trial, the jury declined to convict Wildenstein on the charges of fraud, but there was no way they could acquit him of having sold me goods in breach of the warranty of merchantibility, and I was awarded damages of $450,000. Stripped of its legal jargon, the judgement meant that Daniel had stuck me with a painting which was unsaleable to any responsible buyer.

The award did not even cover my legal expenses, but money was only a secondary consideration. If I were ever to undertake serious business again, it was crucial that my name be cleared, and it was.

My last impression of Daniel Wildenstein was of a man who had achieved much, socially and professionally, but who was consumed by an arrogant disregard, not only of competitors and clients, but even of his own sons. It was clear from Guy's testimony that all important decisions were taken by his father, whatever the legalities. Daniel ruled the Wildenstein empire, and nobody dared to tell him that the time had passed when he should have retired gracefully and left the running of the firm to younger men.

As for Wildenstein's relations with other dealers and galleries, the same ruthlessness persists. Later, I was to come across other examples of what can most charitably be described as adroit manoeuvres by Daniel Wildenstein.

My secretary, Sylvie, after I ceased trading in Paris, joined the Marumo gallery at Fobourg St Honore, where she was appointed a manager. She submitted a Monet pastel to Daniel Wildenstein for an opinion. He approved of it and said that it would be included in a catalogue raisonnée which his firm would publish. This would of course enhance the value of the picture and Marumo sold it on this undertanding. Suddenly Daniel did not like it any more; it would not be included in the catalogue. The effect of such a switch would be to discredit Marumo with their customers and to reinforce Wildenstein's grip on the market where the galleries which are their competitors are dependent on their good offices in such matters as research and their learned publications.

# 33

# Mosaics

Shortly after I had moved to Amsterdam, Bob Fitzgerald brought to me a gallery owner anxious to buy something outstanding. Peg Goldberg was very much the senior partner of Goldberg and Feldman which was located in Indianapolis where Bob now lived. She had come to Europe to tie up the purchase of a Modigliani nude for $5.5 million. She had a buyer, and finance had been made available to her by the Merchants National Bank, also based in Indianapolis, whose chairman, 'Nick' Frenzel was a friend of hers. Everything was perfect except the painting, which turned out to be a fake. Goldberg was bitterly disappointed but resolved to get hold of some really important work before going back to the States.

Peg Goldberg was a heavily built middle-aged woman, active in local politics, a commissioner of Hamilton County, who had access to influential people. She was not a talkative person but I soon judged that she had a keen business sense.

'Bob says you have some fantastic pieces and I am interested in any sort of work, so long as it is top quality.'

I immediately thought of those beautiful, luminous sixth-century mosaics from Cyprus which were still in Aydin's Munich apartment. Certainly not what one might expect to find in a minor Midwestern gallery, but I told her about them.

'Have you got photographs or transparencies?'

I showed her reproductions of the Christ child held by the Virgin and some of the roundels of the apostles. The effect on this big, tough woman was dramatic: quite simply she fell in love with them.

'Michel, these I must have,' she enthused.

'Listen, Peg,' I said. 'I shall be delighted if you buy some of them but I don't know if Bob has ever discussed the mosaics with you, so let me make the position absolutely clear.'

And I recounted how Aydin had told me of the destruction of the church at Lythrankomi and how he had rescued the ravaged mosaics from the ruins and brought them out of Cyprus.

'So if the church was abandoned, the pieces were not stolen?' she suggested.

'That is a question for the legal experts. All I am saying is that it is possible that the Cypriots might try to claim them if you offer them on the market.'

'Leave me to look into the legal angles,' she replied.

She spoke to her lawyer and to her banker and informed her partner, George Feldman, that they would go ahead with a purchase of around a million dollars, provided Aydin could produce the right documentation.

'This Aydin Dikmen was the official archaeologist attached to the Turkish army, right?' she asked.

'No. He is a qualified archaeologist but he made his own arrangements with the army commanders on the spot,' I corrected her.

'Yeah, but I guess we could still describe him as an official archaeologist. Now will he give us a proper bill of sale and evidence that the mosaics were legally exported?'

I checked with Aydin. Like many orientals, he disliked dealing with women and mistrusted Peg Goldberg from the start but eventually agreed, although he did not want his name to appear anywhere. But passionately as she loved the mosaics, Goldberg was not going to rush into a purchase without checking them out, and so she called Sotheby's office in New York. They confirmed that if they were what we stated, each mosaic could command a price of several million dollars.

Goldberg now saw the prospect of making a huge profit. She offered to buy four of them for a total price of $1,080,000, and she sent a Los Angeles lawyer who acted for us, Ron Faulk, to Munich where he got from Aydin a sales invoice, dated March 1979, on stationery of 'Goklaney's Cash & Co' in Lefkosa, as the Turks have styled Famagusta, indicating that the works had been exported to West Germany and also a document from the office of the prime minister of 'the Turkish Federated State of Cyprus' purporting to be signed by Osman Orek, who was Prime Minister at that time, stating that the works had been legally exported from Cyprus in 1978. She called Frenzel from Europe who sent overnight $1.2 million to the Swiss Bank Corporation in Geneva. Of this money, she kept $120,000 and paid $350,000 to Aydin, $325,000 each to Bob Fitzgerald and myself and $80,000 to Ron Faulk, all in cash. The balance was taken up by shipping, bank and insurance charges. In addition, Bob and I each retained a 25% interest in the net profit when Goldberg sold the four mosaics. However, in September 1988, I sold my stake to an investor, Stewart Bick, for $780,000 but bought half of Bob's share, so I was left with a 12.5% participation at a cost of $390,000.

Meanwhile, Goldberg had the mosaics shipped to Geneva where the contract was signed and the deal completed in July 1988 in order, if there were to be a challenge from the Cypriots, that the lenient provision of Swiss law might apply. Then, knowing all the time where the pieces had come from, she set up enquiries to prove that she had taken every reasonable precaution to ensure that they were not stolen. She claimed to have checked with UNESCO and with IFAR (International Federation of Art and Research) who in turn consulted Interpol, and all these bodies stated that the mosaics had not been reported to them as stolen. There were negative results also from customs in the United States, Switzerland, West Germany and Turkey. This tactic was intended to show that the Cypriots, if the objects did turn out to have been stolen, had not 'exercised due diligence' and so could not reclaim them from a bona fide buyer. But a bona fide buyer, knowing the provenance, would have consulted the Church of Cyprus and the government of the Republic of Cyprus before anybody else. Peg Goldberg did not attempt to approach either. In addition, because of her political contacts, she was able to obtain an official letter from the US Commissioner of Customs stating that the mosaics had been properly and legally brought into the country: such a declaration is most unusual.

But now that she was satisfied with her measures to establish good title, Goldberg wanted a more definite evaluation than that which she had obtained from Sotheby's in New York, who of course had not been shown the mosaics. So, during the fall of 1988, she brought one of them, a head of St Matthew, to London. Paul Polak got in touch with Gordon Balderston at Sotheby's and showed him photographs. He recognized them at once as the Lythrankomi mosaics and was enthusiastic but naturally wanted to see one before committing himself to an estimate. He was shown also the certificates Goldberg had obtained from Aydin and consequently he did not at once raise the question of title. So representatives of Sotheby's were waiting for her at Heathrow.

However, while they waited for her at the red channel to come through customs, Peg Goldberg, 'by mistake', brought the mosaic out undeclared through the green channel. Balderston was alerted by this strange behaviour and it prompted him to look more closely into the background of the pieces.

Paul called to fix a definite time for the mosaic to be brought round to Sotheby's. Balderston advised him that he had discovered that the piece was stolen and recorded as such. 'If you bring it here,' he warned, 'I shall be obliged to communicate at once with Interpol.' Paul reported this to Goldberg who took fright and fled the country.

This was not the first time that the experts in London had been consulted over the mosaics. Back in 1986, I had been amazed at the failure of Dr Charles Avery at Christie's to recognize the significance of the works. At Sotheby's, Richard Camber described them as 'provincial' and of far less importance than a mosaic from Torcello which Sotheby's sold in 1987. The Torcello piece was about six hundred years more recent than the Lythrankomi mosaics, and had been stolen by a restorer but, as Camber boasted, it had been in Britain for a hundred and thirty years. However, Dr Robin Cormack at the Courtauld Institute, who later produced the expert report which was the core of the report submitted by the Council of Europe on the cultural heritage of Cyprus, was greatly impressed and told me how pleased he was that works of such importance were in good hands.

Her flight after the Balderston fiasco revealed even more clearly the falsity of Goldberg's claim to have bought the mosaics in good faith. Now she had been definitely warned that they were stolen; nonetheless, she went ahead to find a buyer. Geza von Habsburg offered to arrange a private sale with an offered price of $20 million and was ready to advance $5 million. Goldberg could hardly pretend that the potential profit on her outlay of a million dollars was normal in the trade. However Habsburg approached the Getty Museum whose curator, Marian True, at once informed the government of Cyprus; but before they were able to take formal action, the story broke in the press of the purchase of that other spectacular treasure from Cyprus which had evaded me on the island and which Aydin had later offered to me again: the Lysi frescoes.

I now received an unexpected demand for money. Max had collected my things from Paris, and we agreed on a payment of a hundred thousand guilders. Then he called me.

'Michel, I've had a quick estimate made of these goods. This is no ordinary removal job, you know.'

'Of course not,' I agreed. 'You knew that from the start. That's why I am paying you a hundred thousand.'

'Sure. But I reckon that the bill should relate to their value. I want three million guilders.'

'What the fuck are you talking about?' I shouted.

'Three million, and you had better pay up quickly if you know what is good for you and your family.'

When I checked around on Max, I was told he had connections with the most brutal gangs in Holland, but I had no intention of caving in to his blackmail. Still, I took his threat seriously: I knew he would not simply go away and I told Sonia to stay in Spain for the time being.

Throughout my time in prison, Sonia had efficiently carried out my instructions and she was obviously relieved when I got back to Marbella. But she was very unhappy at the move to Holland. A tension grew up between us and we quarrelled often. Slowly, I came to realize that what mattered to her was the Marbella life. She told me she still loved me, but for her I was the key that opened the door to Marbella. Now that I was not able to live in Spain, she had to choose between me and Marbella. We spent time together in Amsterdam, but she always wished to return to Marbella, and with things getting tough in Holland, I did not want an unhappy woman clinging to me, so I decided to break with her.

However, I trusted her and took no precautions such as withdrawing money from her account, but I was disappointed when she took off without warning. I had thought Sonia had more character than to fall for the tinsel glitter of the coast. I had trusted her completely, and had opened the bank account in her name in Geneva into which I paid the proceeds of my business deals. I never tried to control her spending, but it was essentially our account, the working capital of my business. What with the balance in the bank and other assets, the end of our relationship cost me close to a million dollars.

I was staggered. Of course, I was willing to share what we had and in addition to the money in the account, I had bought her millions of dollars of jewellery on the understanding that if anything should happen to me, they would provide for her and our son. Now she held on to all the money as well as the jewellery, which was a crippling blow, coming as it did when I was negotiating a deal on more of the mosaics.

I am not bitter at Sonia. She did present me with a son of whom I am immensely proud and we had some great times together.

I was still reeling from the shock of her desertion when I received unwelcome visitors. Two men strode into the house.

'We are friends of Max,' one announced, 'and we have come to see about the money you owe him.'

They carried pistols; one of them put a bullet into the ceiling to show they were in earnest. After threatening me with a beating, they said they would be back to collect.

I went to see a police inspector whom I knew. He sympathized but told me there was nothing he could do before an assault was actually made, so I was obliged to take my own measures.

I had come into contact at one time with one of the leaders of a Yugoslav gang which virtually runs the Amsterdam underworld, a man called Jeri, and I asked if he and his friends would offer me protection. He was with another leading member of the group called Paia, a huge man with the physique of a heavyweight wrestler, a man who could kill with his bare hands. Jeri was tall and dark with deceptively soft eyes. I learned that he had to date killed three men.

'We know the men Max is using,' Jeri told me. 'They are heavy guys, but we can handle them. It will cost you at least two hundred and fifty thousand dollars.'

'Let's meet tomorrow and settle terms,' I replied.

The Yugoslavs were into everything – dope, prostitution, robberies and protection. Their normal method of debt collection was first to announce who they were and demand payment. If their victim were foolish enough not to pay promptly, they usually put a bullet into his kneecap as a reminder.

However, when we met the following day, they informed me that the job had already been taken care of. They had checked on me, and concluded that I was very wealthy and they would have no difficulty collecting from me. They were about a dozen strong and they had gone out in force, beating up some of Max's men and ordering him to lay off me. I need not worry about them any more.

'Max told us you owe him three million guilders,' he went on, 'for some things he has brought to Holland. We will deliver for a million and a half guilders.'

'Yesterday we were talking about quarter of a million dollars.'

'That did not allow for recovering your goods. The price is a million and a half.'

Of course they did not expect me to have the money on me and I suggested that they call at my hotel the following Saturday.

After Sonia's taking off, I was not in financial shape to buy off the Yugoslavs, but to fail to keep our rendezvous would be asking for a bullet. We met in the lobby of the Memphis Hotel, Amsterdam. It was unlikely that they would try any rough stuff in such a public place, so I came right out in the open.

'Look,' I said, 'I don't know what Max has told you but I don't owe him three million guilders.' I explained what had happened. 'What is more,' I concluded, 'I deal in works of art and earn good money but I do not have your million and a half ready now.'

They listened quietly and then Paia asked me about the kind of deals I did.

'You have to realize,' I told him, 'that you can go for months without earning a cent; you only collect when you clinch a deal.'

Max had told them a story about how I had stolen money from him and, as I had guessed, they had no high regard for him.

'Max is just a piece of shit,' Paia pronounced, 'but if he thought that he could screw three million guilders out of you, your things must be worth a hell of a lot more. You will get your things and we protect you from Max for half what he wanted. You say it takes time for you to pull off a big sale. OK, we can wait, but not too long you understand.'

When they left, we were on quite cordial terms. I was more than satisfied; they believed they could get more from me than from Max, so that was the end of my problem with him. Now I had some time to find a way of dealing with their million and a half without actually paying it.

# 34

# How to Acquire a Stolen Masterpiece

'How to acquire a stolen masterpiece' was the title given by Thomas Hoving to an article he wrote for the November 1988 issue of *Connoisseur*, describing the complex and hazardous negotiations through which the frescoes from the church at Lysi were bought by the Menil Foundation of Houston and saved for posterity.

Other journalists took up the story of the frescoes, notably Sourcn Melikian, the art critic of the *International Herald Tribune*, in an extensive article in *Art and Auction*. I had been involved with the frescoes since Aydin had removed them from the church at Lysi and I was angry and indignant at what I read. The press release and the accompanying stories were a contrived cover-up of the truth.

According to the press version, a London dealer, Yanni Petsopoulos, had approached the trustees of the Menil Foundation in June 1983 with a proposition that they should rescue some priceless frescoes which were in the hands of 'an anonymous Turkish gentleman'. Petsopoulos said that the Turk had claimed that the frescoes came from Anatolia and he brought Walter Hopps, one of the trustees and the museum director, with curator Professor Bertrand Devezac, to see the frescoes in Geneva where they were waiting to be broken up and commercialized. The negotiations with the anonymous Turkish gentleman had to be carried out with the greatest discretion since, according to Hopps, a seller of such works might become nervous and simply remove the evidence against himself by pulverizing the pieces.

There was not a word of truth in this story. The frescoes had never been anywhere near Geneva but had remained in Aydin's apartment in Munich where he showed them to Petsopoulos about the same time that he offered them to me. As early as the middle of 1981, Aydin told me that he was engaged in serious negotiations on the frescoes and, as he had promised, he gave me the chance to match the million dollars proposed. I then offered them to Johnny Stuart at Sotheby's but he had advised me that they were too hot and that Sotheby's already had more than enough pieces from Cyprus whose provenance was a problem.

Petsopoulos knew there was no truth in the Anatolia story and had to work out how a public body such as the Menil could buy the works without the Cypriots claiming them as stolen property. Aydin did not want his name disclosed, and it suited Petsopolous and the Menil trustees to give the impression of their having to deal with some sinister vandal so that they could pose as saviours, rather than the knowing buyers of stolen goods. Petsopoulos certainly knew that this 'vandal' was an archaeologist and a highly skilled restorer.

So a sham search was set up to establish where the frescoes had come from. Surprisingly, they met with no success when they checked with the Dumbarton Oaks Museum in Washington or the Courtauld Institute in London. But for their scheme to succeed, the frescoes had to be identified so the Menil commissioned lawyers to contact different countries and they were able to report that the Republic of Cyprus had recognized them as coming from the church at Lysi. The fiction had Petsopoulos now entering into delicate negotiations with the anonymous

Turk to save these treasures, which of course were not under any threat at all, while the Cypriot embassy put the Menil trustees in touch with Constantin Leventis, a well-known businessman and Cypriot ambassador to UNESCO, who in turn told them to contact Vassos Karageorghis, the director of the Department of Antiquities of Cyprus. The deal was that the Menil Foundation should buy the frescoes and donate them to Cyprus. As a reward for such altruism, they were to be allowed to keep the frescoes in their museum in Houston, where they built a special chapel to house them, for fifteen years. There would be 'periodic reviews', but the terms of reference of these reviews were kept deliberately vague. 'After fifteen years', Dominique de Menil who together with her deceased husband, John, had set up the Foundation commented, 'who is to know what things will be like in Cyprus?' Hoving was more blunt, stating that the frescoes 'could well remain in Houston for perpetuity'.

Other conditions surrounding the transaction were not released to the press. Dominique de Menil came to Aydin's flat in Munich to clinch the deal. The venerable old lady, patron of the arts, behaved like a child in a sweetshop, eagerly examining all Aydin's treasures. While negotiations were in progress, she slipped three small objects into her handbag: a Sumerian seal in the form of a reclining animal, an amulet representing the sun, and a neolithic fertility idol of a sitting figure. She told Aydin that if the frescoes deal broke down, she would pay him $25,000 for them, but if the Foundation bought the frescoes, she would take them as a present. It was not clear whether she was acquiring them for the Foundation or for her private collection. She also selected a Sumerian statue which she later showed to experts at the Louvre and at Oxford. When they approved of the piece, she agreed to buy the statue.

Aydin was to receive around a million dollars, but this was paid into an escrow account and he was obliged to wait for a year before he got his money. But Petsopoulos also had his eye on the mosaics. As part of the deal with the Cypriots by which the Menil were allowed legally to hold on to the frescoes, pressure was put on Aydin to part with some of the Lythrankomi mosaics, so a couple of the less well-preserved pieces were sold and sent back to Cyprus unannounced. Later another wild story had to be invented to explain this.

The Menil paid another million dollars for restoration work on the frescoes. A considerable amount of money was required, so the world was informed, to repair the heavy damage which the works suffered during their removal by the anonymous Turk, who had crudely flattened the curved paintings.

However, I knew that Aydin used highly trained restorers in Budapest and in Munich, and I have photographs he gave me showing how each fresco was carefully divided to avoid cutting into important features, then covered with adhesive strips to remove and protect them. From a drawing, I was able to see with what painstaking care the segments of the Christ Pancrator fresco had been delineated to avoid damage.

Aydin was unable to do the restoration as he had broken a wrist in a car accident. Stavros Mihalarias, in London, would have done a first-rate job, but he would have been expensive. Instead, Petsopoulos had the work given to Laurence Morocco, although Morocco's wife did much of the painting. A consultant from the hi-tech firm of Ove Arup was retained and the work was protracted over four years. Aydin formed a low opinion of their efforts. According to him, the work could have been completed in a few months and he was emphatic that there was no truth in the allegation of the pieces having been flattened.

The crowning irony was that the Menil, having portrayed Aydin as a destructive barbarian, used him as an adviser on the construction of the chapel to accommodate the frescoes, which was to be a replica of the church in Lysi. But then, who would know better the layout of a church than the man who had stripped it bare?

When I read these lies and suppressions of facts, I was sickened, particularly by the manner in which the Menil, a supposedly charitable organization, was whitewashed; so I gave an interview to the British journalist who had so frankly exposed de Bry. But now that the Cypriots were preparing to take Peg Goldberg to court over the mosaics, it would have been highly embarrassing if it became known that their officials or agents had been fully aware that the mosaics had been in Munich and they had made no attempt to reclaim them but had accepted some of them as part of a deal. So now the story was invented that, following an anonymous phone call to the Cypriot embassy, two complete and two damaged mosaics were found in a garage in Frankfurt, together with a bag of loose tesserae, the little glass bricks with which the mosaics were constructed. This was followed by a further report that the damaged mosaics were fakes and they were later allowed to drop out of the story altogether. Finally, Petsopoulos was obliged to admit that the whole story about the Frankfurt garage was a fabrication.

But what brought matters to a head was my revealing the identity of the 'anonymous Turkish gentleman'. Petsopoulos, anxious to maintain his pretence of being the virtuous protector of works of great religious and artistic significance, let it be known that he had a furious row with Aydin, endeavouring to persuade him to return all the pieces of mosaic in his possession to the Cypriots, and such was his righteous fury that he had hurled a decanter at his fellow conspirator.

The Menil, too, came under press scrutiny and made every attempt to represent themselves as altruistic and scrupulously honest. But, not only had they played along with Petsopoulos in the cover story of the Turkish vandal in Geneva, they had collaborated with him in withholding payment to Aydin until he had consented to the sale of the mosaics which were returned to Cyprus. They did not have even the shred of a justification that they were buying the mosaics to present to Cyprus since the funds came from quite a different source. Subsequently, Walter Hopps resigned as the museum's director.

The press ran Aydin to earth and he declared that he had disposed of every last fragment of the mosaics and that was the reason for the unexplained bag of tesserae. That was just one more lie, since he was actually holding another three pieces on which I had an option to buy and their sale was being negotiated at that time.

I abandoned the house in Amsterdam and moved into a large suite in a hotel in The Hague, a pleasant, elegant city, lacking the bustle of Amsterdam but with an aristocratic charm. My new premises enjoyed one feature which was to be an unexpected advantage; I shared the royal park with the Queen's palace and hence profited from the royal security arrangements.

One of the mosaics Peg Goldberg had acquired was the top half of the representation of the Virgin holding the adolescent Christ; Aydin still had the lower half. I had strongly disapproved of the division of the piece which I ascribed then to a belief by Aydin that he would realize more by selling the parts separately. I fervently wished that the mosaic, the centrepiece of the series, should be reunited and thought I could achieve this since I had negotiated an option with Aydin to buy the lower half as well as two complete mosaics, a St Thomas and a St Andrew. Meanwhile Goldberg had found a buyer for her pieces who was prepared to meet her asking price of $20 million and to donate them to the Cloisters Museum in New York. But now an action for their recovery was filed by the Church of Cyprus, backed by the government of the Republic of Cyprus, and that stalled the sale until the case had been decided.

Goldberg was sufficiently confident to enter into negotiations with me to buy the lower half mosaic and the St Andrew. I was prepared to go on with a deal with her as long as she had possession of half of the Christ and Virgin mosaic, in order to ensure that the two halves were reunited.

But another reason weighed heavily with me. Aydin had told me that the church at Lythrankomi had been completely destroyed by Turkish soldiers and that the mosaics had been saved by him from the rubble. If Goldberg were to win her case, I was confident that the mosaics would be properly looked after in a leading American museum whereas I was by no means certain of their fate if they were to go back to Cyprus. However, Goldberg failed to keep a rendezvous with Aydin and the deal on the lower half and the St Andrew broke down.

But when I learned of the return to Cyprus of the St Luke and St Bartholomew, and the damaged St Philip and St Paul which Petsopoulos had extracted from Aydin, I wondered whether I ought not to reconsider my attitude towards the Cypriots, so I got in touch with the Cypriot consul in The Hague, Tasoula Georgiou. I explained that I had the opportunity to get hold of more of the mosaics and suggested that I acquire them and present them to Cyprus on condition that they allow me to retain one mosaic which I could sell to finance the operation.

'But when we win our case in the United States, we shall have the right to take back all the pieces without having to pay anybody,' she objected.

'It is by no means sure that you will win,' I replied. 'If Goldberg can persuade the court that neither the Church nor the government of Cyprus took the trouble to inform Interpol or UNESCO that the pieces were missing, she will argue that she had good title since your people did not exercise due diligence. My offer would guarantee that some of the pieces go back to Cyprus whatever the outcome of the trial.'

She promised to pass my proposition back but the authorities were busy with the preparation of their case and so we agreed to meet without waiting for a formal reply.

Aydin did not know I was in contact with the Cypriots. He was furious with me for my revealing that he was the 'anonymous Turkish gentleman', and saw himself being cast as villain in the forthcoming trial. Despite his anger, he was willing to offer me fresh objects from Cyprus including a monumental Christ Pancrator. He insisted that he was offering works from churches which had been devastated. He still claimed to be the dedicated archaeologist, saving fine works from destruction, but I was beginning to hear reports from Cyprus which forced me to revise my opinion of Aydin.

* * *

Tasoula Georgiou was a passionate young woman, utterly devoted to the cause of the suffering people of her country and to the fight for saving their cultural heritage. What she brought home to me was not the ordeal of a nation, but the agony of flesh-and-blood people.

Her home had been in the occupied zone and she had lost friends and relatives in their dispersal. As a child, she had worshipped in the little church and each day she had venerated one particular icon, praying to it and kissing it until forced to flee, aged fifteen, a refugee in her own country. That icon was not an object to be bought and sold in the marketplace, but a precious part of her life; now it had been pillaged and desecrated.

She gave me a copy of a publication, *Flagellum Dei*, which the Greek Cypriots had produced explaining how their country had been plundered. From this, and a later Council of Europe report, I began to realize how much things had changed since I was in Cyprus. I had smuggled works out for profit, but it had also been an act of salvation. Now I discovered that many of the churches which were supposed to have been blown up were still standing. The tales of destruction were merely an excuse for looting. I ascertained that the Christ Pancrator Aydin was offering was from an undestroyed church and, contrary to what I had been told, such buildings as the Monastery of Antiphonitis had never been dynamited by Turkish troops. Among other churches damaged but still standing was Panagia Kanakaria at Lythrankomi.

I still respected Aydin's knowledge and skill as a restorer but I was forced to recognize that he was abusing his scholarship and his sole interest now in these works was how he could exploit them. Cyprus was being ravaged by robbers and I felt revulsion at being associated with such people.

'Look here,' I said to Tasoula Georgiou when we next met, 'I thought that smuggling out works of art was probably the best if not the only way of ensuring their safety when I was operating in your country. Now it seems to me that your people have the determination and organization to look after these things themselves. We should be looking beyond winning the case of the mosaics, important as they are, to the recovery of all the other treasures which have been taken out of Cyprus over the past years and I am willing to do everything in my power to help you in this.'

'But you would make a lot of money if the Indianapolis trial were to go against us,' she exclaimed.

'That's right,' I said, 'but for me the business has gone sick. Understand, when I started in Cyprus, it was an adventure and I do not regret for one moment what I did then. And you should bear in mind that a lot of your own Greek people, including some high officials, were stealing and smuggling as well. But now the time is right to start getting these things back to the country where they belong. I have handled so many of these pieces and seen others that I probably have a better idea than anybody where they are.'

The consul realized that I was sincere and she was eager to recruit my help, but my decision to assist the Cypriots involved more than financial sacrifice: it threatened my very life.

I got a terrible shock one day, shortly after returning from a holiday in Mexico, when I bumped into Paia in the street.

'We have been looking for you,' he said grimly, 'and see, wherever you try to hide, we find you.'

'I haven't been hiding,' I told him. 'You know that my business is international. I had to go abroad.'

'Well, now we know where you are living, so don't try to slip away again. We have an account to settle with you. This time we just want to talk, but if you run, we shall find you, anywhere in the world.'

I had no intention of trying to run away. Holland is too small a country to hide in from men determined to find you. The Yugoslav gang were to visit me at eight the following evening.

'And you had better have the money ready,' Paia warned.

But only hours before they were due, I received a hysterical call from Aydin. There was growing press interest in the forthcoming trial; repeatedly his name came up and it was clear that Goldberg intended to hold him responsible for the legality of the deal. She would insist that she had taken every reasonable precaution and that she had looked to Aydin for the pieces having been properly acquired and legally shipped out of Cyprus. Aydin regarded me as the central figure and demanded that I stop the trial going ahead. There was absolutely nothing I could do to prevent the case coming to court, but Aydin was beyond reason.

'Do it,' he screamed, 'or you are a dead man!'

This was no empty threat. I was phoned immediately afterwards by a man called Savo. 'Michel van Rijn, you have three days to do what our friend has asked. If not, we shall find you. Tonight, you will be visited by some of my group in Holland who will tell you what we want.'

I spent most of the day shopping and cooking. As I left the hotel, I was aware of members of Paia's group, in the lobby and outside the entrance, keeping an eye on me. I bought a magnificent leg of lamb and prepared it in a traditional Balkan manner, smeared with mustard and with fresh herbs and spices, sitting in a bed of onions, peppers, mushrooms, potatoes and fennel, all liberally sprinkled with salt, pepper and garlic. The dish was soaked in virgin olive oil and placed in the oven to roast gently.

My guests arrived a couple of hours early but I invited them up. In addition to Paia and Jeri and the other Yugoslavs, there was a squat, unsmiling Indonesian called Cliff and a tall, fair Dutchman named Frank. They practically took the dining room over with their portable telephones and their guns; heavy Smith and Wessons and Colt Cobras were dropped on to the table beside their plates.

'You should not have gone away,' Paia rumbled, with menace. 'When you were missing, we let Max know you owed us money so you were no longer under our protection. If you don't pay us off, it is just a matter of who gets to you first.'

'If you want to beat me up or shoot me, you can do it now or wait until we have eaten,' I bluffed. 'A couple of hours won't make any difference, but it will give me a chance to explain some things to you.'

The odour of the roasting meat was persuasive. They took a few beers while they waited for me to serve dinner. I had made a sauce of yoghurt, cucumber and garlic, a dish called *chiqchiq*, which must have been made by their mothers. The Yugoslavs gazed at my offerings in astonishment.

'Where did you learn to prepare meat that way?' asked Jeri.

'In Montenegro.'

'You were in Montenegro?'

As I carved and served, I described how I had smuggled icons out of Yugoslavia. From the way they smiled and nodded, I could see that they thoroughly approved, and with the third magnum of wine they became almost sentimental. Cliff and Frank simply went on eating solidly but I have never in my life seen a man who could compare with Paia when it came to demolishing food.

I was waiting each minute for the arrival of Savo's men but as the others went on with the meal, I told them about deals I had done and showed them books I had written, pointing out pictures of icons which I had smuggled out of Montenegro. I knew I had to make an impression, partly by my standing in the art world, where they were completely out of their depth, but even more by my being accepted in a society of which they would desperately love to be part. I had left newspapers and magazines on side tables, apparently casually, with articles about me, and photographs of me with celebrities at Marbella parties. As the climax to this ostentatious display, there was a mounted photograph of me with Queen Beatrix and a framed letter signed by her congratulating me on my exhibition in Delft beside my letter of appointment as Minister Plenipotentiary to Japan from the Order of the Knights of Malta. It was an outrageous display, but it was necessary for my survival, exploiting their one vulnerability. They had money and were pleased to demonstrate their wealth. Looking at a picture of me in my garage, Frank said, 'I have a Corniche too,' and Cliff eagerly boasted of his Ferrari Testarossa. There was a discussion about the advantage of the Bentley Turbo R over the Bentley Turbo, and at that moment I felt I had broken through.

Then I led up to the story of the mosaics and the pending court case. When I mentioned that Peg Goldberg had a contract to sell her four pieces for $20 million, they were electrified. I brought them some newspaper articles which bore out my story. Seeing it in print impressed them and I made sure that Frank read them the account which stated that I had a 25% interest in the pieces. The pieces had only cost Peg a million dollars, so even after her expenses I must be worth a large part of the $20 million.

'But what is this about more mosaics?' Frank asked.

I told them of the three pieces on which I had an option. 'The St Andrew and the St Thomas are wonderful, but the real prize is the Feet of Christ.'

These were men who risked their lives practically every day dealing with rival gangs or in drug traffic. Suddenly, they saw the prospect of making a lot of money in what they saw as straight, respectable business; at the same time, I would be their springboard to the charmed circle of society.

'What sort of people will buy these mosaics from you?' asked Jeri.

'If the case is won, they can be sold to museums privately or by open auction,' I told him. 'Every museum in the world would fight to have these unique works. Just think, people are willing to pay $20 million to Goldberg before the trial. Once she wins the case, she can ask what she likes. The price will take off like a rocket.'

'And you have more of them,' Paia repeated. 'We should be partners. You can cut us in on a deal.'

'All right,' I agreed. 'But you know, it might mean waiting for months before clinching a deal and receiving money.'

'Why is this half a mosaic so special?' Jeri asked.

'Whoever ends up with the top part would give anything you cared to ask for the missing part. And if the Cypriots were to win the trial they would still pay up for the missing half.'

'That is the piece in which we must have a stake,' Paia boomed. 'You say you can get these things?'

'That's right, but I am not ready to buy them yet.'

Paia frowned. 'Why not?'

'Let me be frank with you,' I said. 'At the moment, I am short of ready cash.'

'Listen,' said Paia. 'You get hold of those mosaics, especially that lower half, and get on with selling it. We shall be your partners: we'll decide on how to divide up the money later.'

'But there is one other problem,' I told him. 'I am due to be killed within three days.'

Paia stared. 'What are you talking about? Who is going to kill you?'

'A guy called Savo. I am expecting his friends tonight.'

'Savo! We won't have any trouble from him,' Paia swelled up in indignation. 'Jeri knows him well, another Montenegran. His people do operate here although he stays most of the time in Munich, but we are stronger than they are.'

He was interrupted by the phone ringing. I picked it up.

'This is Savo. You won't be seeing my men tonight. Instead, I shall come to Holland myself with some of my people. You can expect us in three days. Don't do anything stupid like running away.'

'It's Savo,' I told Paia.

'Pass the phone to Jeri,' he ordered.

Jeri had always looked goodnatured, almost gentle. Now, his face hardened, his body was taut and there was a cutting edge to his voice. His eyes were hard and glittering. I knew then that I was watching a coldblooded killer.

'I told him you are under our protection,' he explained to me. 'So to touch you would spark off a gang war. I said he had made the threat, so now he must come here, alone. He is to fly in tomorrow.'

'Good,' boomed Paia. 'He should know that if anybody is

going to kill you, it would be us. But now we are partners, so let's drink to the Feet of Christ.

'Futa!' he shouted.

'Futa!' we echoed.

They scented money and believed that they had me in their power. I was pleased that I had won time and got both Max and Savo off my back. By letting them push their way into the mosaics deal, I had turned killers into my protectors.

Paia informed me that three or four of the gang would always be with me, and sleep in the house. I knew they would be there as much to keep an eye on me as for my protection.

At one point Paia asked me, 'Do you have enough money to go on until the end of the trial?' These men had only contempt for weakness, so I smiled bravely and answered that I would manage. 'You are not to go short of money,' Paia assured me. 'We must keep up appearances.'

They each threw on the table bank notes of all sort of currencies and denominations. I collected about twenty thousand dollars. To take money from the men who had come to collect, this was *kavla*!

Frank, the hard-headed Dutchman, handed over his contribution reluctantly. 'What shall I tell my wife?' he asked. 'How do I explain my giving you money when I told her I was coming here to shoot you or take your money?'

As they rose to leave, I pushed their money into my pocket and proposed that we go to a nearby restaurant for a last drink. I understood how important it was to demonstrate that I was man enough to drive with them unarmed across the square at the dead of night.

I took them to the most refined restaurant in The Hague, which they would never have entered on their own. I had been considering buying the place so I was on excellent terms with the owner, who greeted me warmly. I presented each of them to him. This was further proof that they were getting value for their investment in me.

They offered to see me back to the hotel, but I refused.

'Tonight I can still walk alone,' I assured them. As I paid the bill with their money, I added, 'The drinks are on me.'

Next day, Paia, Jeri and I met Savo at the airport. He showed courage by coming alone and unarmed, and although I did not like the man I admired this.

Aydin had dropped his unrealistic insistence that I stop the trial going ahead but wanted me to return every document in my possession which linked him with the mosaics. Although he was in no position to bully me, Savo put up a brave front, telling me he had sworn to Aydin that he would bring back all the papers.

But Paia and Jeri would not stand for this. The three Yugoslavs shouted and hammered on the table, but when the chips were down it was Paia and Jeri who called the shots.

'Listen,' Paia said to me, 'fetch all these papers and let Savo see you have them. He is a man from Montenegro; give him something to take back, so that he does not lose face. But keep whatever you regard as important in case Aydin makes trouble.'

I made sure that Savo saw that the papers I held on to could break Aydin totally. Two documents which he demanded I was unable to give him even if I had wanted; the original sales invoice from Turkish Cyprus and the letter bearing the signature of Osman Orek, both held by Goldberg.

'You go back to Aydin,' Paia told Savo, 'and tell him that he must sell the mosaics he still has to Michel. We are Michel's partners in this deal and you can make whatever terms you want with Aydin. But we want those mosaics. So, tell Aydin he has to come and talk with Michel. They have been doing business for fifteen years: it is up to them to come to a deal.'

'I don't know whether Aydin will agree to come.'

'You have our word that he will not be harmed,' Paia retorted. 'And the same applies to you, but the rest of your men stay behind. You tell Aydin that he made the threat so he has to come to us.'

'OK. Aydin will call you with his answer but you should know that he is very bitter with Michel. He holds him responsible for the death of his brother and is burning for revenge.'

'I have no idea what you are talking about,' I said. 'I did not even know his brother was dead. How am I supposed to be involved?'

Savo told us that, following my disclosure that he was the man behind the Menil deal and his being named over the mosaics, the police had arrested Aydin. They had seized more of his pieces and held him in custody. His brother was driving to arrange for his release on bail when he was killed in a car accident.

'The way Aydin sees it, if Michel had not given his name, none of this would have happened,' Savo explained.

'That's bullshit,' I snapped. 'His name was well known to the authorities long ago. He was first busted in 1966; it was stupid of him to keep unregistered pieces in his house again. Of course, I am sorry about his brother, but it is nonsense to blame me.'

Savo continued, 'He has big problems in Cyprus. His interests on the Greek side are in danger. And with his arrest in Turkey, not only his private collection is under threat but also his business interests there. You remember that he owns a shipbreaking yard there.'

Paia and Jeri looked thoughtful and I wondered whether they were reckoning to change sides in the light of Aydin's wealth.

'I am sorry about his problems,' I intervened, 'but the solution for all of us is to get the mosaics and sell them. And while Aydin found them, I am the one to sell them. Remember that I have already pulled off the deal with the Americans and got a high price. We have done a lot of business together, but I am the one with the clients. He might have money, but with his reputation nobody will buy directly from him.'

'That's right,' Paia said. 'Let Michel sell those mosaics, especially that lower half, the futa.'

'But Aydin thinks that if Goldberg loses, that one would be

unsaleable after all the bad publicity. He told me that he is going to break it up and use the pieces to make new mosaics which could not be identified,' Savo told us.

I was shocked. How could a man with Aydin's skill and learning contemplate such an action? I had to act quickly to save the mosaic, even though it meant that it would be in the hands of Paia and Jeri whose motivation was also simply greed. But I could turn their greed to my advantage and use it to save the mosaics.

'Aydin is not right,' I said to Savo. 'Goldberg will probably win and that work will be worth an unbelievable fortune. But the lower half can be sold, and I have told Paia and Jeri how we can do it, even if the Cypriots were to win. Tell Aydin he must not touch that mosaic until we have had our meeting.'

I chose the Hôtel des Indes as our venue, partly because, surrounded by the heavily guarded embassies of the Hague, it was an unlikely setting for the rival gangs to resort to open warfare but also since it was not the sort of place to which these gunmen, or even Aydin, were accustomed, and this put them at a psychological disadvantage.

Aydin glared at me with hatred. He was here under coercion but he knew that something had to be worked out as long as I had the support of the stronger gang. But I was after more than sullen acceptance until he got the chance to turn the tables and destroy me; I wanted his co-operation – that from the man who blamed me for the death of his brother, his arrest and loss of the goods which had been seized and his being branded by the press.

'I should never have let you talk me into dealing with this damned woman, Goldberg,' he complained. 'Through her stupidity, letting the things be offered openly to the Getty, she started all the trouble.'

'Don't start crying about it now. You made good money on the deal and nobody forced you to do it,' I replied. 'And once the trial is out of the way, you will make a lot more. It was the Menil deal that started your problems.'

'Yes,' he flared up, 'because you shouted my name!'

'Wrong, Aydin. Enough people knew that you had been selling things from Cyprus for years. It was Janni Petsopoulos and the Menil people who put out the story about the Turkish gentleman who had smuggled the pieces and was prepared to destroy them, so they could pose as the good guys.'

He shrugged angrily but I knew that my point had got home.

'But the frescoes are over and done with. What I told the press cleared you of the lies they were putting out about how you damaged the frescoes. Let's get on with the mosaics where there's even more at stake.'

Negotiating with Aydin is always a long, hard affair and our discussion dragged on for hours. But there had to come a climax when I would break through or fail.

'So what do you want from me now, Michel?'

'I have an option to buy the lower half of the Christ mosaic; I want to buy it now. The Andrew and the Thomas we can deal with after the trial has been won.'

'A lot has happened since we struck a deal on the option.'

'I am prepared to discuss price.'

By leaving terms for the other two mosaics open, I wanted him to see that he stood to gain if they were to be sold at a far higher price than he could have envisaged, once Peg Goldberg won her case. I was prepared to do everything possible to help the Cypriots, as I had assured Tasoula Georgiou, but I had to convince my Yugoslav 'partners' that all my efforts were in support of Goldberg, and I had to manoeuvre Aydin into supporting the woman he detested. Once he began to argue price for the lower half mosaic, I sensed that he was coming over. He should stop opposing Goldberg even though she was trying to use him. Let her win and we would all make money. Meanwhile, if instead of his breaking up the lower half mosaic, I would buy it from him at a good price, he would be rid of an acute embarrassment, if people began to ask why he had ever cut the mosaic in half.

We agreed that I would pay him two hundred thousand dollars and the piece would be brought to Holland.

When we got to talking money, Paia, Jeri and Savo got in on the act. I was sure that Savo would make some sort of deal with Aydin, but the suspicions between the two groups resurfaced. If Savo were to bring the mosaic to Holland, how could he be sure that I would not keep it without paying, under the protection of my group? To which the others countered, if I paid first, what guarantee would they have that the mosaic would ever be shipped out of Munich where Savo's men were in control?

Eventually a formula was thrashed out by which I would send Paul Polak to Munich with the money accompanied by one of my group who would be protected by their code of honour since he was only a boy. He would watch that I did not get Paul to do some deal behind their backs, and the two of them would bring back the mosaic.

Everything was settled. Then, like the sun breaking through the clouds, Aydin's face broke into a broad grin.

'Michel, you are right. Now we have to make sure that this Goldberg wins the trial. We are together again, like in the old times in Cyprus. Why do we fight? I have lost a brother, but you are also a brother to me.'

He pulled me to him and kissed me on both cheeks. The Yugoslavs were all smiles. They were going to get the futa, Goldberg was going to win in Indianapolis and they would use me to make a lot of money. With Aydin now a friend, the split with Savo was a thing of the past. He too believed that he was now in control, especially when Aydin told me to make all future contacts through Savo because he thought his phone might be tapped.

My Yugoslav bodyguards virtually took over my suite; it was like any other peaceful domestic scene, only instead of women knitting in front of the fire, the gunmen would sit, cleaning their pistols. Having spent a considerable part of their lives in prison, they had become used to sitting for hours on end, doing and saying nothing. It was unnerving having them about. They listened to everything I said and watched all visitors.

Feeding Paia kept me busy. One day when he looked in at midday, he asked for something light to eat, so I prepared an omelette, using six eggs. He devoured it and then wanted the other half, so I made him another six-egg omelette. He then got to his feet, announcing that he was going home to his wife for lunch.

The trial was hot news, but the Yugoslavs were not readers of the world press. They grasped the essential fact that if the court upheld Peg Goldberg's claim, this would give the green light for the sale of the Feet of Christ, so they looked to me to do whatever was necessary to make sure that she won.

I made no attempt to conceal from them that I was in touch with Tasoula Georgiou. To have done so would have been signing my own death warrant, and they watched me so closely that they would have found out anyway.

'It is our insurance policy,' I explained. 'This is a very complicated case and it is just possible that Goldberg will lose. Then what do we do? We still have the mosaics, and the Cypriots want them. But we need to make plans now if we are going to sell the mosaics to them and I need Tasoula to be friendly.'

They were only half convinced. They insisted that I tape her calls so that they could hear what she was saying as well as my carefully chosen words. I dared not warn her since if it had become known that the Cypriots were in touch with me, the man who had introduced Goldberg to Aydin, it could have seriously prejudiced their case. They would have disowned our talks and Tasoula would have broken the contact. I had to manoeuvre our conversations so that her replies would not trigger off an alarm.

Paul and Michael flew to Munich with the money and back the same day with the lower half mosaic which they brought in, undeclared without any problem. I held the mosaic in my hands. Although only a fragment, it was still a thing of great beauty as well as a chunk of living history. Paia took it and looked at it with total lack of comprehension. It was like an illiterate clutching the bible; for Paia and Jeri, it was merely a meaningless jigsaw of glass and marble.

'Is that all it is?' demanded Paia. 'We go to all this trouble and expense just for this?'

'It may not look impressive, but believe me it is a unique treasure. And it will sell for an enormous price.'

They grasped that it represented money, so they eagerly held on to it.

I let them all think that they were using me, but as the lawsuit approached its climax I was able to influence and eventually control them. It was like playing several simultaneous games of chess with Paia and Jeri at one board, Savo another, Aydin, Goldberg and the Cypriots each playing on their own. The strain was terrific, but the challenge kept the adrenalin pumping. The more I contemplated these people who treated works of art as a mere commodity, to be bought and sold, the more my resolve was strengthened. My exposure of the Menil cover-up and the oncoming trial had focussed attention throughout the world. This case would determine whether occupying armies could destroy and bandits pillage with impunity. If we won, such people, even nations, would be held accountable: the rules would be changed for ever. And that would vindicate the suffering of Cyprus.

But for me, the stakes were high: my life against the fate of great art. Rather than chess, it was like playing Russian roulette, but with only one unloaded chamber in the revolver!

# 35

# Trial in Indianapolis

The case of the Autocephalous Church of Cyprus and the Republic of Cyprus versus Goldberg and Feldman opened before Judge James E. Noland on 30th May 1989. At once, the Turkish Republic of Northern Cyprus demanded the right to join in the action against Goldberg and Feldman, on the grounds that the theft had occurred in their territory and the documents proving legal exportation were forgeries, as was the signature of Osman Orek, and the former Prime Minister was prepared to come to court to say so. The request was denied because the Turkish Cypriot state is not recognized by any country apart from Turkey.

But there was a more profound reason for the concern of the Turkish Cypriots. They were embarrassed by the revelation of the army's atrocities and their neglect of abandoned churches, and wanted to establish that they were a civilized state. That was the reason for their permitting the Council of Europe commission to enter the territory to investigate and report. The fact that the Turks and Turkish Cypriots were on the defensive, and taking steps to protect works of art, meant that the publicity I had courted had already achieved something. They were being held accountable before the whole world.

Another vital decision which the court had to make was

whether the case would be tried under the laws of the state of Indiana or, as Goldberg claimed, Swiss law. Should the purchase by an American from a Turk of objects allegedly stolen from Cyprus and kept in West Germany be regarded as subject to Swiss law simply because the mosaics were taken for a few hours to the Geneva free port and the contract signed in Switzerland? Judge Noland was not impressed. The complaint had been brought before his court and Indiana law would apply.

At the end of each day's hearing, I would get a progress report from Goldberg or sometimes Bob Fitzgerald. The Yugoslavs listened. A setback, such as the refusal to allow Swiss law, would lead to furious outbursts. It was almost as if they held me responsible for the way things were going. On the days when there was some spirited argument from a defence witness, they were all smiles and would demand drinks. With all their cruelty and violence, their reactions could be dangerously irrational.

Two of the witnesses called by the Cypriots were Constantin Leventis and Dr Athanasius Papageorghiou, the acting director of the Cypriot Department of Antiquities, who told how their country had pleaded with UNESCO to send in a mission but that the Turkish Cypriots had refused permission. Nevertheless, Leventis insisted that he had notified UNESCO that the mosaics had been stolen although Goldberg claimed that she had checked with their office in Geneva. As for Interpol, Papageorghiou informed the court that they refused to list the works as stolen unless they were provided with a description, the name and address of the thief and the name of the informant. But other witnesses bore out that the refusal of the Greek Cypriot government to have any official dealings with the Turkish Cypriot administration led to their refusing to negotiate over the fate of antiquities in the north.

The Menil case was brought up when the press secretary at the Cyprus embassy in Washington, Marios Evriviades, testified that the Cypriots had demanded to know from whom the Menil was buying the Lysi frescoes but the trustees refused to divulge.

'Should you not have reported the Menil to the police for their failure to co-operate?' demanded Goldberg's attorney.

'No, it was not my job,' replied Evriviades, although he admitted playing a part in the negotiations.

Although I kept in contact with Tasoula Georgiou throughout the trial, the Cypriot lawyer, Michael Cypreanou, who conducted their case together with their American attorneys, made a determined attack on my character, bringing up the unproved case in France that I had forged Chagalls and saying Goldberg should have been on her guard in dealing with me. I was already taking the first steps towards clearing my name on this charge, but this onslaught helped to allay the suspicions of the Yugoslavs.

A lot of the testimony offered by the Cypriot Church was aimed at winning sympathy because of the religious significance of the mosaics, but the solid legal arguments were based on attacking Peg Goldberg's claim to have bought in good faith. There were contentions over whether the statute of limitations applied or whether the provisions of an international treaty on stolen works of art and antiquities was relevant since the United States had ratified it after the mosaics had been removed from Cyprus. Goldberg remained optimistic in her reports, and the Yugoslavs were satisfied. The Archbishop of Cyprus had no more claim to the mosaics than the Vatican has to paintings from European churches displayed in American museums, asserted André Emmerich, a former president of the American Association of Art Dealers. 'As an art dealer, you deal with the powers that be,' he stated.

After a week of arguments and testimony, both sides renounced their right to make closing statements and the judge retired to consider his verdict. We had to wait for two months for it, during which the Yugoslavs never let me out of their sight.

* * *

Michel de Bry was exultant at the news of my arrest in Spain. This, so he claimed, proved that he had been the innocent victim, cheated by an unscrupulous trickster. All he had to do was sit back and wait for an English court to order Coutts to give him back the modello. Then, with the expert witness of Hartt, he would be able to sell it for an astronomical sum. After that, out of the tens of million dollars, he might get round to endowing the Honegger Foundation he had finally been obliged to set up at least with sufficient capital to offer a scholarship every two years.

But my release and flight to Holland cut short his rejoicing. 'What? Is he out of prison?' de Bry sneered in December 1988.

I had given an interview to the British journalist who had exposed his deceit over the Skopas Head and who had seen through the illusions of the fabulous de Bry collection when she visited him in Paris. Some papers had already raised questions about the elusive Honegger Foundation. Now, for the first time, it was revealed how Hartt had changed his manuscript to back up de Bry's lie about the modello being seen in Geneva instead of Paris, as well as the correspondence in which Hartt claimed recompense on the sale of the piece.

De Bry refused to comment while Hartt, relying on the stringent libel laws in Britain and on a trend to inflict punitive damages on the more strident tabloids, decided to sue *The Independent*, in which the article appeared.

He could not deny the changed manuscript nor the letter, but his contention was reported to be on surprising grounds. On 11th November 1985, de Bry had sent him a letter confirming their financial arrangement and countersigned by his son and daughter as well as himself. He had invited Hartt to return a copy of the letter, signed and with the words '*lu et approuvé*' added and initialled. Such a letter was given by de Bry to Smyth, his London lawyer, and it was naturally assumed that these words and the signature were written by Hartt. However

Hartt later claimed that both the added words and his signature were forgeries.

If Hartt's contention was correct, the obvious question is who could have committed the forgery, implicating as it does Hartt in de Bry's scheming? Since de Bry sent the letter directly to Hartt and demanded that the copy be returned to him, only the two of them would have had access to the letter before it was given to Smyth, so either Hartt was lying or de Bry stood accused of forgery.

But just a few weeks later, de Bry's carefully constructed fiction over the discovery and ownership of the modello received a shattering blow. One of the directors of Sotheby's was dining in a Paris restaurant with an antiques dealer and the subject of the Michelangelo statuette came up in conversation. A stranger at a nearby table walked over, apologized for the intrusion but said that he could not help overhearing their discussion and their reference to de Bry. Neither Michel de Bry nor any member of the Honegger family had any legal right to the object, he told them.

'Then who is the owner?' he was asked.

'I am.'

The man told them that he had left the modello with de Bry for research and possible sale. Could he be serious, they wondered.

'And I have instructed my lawyer to start an action against de Bry to have the piece restored to me,' he informed them.

The story got back to me.

'What is his name?' I asked.

'We never asked,' I was told. They had not taken the man's claim seriously.

'Anyway, you can give me a description of him?' I pressed.

I was told that he had a compound Belgian name, 'van something or other', was about forty and appeared to be gay. In direct contradiction to this information, using my contacts in Paris, I learned that the claimant was a macho Italian, Gianni Ongaro, although he styled himself Jean-Baptiste Ongaro when operating in France. I put a call through to Ongaro. When he heard who I was, he readily confirmed the report of his conversation.

'And where did you get the statuette?' I asked him.

'In Antibes. I bought it in a street market in 1982.'

'And you can prove this?'

'I have documents which will blow de Bry's case sky high.'

He knew about the case due to come before the English court. Of course, if Ongaro's case were proved, not only would it destroy de Bry's claim but also that of Bob and myself, but when he told me what he had, I offered to buy the documents for a hundred thousand francs.

'I need to see what I would be buying,' I pointed out.

'I am attacking de Bry through my lawyer. He has everything. I really am going to take him to court, you understand.'

'Let me send my assistant, Paul Polak, to your lawyer to see the papers.'

He agreed, and Paul reported back.

'The most damaging evidence,' Paul told me on his return, 'are two statements signed by de Bry. One is on Academie du Disque stationery and is dated 17th February 1987, which confirms that he has received from Ongaro a statuette representing the David of Michelangelo in stucco, as shown in a photograph in his possession, for research and eventual sale.'

The second document Paul had seen was a photograph of the modello on the back of which de Bry had signed a more formal statement, the wording of which could be translated as:

> Paris, February 1987
>
> I, the undersigned Michel de Bry, living at 68 Boulevard de Courcelles, Paris 17e, acknowledge having received delivery from Monsieur Gianni Ongaro for study and eventual sale a statuette in stucco of the David of Michelangelo as in the photo on the reverse.
>
> Read and approved in good faith,
>
> Michel de Bry

I told Paul to let slip the information to Famchon, Ongaro's lawyer, that the piece was deposited with Coutts and could only be released with the consent of both de Bry and myself. This was news to him and Ongaro although it had been reported in the British press.

While I was excited by Ongaro's allegation, I did not intend to buy the evidence. I knew Ongaro would be obliged to put Coutts on formal notice and that this would automatically result in the release of all relevant documents.

On 10th March 1989, Ongaro wrote to Coutts informing them of his claim and that a criminal action against de Bry was before the *juge d'instruction*, Madame Leroux. He ordered Coutts not to release the modello to any unauthorized person and that they should communicate with his lawyer, Maître Yves Famchon. The bank passed the letter to their lawyers, Farrer and Co, who at the end of March wrote to Ongaro and Famchon, suggesting that he provide full details of his claim and get in touch with Smyth and Schilling, representing de Bry and Fitzgerald and myself respectively. Farrer of course wrote to both lawyers; Keith Schilling demanded that Famchon send him a copy of the dossier and so I got access to it without paying Ongaro a cent.

The story hit the press in June: once more the modello was hot news. A statement of de Bry's case had been submitted by Smyth in a reply to Farrer. He categorically denied that Ongaro had brought any action against his client and commented that it was strange that Ongaro should have waited two years before making his claim. He went on to counterattack. De Bry had in fact taken Ongaro to court for fraud in connection with a painting by Largillière and another attributed to Rubens, and the court had ordered Ongaro to return the paintings to their rightful owners. Smyth made no mention of the written admissions by de Bry, but that was taken up by Harry Donckers, de Bry's Paris lawyer and associate, who was interviewed by Geraldine Norman for *The Independent*. He admitted that Ongaro and de Bry had been doing business together for years, and confirmed that the two signed statements were authentic, but claimed that Ongaro had some sort of hold over de Bry through their other dealings and had bullied de Bry into giving them.

That was a strange excuse. What sort of business was de Bry involved in which would give Ongaro such a hold and allow him to be blackmailed?

As for the Largillière and Rubens, it transpired that Ongaro had taken them on consignment from a man called Heim, who had a reputation for going opportunely bankrupt but had succeeded his father who had been a highly respected dealer in Paris. Ongaro left them with de Bry to whom he was trying to sell them, but when the dispute broke out between them over the modello, de Bry went directly to Heim. Together they conconcted a plot to discredit Ongaro. Heim claimed the money for the paintings from Ongaro who had never been paid by de Bry, so Heim asserted that he had no title to the paintings and was trying to sell them dishonestly to de Bry who once again posed as the wronged victim.

But of course the ownership of the paintings had no bearing on the statuette and although Smyth had stated that there was no case pending against his client, the French police were homing in on him, investigating not only the Michelangelo but also his earlier activities. It was the crowning irony that the French who had brought such a collection of wild, even ridiculous accusations against me and had pressed relentlessly for my extradition should now be forced to plead for my help.

Additionally, the Getty Museum made a formal complaint against him; the scandal of the Skopas Head which he had sold them was so blatant that they were unable to sweep it under the carpet.

I agreed to a meeting with the French in The Hague which was also attended by two Dutch police inspectors. My relations with the Dutch police were now excellent and I reckoned that it would be a good thing if the French were aware of it.

Inspector d'Allem, a pleasant man of about thirty, intelligent and quietly spoken, had brought a number of prepared questions but as the meeting went on, his indignation at de Bry bubbled over and at one point he switched off the tape recorder in order to tell me exactly what he thought of him. What had particularly incensed the inspector was de Bry's pretentiousness, as when he came to a meeting with notepaper from the Elysée Palace sticking out of his pocket, as if to proclaim that the humble policeman had better not get on the wrong side of a friend of President Mitterrand. This only made the inspector more determined than ever to nail de Bry.

The emergence of Ongaro, the third man, prompted me to make one final appeal to reason. As long as the three of us were in dispute, the modello would stay in a bank vault, and none of us could profit. Ongaro and de Bry were old associates who had fallen out and their squabble only made the fate of the piece yet more uncertain. So, I suggested, why didn't we make common cause, take the piece out of the bank, sell it and divide the proceeds equally among us? The proposal fell on deaf ears. De Bry, on the verge of exposure and prosecution, refused any deal or compromise.

In September 1989, Michel de Bry was arrested and formally accused of fraud. In view of the sworn statements he made about his claim to the modello before the English court, if convicted in France, criminal charges could also be brought in England.

De Bry, in his eighties, was released on bail, but while awaiting trial, the whole tissue of lies he had woven began to unravel. Obviously, if Ongaro had bought the statuette in a flea market in Antibes, it could not have been reposing for years in Arthur Honegger's shoebox. Journalists tried to get a statement from Pascale Honegger whose first response was that she was sick of the whole business and refused to answer questions. When Ongaro's claim was first reported, she did tentatively suggest that what he had produced was not the same statuette, and this was the line adopted by Smyth on behalf of de Bry, but once de Bry's signature on the back of the photograph was produced, that defence collapsed.

But Pascale could not refuse to answer the police. She must

have been under terrible stress but finally admitted that the whole story about the modello in the shoebox was pure invention. Why did a respectable elderly woman help to propagate a pack of lies and run the risk of being prosecuted as a party to fraud? The answer is simply that de Bry had been a friend of her father, had helped to arrange his funeral, paid tribute to his memory and even promised to set up the foundation in his honour. How could Pascale refuse this sweet old gentleman a little favour which she was assured could do no harm? But the innocent story had become a nightmare.

And soon there came an even more startling disclosure. Ever since Hartt had disclaimed his signature on the copy of de Bry's letter of 11th November 1985 which had allegedly been returned by him to de Bry, questions over the letter had been raised. Smyth was now also retained by Hartt: presumably he satisfied his own conscience that there was no conflict of interest and that his conduct was professionally correct. As de Bry's lawyer, he had produced for the court a copy of that letter with the words *lu et approuvé* and Hartt's signature added. Now, as Hartt's attorney, he showed a copy without these additions.

But Michel de Bry's own daughter had agreed to testify in the case brought by Ongaro in Paris against her father. To convey to Hartt the solidarity of the support of his family to their pact, de Bry had the letter countersigned by his son and daughter. But his daughter is prepared to go on oath that the signature is not hers!

I thought from the first that there was something intrinsically wrong, even evil, about de Bry, which was why I was prepared to counter his plots with my own, to challenge and defeat this magician who could appeal to men's love of myths as well as to their greed. For de Bry is, or has been, a genius in his own perverted way. But when he refused to come to terms with reality over the modello, once it was in Coutts, I recognized that he was a victim of his own illusion. Now that I have seen the extent of his exploitation of people, even his own daughter, I have only contempt for such a character and disgust at the misery he has inflicted without a trace of remorse on so many people.

The modello remains an enigma for as long as it stays hidden from the world. The speculation over whether it is the actual model used by Michelangelo will continue. I have handled the piece, and I know that it is a thing of great beauty in itself, regardless of the identity of its creator.

Of course, if it turns out to be the work of Michelangelo, it will be enormously important for the history of art and our understanding of the artist. I feel privileged that, through me, the cheap lies which had been created around this piece were exploded, and that I was able to have it presented at its own true worth. To decide on its authenticity, I would suggest that a symposium headed by an authority such as Pope-Hennessy or Frederico Zeri should examine the piece, supported perhaps by more specialized technical research than that commissioned by Hartt from the University of Bordeaux. This could be obtained from the Research Laboratory for Archaeology and the History of Art at Oxford which, under its director, Professor Edward Hall, and with such authenticators as Doreen Stoneham, is pre-eminent for its expertise in art research.

Even if it transpires that the modello is not by Michelangelo, it will always retain its own mystery, its romance; it is a work to make men dream.

# 36

# WIN THE APPEAL

Now that the frescoes trial was over and the judge's decision was awaited, it became possible for me to talk directly with Michael Cypreanou, the Cypriots' lawyer. He was willing to discuss my offer to help with the recovery of works and invited me to meet him in Cyprus. But the Cypriots had attacked me during the trial and when he refused to give me written confirmation of his promise of a safe conduct, I said that I would meet him, or anybody he wished to send, but only on Dutch soil. All the time, I had to keep up the pretence with the Yugoslavs that I was working for the sale of 'their' futa in the event of the verdict going against Goldberg. When Cypreanou proposed sending a couple of Cypriot police inspectors who specialized in the tracing of stolen works of art, Jeri and Co insisted on being present.

On 12th July, the inspectors arrived and we met in the presence of Tasoula Georgiou. Paia and Jeri, whom I presented as my bodyguards since the Cypriots knew that I was under threat, sat silently at the back of the room. As far as they were concerned, I was proposing that I could get hold of stolen works and sell them to the Cypriots and I had to be careful not to say anything to raise their suspicions.

The policemen had brought lists of important works which

were missing, believed stolen. I was able to identify many of them and confirmed that I knew where they were.

'Quite a number are in the hands of private collectors who, if approached, could probably be persuaded to part with them for a sensible price if they were going to be restored to Cyprus,' I explained. 'I sold a lot of them so I know the sort of prices they paid. Give them their money back and at least acknowledge that they have cared for the pieces.'

I knew that inspectors were not empowered to make any sort of deal but I wanted a message to get back to Michael Cypreanou.

'I am ready to help you by approaching these people and negotiating on your behalf,' I said. 'But I ought to be given some sort of official status by the government of Cyprus so that they know I have the right to speak for you.'

I could not say anything more openly. The inspectors told me they would report back. I confirmed that I would stay in touch through Tasoula, and the meeting was concluded on a formal note for the benefit of the eavesdroppers.

One night, I received a call from someone I knew in Marseilles who told me that Jacky Lebreq had been butchered in his car, with four bullets in his head. His death was a shock but not altogether a surprise. The things he did brought him into contact with violent men.

I had not been particularly fond of Jacky but had been prepared to assist him in Holland out of regard for Stephan. But when he tried to enlist my support in finding people and locations for new drug laboratories, I turned him down flat.

But with both Stephan and Chantal now in prison, I could imagine the sort of case the French police would try to build up of a *crime passionel* so I judged that the time had come for me to step forward and help my friends. I contacted d'Allem.

'Some of your people from Marseilles visited me a little while ago and asked about Jacky Lebreq. I was not able to tell them anything then, but now that he is dead, things have changed.'

He was surprised that I knew already of the murder but knew better than to ask me my source. He told me that two men from the homicide division from Marseilles would come to see me but that also he wanted to see me about my own business and that he would be accompanied by his boss, a Chief Inspector Mirelle Ballestrazzi.

I invited them to dinner the night before our formal meeting and took great pains that the setting and company would create an atmosphere conducive to the serious business the following day. My previous lunches and dinners with policemen had paid off well. It would have been foolish to abandon such a successful formula, so I chose one of the best restaurants in the country outside The Hague and invited the two Dutch inspectors, whom I now knew well, to meet the couple from Paris and bring them to the restaurant where I would be waiting, escorted by a stunningly pretty girl to help keep the mood relaxed.

That was a miscalculation since when d'Allem presented his chief, I was confronted by an extremely attractive woman in her mid-thirties, self-assured and obviously intelligent but with hard, cold eyes which gave a clue to how a woman, still so young, could have achieved so powerful a position.

I hid my surprise. A flowery compliment would not be appreciated, but I allowed myself the indulgence of kissing her hand which she accepted with a smile.

'I am so glad you have been able to accept my invitation,' I said, 'since the French have issued so many invitations to me which I have been obliged, regretfully, to decline.'

She was quick to respond. 'We would not like you to get the impression that we want to take advantage of your hospitality, so we have brought you a little present.'

As an acknowledgement of the assistance I had given d'Allem, it had been decided, she informed me, to send a *commission interrogatoire* to question me on the Mirò forgery.

'That means,' she said, 'that, in this particular instance, the demand for your extradition has been dropped.'

'Fine,' I said as we sat down to dinner, 'but that still leaves the other requests for extradition over the forged Chagall signatures.'

'Of course, at the moment, the other demands still stand, but it is a first step. We are looking into these others,' she said. 'We are hoping for your continued co-operation, but these things take time.'

I shook my head. 'Chief Inspector, let me be frank. I love your country, where I have many friends. I want to be free to walk into a Paris bistro, to go to an auction at Drouot, or visit a gallery. It was thoughtful of you not to come emptyhanded, and I much appreciate your coming personally to Holland. But you must understand that I have been persecuted in Spain, chased all over the world and forced to assume another name when I travelled. And all this on the strength of ludicrous, petty charges!

'Now, I know that your people are aching to get details on the laundering of money, but you might have brought charges which could be taken seriously. I want to get the whole business over with and finally clear my name. The clearance of the Mirò demand is not enough. I want an assurance on these last extradition demands.'

I think that she approved of my directness: I had too much respect for her to try to flatter her. 'Very well,' she said. 'I shall speak with Paris. We have a formal meeting tomorrow. You will have an answer at midday.'

'Good,' I smiled. 'Now let us enjoy a pleasant evening. We shall talk about every subject under the sun with one exception. Not a word about my case.'

'Agreed,' replied Chief Inspector Ballestrazzi with a laugh.

As dinner progressed, she began to talk more freely and my admiration for her charm and wit grew while I got the impression that she had revised her opinion of me.

Next day, the French detectives were businesslike when we

met, but there was a sense of mutual respect and something of the cordiality of the evening persisted.

'First let me explain the situation, Monsieur van Rijn,' said Chief Inspector Ballastravi. 'We are serious about working for your rehabilitation and that is why we are giving you the chance to deal with the Mirò in Holland. But the Chagall case presents us with a difficulty since there is a judgement against you in the French courts in absentia and that can only be challenged by you personally appearing in France. So we have a problem. We cannot change the law for you, but we are working on how to get round this and you have my word that a way will be found.'

In the light of her assurance, I went ahead with the meeting.

'Now I am not going to give you names or Swiss bank account numbers,' I told them, 'but I am prepared to tell you how the money was moved and the routes which are still being used.'

So I told them in detail of the leaking sieve which was Charles de Gaulle.

This was a revelation. '*C'est pas possible*!' she exclaimed to d'Allem.

'I can tell you that in preparation for your visit, I had both channels checked by my assistant. They still work perfectly.'

At the close of the meeting, we shook hands and as they got ready to leave she turned to me. 'We shall keep in touch and you will hear from us again by the twentieth,' she said. 'Let me assure you that things really are moving. I think we understand each other now.'

One hour later, the two men from Marseilles arrived. There could not have been a more complete contrast. They did not seem to realize that they were not in France and started to order me about.

'Tell us all you know about Jacky Lebreq.'

I was not prepared to stand that sort of treatment so I ignored the question and walked out to the bar. After a few minutes they got the message and came and apologized.

I repeated that since Jacky had been murdered and they might be trying to forge a connection between his death and Stephan, I was ready to talk about it.

'Monsieur van Rijn, it must be very lonely for a man in prison. He is away from his wife, and hears that she is going about with his friend. They come together to see you; the wife takes money from you. Maybe nothing is going on, but wouldn't that sort of conduct make a man jealous? And jealousy in a jail where the man is helpless, that must be torture. Perhaps it could drive a man to plotting the death of this friend?'

I shook my head. 'I know Stephan. Sure, he gets depressed in jail, we all do. But he is far too intelligent to jump to the conclusion that Jacky was playing around with his wife. He knows how your people had been hounding Chantal and would expect Jacky to do what he could for her. You are looking in the wrong direction.

'Jacky told me that the top men in the French Connection are coming out of prison now,' I continued. 'Holland is notoriously soft on drugs, so they have chosen to set up new laboratories here. That's what Jacky was doing, looking for sites and suitable people. I know because he invited me to join him, but I turned him down. I am not in the drug business. I hate it.'

They confirmed that they had observed him with some of the people from the French Connection who were already out of prison. They had wondered what he was doing there: they now understood what had been going on.

On 3rd August 1989, Judge Noland delivered his verdict in Indianapolis. He ruled that Peg Goldberg never obtained the right to possess the mosaics and ordered that they be returned to Cyprus. The decision was hailed by the museum world as a milestone. Gary Vikan, Curator of Medieval Art at the Walters Art Gallery in Baltimore told the press, 'The significance of the decision is quite profound. We are going to use it as a basis for formulating a policy on the purchase of antiquities.' This was ironic since Vikan, testifying for the Cypriots, had denigrated my character and said that any deal coming from me was suspect but then had to admit that he was at Dumbarton Oaks when they bought the St Peter, their star exhibit, from my collection.

In Cyprus, the President of the Republic interrupted ceremonies in commemoration of the tenth anniversary of the death of Archbishop Makarios to announce the news. Church bells were rung and thousands thronged the streets to celebrate.

The Yugoslavs reacted with fury. They listened to every word when Goldberg called me. She claimed to be shattered by the verdict. What made things worse was that the Cypriots accused her of allowing the mosaics to be damaged in transit for which they intended to sue her.

'I guess that the packaging was not good enough,' she confessed, 'but the things these guys are saying are absurd. They talk as if the tesserae had been shattered but all that happened was there were some clean fractures into segments. The pieces were not in perfect condition when Aydin sold them, you know, and we spent a hundred thousand dollars on restoration. The fractures were straightforward.'

I thought it did not say much for Peg Goldberg's attachment to the mosaics that she had not bothered herself with their despatch from Geneva, but photographs of the pieces, taken in Aydin's apartment and when they arrived in the States, do support her version.

A few days later, she confirmed to me that an appeal would be lodged.

The pressure on me from both groups of Yugoslavs, from the Americans and from Aydin, was to work to win the appeal, but a new onslaught on Goldberg's position came with a report that a federal grand jury was being empanelled to investigate whether the loan which 'Nick' Frenzel had so opportunely arranged for her and his sending of $1.2 million dollars to Switzerland at a moment's notice had been in breach of federal banking regulations. In his deposition, he had stated that he had paid $390,000 for a stake in any future profits from the resale of the mosaics, but it was not clear whether that was on behalf of a client or for himself. He said that the money had been paid to Bob and myself but my sale to Bick and buy-back from Bob was the only occasion when I received such a sum.

I reckoned that if she were to have any chance at all in the appeal, Goldberg would have to come up with something very dramatic. One night, she called.

'Listen, Michel.' Her voice was triumphant. 'We've got them. This is going to knock those goddammed Cypriots right out of court. When they hear what we have on them, they won't even bother fighting the appeal.'

She had received a call from Savo. All the Yugoslavs had been around so often when Peg and I talked, it was no surprise that he got in touch with her direct. He had a fantastic story which would incriminate the Greek Cypriot clergy in the rape of Lythrankomi, and he had documentary evidence.

'He asked if I would buy what he had to offer. Would I buy air to breathe! I told him that I was not going to buy evidence but that he should talk through you. Now you know, Michel, there's no way I am going to pay a cent before the story and the documents are thoroughly checked and even then I will only pay the guy after I have sold the mosaics. All negotiations should go through you, so, Michel, get those documents. I don't need to tell you how important it is. We shall all be rich, including you, so we are all relying on you.'

# 37

# THE CLERGYMAN AND THE COLONEL

Paia and Jeri had heard this conversation, and insisted on a general meeting. Savo sounded supremely confident about his story and raised no objection.

'Aydin has always told us how he removed the mosaics himself from the church,' Savo commenced when we met.

'No,' I contradicted. 'His original tale was that the church had been destroyed and he picked up the pieces from the rubble.'

'Well, we know now that the church was not destroyed, but he did pick up the pieces of the mosaics,' Savo said. 'After the Turkish occupation the church was deserted and then it was looted, but not by the Turkish army nor by Turkish Cypriots. The man who ripped great chunks from the walls was a priest, one of the clergy of the Greek church who are claiming the pieces back.'

'Do you have his name?' I asked.

'He is named in a formal document, one of those which are for sale,' replied Savo. 'It appears that these mosaics are tremendously revered among the clergy, and there was a tradition that they had great value. To this simple priest, that could only mean that they were made of precious stones and gold. So he decided to take the stones and sell them to a jeweller. His problem was how to get over the Green Line into the Turkish sector.

'Well, some of the United Nations troops have been involved in smuggling, Aydin had some working for him. This priest got to know a Finnish colonel, and they came to an agreement. He would take the priest over in a UN truck, they would take the precious stones and divide them between them.'

'Do we know who this colonel was?' I asked.

'Yes, Michel. There are attestations, some on United Nations paper, which give his name and rank.'

'So the two of them went over and stripped the church?' asked Jeri.

'That's right. They could not take everything, but they hacked out the stones which looked most valuable, sixty kilos of them. The priest took his treasure to a jeweller in Nicosia where he found that what he had thought were rubies and amethysts were simply coloured glass. But the jeweller recognized something highly unusual, and showed them to Aydin. Aydin bought them and set about finding any more of the tesserae.

'The colonel's hoard got into the hands of a dealer called Schoeller, who was known to Aydin, who was able to buy these tesserae as well. Aydin went back to the church and skilfully removed whatever was left that was salvageable. Then, working from photographs, he gradually rebuilt the mosaics.'

This story explained why some mosaics were in so much worse condition than others. It would also be consistent with the two damaged mosaics in the Frankfurt garage being considered fakes, and the bag of loose tesserae, since Aydin would not have been able to reassemble all the mosaics and there would have been some pieces left over. It would also make sense of the Cypriot assertion that the mosaics had been damaged by Goldberg if they had merely been put together again in this manner.

'So, Michel, you get hold of Goldberg and tell her what she can have,' Savo concluded. 'What do you think she will pay?'

'Let me see how keen she is,' I replied.

After Savo had left, Paia pressed me. 'I understand that you did not want to stick your neck out in front of Savo, but tell me how much we can get out of them.'

'If they believe that this is going to enable them to sell their mosaics, maybe they will go to two and a half million.'

'Fine,' smiled Paia. 'That's two million for us and half a million for Savo.'

When I reported this to Goldberg, she blew her top. 'Is he fucking crazy? After this trial, I don't have two and a half million ready, and even if I did, I wouldn't pay until we have won the appeal and I have sold my mosaics. Make them see that unless Savo hands over what he's got, they won't get anything.'

'I'm sure that he won't give without being paid something up front.'

'Well, Michel, it's up to you to persuade him!'

There were stormy meetings of both gangs and I argued that they could not expect Goldberg to pay or even agree a figure without a detailed description of what she would be receiving. Savo would not even show me the documents but agreed to let me have a more precise description, in return for his share up front.

Paia grudingly agreed that Savo could have his half million as soon as we had an agreement but they stood firm on a total of two and a half million dollars. They were prepared to wait for their share until after Goldberg had won the appeal, but that was their final offer.

I realized that such documents would be dynamite. But the Cypriot case was that the mosaics had been stolen from the Church of Cyprus, and the identity of the thief, even if it turned out to be one of their own priests, made no difference to the facts. It would be an embarrassment, but neither the morality nor the legality of their case would be altered in the slightest. But as long as the Yugoslavs and Goldberg believed that they would win, the pressure on me to deliver was enormous.

Savo was not willing even to show what he had until he saw

the moeny. And Goldberg was not ready to put up any money without first seeing what she was buying. It was Catch 22, and I was sitting in the middle.

Then the Yugoslavs put their menace into words.

'This is your final warning,' Paia told me. 'Either you have money for us by the end of the week, or we start on you. And don't try to hide.'

That usually meant a heavy beating or a smashed kneecap which would leave one crippled for life. So I decided that I had to escape. Nowhere in Holland would be safe from them because of the French Interpol warrant but I had to remain on Dutch territory. My persecutors would find it more difficult to use force against me and get away if I were on a remote island, so I called Goldberg and said I needed to meet in a few days' time, but it would have to be on Curaçao.

'Are you bringing the documents?' she demanded.

'I must have a meeting in order to make arrangements for me to collect them,' I told her.

'I'm not coming all the way to Curaçao if you don't have the goods,' she replied. 'I'll send George. Call when you know where you will be staying and when you'll be there.'

'I know already. I shall be in the Curaçao Caribbean on Friday evening.'

On the Thursday evening I called Paia. 'Good news,' I said. 'I am expecting to hear something tomorrow around midday. I suggest we all meet here at two.'

Next day, at around eleven, I told my watchdog that I wanted to rest before the meeting, and asked him to see that I was not disturbed.

So while he stood guard outside my bedroom door, I put a few clothes and some important papers into a case. I also took the tapes of my conversations with Tasoula for safekeeping. Very quietly, I opened the bedroom window, stepped on to the fire escape and hurried on tiptoe down the iron staircase. I ran across the small hotel garden, climbed over the low wall and dropped on to a footpath in the Royal Park. The spot was deserted and well out of view of the sentries outside the palace.

I took a taxi to Schiphol, collecting my ticket at the airport. I called the hotel from the airport shortly before embarking and was put through to my suite where I spoke to Paia.

'I am on my way to Curaçao,' I told him, 'but don't get the idea that I am running away. I have an appointment there with George Feldman, Goldberg's partner, and I hope to do a deal which will mean money for all of us. If you want to contact me, I shall be in the Curaçao Caribbean Hotel.'

'Come back here at once,' Paia shouted.

'I did not tell you about this before,' I went on, 'because I knew there would be endless discussions and I would miss the chance to pull this off. You know where you can reach me: I'm leaving now, my flight has been called.'

He was still screaming when I put the phone down. As I entered the plane, for the first time for months I felt a free man again.

George Feldman was waiting for me in Curaçao. A short, tubby man in his early forties, he had invested in the art gallery, but there was no question who was the boss. George had the title of partner but did what Peg Goldberg told him. Right now, he had been ordered to do whatever was necessary, short of paying, to get possession of the evidence which Savo had promised.

We both checked into the Curaçao Caribbean and when George was not scuba diving or on the phone to Indianapolis for orders, we had a series of meetings.

George informed me that he had full authority to negotiate, not only on behalf of himself and Goldberg, but also Bob Fitzgerald, my supposed partner, and Stewart Bick, my investor. That sounded fine but I soon found that he would not order a glass of water without getting the go-ahead from Goldberg.

Although we talked for a week, the basic positions had not

changed, with the Americans eager to get their hands on the evidence but not willing to pay anything up front.

'Listen, Michel,' he said after one of his phone conferences, 'why don't you get these guys to accept our word that they will be paid, if they have a proper legal contract?'

'Are you willing to give them a contract?' I asked.

'No way!' George shuddered at the prospect of having to confront them. 'You are the one talking with them. With the appeal pending, we cannot be caught negotiating to buy evidence, can we?'

'Well, you don't expect me to make a contract to pay them, do you?'

'No,' he smiled. He had obviously been carefully rehearsed. 'But we could make a contract with you in which we would agree that a stated sum of money would be paid when certain conditions were fulfilled. You could give them your word that you had a formal contract binding us to pay and that ought to satisfy them that we are legitimate. Of course,' he went on with a sly grin, 'we would not want the contract to be generally known so we can deposit it here with a bank in both of our names. As a matter of fact, Peg has already talked with our lawyer and sent me a fax of what he has drafted.'

I glanced at the paper and told him that I would like to get the opinion of my own lawyer, but I could already see the trap they had set. If I could persuade Savo to part with his evidence on the strength of my having signed a contract, George need never agree to return to Curaçao and withdraw the contract. Since it would need both our signatures to take it out, in effect, the contract would have ceased to exist, leaving me to satisfy a band of killers who had been swindled out of money they had been promised.

Back in my room, I put in a call to Bob. 'What the fuck are you guys playing at? I knew this trick with the two signatures twenty years ago. Don't treat me like a child!'

'Calm down, Michel,' he said. 'I never expected you to go

along with it, but it was Peg's idea and you know how much she hates you.'

'Sure! But this would kill me! You know I can't fuck about with these Yugoslavs. Peg is sick. She should be under a shrink instead of pretending to deal in art.'

'Yeah, I know, Michel, but you play along and I give you my word that I shall keep Peg under control.'

But I knew very well that Peg Goldberg was not that easily controlled, whatever Bob might promise.

I had got to know a prominent local lawyer, called Komdeur, an elderly Dutchman. He looked quizzically at the bizarre contract from Goldberg which involved me in their obligations towards some other unnamed people.

'Well, if for some reason which is none of my business this is the way you want it, there is nothing to prevent such a contract being valid under Dutch law,' he told me.

'You must be in touch with the notaries on the island,' I said. 'If we finalize a contract, would you make arrangements for it to be signed in the presence of one and deposited with him?'

He agreed, and I went off to give George my answer. 'You can tell Peg I am prepared to go along with this contract.'

His face lit up; they had anticipated a long drawn out struggle.

'But,' I continued, 'forget the bank. We go to a lawyer. He can read the contract, draw up the document and hold it for us in his office.'

'Now, Michel, be reasonable,' George pleaded. 'The fucking paper has been written by a lawyer. Why go to the expense of bringing in another one?'

'Because your lawyer is American,' I explained patiently. 'He may be the greatest on the law of Indiana, but Curaçao happens to be Dutch territory, and we need someone who practises Dutch law.'

'I'll have to ask Peg,' he replied. 'That means more phone bills. Christ, Michel, do you know what this is costing us?'

'And while you are talking, tell her that we leave the contract with the lawyer and I want it to be a notarized contract. You can give the same instructions as you would give a bank and it will be perfectly secure in his safe.'

George departed for his conference with the boss. I counted on their assumption that a notarized contract here would mean the same thing as in the United States, simply legally confirming the signatures. In fact, a notary in Holland plays an important role, bearing a legal responsibility to both parties; he is a member of a highly restricted profession with correspondingly high status. To put it bluntly, a Dutch notary cannot be manipulated, but that was something, as was soon to be proved, none of the Goldberg crew realized.

My hunch was correct. A few hours later, George reappeared with a big smile on his face. 'OK, Michel, I finally got Peg to agree to using a lawyer here, and having the contract notarized, but it has to be understood that he acts for and takes instructions from both of us.'

'Agreed.'

Komdeur made an appointment for us at the office of a Mr Thesseling the following morning. George and I met for dinner the night before and I said something which took his appetite away.

'George, I've been thinking. This arrangement by which the contract can only be taken out of the safe if we both agree does not work.'

'What!' he howled. 'Michel, you gave your word. You can't back out now. Everything has been agreed.'

'Hold it,' I interrupted. 'I'm not backing out. Think for a minute. You want me to tell Savo I have a contract binding you to pay up after he has delivered the goods. He's not an idiot, he will want to see the contract. I shall tell him it cannot be taken out of Curaçao but that he is welcome to come and see it for himself.'

'That's right,' George assented. 'I'll come back, and we'll show him the contract. What's wrong with that?'

'What if something happens to you? Maybe you fall sick or whatever?'

George thought for a moment. 'I don't think that is a problem. I could send somebody with a letter of authorization to act in my place.'

'Could you? Suppose you had an accident or you die? I tell you what we do,' I went on. 'We go ahead as planned only we tell the lawyer that he is to show the contract, not let it out of his office, simply show it, if either of us requests.'

George rolled his eyes miserably. 'Peg will not be happy, Michel.'

'It's my last word. The contract can be shown on the demand of either one of us, or there is no contract. Tell her, George.'

'You don't realize, Michel, it is not just Peg. I have to get Stewart and Bob as well and Bob is so often out of town. This can put us back days.'

'Well, you had better skip dinner and get busy,' I suggested.

He gazed at me resentfully, gobbled down his meal and ran off to put in a call.

The discussions took some time, and we had to put off the appointment with the notary but at last George came back to me.

'Look, Michel, you and I are on the same side. I trust you but the others want some sort of assurance about whom you show this document. You told us you had tapes of your conversations with the Cypriot consul with you. So this is the deal. We accept that the lawyer be told that he can show the contract, and you hand over the tapes to us.'

I could see the way their minds were working. Get the contract signed, get hold of the evidence, then tell the lawyer we had decided not to go ahead and that he should destroy the document. I would be left to face Savo, and they would produce the tapes to convince the Yugoslavs that I had been negotiating behind their backs all along with the Cypriots. They did not appreciate that Paia and Jeri had been listening in during my talks with Tasoula.

At last we assembled in Thesseling's office. He read the draft carefully, in which they promised to pay $2.5 million dollars on condition that they were given certain documents and they won the appeal. He made some minor amendments and, with our approval, inserted a clause stipulating that the contract was to have a validity of two years, by which time the appeal would be long over. The contract was typed out, signed and witnessed. Thesseling solemnly placed it in an envelope which was closed and sealed, and we initialled the seals.

I could see that George was surprised at the prominent part the notary had taken and even more surprised when Komdeur proposed that the documents be left, not with him but with the notary. Only after Komdeur explained that under Dutch law a notary is a qualified lawyer and highly specialized, did George hesitantly agree to leave it there. A paper was then typed, stating the conditions under which the envelope could be opened and its contents shown in his office but not photocopied, not even handed to anyone.

George flew back home and I awaited developments.

I managed to get a call through to Tasoula Georgiou and described how the situation in Holland had become so dangerous that I had come to Curaçao until things were under control. I told her how Goldberg was trying to use me to buy evidence against Cyprus. 'I want you to know,' I concluded, 'that my commitment to your case remains absolute whatever the Americans might say. And you can rest assured that I am not going to pay some Yugoslav gangster two and a half million dollars in order to help Peg Goldberg.'

I kept in touch with what was going on in Holland through my brother, Guy. Shortly after George's return, I learned that Jeri had called on him.

'He wanted to know where you were,' Guy said, 'so I told him you had not moved out of the hotel. "You tell your brother that even on Curaçao he is not safe," he threatened, "and if we cannot punish him immediately, we can take it out on his family.

Remind him that we can and will hit you if he does not come up with money."'

I was white with fury. 'They are the lowest shits, just fucking animals! You know, Guy, I would never leave you to take the rap for me. Get yourself on the first plane out here.'

'No, Michel.' Guy's voice was very calm but firm. 'I have followed every move you have made, I understand your decision to help the Cypriots and I am backing you all the way. You are not to give way to threats to protect me. You stick to your guns. But I am not going to run away. For the time being, your place is in Curaçao but mine is here. I have my own business to look after and I am of use to you in Holland. But don't worry, I shall lie low, move into the country for a bit. And I'll see that steps are taken to protect your daughter. Don't get diverted, Michel. You are their prime target.'

I have always loved my brother but I do not think that I have ever admired him so much as at that moment. But I knew what I had to do. I called Paia and Jeri.

'Understand this,' I said. 'It was necessary for me to go to Curaçao to conclude an agreement with Feldman. If any member of my family is hurt, or if you so much as threaten any of them again or I meet with a sudden accident, my lawyers have instructions to send the police a complete record of every one of your gang, including photographs. And then you will find out how easy it will be to live in big houses and drive expensive cars while you draw social security to keep a low profile. And as for getting Dutch nationality, forget it! I promise that each of you will be hunted down. You won't be given a moment's peace, you won't even get away with a parking ticket.'

I did not expect to scare them off permanently, but reckoned I could win some time for my family and myself, and I was ready to use the contract with Feldman to string them along.

I received a call from Savo, and explained the contract. 'I am willing to take you to the notary and let you read it,' I told him.

'I don't want to set foot on Dutch soil,' he countered.

'Tell me what is in the contract and how much is being paid up front.'

'There is nothing in it about up front money.' And I told him the other conditions.

'You tell that cow there is no deal. I want six hundred thousand dollars and I want it now. Get this done at once, or you have to reckon with me. I have invested a lot of money in these papers and I could not buy them on promises.'

'Let me make this clear,' I told him. 'I am not paying your front money. If you can get it from Goldberg, that is up to you.'

'No, you fix it,' he shouted and slammed down the phone.

Within half an hour, I had a call from Paia.

'I've just heard from Savo that you are fucking things up. We talked about them paying two and a half million. Savo says that you are to get him six hundred thousand. That's OK, it still leaves us with $1.9 million, and we want it. We want our share of the original deal and we want our futa sold. Or we come and find you in Curaçao!'

The last straw was a call from Goldberg, asking when she could expect to receive the papers.

I had been threatened and blackmailed enough and I judged that the best defence would be to make the true story behind the mosaics known to the world. Over the next two days, I gave a series of interviews to the *Indianapolis Star*.

That night, I ran into Komdeur in a restaurant.

'I had a phone call this morning from your associate, Feldman, with a highly original proposition.' He spoke drily but there was a glint of amusement in his eye. 'He wanted me to destroy the contract. I told him that would be unethical and anyway, as he knew, the contract is held by the notary. Feldman said Thesseling must be a friend of mine, that presented no difficulty. I was to have a word with him, and Thesseling should destroy the contract. And he took care of my ethical objections by trying to bribe me. Can you guess, Mr van Rijn, what the fat bribe was?'

I shook my head.

'If I were to persuade Thesseling to act in this unheard of manner, Mr Feldman offered to pay my bill which is still outstanding. In effect, since he owes me that money, he wanted me to pay my own bribe.'

So my suspicions had been justified. That contract was the only written proof that Goldberg was prepared to buy evidence; with it out of the way, if Savo had delivered, the Yugoslavs would have looked to me for their money and I would not have had a shred of evidence to implicate her.

A journalist had flown out to Curaçao to prepare a story on the modello for the London *Sunday Correspondent*, and I had agreed some months before to give an interview about it to French television. So I secretly flew back to Holland, leaving a message with hotel reception that I was taking a few days' rest, sailing. Paia and the others never even realized that I was in Holland. The interview strengthened my belief that the story of the modello was attracting a lot of interest, and the interviewer allowed me to present my side of the story fairly.

While in Holland, I had another meeting with Tasoula Georgiou, this time on the record. My offer to help the Cypriots recover works of art had been favourably received.

'But before giving you some kind of official appointment we would want a written statement confirming your willingness to help us. Would you be prepared to write such a letter?' Before I left Holland, my formal letter was in her hands.

Back in Curaçao, I moved into a simple, native house where the constant breeze blows through the windows and over a patio, protected from the glare of the sun by a long, sloping roof. It stands above a bay where a handful of small fishing boats bring in their daily catch at the western end of the island, Westpunt. The view through the pergola is of two or three tiny boats lazily bobbing up and down on the shimmering sea, clear as crystal, sometimes emerald, sometimes every shade of blue, and in the evening, an expanse of silver as the sun suddenly falls below the horizon.

Each day, I walk past a cemetery where the tombs of stone or coloured tiles are ranged like an army of the dead on parade, past clumps of trees, some dead, others with roots exposed by storms, like writhing limbs. In the middle stands a pile of stones, a ruin, perhaps of a voodoo shrine. From one side, it looks like a giant skull with a row of menacing teeth. The air is scented by shrubs, but in this spot the aura is one of black magic.

I row out to my fish trap: the catch of the day is a painter's palette. Down by the pier is a bar, no more than a shed, where I sip beer with the locals. At night, we gather at another, rather bigger bar, to gossip, play dominoes, or watch the latest instalment of a horror movie from Venezuelan television. Behind the bar is a cabinet full of silver cups and trophies, mostly quite small. 'What are they for?' I asked the owner one evening.

'The big ones are for football, the others for dominoes.'

'How about a trophy for arm wrestling?' I asked. 'Anybody can enter, there's no fee, but I will give a couple of hundred guilders as prizes and some silver cups.'

The idea was a terrific success. The coming event was a topic of conversation for days.

I called Bob to check the latest news from Indianapolis. It was clear that the Americans were getting desperate. Time was running out and they still did not have those precious documents. Since I was clearly not going to act as their ambassador, Bob told me that he was speaking with them and I let him know that I thought that he ought by now to have realized that the Cypriots were justified in claiming what had been stolen from them. But he, like the Yugoslavs, was only swayed by the consideration of how much money could be made if they were to overturn the judgement. As a last desperate throw, Peg Goldberg, abandoning all pretence at ethical conduct, had flown to Europe herself for a meeting with Savo and Paia but apparently had not achieved anything.

The arm wrestling proved wildly popular. I made it to the semi-final, and fought with everything I had; but after so many bouts my arm felt as heavy as lead, and my opponent was a solid lump of rock. He went on to win the final, to his great delight. The prizes were presented, and he was photographed drinking from his silver cup.

Such a triumph had to be followed up. I wanted it to be something new and unfamiliar, but easily mastered without complicated rules. I thought of the Highland Games, and brawny Scots hurling tree trunks. I doubt whether there has ever been a more unlikely setting for tossing the caber.

Again, the idea swiftly caught on. The major problem was finding a caber. Most of the trees at this end of the island were small and twisted. Then two fishermen staggered to my house, bearing a sawn-off section of telegraph pole on which I painted Dutch and Curaçao flags. There was an interruption of telephone communications for a while, but it was in a good cause. I had tapes of bagpipe music flown in, and ordered the trophies.

On the morning of the contest, the restaurant owner told me that someone had telephoned for me and left a Paris number. I recognized it as Inspector d'Allem's. Because of the time difference, it was too late to catch him.

The caber-tossing went with a swing. I didn't disgrace myself, throwing four metres eighty and coming third, but the winner was Paco, our arm-wrestling champion, who cleared five metres. We drank and danced in celebration.

One of the older men took me on one side just before I left.

'At Westpunt, we have a good life, *tranquillidad*. Tourists stay at the other end of the island and we don't see them much. But it is great to have a bit of action, and that is something you have brought us.'

It took some time getting through to Paris but d'Allem came to the phone immediately.

'Monsieur van Rijn, I wanted to let you know as soon as possible that the review of all the outstanding cases against you has been confirmed. It will take a few days for the formal notification to come through but you can be certain that the extradition demands will then be withdrawn. May I be the first to offer you my congratulations.'

I thanked him and walked home up the hill. That evening, I rowed out to sea and hauled in my fish trap. The sunset seemed more glorious than ever, the sea more iridescent, but perhaps it was simply my awareness that I had only a few more days in which to enjoy this unspoilt corner of the world, a vestige of paradise. The time had come for me to return to the turmoil of the world.